4.50

THE FEDERAL PRESENCE

**The MIT Press
Cambridge,
Massachusetts,
and
London, England**

Lois Craig

and

the staff of the
Federal Architecture
Project

THE FEDERAL PRESENCE
Architecture, Politics, and Symbols
in United States Government Building

This project was supported with the assistance of the
National Endowment for the Arts, a federal agency.

Foreword

In 1972, on the recommendation of the National Council on the Arts, the quality of federal government architecture became the subject of inquiry for the National Endowment for the Arts. Our studies were carried forward by a task force and a small staff, which came to be known as the Federal Architecture Project. Major and influential recommendations for change developed.

In the process of the task force's work we discovered that we needed to grasp the extent and influence of government building before we could consider quality. We soon had a growing collection of visual and written material on the history of the government's attempts to house its services and activities. Characteristically, task force member Charles Eames was one of the first of our group to recognize the potential of an informal display in the project office. With his encouragement and the advice of other task force members, especially Harry Weese and Eliot Noyes, the Endowment supported the continuation of the staff's historical research for the preparation of a book. The result is *The Federal Presence: Architecture, Politics, and Symbols in United States Government Building.*

Neither the National Endowment for the Arts nor its advisors were asked to take responsibility for the book's conclusions. But it was clear that this serious and engagingly presented effort to understand the heritage and the future of our far-ranging federal programs merited wide attention.

Our public buildings and spaces are the products not only of designers but of the society that pays for them, uses them, and looks at them. The public is, after all, the ultimate client. Perhaps the knowledge gained from this historical look at America's national image will help us answer questions about the government's future effect on the quality of the environment.

Nancy Hanks
Chairman, National Endowment for the Arts, 1969–1977

Introduction

Many have noted that the federal government is one of the world's largest volume builders, as well as one of its most ubiquitous landlords. Taken together, these construction and management activities have long exerted a pervasive, if often unconscious, influence on the way Americans think and feel about their government. As the authors of this book state, the various governmental strings attached to subsidized building projects have dictated the design of two-thirds of this nation's health care facilities, one-fourth of its schools, and "virtually all of its housing." Indeed, Uncle Sam's real estate holdings have become so expansive in the years since 1949—when most civilian federal building programs were consolidated under the General Services Administration—that the innocent sojourner might wander the republic's length and breadth without ever departing an environmental web created by federally commissioned architects and engineers.

In recent years the federal government was not, as the young phrase it, "into" architecture. It was "into" building. So much so that after I became Director of Architecture + Environmental Arts at the National Endowment for the Arts, one of the first thoughts that struck me was that our section at the Endowment was the only unit in the entire federal government which contained the word "architecture" in its name. That was in 1971.

In the spring of 1972, Nancy Hanks, Chairman of the National Endowment for the Arts, reported at a National Council on the Arts meeting that a President's directive had called on the Endowment to assume the task of re-examining standards for architecture, graphics, and the related professions at the federal level. This directive touched off a truly significant breakthrough. Among the tasks it mentioned was the need to update and revise the 1962 "Guiding Principles for Federal Architecture," a product of the Kennedy Administration's policy of promoting all manner of cultural and aesthetic interests. But as guidelines go, these didn't go far enough.

Thus our work at the Endowment was cut out for us. We took an essential first step when we assembled some of the nation's most gifted and thoughtful design professionals, together with a spare but zealous staff, and set them to work as a body called the Task Force on Federal Architecture. Ideas proliferated. One in particular, expressed over and over, served as a philosophical form of aggregate to which other ideas and attitudes were bonded. That central idea is simply that federal architecture, in addition to fulfilling its functional purpose, should bring enjoyment to people. The task force members felt, as one, that public architecture should never intimidate, never repel, never lord it over the ordinary citizen. Instead it must respond to his innate appreciation of such environmental and human attributes as color, light, comfort, convenience. Also safety, spontaneity, and free movement. Also sensory and spiritual delectation.

Of the many ideas germinated by the task force, the Public Buildings Cooperative Use Act is potentially one of the most fruitful. The act was passed by Congress in 1976, and in the short period since, its provisions have served admirably to liberalize bureaucratic thinking as to the uses and reuses of federal buildings. Specifically, this legislation authorizes the General Services Administration to accommodate a great many social and commercial uses hitherto excluded in both new and restored buildings. Federal architecture may now allow not only for official space but also for *tenants*—restaurants, shops, and a full range of service-dispensing businesses. GSA is also encouraged by the Cooperative Use Act to promote the use of courtyards, auditoriums, corridors, and other assembly facilities for a wide range of social and cultural events. And, under the act, GSA began a living buildings program of public events in federal buildings across the nation.

To be sure, events cannot be the whole of federal architecture. Nor is merely living over the store, or vice versa, more than a minor variant on the central theme of government-shaped elements of the manmade environment. Increasingly, we must look to the federal government for a new form of architectural symbolism, a means of physical and social expression that transcends the traditional importance of architecture as an affirmation of national seemliness. I am suggesting that federal architecture must reward rather than penalize the innovative, the risk-taking design. For, as at no other time in history, our success as a society will depend henceforth on how well, given our limited and shrinking resources, we literally design our future. By what it builds and by the research and development it supports through subsidy and incentive, the federal government can exemplify the conserving society that will face the future with a new confidence.

Bill N. Lacy
Director, Architecture + Environmental Arts Program,
National Endowment for the Arts, 1971–1976

Acknowledgments

When I established the office of the Federal Architecture Project for the National Endowment for the Arts it was my good fortune to serve a lively task force and an enlightened agency. And to find a staff that shared my interest in history as the foundation for addressing issues of public policy.

Originally, our historical research was to be embodied in a section of the task force report, "Federal Architecture: A Framework for Debate" (1974). But our interest and the material outgrew the confines of a report. In 1974, with the support of the Endowment and its Architecture + Environmental Arts Program, I began to shape the accumulating archives into a book.

Over the next four years a number of staff members and consultants worked under my direction. Inevitably, responsibilities shifted back and forth to accommodate individual strengths and interests as well as the other work demands of the office. Acknowledgments can only suggest the extent of dedicated and imaginative collaboration required to develop an ambitious new subject into a book.

During the planning stage staff members Lisa Hirsh, Joseph Flores, and Robert Feild assisted with the research and outlines that became the foundation for further efforts. Initially we were guided by a paper prepared by Frederick Gutheim. Robert Feild provided a draft design scheme, which influenced future research directions.

In the subsequent preparation of the book William Barnes directed the research that furnished the essential framework of chapters 1 through 5. Robert Peck contributed substantially to chapter 6 and Vicki Reed to chapter 7. Joseph Flores served as chief research assistant and Vicki Reed as chief editorial assistant. The director of photo research was Shirley Green, assisted by Debra Kayden.

Additional help with editing was provided by Simpson Lawson and with photographs by Sally Evans and John Guard. Catherine O'Neill was in charge of preparing the bibliography. Throughout the project my administrative assistant, Hope Gray, kept all the parts—and people—working smoothly and supervised the preparation of a changing manuscript. She was also responsible for securing illustration permissions. Carolyn and Jennifer Craig were tireless photocopiers and collators.

Too numerous for the list of credits are the names of the many persons and organizations that ably and courteously responded to our requests for help. Particularly heartening was the cooperation of a committee of federal agency representatives, originally appointed as a resource for the National Endowment for the Arts in formulating new policies for federal architecture. The research facilities of the Library of Congress, the National Archives, and the Library of the American Institute of Architects provided major assistance.

Federal buildings should be understood in a context of government policies that influence the shape and quality of our physical surroundings. William Barnes, especially, was helpful in formulating this connection. Much of my research and reflection on that aspect of the book was done during the tenure of a Loeb Fellowship in Advanced Environmental Studies at Harvard University, where I had the privilege of studying with John Brinckerhoff Jackson.

The contribution of MIT Press deserves special comment. The editorial and design staff worked with skill and patience to give extraordinary attention to the integration of words and images.

Lois Craig
Director, Federal Architecture Project,
for the National Endowment for the Arts, 1972–1977

PROLOGUE

Footholds, Blueprints, and Inventions

Buildings and landscapes express subjective values. Particularly in its public works— its architecture and land planning—a society projects its views of the world and of the good life. From the beginning of the American nation such design choices have embodied many forces, political and economic as well as cultural. Government building, then, must be understood in the context of the American experience, which has been encompassed in the dimensions of American space.

Americans have always been space explorers. The first settlers found in their new country a paradoxical wilderness, richly full and starkly empty. Varying with their notions of what they wanted from this vastness and with the cultural baggage they carried, the newcomers planned their settlements. At times they imposed Old World patterns on the new. Plans were successful, however, insofar as they met pragmatic needs and took into account the American context. Abstractions and utopias fared poorly in the relentlessly empirical wilderness. In the tension between the land and their aspirations, the Europeans fashioned their new-found land.

With them, these mostly English settlers brought an acquisitive ethic, a biblical sanction to "subdue and replenish the earth" and a popular belief that the course of empire must move from classical Rome westward. The wilderness absorbed the newcomers' enterprise and shaped it, replacing European notions of severely limited resources with an expansionist mentality that historian Michael Kammen has called "resourceful wastefulness." These views brought conflict with native Americans and established habits of development that increasingly trouble modern America.

The organization and use of space—clearing stumps, arranging farm patterns and town layouts, constructing buildings of all sorts—were at the heart of the colonial enterprise. Land use patterns reflected the colonists' images of themselves as participants in physically grounded communities. Attempts to plan these patterns through public policy—attempts to implement particular images—have a lineage that extends from the Puritan ideal of a city on a hill, through a grandiose Georgia scheme, the Indian removals, and the homestead laws to the conservation movement and highway construction programs of the twentieth century.

On July 3, 1573, Philip II of Spain proclaimed the Laws of the Indies, characterized by scholar John Reps as "America's first planning legislation." These detailed regulations were closely followed in the construction of towns throughout Spain's possessions in the Americas. The laws mandated everything from site selection through a provision that Indians were not to enter a town until construction was complete "so that when the Indians see them they will be filled with wonder . . . and will consequently fear the Spanish."

No such document governed the settlements of the English, French, or Dutch. Here individual explorers, entrepreneurs, and religious leaders brought small bands of settlers to the new land in search of opportunities not found in Europe. Their needs and desires differed and, thus, so did their settlement patterns. Probably the densest settlement in the colonies occurred at New Amsterdam, later New York, which represented one end of the spectrum of colonial land use patterns. At the other end were the autonomous farms of the southern river valleys, discrete and isolated atoms in the wilderness. Most numerous were the varieties of town settlements and dispersed family farms that characterized New England and Pennsylvania.

One of the first tasks immigrants undertook in establishing footholds in the American vastness was the building of forts, in whose protective shadow settlements sprouted. Limited resources in a threatening environment permitted little more than crudely fashioned structures, and early forts were often in a triangular form that required minimal effort to enclose a space. Later efforts were more substantial.

Construction priorities in the first years of a village settlement were simple: the perimeter fortifications, public structures such as the storehouse and the church, and private houses. Architectural expediency prevailed well into the eighteenth century. Where government only gradually separated from religion, the church was often used for the business of government. It was common practice for these churches to be built and maintained by public taxes. They were the focal points of their communities and offered ample space for legislative meetings. Not surprisingly, the earliest legislative buildings were often adorned with a churchlike turret capped by a spire, a visual symbol of the center to be seen from the surrounding countryside.

The emerging variety of public buildings and their uses reflected diverse colonial notions of the extent of the public domain. Centers built for governing often accommodated more than one use—an expedient and perhaps philosophical statement of the proximity of government to the daily life of the governed. America's first public building, the Palace of Governors, built at Santa Fe, New Mexico, in 1610, contained barracks, offices, a chapel, magazines, and a prison. The Colony House in Rhode Island housed the legislature and also served for social and religious functions. In Annapolis, the State House provided offices for officials of the colony, the county, and the town. The first Town House at Boston, authorized in 1657, contained an open air public market at ground level and above this a public library, courtrooms, an assembly room, a council room, and an armory. Massachusetts and Boston officials shared the second Town House, the bottom level of which was a merchants' exchange in the medieval tradition.

Capital plans also revealed society's intentions. The 1718 plan for Annapolis, Maryland, demonstrated the relationship between church and state with the "Public Circle" situated on the crest of the highest point of land as the site for the State House; a smaller "Church Circle" was located at a short distance from the Public Circle. In the plan for Williamsburg, the first monumental capital in America, the General Assembly in 1699 called for "a healthy, proper, and commodious place, suitable for the reception of a considerable number and concourse of people, that of necessity must resort to the place where the assemblies will convene." The legislators not only stipulated the dimensions of the new town and the locations of public buildings, but also gave detailed instructions for the design of the new House of Burgesses, specifying everything from the furniture to the cupola. The form for the building itself was

reminiscent of the Roman Capitoleum, the building duplicated in Rome's colonial out-
posts to establish the imperial presence. The town plan clearly described the needs
and functions of the colonists. It was an orderly society.

In an epoch for learning by doing—a time for generalists, dilettantes, and experimen-
ters—yeoman architects were bound to their own experience and to the few available
books on building design. Most men had designed their own homes and consequently
felt confident about helping to shape the design of a public building. Although a few
emigrants from England had some architectural training, most important colonial public buildings were designed by well-read amateurs or talented craftsmen. Moreover,
the often vigorous involvement of the legislators themselves in the design and construction process combined to obscure the specific contributions of individuals.

As in their political economy, so in their architecture and other spatial arrangements,
the Americans' activities resulted in amalgams of inheritance and adaptation. With no
substantial indigenous architecture to copy, European style importations were necessary, but so was a spirit of innovation.

By the Revolutionary era, the conjunction of the individualistic ethic of Locke and the
land, of inheritance and adaptation, had pushed the Americans into deviations from
appropriately colonial roles and mentalities. The British attempt to rectify proclaimed
abuses pinched the colonists where it hurt most—in their self-images and especially in
their self-interests. Their perspective shifted: what had been deviations became rights,
what had been British blundering or straightforward conflicts of interest became "a
long train of abuses and usurpations."

The drive to nationhood was no smooth, ineluctable process. The conflicts of the colonial era were numerous and significant, the paradoxes myriad. Perhaps the most
glaring contradiction was the juxtaposition of slavery with the claim that all men are
created equal. The Revolution did not give birth to a model society, a mellow blend
of harmonious elements. The ringing phrases of the Declaration of Independence anticipated the time when the weight of responsible choices would take its toll of this
"first new nation." Following the violent climax of their colonial era, the Americans
confronted the question of whether their revolution had created circumstances that
would make if possible to solve the problems of their society.

Diversity had characterized the public buildings scattered throughout the colonies as
well as early efforts to find acceptable symbols for the rebels facing expedient unity.
With the coming of nationhood the search would begin for patterns that symbolized
collective identity. New public buildings would be lectures on moral philosophy, at
once reminders of ideology and instruments of ideological persuasion. The patterns of
land design would mirror the common belief in equality of opportunity and private
ownership.

"Our land is more valuable than your money. It will last forever. It will not even perish by the flames of fire. As long as the sun shines and the waters flow, this land will be here to give life to men and animals.

We cannot sell the lives of men and animals; therefore we cannot sell this land. It was put here for us by the Great Spirit and we cannot sell it because it does not belong to us. . . . As a present to you, we will give you anything we have that you can take with you; but the land, never."

Blackfoot chief, recorded in a nineteenth-century treaty council

Sixteenth-century portrayal of Indians worshiping a column placed by the French to memorialize their landing in Florida. Later, as the native Americans realized the Europeans' intentions, their attitudes toward such symbols of permanence changed.

"The land was ours before we were the land's.
She was our land more than a hundred years
Before we were her people. She was ours
In Massachusetts, in Virginia,
But we were England's, still colonials,
Possessing what we still were unpossessed by,
Possessed by what we now no more possessed . . . ."

Robert Frost, "The Gift Outright"

Pennsylvania State House (Independence Hall), 1731–1753. Although it was modeled on English palaces, its plan symbolized the evolution of government. The large assembly rooms contrasted with the first colonial assembly house constructed a century earlier at Jamestown, Virginia. There, historian Henry C. Forman observed, the interior had reflected social and political stratification: small meeting rooms where decisions were made by a few men.

BEGINNINGS: "A MODEL . . . SUFFICIENTLY CHASTE"

1

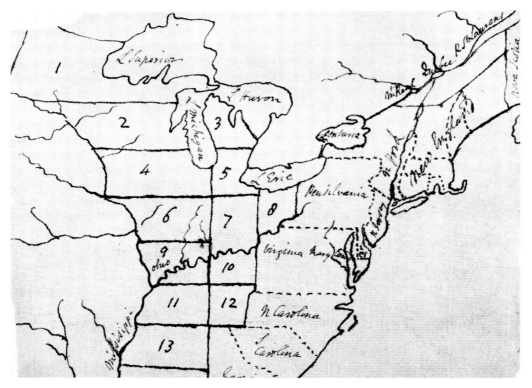

Thomas Jefferson's proposal for making states by imposing great quadrangles on an unknown landscape was rejected by Congress. His geometric scheme was used, however, to mark off individual lots of 640 acres to a section. The precise definition of state boundaries was left to the future and the acquisition of more detailed topographical knowledge.

Model for State Capitol, Richmond, Virginia, built by Thomas Jefferson and Charles Louis Clerisseau, 1785, copied from the Maison Carrée, Nîmes, France. In the explanation of the Roman temple plan for the Virginia building, Jefferson described it: "Erected in the time of the Caesars and which is allowed without contradiction to be the most perfect and precious remain of antiquity in existence. . . . I determined, therefore, to adopt this model and to have all its proportions justly drewed."

Thomas Jefferson was the guiding spirit for the first federal architecture. His influence, however, was not limited to buildings, but pervaded federal designs for American space, from land use to architectural style.

Jefferson worked at a time of major change. Republican government was rising in France; belief in order, harmony, and reasonableness as reflections of natural law was replacing earlier standards in art and society, standards viewed as capricious and immoral. Coincidentally there occurred the discoveries of the ancient cities of Herculaneum and Pompeii. And fortuitously, the new values could be linked to the newly discovered forms of classical civilization. Capitalized virtues could be imagined clothed in togas and strolling the streets of republican Athens or Rome. No longer would society condone a Marie Antoinette playing at milkmaid on an aristocratic estate. "Be stern like the grand old Romans!" said the French painter Jacques Louis David. In architecture the conjunction of the classical scholarship and the new public virtues replaced the Renaissance classicism of Palladio. The replacement was essentially romantic. Romanticism, as Geoffrey Scott wrote, "cast upon the screen of an imaginary past the vision of its unfulfilled desires."

Jefferson, as the new emissary from the United States, was an impressionable visitor in the midst of the artistic and political ferment of France. The linking of form and meaning, of form and moral standards, was made to order for his sensibility and his perception of the need in his fledgling country for a unifying order and vision, for a national identity. He lamented the cultural inexperience of his countrymen, complaining of the absence of "a model among us sufficiently chaste" to elevate the sights of mostly self-taught designers with a bent for unruly ornamentation. In 1785 he advised the Virginia legislature to construct its new capitol in the image of the Roman temple at Nîmes, France. Social meaning, not everyday activities, should determine the form of a public building. This use of classical form for an institutional building preceded by decades the European practice of fitting institutional buildings to archaeological antecedents.

When Jefferson returned to America there was much for his classical predilections to model: a new national capital and an unknown continent. Jefferson believed that the lofty values of Reason and Order could work their designs upon the visual environment, both architectural and spatial, to fashion compelling models. And his classical sense of composition influenced both the architecture of the new republic and the planning of its public domain.

As the author of a series of land ordinances, Jefferson organized the spatial and political geometry of the national territory. Upon the diverse contours of a vast and growing public domain, the ordinances and the Land Act of 1796 imposed a rectangular survey system. In the country west of the Alleghenies, government surveys formed the basis of land division, the guide for laying out of roads and streets, even the pattern for aligning fences, plantings, and houses. Later, utilities and transport lines would conform to the grid that now covers three-quarters of the continental United States. The chief module of this rectilinear pattern was the 640-acre, or one-mile-by-one-mile, section.

The application of such a scheme over an entire continent had its disadvantages. In the fertile lands of Ohio the presumed uniform value of the section was, in fact, roughly consistent. But later, when settlement reached the arid Great Plains, the notion of equal value for equal size was totally inapplicable, although it was adhered to.

When the speculator followed the surveyor he found the rectangular parcels of land, which could be sold by the front foot and easily platted, well suited to real estate market needs. The result, wrote Lewis Mumford, was "a frame for the architect . . . where site-value counted for everything, and sight-value was not even an afterthought." The grid's disregard for topography became particularly conspicuous at the city planning scale. "Such regular plans," complained city planner Pierre L'Enfant, ". . . must even when applyed upon the ground best calculated to admit of it become at last tiresome and insistent."

But when the task embraced millions of square miles and the planning experience of the nation's designers barely extended beyond the eastern seaboard, the grid was a reasonable framework for ordering a continent. To grasp such an awesome unknown the human mind had to reach for some form of measurement. To Jefferson and others of the classical persuasion, the methodical and orderly qualities of the grid were compatible with their philosophic view of the world—a compatibility that had also argued for Greek acceptance of grid planning in the colonial towns of the sixth century B.C. And, in the early days, at least, the marketable, equal section of land reflected democratic assumptions of equal opportunity and of land ownership as an important basis for citizenship.

In the sparsely peopled landscape of America of this period no group felt more deprived of a sense of permanence than the Congress. The sojourning legislators met in nineteen separate halls in eight towns from 1774 to 1800 before they finally convened in the still unfinished capital in Washington.

The street plan envisioned in Pierre Charles L'Enfant's 1791 scheme for the city of Washington rivaled that of European capitals and some of the celebrated cities of antiquity. It was also a city very much of its time, following the new principles of rational taste. Its plan provided for the separate functions of government and for the measured, dignified spaces believed to be conducive to measured, dignified conduct. The city itself would be a symbol of Reason and Order, values upon which the new nation should build its future.

Influenced by Thomas Jefferson and delineated by Pierre L'Enfant, the federal district reflected the latter's conviction that "although the means now within the power of the country are not such as to pursue the design to any great extent, it will be obvious that the plan should be drawn on such a scale as to leave room for that aggrandizement and embellishment which the increase of the wealth of the Nation will permit it to pursue to any period however remote."

Designs for the Capitol and the President's House, on Jefferson's recommendation, were chosen by competition. The 1792 advertisement for entries declared "that public buildings in size, form and elegance should look beyond the present day." As with the city plan, the clear intention was that the first federal architecture and urban design should represent the best. The resulting neoclassical designs, bearing traces of intervention by officials, craftsmen, and other designers and of influences from colonial and European styles, were by no means universally acclaimed. Critical salvos, often exchanged by designers with ties to opposing factions, frequently had political overtones. But the designs responded to the increasing scale and aspiration of society's needs and symbolically helped correct the immediate realities of an undeveloped wilderness and a small army and navy.

As the third President of the United States, Jefferson continued to shape the country and its capital. Benjamin Latrobe, Jefferson's protégé and appointee as Surveyor of the Public Buildings, exerted significant influence on the future form of the Capitol. The British-born and -trained Latrobe was a new phenomenon in America—the professional architect—and a sign that the tradition of amateur architects and anonymous builders was beginning to yield to professionalism. As with his patron, Latrobe's talents spanned many disciplines, in his case bridging the separate professions of architecture and engineering. He also contributed early transportation studies that would be used as part of a major report on national planning. In a later age of increasing specialization, neither Jefferson's span of design control nor Latrobe's span of design practice would be possible.

Before he left the Presidency Jefferson also made another lasting impression on American space. With a few strokes of the pen the domain upon which his grid would work its designs was more than doubled on April 30, 1803, when he purchased the Great Plains from Napoleon Bonaparte. For the so-called Louisiana Purchase Jefferson's emissaries, James Monroe and Robert Livingston, agreed to pay Napoleon $15,000,000—more than authorized by the President and still more than authorized by Congress. When Livingston had asked Napoleon's representative how to construe the bounds of a Louisiana territory, the French Minister reportedly replied, "I can give you no direction; you made a noble bargain for yourselves and I suppose you will make the most of it."

Making the most of it was the American way. And Jefferson offered an amendment to the Constitution to allow incorporating the foreign territory into the nation. The amendment envisioned for settlers the rights of occupancy and self-government then limited to the Indian inhabitants. To Congress he urged, "The Legislature, in casting behind them metaphysical subtleties and risking themselves like faithful servants, must ratify and pay for it, and throw themselves on their country for doing for them unauthorized what we know they would have done for themselves had they been in a situation to do it."

"I stretched the Constitution until it cracked," Jefferson told Congress, ". . . yet the fertility of the country, its climate and extent, all promise in due season important aids to our treasury." He shortly dispatched the Lewis and Clark expedition to back his faith with more compelling evidence. While Jefferson was eager to acquire scientific information he also valued the expedition as a practical way of securing political ends.

Imagination had dared the acquisition of this huge territory. The journals of its exploration suggested the greater imagination it would take for Americans to conquer the immense space that would complete the outlines of the continental United States in the next half century. According to historian Daniel Boorstin, Lewis and Clark expanded the very language to convey the new landscape, adding many make-do expressions that became part of everyday speech and increasing the vocabulary of natural science by hundreds of terms, mostly borrowed from Indian languages. Not long after, Noah Webster included in his dictionary the words "locate" and "location"—words not found in the English dictionaries of the day. "This," he reportedly said, "was one reason why I compiled mine. How can the English *locate* lands, when they have no lands to locate!"

In less than half of its first century the new nation built and, after the War of 1812, rebuilt, the foundations of a national capital. Although none of his designs for federal buildings was ever used, Jefferson's choice of the columnar style of ancient Greece and Rome would project a symbolic image of the federal presence that would continue to influence and eventually plague federal architecture. The map he designed for America, although broken by blank spaces still to be filled, followed a pattern that would continue to affect architecture and the other uses of space, both public and private.

In the first years of the new republic, rhetoric extolled the nation's guiding principles in capitalized nouns: Liberty, Justice, Equality, the Rights of Man. As these abstractions gained rallying power they took visible form in the shape of symbols, replacing the colonial clutter of insignia and styles, the diversity that had tied social identity to the national origins of peoples away from home.

"The language of symbol was a common, not a rarified, means of communication," writes art historian Joshua C. Taylor. "Once an allegorical state of mind is established, only a slight clue is needed to draw the earthly image into the realm of idea." The favored antique references of the day could make a building, a hero, a certificate part of the common language and aspiration. In a nation newly formed and struggling for unity, such symbolism had a special, vital force, unlike the accumulation of symbols that would later be dragged out to remind Americans of their heritage.

The search for symbols of national unity, of a shared past and common expectations for the future, began immediately, especially in the form of the apotheosis of George Washington. The pantheon of Revolutionary War heroes filled gradually; folk heroes such as Davy Crockett and Mike Fink emerged later. The Constitution itself, the national flag, the Declaration of Independence and the Fourth of July, and later the President's

House, the Capitol—all these became venerable, outward, and visible signs of an invisible knitting together of local and regional loyalties into a national heritage and identity.

The Continental Congress apparently believed it important to assert the identity of the new union with a single lasting symbol, for on the evening of the same day the Declaration of Independence was signed, the Congress voted it "Resolved, that Dr. Franklin, Mr. J. Adams and Mr. Jefferson be a committee to prepare a device for a Seal of the United States of America."

It would take six years, three separate committees, two consulting artists, and a secretary of the Continental Congress to reach the final selection. The choice was the American bald eagle, an adaptation of the ancient personification of Zeus to the native fauna of North America. At one point in the official deliberations the favored symbol was the personage of America, or Columbia, the Greek descendant of the Indian princess whom Europeans had long identified with the Garden of the New World.

With the signing of the Treaty of Paris in 1783 the United States officially became a country, encouraging a mania of eagles decorating everything from architecture and furniture to quilts and certificates. Although Columbia appeared on neither the seal nor the flag she continued to be a popular symbol of the American republic. Uncle Sam made his first appearance in 1830.

The BLOODY MASSACRE perpetrated in King Street— BOSTON March 5th 1770 by a party of the 29th REG^T., engraving by Paul Revere, which appeared in a broadside, March 12, 1770: a colonial view of one of the events that precipitated the Revolutionary War.

Patriots pulling down the statue of George III in New York, 1776, painting by J. A. Oertle. Musket balls were made from parts of the statue so that the king's men could feel, as one New Yorker wrote, "melted Majesty fired at them." Other pieces of the statue, including the horse's tail, were turned up in 1871. A recent investigator estimates that 1,500 of the statue's 4,000 pounds remain to be accounted for.

The Phoenix or Resurrection of Freedom, print after painting by Irish painter James Barry, 1776. John Locke mourns the Memory of British Freedom, the recumbent figure, while his followers greet the rebirth of his ideas in America, represented in a distant vision of figures dancing near a classical temple inscribed with the words "Libert. Ameri. . . ." and topped by a phoenix from whose wings Liberty arises. Time scatters flowers on fragments of earlier republics of Athens, Rome, Florence—a theme in the popular tradition that the course of empire historically moves westward.

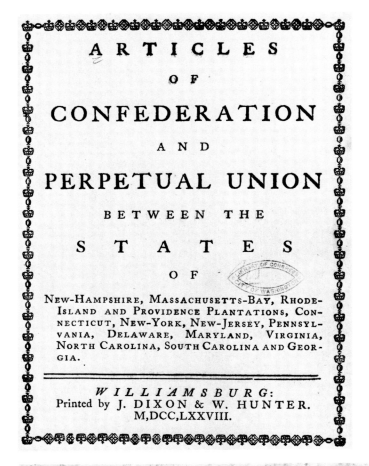

Articles of Confederation, 1777, Williamsburg edition published in 1778 and bordered with a design of crowns, a curiously symbolic link with the past.

This cartoon in the July 26, 1788, *Massachusetts Centinel* was occasioned by New York's ratification of the federal Constitution. It urges North Carolina and Rhode Island to ratify and thus complete the "Federal Edifice." North Carolina joined the Union in November 1789; Rhode Island resisted until May 1790, when Congress threatened to treat the state as a foreign nation.

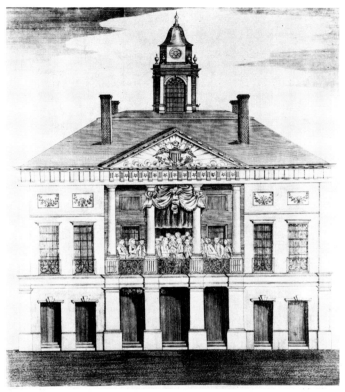

Laying the cornerstone of the Capitol, September 18, 1793, from Duncan S. Walker's *Celebration of the One Hundredth Anniversary of the Laying of the Corner Stone*. The *Columbian Centinel* of Boston reported on October 5, 1793: "The Plate was then delivered to the President, who, attended by the grand master P.T.—and three most worshipful masters descended into the cavasson trench, and deposed the plate, and laid on it the cornerstone of the Capitol of the United States of America—on which was deposed corn, wine, and oil,

when the whole congregation joined in awful prayer, which was succeeded by Masonic chanting honours and a volley from the artillery. . . .

"The whole company retired to an extensive booth, where an ox of 500 lbs. was barbecued, of which the company generally partook, with every abundance of other recreation. The festival concluded with fifteen successive vollies from the artillery, whose military discipline and manoeuvers, merit every commendation."

Inauguration of George Washington on the balcony of Federal Hall, New York City, April 30, 1789. Engraving by Amos Doolittle after a drawing by Peter Lacour, 1790.

Federal Hall was built in 1699 as the city hall. In 1788–1789 Pierre L'Enfant remodeled it for use by the new national government. It was richly decorated with marble pavements, painted ceilings, and crimson damask hangings. Such were the swaddling clothes of the infant nation.

This first image of federal architecture would reappear—

in a competition proposal for a new capitol in Washington and in 1933 as the presidential reviewing stand for the inaugural parade of Franklin D. Roosevelt.

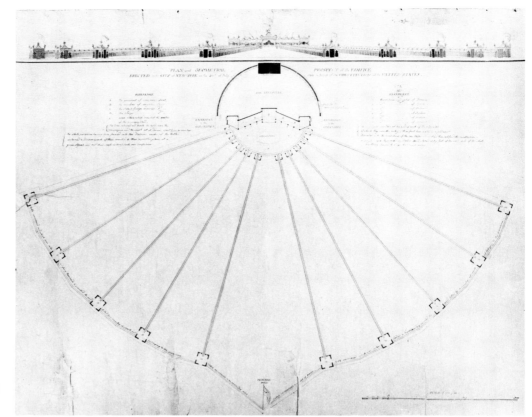

Plan and Geometrical Prospect of the Edifice Erected in the City of New York on 23 July 1788 in Honor of the Constitution, drawn by Major Pierre Charles L'Enfant. L'Enfant was in charge of the celebration, attended by more than 6,000 people. The pavilion was his first important design commission in America. He later remodeled Federal Hall in New York and laid out the plan for the new capital city of Washington, D.C.

Symbolic design dedicated to the Congress of the United States, by Charles Buxton, M.D., engraved by Cornelius Tiebout, 1783. Behind Washington is the fort, Bowling Green, with the pedestal from which the statue of George III had been torn, July 9, 1776. Dr. Buxton's design foreshadowed the classical revival soon to dominate American architecture.

"Every American considers it his sacred duty to have a likeness of Washington in his home, just as we have the images of God's saints."

Paul Svinin, Secretary to the Russian Legation in Washington. 1815

"O Washington! How I do love thy name! How have I often adored and blessed thy God, for creating and forming thee the great ornament of human kind."

Ezra Stiles, 1783

"In vain may . . . Plutarch and Polybius vaunt their Alexanders and their Scipios and Caesars, all their boasted virtues would but serve as an appendix to the biography of our Washington."

George Blake, "A Masonic Eulogy on the Life of the Illustrious Brother George Washington," 1800

Triumphal arches erected for
reception of General Washington at Gray's Ferry, near
Philadelphia, April 20, 1780.

*Sacred to the Memory of
Washington*, after John J. Bar-
ralet, c. 1800, painting on
glass by a Chinese artist, apparently commissioned for the
American trade. An identical
composition, with the substi-
tution of President Lincoln's
face, appeared in a popular
print of 1865.

Great Seal of the United States, final design, 1782. The banner motto, "One out of Many," is restated by the symbols: the stars and stripes, olive leaves, arrows, and even the letters in the motto all number thirteen. In 1904 the tail feathers were changed to nine to represent the Judiciary. From time to time the seal has been remodeled, but the basic elements remain the same.

Eagle carved by Samuel Mc-Intire, Salem, Massachusetts, 1805, an early horizontal adaptation of the Great Seal. It has been characterized as the archetype of American eagle carvings. McIntire was a famed New England wood-carver and builder. Among his building designs were the first Salem customhouse and a proposal entered in the design competition for the U.S. Capitol.

Reverse of the Great Seal of the United States, 1782. The Latin rendition of the motto, "God has favored our undertakings," contains thirteen letters. The thirteen layers of the pyramid refer to the original thirteen colonies; the stones stand for self-government. The banner displays the Latin for "New Order of the Ages." The incompleteness of the pyramid symbolically anticipates the addition of new states to the nation.

"Man . . . values animals by their capacity to become his slaves. But for his coats-of-arms, he has chosen, not the pig, but lion and eagle. Here man judges the animal as if it were human, and there is deep within him a loathing for the traits of domestication in man himself. This loathing is a protection against that self-domestication which is one of the consequences of civilization."

C. F. von Weizacher, The History of Nature, 1949

"For my own part, I wish the bald eagle had not been chosen as the representative of our country; he is a bird of bad moral character; he does not get his living honestly . . . too lazy to fish for himself . . . he is generally poor, and often very lousy. Besides, he is a rank coward; the little kingbird, not bigger than a sparrow, attacks him boldly and drives him out of the district."

Benjamin Franklin

First meeting of the Continental Congress, 1774, in Carpenters' Hall, Philadelphia, engraving by Godefroy after Le Barbier in Hilliard d'Auberteuil's *Essais historiques et politiques sur les Anglo-Américains*, Brussels, 1782.

The alliance among the colonies evolved toward an ever-stronger central power—from the early Continental Congresses through the Articles of Confederation to the plans for a federal constitution. That evolution persisted even while Congress itself could sometimes hardly muster a quorum: even ratification of the Treaty of Paris was delayed beyond its deadline for lack of sufficient state representation, and many members fretted lest the British reject the tardy document.

Through this time of troubles, Congresses met in no less than eight different towns. They were thrice driven from Philadelphia between 1774 and 1783—

twice by the British and once by a band of mutinous (and unpaid) American soldiers. During 1783 and 1784, Congress wandered from Princeton to Annapolis to Trenton amidst a flurry of invitations from towns desirous of becoming the seat of national government. The issue of places for a temporary and then a permanent seat became, for a time, "the principal pabulum" of Congress's deliberations. At one point in 1783 the Congress approved tandem capital cities, one in Virginia and one in Delaware. According to John Reps, "This bizarre arrangement was repealed in the following year, but not before one wit suggested that a single town on a wheeled plat-

form could be built and moved from one site to the other as the need arose. The statue of General Washington, just authorized by the Congress, was also to be portable so that it could accompany the mobile town!"

In early 1785 Congress settled itself into New York City, and until the "ten-mile-square" on the Potomac was finally chosen, the question of a permanent home filled the thoughts and proceedings of the national legislators.

States and cities vied to pluck this promising plum. A consensus emerged—

and was incorporated into Article I of the Constitution—regarding the need for a seat solely under federal jurisdiction. The question of location was not resolved, however, until the Residence Act of July 16, 1790 chose a Potomac River site "at some place between mouths of the Eastern Branch and Connocheque." The law provided for a ten-year interregnum at Philadelphia while the new capital was being planted in the Potomac wilderness. The ambitions of other localities were not easily squelched: serious proposals to remove the capital to another city were intermittently discussed until the 1870s.

Congress House, Baltimore, Maryland, wood engraving in *Frank Leslie's Illustrated Newspaper*, 1882. Congress rented this house from one Henry Fite and met here December 1776 through February 1777. Of Congress's stay in Baltimore (which one delegate termed an "extravagant hole"), Benjamin Rush wrote "We live here in a Convent, we converse only with one another" (February 8, 1776). The lack of local diversions may have facilitated concentration: Samuel Adams declared that "We have done more important business in three weeks than we had done, and I believe should have done, at Philadelphia, in six months" (January 9, 1777).

Carpenters' Hall, Philadelphia built in 1770–1773 from a design by member Robert Smith. Shown here, the front elevation as engraved by Thomas Bedwell for the 1786 Rule Book entitled *Articles of the Carpenters Company of Philadelphia: and their Rules for Measuring and Valuing House-Carpenters Work.*

This meeting place was selected by the more radical delegates, chiefly as an arbitrary show of strength against the conservatives' offer of the State House. The former argued that using the carpenters' guild hall would be "highly agreeable to the mechanics and citizens in general."

"*Where will Congress find a resting place?—they have led a kind of vagrant life ever since 1774, when they first met to oppose Great-Britain. Every place they have taken to reside in has been made too hot to hold them; either the enemy would not let them stay, or people made a clamour because they were too far north or too far south, and oblige them to remove. . . . We pity the poor congress-men, thus kicked and cuffed about from post to pillar—where can they find a home?*"

New York Advertiser, January 27, 1791

Courthouse in Lancaster, Pennsylvania, scene of a brief Congressional session in 1777. Sketch by Benjamin Latrobe.

The Government House, intended for the residence of the President, New York City, 1790. The capital was removed to another place before Washington could occupy this house. Subsequently it became the Governor's House and then was used as the Customhouse from 1799 to 1815, when it was demolished. A similar house, also never used, was constructed for the President in Philadelphia.

State House, Annapolis, Maryland, home of the Confederation Congress when the Treaty of Paris was signed here in 1783. At the beginning of the Annapolis visit the legislators met briefly in the small building to the right.

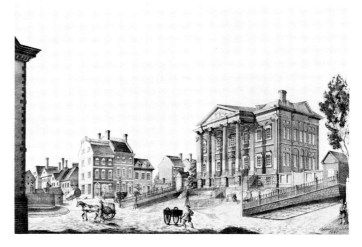

Philadelphia County Building—Congress Hall. The federal establishment that lodged here from 1790 until adequate quarters were ready in a new capital city was something less than multitudinous: the State, War, Navy, and Post Office departments that moved to Washington in 1800 totaled 131 employees.

Cartoon of the day critical of
the Congressional decision to
leave New York for Philadelphia in 1790. Here the Devil
beckons legislators from their
home in Federal Hall to the
wicked pleasures of Philadelphia.

Chronological Table of the Capitals

First Continental Congress

Monday, September 5, 1774 to Wednesday, October 24, 1774	Philadelphia	Carpenters' Hall

Second Continental Congress

Wednesday, May 10, 1775 to Thursday, December 12, 1776	Philadelphia	State House
Friday, December 20, 1776 to Thursday, February 27, 1777	Baltimore	Henry Fite's House
Tuesday, March 4, 1777 to Thursday, September 18, 1777	Philadelphia	State House
Saturday, September 27, 1777	Lancaster	Courthouse
Tuesday, September 30, 1777 to Saturday, June 27, 1778	York	Courthouse
Thursday, July 2, 1778 to Thursday, March 1, 1781	Philadelphia	College Hall, then State House

Congress under the Articles of Confederation

Thursday, March 1, 1781 to Saturday, June 21, 1783	Philadelphia	State House
Monday, June 30, 1783 to Tuesday, November 4, 1783	Princeton	"Prospect," then Nassau Hall
Wednesday, November 26, 1783 to Thursday, August 19, 1784	Annapolis	State House
Monday, November 1, 1784 to Friday, December 24, 1784	Trenton	French Arms Tavern
Tuesday, January 11, 1785 to an indefinite date in autumn of 1788	New York	City Hall, then Fraunce's Tavern

Congress under the Constitution

Wednesday, March 4, 1789 to Thursday, August 12, 1790	New York	Federal Hall
Monday, December 6, 1790 to Wednesday, May 14, 1800	Philadelphia	Philadelphia County Building—Congress Hall
Monday, November 17, 1800	Washington	Capitol

Source: Robert Fortenbaugh, *Nine Capitals of the U.S.* (York, Pennsylvania, Maple Press Co.), 1948.

North, or Senate, wing of the Capitol, 1800. Watercolor by William R. Birch. On November 22, 1800, President Adams congratulated a joint session of Congress, meeting in their new capital city, "on the prospect of a residence not to be changed." On the occasion—huddled in the only finished wing of the Capitol, surrounded by moats of mud, amidst an undulating wilderness where only 3,000 souls dwelt outside Georgetown and Alexandria—Abigail Adams observed, "Congress poured in, but shiver, shiver."

L'Enfant Has a Vision

Pierre Charles L'Enfant (1754–1825). On September 1, 1789, L'Enfant wrote to Washington that planning the nation's capital city "offer[s] so great an occasion of acquiring reputation, to whoever may be appointed to conduct the execution of the business, that Your Excellency will not be surprised that my ambition and the desire I have of becoming a usefuli citizen should lead me to wish a share in the undertaking."

Pursuant to the Residence Act of 1790, President Washington selected the exact site for the District of Columbia along the Potomac River near Georgetown and appointed three commissioners to supervise the development of the new capital. In early 1791, Washington dispatched Andrew Ellicott, the Geographer General of the United States, to survey the District and in March asked the French engineer, Pierre L'Enfant, to undertake the design for the city of Washington.

L'Enfant prepared an initial map in June and completed a plan in August 1791. He had combined the radiating avenues of his native French tradition with the grid of streets currently favored in American planning. Following the prevailing principles of rational taste popularized by the European Enlightenment, the measured spaces of his plan symbolized a rational, orderly society and provided for the separate functions of government.

L'Enfant viewed his role as that of an artist with sole control over his project. This notion led to direct conflict with the District's three Commissioners, and, eventually, to L'Enfant's dismissal in February 1792. Not particularly helpful to his cause was his removal of a house that lay in the path of a street proposed on his plan; the house belonged to one of the Commissioners. He predicted that "the same Reasons which have driven me from the establishment will prevent any man of capacity . . . from engaging in a work that must defeat his sanguine hopes and baffle every exertion." L'Enfant sought for many years—unsuccessfully—to obtain from the government what he considered a just reward for his contributions.

The notes accompanying L'Enfant's map described the vistas and scale, the "reciprocity of sight," the fountains and gathering places, the interrelation of activities that would bring it into a third dimension.

But the vicissitudes of city development and successive planning attempts have left little of L'Enfant's original concept except the street plan. He envisioned a city. A century later his self-acclaimed interpreters would convert his Grand Avenue into the greensward of the parklike Mall. Writing in 1935, planner Elbert Peets observed, "L'Enfant, when the site of Washington was a forest, dreamed of the Mall as a fashionable Parisian avenue, while the Commission of 1901, with a big city spreading all about them, dreamed of the Mall as a quiet sanctuary from the city's noise and bustle."

The proceeds from the sale of lots in the federal city were to finance most of the cost of the Capitol and other public buildings. These lots were sold to foreigners as well as American citizens who had faith in the future of the new republic.

TERMS of SALE of LOTS in the CITY of WASH-INGTON, the Eighth Day of *October*, 1792.

ALL Lands purchaſed at this Sale, are to be ſubject to the Terms and Conditions declared by the Preſident, purſuant to the Deeds in Truſt.

The purchaſer is immediately to pay one fourth part of the purchaſe money; the reſidue is to be paid in three equal annual payments, with yearly intereſt of ſix per cent. on the whole principal unpaid : If any payment is not made at the day, the payments made are to be forfeited, or the whole principal and intereſt unpaid may be recovered on one ſuit and execution, in the option of the Commiſſioners.

The purchaſer is to be entitled to a conveyance, on the whole purchaſe money and intereſt being paid, and not before. No bid under Three Dollars to be received.

"A European, when he first arrives, seems limited in his intentions, as well as in his views, but he very suddenly alters his scale. . . . He no sooner breathes our air than he forms new schemes, and embarks in designs he never would have thought of in his own country. . . . He begins to feel the effects of a sort of resurrection; hitherto he had not lived, but simply vegetated; he now feels himself a man, because he is treated as such. . . . The American is a new man who acts upon new principles; he must therefore entertain new ideas, and form new opinions."

Hector St. John de Crèvecoeur, Letters From an American Farmer, 1782

"It was a supreme irony that the plan forms originally conceived to magnify the glories of despotic kings and emperors came to be applied as a national symbol of a country whose philosophical basis was so firmly rooted in democratic equality."

John Reps, Monumental Washington: The Planning and Development of the Capital Center, 1967

George Washington and His Family Looking at the L'Enfant Plan, painting by Edward Savage. Convinced that the site just below Georgetown lay at the junction of natural thoroughfares, Washington prophesied the rise of a great city. This conviction may have derived partly from his earlier involvement in land speculation in the area. Nonetheless, he successfully kept secret his choice for the exact location of the city of Washington within the District in order to play the landowners off against one another and thus minimize the cost to the government.

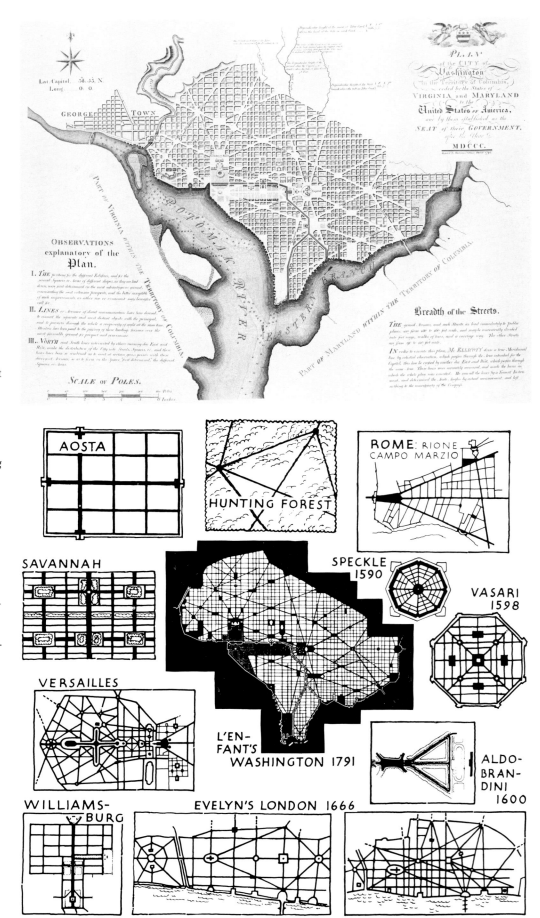

The official plan of Washington, engraved in Philadelphia by Thackara and Vallance, October 1792. Andrew Ellicott, surveyor for the District, prepared the plan after L'Enfant had been dismissed. L'Enfant refused to surrender his drawings to Ellicott, and, although the latter's version does not differ significantly from L'Enfant's plan of August 1792, the official map does not mention L'Enfant at all.

Antecedents of the L'Enfant plan, from Elbert Peets, "Famous Town Planners III—L'Enfant," *The Town Planning Review,* July 1928. In determining the genealogy of L'Enfant's plan the problem, according to civic planner Elbert Peets, was "to account for the two conspicuous distinctions of the Washington plan. The first of these, and the most obvious, is that it comprises a system of diagonal streets laid over a plaid or irregular gridiron of rectangular streets. The second is that the plan has a central controlling axis scheme or organization, intended primarily to give the Capitol and President's residence effective places in the design and to enable them to dominate it."

Thomas Jefferson advised Americans that "architecture is among the most important arts; and it is desirable to introduce taste into an art which shows so much." Their taste would be developed only if "we avail ourselves of every occasion when public buildings are to be created, of presenting them as models for their study and imitation."

Of the existing American patterns for a national architectural presence he decried their "burden of barbarous ornaments." The first principles of the art of architecture, he claimed, were unknown, and "there exists scarcely a model among us sufficiently chaste to give an idea of them." He dismissed the foremost model, Williamsburg—the Capitol, "tolerably just in its proportion," but "its ornaments not proper to the order"; the Palace, "not handsome without"; the College and Hospital, "rude, misshapen piles which, but they have roofs, would be taken for brick kilns."

Jefferson owned the largest architectural library in the country. His personal taste in private buildings was for the Renaissance classicism of Andrea Palladio. During a diplomatic tour in France, however, his political sensibilities responded to the congruence of Republican virtues and Roman forms. He concluded that classical forms, particularly of the Roman republic, were most suitable for the public architecture of the new American republic.

Today it would seem that Jefferson's politics was visionary, his architecture antiquarian. But when he selected a temple for the state capitol of Virginia in 1780—that "favorable opportunity of introducing into the State an example of architecture in the classic style of antiquity"—his choice was imaginative. In Europe the classical structures were being copied for commemorative monuments but seldom for momumental buildings. No national leader had yet imagined a broad symbolic scheme of housing the work of government in the forms of ancient republics. Ironically, Napoleon would soon emulate Jefferson's example.

As Governor of Virginia and Secretary of State and President of the United States Jefferson was uniquely positioned to influence the architectural ideas of the new nation, to direct popular attention to the models of Greece and Rome—and uniquely empowered to determine that these models would be built.

The culminating and most complete model of his public design philosophy was the University of Virginia. Stylistically it was built on the ruins of republican Rome. Spatially it materialized republican America and Jefferson's views of the society necessary for harmony among men in collective situations. Like Jeffersonian democracy, the university ensemble is composed of separate yet united parts.

Jefferson as gentleman-scientist. His love of classical order was also reflected in his championship of the metric system of measurement and currency. Engraving by Cornelius Tiebout, 1801, after a painting by Rembrandt Peale.

The Oath of the Tennis Court, ink and wash, Jacques Louis David, 1791. Jefferson admired the painter David's revolutionary activities and shared his veneration for classical Roman forms. Like many of their contemporaries they valued antiquity because in it seemed to be the traits compatible with the republican political virtues they desired. "Be stern, like the grand old Romans," said David.

Detail of Ionic column, Stuart and Revett, *Antiquities of Athens*, 1762, one of the numerous volumes of scientific archaeology published in the late eighteenth century and known to Jefferson. The excavation of Pompeii had begun in 1755. These new sources provided a basis for challenging Palladian orthodoxy but stimulated instead an imitation of archaeological styles.

"Architecture is my delight. . . . But it is an enthusiasm of which I am not ashamed, as its object is to improve the taste of my countrymen, to increase their reputation, to reconcile them to the rest of the world, and procure them its praise."

Thomas Jefferson

"Each new age rewrites history in terms of its own ideals; the classic past became all things to all men. It was the Simple Life of Rousseau, the Upright Life of Diderot; to the Revolutionists it was Democracy, and to Napoleon Empire."

Hugh Morrison, **Early American Architecture**, 1952

"When the empire of America shall fall, the subject for contemplative sorrow will be infinitely greater than crumbling brass and marble can inspire. It will not then be said, here stood a temple of vast antiquity, here rose a Babel of invisible height, or there a palace of sumptuous extravagance, but here, ah painful thought, the noblest work of human wisdom, the grand scheme of human glory, the fair cause of freedom, rose and fell."

Thomas Paine

"Pray get me by some means or other a compleat set of Piranesi's drawings of the Pantheon. . . . I wish to render them useful in the public buildings now to be begun at Georgetown. . . ."

Thomas Jefferson, letter to William Short, 1791

Maison Carrée, Nîmes, France. Jefferson wrote that he had sat before this Roman temple for hours, "gazing . . . like a lover at his mistress." He sent the Virginia legislature sketches of the Maison to provide classical authority for his proposed design for a state capitol at Richmond. To adapt the windowless Roman temple to a legislature building Jefferson inserted rows of windows and a gallery that later collapsed with some loss of life. He may have substituted Ionic capitals for the more complex Corinthian order on the Maison because of the dearth of trained sculptors in America.

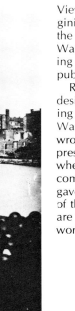

View of Richmond and Virginia Capitol, 1865, records the devastation of the Civil War as well as the commanding presence of Jefferson's public temple.

Robert Mills, famed for his designs for the Treasury Building and Patent Office and the Washington Monument, wrote: "I remember the impression it made on my mind when first I came in view of it coming from the South. It gave me an idea of the effect of those Greek temples which are the admiration of the world."

"Jefferson's architecture combined excellence at the level of design and symbol with specific gadgetry-inventiveness. As a patrician-amateur, however, he lacked the training and background that would connect elegance invariably with utility. His Richmond Capitol was plagued with an incommodious interior. His copyist tendencies approached absurdity when, in 1805-06, he insisted—over Latrobe's specific practical objections—that the domed roof of the House of Representatives in the Capitol be lighted with wedge-shaped skylights copied from the Halle aux Blés in Paris. He rejected Latrobe's more effective lantern concept because, among other reasons, he could find no ancient classic precedent for it."

Talbot Hamlin, Benjamin Henry Latrobe, 1955

"There is an expression in music, 'doubling in brass.' You play in the strings but you can double in the brass section. Jefferson could double in brass. In the Jeffersonian sense, everything is architecture: his design for the University of Virginia not only concerned the building, but the curriculum, the professors, the faculty. His Land Ordinance for the settlement of the West was the grandest conception of land use America has seen—and to Jefferson it was pure architecture."

Charles Eames, in Observer Magazine, November 2, 1975

Jefferson's plan for Washington, 1791. Jefferson served as Washington's liaison with L'Enfant and the District Commissioners. L'Enfant's final plan for the new city incorporated the grid design favored by both Washington and Jefferson.

Study for the Capitol, Thomas Jefferson, c. 1792. A Pantheon-inspired rotunda was in Jefferson's mind before the competition for the design of the U.S. Capitol was held. He wrote to L'Enfant in 1791: "Whenever it is proposed to prepare plans for the Capitol, I should prefer the adoption of some one of the models of antiquity, which have had the approbation of thousands of years."

Although Jefferson was not a contestant in the Capitol competition, he had a lively and active interest in the outcome. This sketch—strikingly like the Capitol of today—was probably done to convey his ideas to the competitors, especially Hallet.

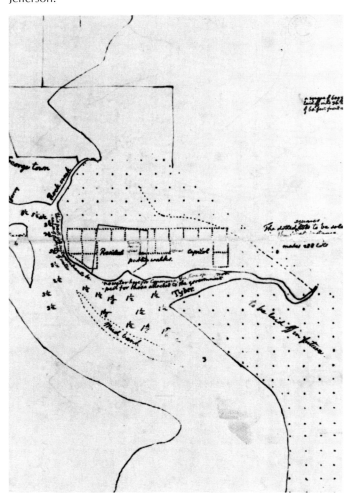

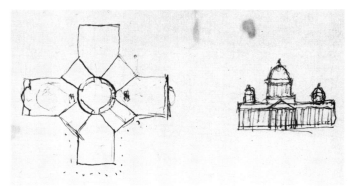

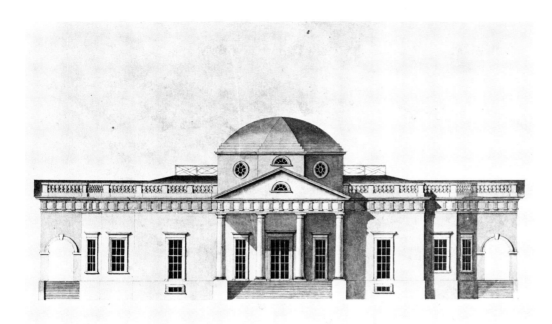

West elevation of the final version of Monticello, drawing attributed to Robert Mills, 1803, who studied architecture with Jefferson at Monticello and would later be the chief public architect of Andrew Jackson's administration. Jefferson's house, along with Washington's Mount Vernon, was destined to join the panoply of American symbols. The Jefferson-style rotunda would later be copied for the twentieth-century memorial to him in Washington, D.C.

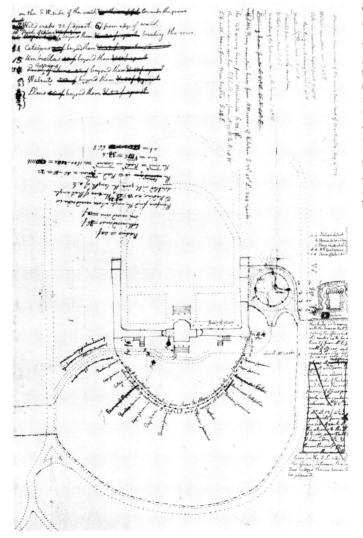

General plan of the summit of Monticello mountain, 1771–1772. Architectural historian Vincent Scully observes that Monticello and "much of Jefferson's work should be seen, metaphorically speaking, as a struggle between the fixed European past and the mobile American future, between Palladio and Frank Lloyd Wright, between a desire for contained, classical geometry and an instinct to spread out horizontally along the surface of the land."

Thomas Jefferson, Gentleman Architect

28–29

Section of the Rotunda, University of Virginia, c. 1821.

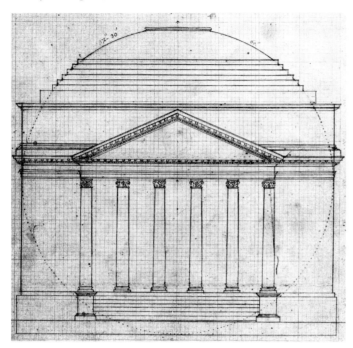

Elevation and plans for Pavilion X, University of Virginia, 1819. Each pavilion represented a different classical model. The Rotunda, overlooking the ensemble, was a model, in Jefferson's phrase, of "spherical architecture," as the pavilions were a model of the cubical.

Jefferson is believed to have been the first American to use graph paper for architectural drawings, which provided a modular system for sizing elements as multiples of a common measure.

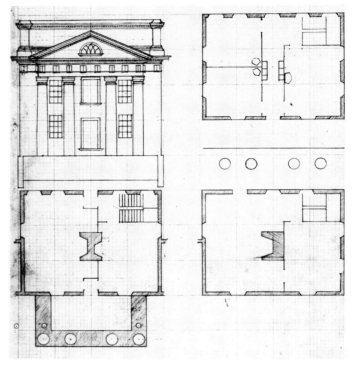

University of Virginia, 1826 (the Böye Print, believed to be the most accurate drawing of the University).

Temple-like pavilions, housing the classes and the heads of the ten schools, are connected by colonnaded dormitories. At the head, on the highest ground, is the Rotunda, resembling the Roman Pantheon. The architectural rank of dormitory and pavilion, of student and professor, are mediated by the common space of the central square.

Spread out on the land, the University was an important departure from the custom of building one large university building—"a large and common den of noise, of filth, and of fetid air."

"We are commencing here the establishment of a college," Jefferson wrote. ". . . This village form is preferable to a single great building for many reasons, particularly on account of fire, health, economy, peace and quiet. . . . These pavilions . . . shall be models of taste and good architecture, and a variety of appearance, no two alike, so as to serve as specimens of the Architectural lectures."

WASHINGTON, *in the Territory of* COLUMBIA.

A PREMIUM

Of a LOT, in the City, to be defig-
nated by impartial Judges, and FIVE HUNDRED DOLLARS,
or a MEDAL of that Value, at the Option of the Party, will
be given by the Commiffioners of the Federal Buildings, to the
Perfon who, before the Fifteenth Day of July, 1792, fhall produce to them the moft approved PLAN, if adopted by them, for
a CAPITOL, to be erected in this City; and TWO HUN-
DRED and FIFTY DOLLARS, or a MEDAL, for the Plan
deemed next in merit to the one they fhall adopt. The Building to be of Brick, and to contain the following Apartments,
to wit:

A Conference-Room, ⎤ fufficient to ac- ⎤
A Room for the Repre- ⎬ commodate 300 | Thefe Rooms
   fentatives, ⎦ Perfons each. | to be of full
A Lobby or Antichamber to the latter, ⎬ Elevation.
A Senate-Room of 1200 fquare Feet Area, |
An Antichamber or Lobby to the laft. ⎦

Twelve Rooms of 600 fquare Feet Area each, for Committee-
Rooms, and Clerks' Offices, to be of Half the Elevation of the
former.

Drawings will be expected of the Ground-Plats, Elevations of
each Front, and Sections through the Building, in fuch Directions
as may be neceffary to explain the internal Structure; and an
Eftimate of the cubic Feet of Brick-Work compofing the whole
Mafs of the Walls.

March 14, 1792.   THE COMMISSIONERS.

Advertisement of the competition for design of the Capitol, published April 3, 1792. A similar advertisement, drafted by Jefferson, announced the competition for the President's House. That program, without the precise specifications of the Capitol, left more freedom to the designer.

After the dismissal of Pierre L'Enfant, Thomas Jefferson persuaded President Washington to select the designs for the Capitol and the President's House through design competitions, an approach Jefferson had favored during the earlier stages of planning for the new capital city. In March 1792, the District Commissioners announced the competitions that were to be a major effort to depart from the style and scale of colonial public buildings.

The entrants still turned to the architectural handbooks and texts that had traditionally helped the carpenter-builder achieve architecture. The results reflected both colonial antecedents and the newer classical authorities plus a seasoning of American symbols—various eagles, a garland of American roses. On July 18, the day after the judging by the President and the three Commissioners, first prize for

the President's House was awarded to the Irish-born architect James Hoban, who was also engaged to supervise construction.

The Capitol competition dragged on through a year of controversy. When none of the submissions was satisfactory, Stephen Hallet, as best of the lot, was asked to revise his drawings. Despite the July 15 deadline for submissions the Commissioners accepted a new entry from a Dr. William Thornton in November, which he subsequently revised. With the blessing of Washington and Jefferson, Thornton was awarded the long-delayed prize in April 1793. To assuage the second-place Hallet, the Commissioners gave him a compensatory award equal in value to Thornton's prize and allowed him to supervise construction. The cornerstone of the Capitol

was laid by Washington in a grand Masonic ceremony in September. After continuous difficulties, including a war, the first edition of the Capitol was completed by Charles Bulfinch in 1828.

The open and lively exchanges, the unruly procedures of the competitions would today seem either odd or unethical. But the leaders were bent on finding a design idea, not an architect. Indeed, the only architects among the contestants were Hoban and Hallet. A builder could always be found, and, as it happened, architect Hallet was hired to assist with the construction of Thornton's design; architect Hoban supervised the building of his own design.

Not everyone was pleased with the results. There were no professional restraints in those days governing architects' criticism of building designs. Architect George Hadfield, for instance, noted that the

Capitol competition occurred "at a period when scarcely a professional architect was to be found in any of the United States; which is plainly to be seen in the pile of trash presented as designs for said building." Benjamin Latrobe did not like Hoban's President's House. He found the south entrance "disproportioned," the north entrance "undistinguished." He would amend Hoban's design when Jefferson was in residence, adding the now-familiar south portico that today overlooks the Ellipse and, once a year, the national Christmas tree.

The building and redesigning process would long continue for the government's first two principal buildings, especially the Capitol. That they would also continue to exhibit a basic architectural unity suggests an agreement about the symbolic confluence of classical design and federal power.

East front of the Capitol as proposed by Thornton, 1795–1797. This version is a later adaptation by Thornton to suit the foundations started by the second prize winner, Stephen Hallet.

Hallet's alterations of the winning design during construction incurred the wrath of Thornton and the displeasure of the President. Jefferson suggested that Hallet's revisions would be "considered as Dr. Thornton's plans rendered into practical form," but Hallet was dismissed in November 1794. The next supervising architect, George Hadfield, soon came to resign on principle, believing the Thornton-Hallet hybrid could not be executed.

Dr. William Thornton (1759–1828), charcoal portrait by Charles Balthazar Julien Favret de St. Memin, c. 1800. Thornton was born in the British West Indies and educated in England. After he became a U.S. citizen, in 1788, he won the first architectural competition to be held in America—for a public library in Philadelphia. He wrote that he "got some books and worked a few days, then gave a plan in the ancient Ionic order which carried the day."

Although untrained in architecture, Thornton waged a protracted war on many fronts to protect his design from commissioners, supervising architects, and others lacking what he considered the appropriate sensibilities. His exchanges with architect Benjamin Latrobe eventually culminated in a successful libel suit by Latrobe. Thornton served as one of the District Commissioners and in 1802 he was appointed head of the Patent Office.

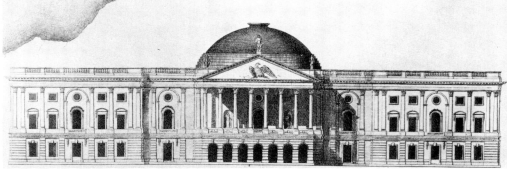

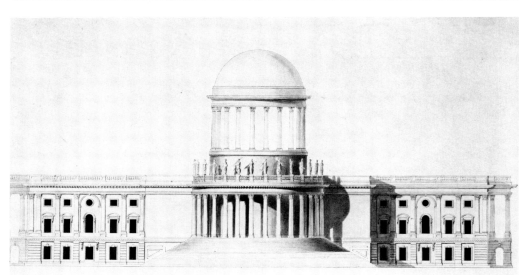

West front of the Capitol as proposed by Thornton, showing an alternative design for the dome, 1795.

Losing entry for the Capitol by Philip Hart, c. 1793.

Losing entry for the Capitol by James Diamond, who also submitted a design for the President's House competition. The same bird decoration appears on his other entry.

"It may be relied on, it is the progress of that building [the Capitol] that is to inspire or depress the public confidence."

George Washington, letter to the Commissioners

"It is surprising that some of the advisers of General Washington . . . did not advise the only method by which the success of the building, in all its stages, might have been ensured, which was, by offering an adequate sum to the most eminent architect in any of the great cities of Europe. . . . Under such a system the whole of the Capitol would have been long ago completed for half the sum that has been expended on the present wreck."

George Hadfield, 1820

"This mode of procuring designs of public buildings, though exceedingly common, is certain of defeating its own end. It brings into competition all the personal vanity of those who think they have knowledge and taste in an art which they have never had an opportunity to learn or practice—of all those who, enticed by the reward, think that personal influence and interest will procure it for them—and of all those who know of design nothing but its execution; and it keeps out of the competition all who have too much self-respect to run the race of preference with such motley companions, and especially of all regularly educated professional men,—who understand their business too well not to know that a picture is not a design. . . ."

Benjamin Henry Latrobe, "A Private Letter to the Individual Members of Congress on the Subject of Public Buildings of the United States at Washington," 1806

". . . if none more elegant than these drawings should appear on or before the 10th. instant, the exhibition of architecture will be a very dull one indeed."

George Washington, letter to one of the Commissioners, July 9, 1792

Winning design for the President's House by James Hoban.

"We wish to exhibit a grandeur of conception, a Republican simplicity, and that true Elegance of proportion which corresponds to a tempered freedom excluding Frivolity, the food of little minds."

Letter from the D.C. Commissioners, January 4, 1793, to the municipal authorities of Bordeaux, requesting permission to recruit French craftsmen for the President's House

Design for a house to have been built in Greenwich, England, James Gibbs, 1720.

The Palladian design by Irish-born architect Hoban resembled designs in James Gibbs's *Book of Architecture, Containing Designs of Buildings and Ornaments*, published in 1728.

"The Palace . . . should stand in the Heart of a City, it should be easy of access, beautifully adorned, and rather delicate and polite. . . ." (Leone Battista Alberti, *Ten Books on Architecture*, 1755).

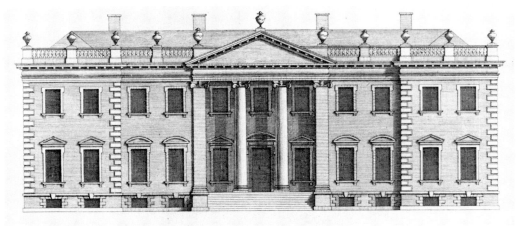

Andrea Palladio's Villa Rotonda, from Giacomo Leoni, *The Architecture of A. Palladio*, Book IV, Plate XLV, 1715. Palladio's popular precedent was used by Hoban and Jefferson as the model for their submissions for the President's House and by two other competitors for their Capitol entries. Palladio's design features were echoed in many of the other entries.

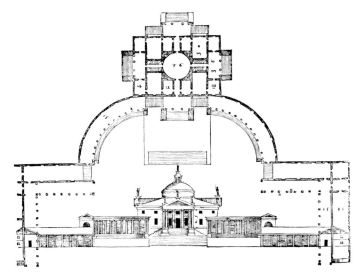

Losing entry for the President's House by Thomas Jefferson, submitted under the initials "A.Z."

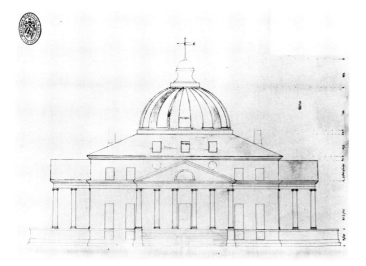

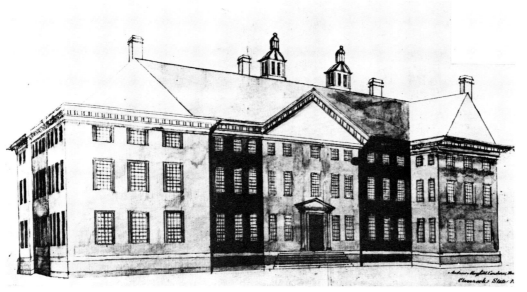

Losing entry for the President's House by Andrew M. Carshore, 1792, the only competition attempt at perspective drawing. Carshore was a school teacher and noted for his fine penmanship.

Detail of canopy and hall doorway for the President's House, Andrew M. Carshore. Beside the doorway was Carshore's instruction, "The Place or Canopy over the Presidents' [sic] Chair these two Columns appear in Front." This was the only entry with such a regal trapping as a throne. Above the door Carshore noted the more acceptable ornament: "Place for a spread Eagle."

Benjamin Henry Latrobe, portrait by Rembrandt Peale, c. 1816.

On March 6, 1803, three days after Congress allocated $50,000 for further work on the Capitol, President Jefferson invited Benjamin Henry Latrobe to be the first "Surveyor of the Public Buildings." In this and related positions, Latrobe spent more than a decade designing and supervising work on both the Capitol and the White House. Other important government commissions came to him through Albert Gallatin, Jefferson's Secretary of the Treasury.

English by birth and training, Latrobe had ventured to America in 1796. By 1803 he had a national reputation as both an architect and an engineer. He was also, incidentally, a fine watercolorist. To his credit especially were his achievements in Philadelphia—the city waterworks

and the vaulted Greek Revival Bank of Pennsylvania. He was among the few architects who were trying to establish themselves as professionals, in contrast to the gentlemen amateurs—like Thornton and Jefferson—and the ambitious carpenters who were designing most of America's buildings. Latrobe's professional skills covered the range of building design. The split between architecture and engineering had not yet occurred.

Latrobe's federal architectural career was a strong brew of aesthetic sophistication and technical innovation, laced with spirited controversy. His close connection with Jefferson was, at once, the foundation of his government practice and a point of departure for attacks from

the opposition Federalist press. Latrobe's outspokenness often fueled these attacks. His running battle with William Thornton, a Federalist adherent, over Latrobe's revisions in the good doctor's Capitol design eventually resulted in a libel suit against Thornton, which Latrobe won. He complained about the criticism of Congressmen and other officials who persistently intervened in what he thought were professional decisions. Even the partnership between the professional architect and the Presidential patron faltered in a battle over the ceiling in the House of Representatives. Latrobe insisted that Jefferson's academically classical solution would leak. A compromise solution did leak and, on Latrobe's part, the matter

did not rest until he rebuilt the ceiling—his way—after the fire of 1814.

Preoccupied by impending war in early 1812, Congress postponed further Capitol construction and also took the occasion to dismiss Latrobe. He moved to Pittsburgh and a reportedly disastrous collaboration with Robert Fulton in a steamboat enterprise. In 1815 he was recalled to Washington to repair damage the British had done to the Capitol. He redesigned the two wings, planned the central, or rotunda section, and rebuilt a large part of the wings. In 1817 he was forced out by an aggressive D.C. Commissioner, an aloof President Monroe, and a suspicious Congress. "Government service," he lamented, "is a ruinous connection."

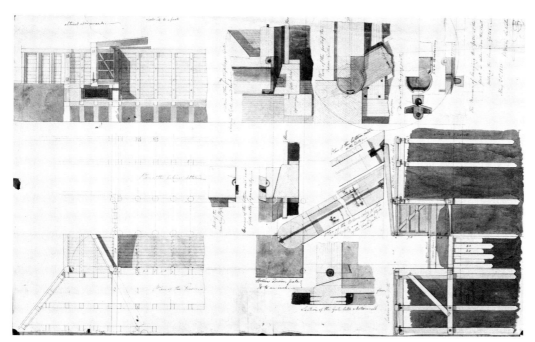

Benjamin Latrobe, Government Architect

Details of gates and locks, Washington City Canal, drawing by Latrobe, 1810.

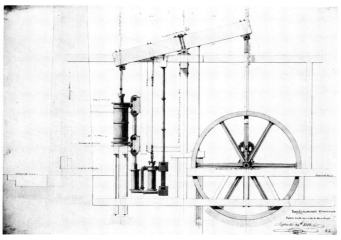

Latrobe's design for an engine for the Navy Yard, Washington, D.C., watercolor by James Smallman, 1809. Latrobe added to his government pay by also holding the position of engineer for the expanding Navy Department.

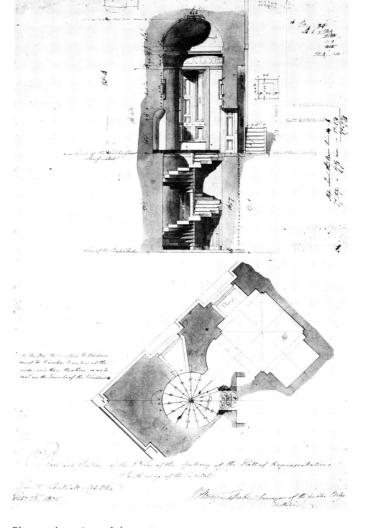

Plan and section of the staircase to the House gallery, House of Representatives, Capitol, watercolor by Latrobe, 1805.

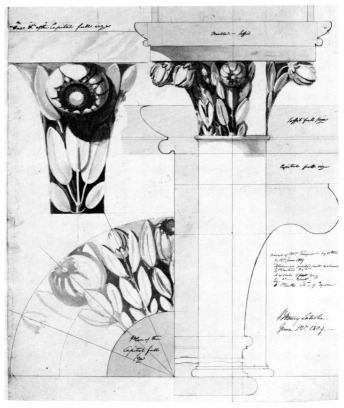

Letter from Latrobe to Jefferson concerning the tobacco plant capital, November 5, 1816, one of the three Latrobe designed for the Capitol using indigenous plants important to the economy of America. "I have composed a capital of leaves and flowers of the tobacco plant which has an intermediate effect, approaching a Corinthian order and retaining the simplicity of the Clepsydra or Temple of Winds."

Indian corn column and capital from Senate stair vestibule, Capitol. Latrobe shipped a model to Jefferson, who used it to support a sundial in his Monticello garden. Latrobe wrote Jefferson that "[T]his capital, during the summer session obtained me more applause from the members of Congress than all the Works of Magnitude."

Detail of cotton capital for columns in gallery of entrance to the Senate chamber, Capitol, watercolor by Latrobe, June 12, 1809.

Arches and vault of the Supreme Court chamber of the Capitol, watercolor by Latrobe, 1808. The justices, who met in this room from 1812 to 1860, reportedly found the room so dim and dank that they preferred to meet at a nearby tavern.

"[I am] bidding an eternal adieu to the malice, backbiting, and slander, trickery, fraud, & hypocrisy, lofty pretensions & scanty means, boasts of patriotism & bargaining of conscience, pretense of religion & breach of her laws, starving doctors, thriving attorneys, whitewashing jail oaths, upstart haughtiness, & depressed merit, & five thousand other nuisances that constitute the very essence of this community [Washington] . . . the more you stir it, the more it stinketh. . . . And, in general, honest & right intentioned as is our cold-blooded President [Madison], you might as well stroke an armadillo with a feather by way of making the animal feel, as try to move him by words from any of his opinions or purposes. . . ."

Latrobe's first farewell to Washington, letter to Nathaniel Ingram, September 1813

"I never heard him speak of his early experience, without dwelling upon the annoyances he had from the beginning, when brought into contact professionally with those who regarded an architect as nothing but a better sort of carpenter. . . . The most important public work in America, with which my father's name is connected, is of course the Capitol at Washington, where he was brought in contact with ignorance in all its forms. Here the architect, his plans and estimates, underwent the criticism of members of Congress, nearly all of whom seemed to fancy that their elections made them competent to determine the merits of works of art. . . . The work on the public buildings requiring annual appropriations, these were never made in those days without debate, when the architect and those in any way connected with the building were dealt with, often without mercy."

Letter from Latrobe's son, John H. B. Latrobe, January 29, 1876

"My principles of good taste are rigid in Grecian architecture. I am a bigoted Greek in the condemnation of the Roman architecture of Baalbec, Palmyra, and Spalato. . . . Wherever, therefore the Grecian style can be copied without impropriety I love to be a mere, I would say a slavish copyist, but the forms & the distribution of the Roman & Greek buildings which remain, are in general, inapplicable to the objects & uses of our public buildings. Our religion requires a church wholly different from the temples, our legislative assemblies and our courts of justice, buildings of entirely different principles from their basilicas; and our amusements could not possibly be performed in their theatres & amphitheatres. . . ."

Latrobe to Jefferson, defending the lack of classical precedent for a practical building solution Latrobe wanted, May 21, 1807

". . . a graceful and refined simplicity is the highest achievement of taste and art. . . . We find ornaments increase in proportion as art declines, or as ignorance abounds."

Latrobe, letter to Congress, 1806

Greek Revival chair designed by Latrobe for the Blue Room of the White House, watercolor by Latrobe. The chairs were destroyed in the fire of 1814.

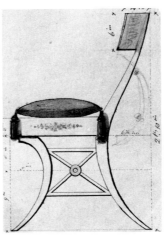

"I believe I am the first who, in our own country, has endeavored & partly succeeded, to place the profession of architect and civil engineer on that footing of responsibility which it occupies in Europe. But I have not so far succeeded as to make it an eligible profession for one who has the education & the feelings of a gentleman. . . ."

Latrobe to Henry Ormond, November 29, 1808

"Your anxiety about me, & regret that I have not yet made my fortune is very flattering & honorable to me. . . . You forget that I am an Engineer in America, that I am neither a mechanic nor a merchant, nor a planter of cotton, rice or tobacco; for you know it as well as I do, that with us the labor of the hand has precedence over that of the mind; that an engineer is considered only as an overseer of men that dig, and an architect as one that watches others that hew stone & wood. . . . The service of a republic is always a slavery of the most inexorable kind, under a mistress who does not even give to her hirelings civil language. This kind of treatment extends from her first political characters to her menials. . . ."

Latrobe to Constantin F. C. Volney, July 28, 1811

"I can still recall, among the shadowy impressions of my earliest boyhood, the effect, approaching awe, produced upon me by the old Hall of Representatives. I fancy I can see the heavy crimson drapery that hung in massive folds between the tall fluted Corinthian columns to within a short distance of their base, and I remember, or I think I remember, the low, gilded iron railing that ran from base to base, and over which the spectators in the gallery looked down upon the members on the floor. I seem to see, even now, the speaker's chair, with its rich surroundings, and the great stone eagle [with a wingspread over 12 feet] which, with outspread wings, projected from the frieze, as though it were hovering over and protecting those who deliberated below. Of course, after so many years, it is not impossible that form and color have been given to the memories of a boy, nine years old at the time, by what he had seen in the portfolios which were almost the picture-books of his childhood."

John H. B. Latrobe, recalling the room his father designed

"With respect to yourself, the little disquietudes from individuals not chosen for their taste in art, will be sunk into oblivions, while the Representative Chamber will remain a durable monument of your taste as an architect. . . . I shall live in hope that the day will come when an opportunity will be given you of finishing the middle building in a style worthy of the two wings, and worthy of the first temple dedicated to the sovereignty of the people, embellishing with Athenian taste the course of a nation looking far beyond the range of Athenian destinies."

Jefferson to Latrobe, July 12, 1812

The Old House of Representatives, painting by Samuel F. B. Morse (inventor of the telegraph), 1822. In 1807, when members moved in, they complained of the acoustics. John Randolph declared the chamber "handsome and fit for anything but the use intended." The British officer who was ordered to destroy it during the War of 1812 reportedly said that it was "a pity to burn anything so beautiful."

The new Capitol and the President's House, rising on opposite shores of a swamp, resembled ruins more than a brave new world. Between their hilltop sites was a landscape of marshes, barren knolls, tree stumps and rubbish heaps. Stones marked the intersection of L'Enfant's intended avenues.

To this desolate spot came the new legislators and their families to conduct the gritty business of government—and of life in a new town.

Whatever the national outcome, the War of 1812 was a disaster for the federal buildings at Washington. After blockading Chesapeake Bay in 1813, the British began localized attacks. The following year L'Enfant recommended improvement of Washington's fortification system, but Secretary of War Armstrong did not believe there would be an attack on the capital city. In August 1814, Major General Ross led the British forces into Washington. The invaders burned the President's House, the Capitol, and Hadfield's two departmental buildings that flanked the President's House. The Patent Office, housed in a rented building, was spared when William Thornton persuaded the British that the records were vital to science.

Benjamin Latrobe was recalled to rebuild the Capitol; the reconstruction of the President's House was given to the original architect, James Hoban. Latrobe's temper and President Madison's contentious interest in building details did not mix. Latrobe was dismissed, and Charles Bulfinch arrived to replace him in 1818.

A romantic watercolor view of the Capitol from Pennsylvania Avenue, by Benjamin Latrobe, 1812. The passageway between the two wings was constructed of rough boards. The quick-growing Lombardy poplars in the foreground were chosen by Jefferson.

An unromantic view of the Capitol showing chained slaves in the federal city. Congress prohibited slave trading in the District of Columbia in 1850, as part of the Compromise of 1850. By 1860, there were still 2,000 slaves in the District. The city had also become a major haven for free blacks.

"We want nothing here but houses, cellars, kitchens, well-informed men, amiable women, and other little trifles of this kind to make our city perfect."

Gouverneur Morris

"Pennsylvania Avenue was little better than a common country road. On either side were two rows of Lombardy poplars, between which was a ditch, often filled with stagnant water, with crossing places at the intersecting streets. Outside of the poplars was a narrow footway, on which carriages often intruded to deposit their occupants at the brick pavements on which the few houses scattered along the avenue abutted. In dry weather the avenue was all dust; in wet weather, all mud."

John H. B. Latrobe (son of Benjamin Latrobe), recalling the capital city of 1811

"The house [President's House] is made habitable but there is not a single apartment finished. . . . We have not the least fence, yard, or other convenience, without, and the great unfinished audience-room I make a drying room of, to hang up the clothes in."

Abigail Adams, 1800

"There is one good tavern, about forty rods from the capitol and several other houses are built or erecting: but I do not see how the members of Congress can possibly secure lodgings, unless they will consent to live like scholars in a college, or monks in a monastery, crowded ten or twenty in one house, and utterly secluded from society. The only resource for such as wish to live comfortably will be found in Georgetown, three miles distant, over as bad a road in winter as the clay grounds near Hartford. I have made every exertion to secure good lodgings near the office, but shall be compelled to take them at the distance of more than half a mile. There are in fact but few houses in any one place, and most of them small miserable

At Home in the Federal City

huts, which present an awful contrast to the public buildings. The people are poor, and as far as I can judge, they live like fishes, by eating each other. . . . You may look in almost any direction over an extent of ground nearly as large as the city of New York, without seeing a fence or any object except brick-kilns and temporary huts for laborers. . . . All the lands which I have described are valued at fourteen to twenty-five cents the superficial foot. There appears to be a confident expectation that this place will soon exceed any city in the world."

Oliver Woolcott, Jr., Secretary of the Treasury, July 4, 1800

". . . So intense was the flame, that the glass of the lights was melted and I have now lumps, weighing many pounds of glass, run into mass. . . . The appearance of the ruin was awfully grand when I first saw it, and indeed it was terrific, for it threatened immediately to fall, so slender were the remains of the columns that carried the massy entablature. If the colonnade had fallen, the vaulting of the room below might have been beaten down, but fortunately there is not a single arch in the whole building which requires to be taken down. In the north wing, the beautiful doric columns which surrounded the Supreme Court room, have shared the fate of the Corinthian columns of the Hall of Representatives, and in the Senate Chamber, the marble polished columns of fourteen feet shaft, in one block, are burnt to lime, and have fallen down. All but the vault is destroyed. They stand a most magnificent ruin."

Latrobe to Jefferson on the burning of the Capitol, 1814

Contemporary British version of the attack on Washington, 1814.

Section of the Capitol Rotunda, Charles Bulfinch. The walls that supported Bulfinch's light wooden dome today support the nine million pounds of Thomas U. Walter's later cast-iron dome.

Charles Bulfinch, from a drawing by Alvan Clark. Bulfinch, a well-known Boston architect, came to Washington in 1818 to finish reconstruction of the Capitol begun by Latrobe, who was fired. Bulfinch left Washington in 1831.

"The people have now more general objects of attachment with which their pride and political opinions are connected. They are more American; they feel and act more like a nation."

Albert Gallatin, a member of the Ghent peace commission, commenting on the aftermath of the War of 1812

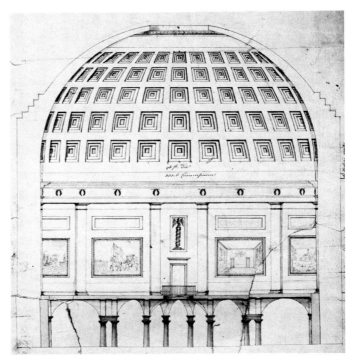

The Capitol as completed by Bulfinch. Latrobe's plan called for a low rotunda dome, but, on the insistence of the Cabinet, Bulfinch built the higher dome seen here. He preferred a dome "about half way between" this one and the very low one Latrobe had designed.

F Street at Fifteenth Street, N.W., looking northwest, 1817, watercolor by Madame Hyde de Neuville, wife of the French minister.

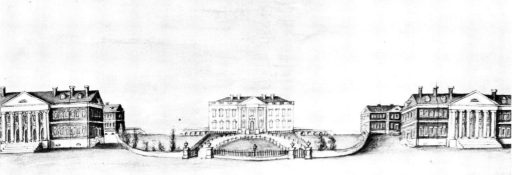

View of the North Front of the White House and the Buildings of the State, Treasury, War, and Navy Department, painting by Madame Hyde de Neuville, 1821. These five structures plus the Capitol were the only major federal buildings in Washington as late as 1836, forty-four years after the city was founded. The four departmental buildings that flanked the White House were all based on a single design by George Hadfield, a striking instance of early standardization for the sake of economy.

"I have received . . . a great number of drawings, exhibiting the work already done [on the Capitol] and other parts proposed, but not decided on. At the first view of these drawings, my courage almost failed me— they are beautifully executed, and the design is in the boldest stile—after longer study I feel better satisfied and more confidence in meeting public expectation. There are certainly faults enough in Latrobe's designs to justify the opposition to him. His stile is calculated for display in the greater parts, but I think his staircases in general are crowded, and not easy of access, and the passages intricate and dark. Indeed, the whole interior, except the two great rooms, has a sombre appearance. I feel the responsibility resting on me, and should have no resolution to proceed if the work was not so far commenced as to make it necessary to follow the plans already prepared for the wings; as to the centre building, a general conformity to the other parts must be maintained. I shall not have credit for invention, but must be content to follow in a prescribed path."

Charles Bulfinch to Hannah Bulfinch, January 7, 1818

"I prepared drawings for domes of different elevations, and, by way of comparison, one of a greater height than the one I should have preferred: they were laid before the Cabinet, and the loftiest one selected, and even a wish expressed that it might be raised higher in a Gothic form, but this was too inconsistent with the style of the building to be at all thought of by me."

Charles Bulfinch, from Ellen Susan Bulfinch, The Life and Letters of Charles Bulfinch, Architect, *1896.*

"Upon the ribs of the dome being boarded, I was so far dissatisfied as to propose to reduce it, stating that the saving in Copper would meet all the expense; but our Commissioner was not a very compliant gentleman and rested upon the Cabinet decision, and, to avoid the altercation which had been so common formerly, I yielded the point. But I should be well pleased if, when the dome requires a thorough repair, which it may in 10 or 15 years, it should be reduced in height,— not to Mr. Latrobe's design, but about half way between that and the present elevation. The foregoing will give my sons a full view of the circumstances under which some of my work was executed; but you will readily see that it is best not to make it too public. Architects expect criticism and must learn to bear it patiently."

Charles Bulfinch, from Ellen Susan Bulfinch, The Life and Letters of Charles Bulfinch, Architect, *1896.*

AMERICAN TEMPLES AND NEEDFUL BUILDINGS

2

Consummation of Empire,
Thomas Cole, 1836, third
painting in "The Course of
Empire," depicting civilization's triumph over obstinate
nature. The fifth and final
scene in the series, titled
Ruins of Empire, portrays the
wilderness invading and over-
running the monumental city.
The grandeur and style of
Cole's vision appealed to
America's romantic mood, but
he pushed beyond the popular optimism to raise brooding
questions about American
destiny.

Customhouse, Ithiel Town and
A. J. Davis, New York, 1842.
The site is at Wall and Nassau
Streets in Manhattan—the former location of Federal Hall,
where George Washington
was inaugurated in 1789. The
structure is now the local
headquarters for the National
Park Service.

"We are under the most imperious obligation to counteract every tendency to disunion. . . . Let us, then, bind the republic together. . . . Let us conquer space!" So urged John Calhoun in 1817 during a Congressional debate on the internal development of the nation.

Within the nation's first half century, the settled frontier tripled its farthest reach inland to over a thousand miles. Congress exercised uncertain control over this even more uncertain and unwieldy public domain, which was larger than the thirteen original states together and larger than any Western European country of the time. Survey and disposal passed for management. In the early heyday of land sales, from 1816 to 1821, the Treasury Department did a land office business, bringing five new states into the Union.

Having secured a nation, Americans bent their energies to securing a continent. New physical evidence of government authority was sparse; beyond the eastern seaboard, the most important impact of the federal presence was in land policy and transportation planning. As historian Daniel Boorstin observed, "Those who came to think that their birthright included a piece of the continent, came also to think it a task of governments to make the land accessible, to increase its value and its usefulness."

"If Americans agreed in any opinion," Henry Adams wrote of the period, "they were united in wishing for roads." Travel in America was at best a trying and at worst a perilous experience. There was little quibble about the need for improved and new transportation arteries that could unite a scattered people and promote their economic betterment. The timeless questions were, Who decides? Who pays? Who profits? In an early version of a highway trust fund, for example, the Ohio Enabling Act of 1802 and later arrangements with other new states provided that a percentage of proceeds from land sales should be used for roads. In 1806 Congress rallied to the cause of a National Road. Wrangling over its highly prized location delayed construction until after the War of 1812. Wrangling over repair bills and toll collections ultimately relegated America's first super-road to the care of the states.

Astute political leaders understood, however, that the clamor for roads and waterways offered a unique opportunity for national planning. In 1807 President John Quincy Adams requested his Secretary of the Treasury, Albert Gallatin, to prepare "a plan for the application of such means as are constitutionally within the power of Congress, to the purpose of making roads, for removing obstructions in rivers, and making canals; together with a statement of the undertakings of that nature now existing within the United States which, as objects of public improvement, may require and deserve the aid of government."

So began the nation's first attempt at national planning. The following year Gallatin sent to the Senate his remarkably detailed *Report on Roads and Canals*, a ten-year plan of national action for a federally supported system of canals and roads. The report concluded, "The National Legislature alone, embracing every local interest, and superior to every local consideration, is competent to the selection of such national objects." It marked the opening of a debate on national planning that would last thirty years.

In this first major effort at national economic and physical planning there was no attempt to go beyond specific engineering projects to social considerations that would characterize the New Deal planning of the 1930s. Also unlike the debate of the 1930s, the heated discussion that went on in the following decades met with little opposition based on any desire of the private sector to do the job itself.

In 1824 a General Survey Act authorized the Corps of Engineers to plan for an integrated network of internal improvement projects. The Corps had originally been established in 1802 to provide and maintain fortifications for the Army. With the 1824 Act the Corps assumed responsibility for civilian public works, an engagement President James Monroe believed would insure that "the military will be incorporated with the civil, and unfounded and injurious distinctions and prejudices of every kind be done away."

The civilian construction role of the Corps of Engineers continued and grew, but local rivalries, sectional politics, constitutional issues, and ultimately the states-rights opposition of President Andrew Jackson defeated the opportunity for effective planning envisioned by the Gallatin report and offered by the 1824 act.

In the design of American space, lack of support for national planning did not reflect any lack of interest in national dollars or favored treatment for internal improvements. There continued a steady flow of appropriations to finance the Corps of Engineers' work for improvements to rivers and harbors, and for military and territorial roads. Substantial appropriations were granted to canal companies through federal subscriptions of stock. In addition, a new form of federal encouragement for state projects was developed in the 1820s when substantial grants of land were made for both roads and canals. Despite their enormous spatial and economic impact, internal improvements remained a series of ad hoc projects—scraps that filled the federal pork barrel.

Building programs were similarly uncoordinated. Federal services struggled to keep up with growth by responding to the mandates of Article I of the Constitution, which gave the government power to "lay and collect taxes . . . to pay the debts and provide for the common defense and general welfare . . . to establish post offices and post roads . . . and to exercise authority over all places purchased . . . for the erection of forts, magazines, arsenals, dockyards, and other needful buildings." Few of these mandates could be carried out without structures of some type.

The forts, magazines, arsenals, and dockyards were familiar enough. Many of them already existed, legacies of colonial beginnings or the prizes of battle. Now, emerging national responsibilities necessitated other structures. A government responsive to a rapidly expanding maritime trade had increased twenty-fold the number of light-houses it operated by mid-century. Excise taxes were collected in the new custom-houses. A major share of public construction went to providing an increased and diversified system of harbor fortifications. Interior forts secured the western trails. And, under a 1798 act providing medical care for seamen, the federal government built its first hospitals.

To handle the government's monies and to try to stabilize the nation's financial affairs the Second Bank of the United States was established in 1816. A federally chartered private institution, the bank was, nonetheless, popularly viewed as public property. Its architectural style, like its economic precepts, was part of the search for national identity. Before the Second Bank system was toppled in 1833 by President Jackson, the bank had scattered twenty-six money temples around the country. These structures, makeshift or magnificent, established a federal presence and a collectively approved architectural symbolism of stability and order, which could impart the aura of real stability to even the most speculative banking enterprise.

With the advent of Greece's war for independence from Turkey in 1821, a Greek Revival mania swept the country. There were Congressional demands for military support. Towns with Greek names and imitation temples sprang up all over the region west of the Alleghenies. A painting celebrating the use of vaccines in medicine was titled *Venus Vaccinated by Aesculapius*. Engines were housed in temple forms. And the temple form packaged all classes of buildings.

The classical revival style appeared peculiarly suited to democratic predilections and the democratization of style. Columns could be added at will—often with little expert knowledge—to provide a temple for everyone, whether banker or legislator or tradesman. This interchangeable, Jack-of-all-trades approach to architectural style was not unlike the attitude toward the land itself, which viewed each measured parcel as theoretically equal to every other parcel.

Thus, as historian Fiske Kimball has observed, Jefferson's dream came true—"to establish the classic as a national style. While it had triumphed in every country, in the older nations of Europe, with firmly established traditions, its success had been tempered by conservatism and common sense. Only on the outskirts of European civilization, in Scotland, in Russia, in America was enthusiasm sophomoric enough to carry through the full classic program. Only in America was it pushed to its extreme consequences."

And, in appropriately solemn versions, the style housed the expanding federal presence. When the full temple form was not used, at least the great colonnade was. In Washington these colonnades graced the new building designs of Robert Mills, a former student of Jefferson and Latrobe and now President Jackson's appointee as architect of public buildings. Begun in the summer of 1836, the Patent Office and Treasury buildings were the capital city's first Greek Revival government buildings and a major influence on the emergence of Washington's classical style. Mills's design for the new

General Post Office also boasted the ubiquitous classical symmetry of columns and pediments. Behind the mandatory facades of antiquity, however, the interiors prophetically responded to the technological and organizational needs of the modern office building. Offices opened off long connecting hallways and fire safety provisions were an important feature. Outside Washington, in his marine hospitals and customhouses, Mills used the imperative American classical style but in standardized, frugal, and technologically innovative versions that spoke of the other government imperatives of economy and the expanding business of bureaucracy.

The first half of the nineteenth century was not a period, however, in which the federal presence was expressed prominently in stone and mortar. Although some notable landmarks appeared, the leaders of the disparate former colonies still felt no strong compulsion to embellish the physical forms of the central government. Most manifestations of the government's presence were small or makeshift. A still limited government satisfied many of its space needs during this period by buying, leasing, and, in at least one instance, as the 1857 annual report of the Treasury put it, "by conquest." The closer to the symbolic center of the institution and the closer to the capital center of the nation, the closer the style of federal structures to the prevailing classical imperative. Urban customhouses, like banks, spoke in the classical tongue—unabashedly of the government's dignity and optimistically of its reliability and permanence. The New York Customhouse, like the Second Bank in Philadelphia, provided the full temple ambience, the full speech about federal authority. Farther from the locus and necessity of symbolism, frontier customhouses were utilitarian structures. Marine hospitals used the classical language sans temple form. Lighthouses exhibited a casual mélange of classical tidbits—a doorway here, a scroll support there.

By mid-century the reconstructed Capitol and presidential mansion held promise of future grandeur. To provide work space for civilian employees, who totaled 1,533 in 1851, there was a scattering of other buildings, some at variance in location and scale with the L'Enfant scheme. Considering the ravages of the War of 1812, which had leveled the city, and the rising tensions of the impending civil strife, the whole ensemble could be considered evidence of progress. Yet even the most chauvinistic Americans had to concede the validity of the recorded judgments of European visitors who recognized that L'Enfant's vision would for decades remain just that—a vision.

The uncompleted character of the capital city reflected that of the nation. With a scattering of government buildings, numerous but uncoordinated federal "internal improvement" projects, the ubiquitous influence of the grid survey and land disposal policies, the national government had laid claim to and supported the Americans' drive to "conquer space." In the 1830s the rhetoric of American destiny was flowing. Tocqueville came to America; Ralph Waldo Emerson wrote "The American Scholar"; James Fenimore Cooper published *The American Democrat*; Robert Mills laid claim to being the first American architect. Paradoxically, the effort to "bind the republic together" eventually would bring the nation face to face with its contradictions.

First Bank of the United
States, built in Philadelphia in
1794. Still standing today, the
building is variously credited
to Samuel Blodgett and to
James Hoban. Reportedly, its
high costs caused "an injurious deviation" from marble
to brick for the side walls. Latrobe commended this building "as bold proof of the spirit
of the citizens who erected it,
and of the tendency of the
community to *force* rather
than *retard* the advancement
of the arts."

From its earliest days, the
federal government sought
a stable and secure means
of handling its own bank-
ing needs as well as a
method for bringing order
to the melees of state and
local banking. The First
and Second Banks of the
United States, each char-
tered for 20 years, were
founded in 1791 and 1816
respectively. As one of the
directors and later president of the Second Bank,
Nicholas Biddle was a ma-
jor protagonist as well as a
victim of the bitter con-
flicts involved in the
young nation's economic

development. He was also
the promoter of a major
design competition for the
Second Bank of the United
States at Philadelphia. His
preferences for classical
style as well as for cau-
tious public expenditure
were exemplified in the
guidelines for the Bank
competition: "We seek a
chaste imitation of Gre-
cian architecture in its
simplest and least expen-
sive form."

As Jefferson's Roman Cap-
itol at Richmond marked
the beginning of a Roman
phase in American classi-
cism, William Strickland's
winning design for the
Second Bank signaled a

turn toward Greece as the
dominant inspiration for
public style. The Bank at
Philadelphia presided over
a system of 25 subsidiary
money temples, all de-
signed in a style that was
fast becoming synonymous
with banking itself.

Toward the end of the
Second Bank's charter
(1832) President Andrew
Jackson led a successful
campaign to destroy Bid-
dle's system. But the monetary Panic of 1837 dra-
matized the need for some
sort of central control
over the money system.
The Independent Treasury
system was set up as the

government's fiscal agent
with regional subtreasuries
and decentralized control.
In addition, acts of 1863
and 1864 established a
chartering mechanism for
privately owned national
banks under federal regu-
lation. This makeshift arrangement persisted until
1913, when a full-fledged
central bank was estab-
lished—the Federal Re-
serve System. With these
mechanisms as a means of
regulation, the Treasury
Department in 1845 used
43 banks as depositories;
in 1895, the number was
160; by 1945, 13,167.

The Second Bank of the United States, William Strickland, Philadelphia, 1817–1824. Strickland, who trained under Latrobe, suggested that the Parthenon was the right classical model for his bank because the ancient building had also housed public treasure. In 1844 the federal government converted the building to use as a customhouse and post office.

Nicholas Biddle (1788–1844), who believed that "the two great truths in the world are the Bible and Grecian architecture." Appointed as one of the five government directors of the Second Bank in 1819, Biddle became president of the Bank in 1823 and remained—even after disastrous battles with President Jackson and the loss of the federal charter in the 1830s—until the Bank's liquidation in 1841. John Quincy Adams remarked that the arrogant Biddle had been "waylaid and led astray by prosperity."

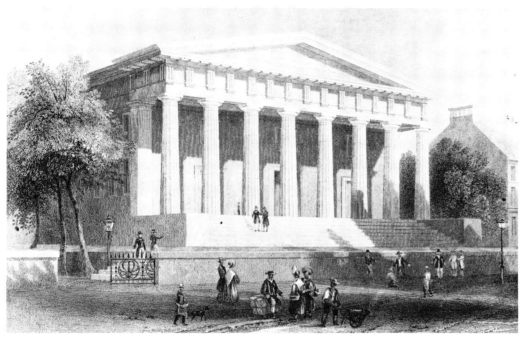

"The public sentiment just now runs almost exclusively and popularly into the Grecian school. We build little besides temples for our churches, our banks, our taverns, our court houses, and our dwellings. A friend of mine has just built a brewery on the model of the Temple of the Winds."

Aristabulus Bragg in James Fenimore Cooper's Home as Found, 1828

"There are certainly a hundred buildings in Europe of a very similar style, and of far more labored ornaments; but I cannot remember one in which simplicity, exquisite proportion, and material unite to produce so fine a whole."

James Fenimore Cooper, on the Second Bank

". . . In terms of public use, it has been an American contribution to make temples of their banks and palaces of their railroad stations and department stores. . . . Splendor once reserved for royal residences and noble mansions was brought to the people and it continually sought out new types of buildings for its province."

Henry Hope Reed, The Golden City, 1959

"Men build temples to the things they love."

C. W. Short and R. Stanley-Brown, Public Buildings: A Survey of Architecture, 1939

Losing entry, Second Bank of
the United States, design and
watercolor by Benjamin Latrobe, Philadelphia, 1818.

Second Bank of the United
States, Savannah Branch, William Jay, 1819–1920. The
building was significantly altered in 1880 and torn down
in 1924.

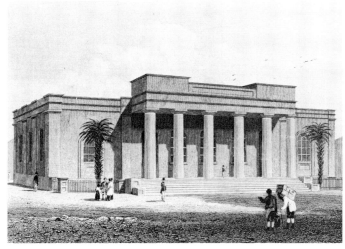

The proclivity for solemn antiquity in banks was not con-
fined to the United States. The
birds-eye view of the Bank of
England conjures up not a
temple but an entire imperial
Forum.

A political cartoon of the 1830s uses architectural images to symbolize President Jackson's victorious campaign to destroy the Second Bank.

"Banks and their money were an even more compelling discovery for the citizens of the young Republic than paper money was for the colonists. . . . The function of credit in a simple society is, in fact, remarkably egalitarian. It allows the man with energy and no money to participate in the economy more or less on a par with the man who has capital of his own. And the more casual the conditions under which credit is granted and hence the more impecunious those accommodated, the more egalitarian credit is. It is also that agreeable equalization which levels up, not down, or seems to do so. Thus the phenomenal urge in the United States, one that lasted through all of the last century and well into the present one, to create banks. And thus, also, the marked if unadmitted liking for bad banks. Bad banks, unlike good, loaned to the poor risk, which is another name for the poor man."

John Kenneth Galbraith, Money: Whence It Came, Where It Went, 1975

Robert Mills,
American Architect

56–57

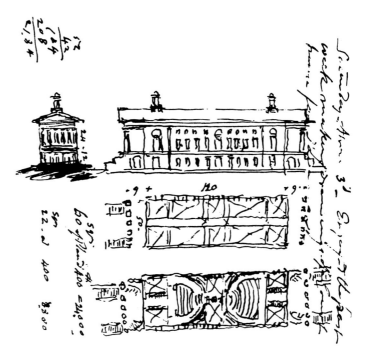

Diary sketch of Savannah Courthouse. Like Latrobe, Mills left his distinctive mark on many parts of the public realm.

Robert Mills (1781–1855).

Beginning in 1813 Robert Mills, a thoroughly trained professional architect, spent 21 years in patient pursuit of the position of architect for the general government. His quest was rewarded by President Andrew Jackson on July 6, 1836—the same day the Congress voted to approve construction of a new Treasury Department building to replace a structure that burned in 1833. Mills served more or less officially in the position he described as "architect of the public buildings" until 1851 when he lost out to Thomas U. Walter for control of the extensions to the Capitol.

Like his predecessors Robert Mills had a wide-ranging mind and imagination. Unlike them he had received all of his architectural training in America—under the tutelage of Hoban, Jefferson, and Latrobe, who represented the Palladian, Roman, and Greek styles. To Latrobe he owed both his professional principles and his engineering skills.

During his career Mills designed numerous marine hospitals and custom-houses. He was also responsible for major portions of the General Post Office, Patent Office, and Treasury buildings in the nation's capital. Perhaps he is best known for his winning design for a monument to George Washington—a commission he

won in a privately sponsored competition. In 1833 a National Monument Society, composed mainly of Washington's fellow Freemasons, advertised for designs that "harmoniously blend durability, simplicity, and grandeur." They chose the obelisk submitted by Robert Mills for the approximate site marked by L'Enfant for a memorial on his 1791 plan.

Mills is identified with the classical in architectural style, but in management skills and technical innovations he was a man of the future. In an early version of fast-track construction, the foundations of the Treasury were poured

before the design of the building was complete; he was an ardent spokesman for and demonstrator of fireproofing of public buildings. His experiments ranged from gas lighting and a heating and cooling system for the Capitol to the design of a monorail. A man of boundless energy, he was also a city planner, a transportation advocate, and the author of several books, including *Treatise on Island Navigation* and *Guide to the Capitol and National Executive Offices of the United States*. In the arena of social issues, he opposed slavery and sought prison reform and better treatment for Indians.

Mills's customhouse at New Bedford, Massachusetts, like his other customhouses, states an American preference for both the classical and the economical.

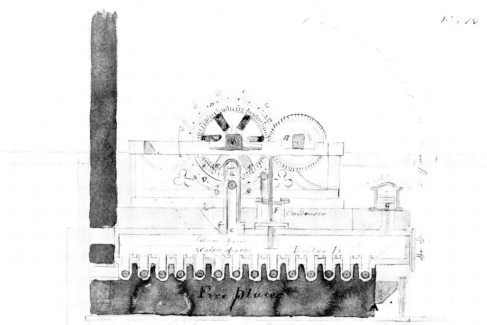

Mills's design for a rotary engine.

Robert Mills, American Architect

"The author [has] the honor of being the first native [born] American who directed his studies to architecture as a profession. . . . The author is altogether American in his views."

Robert Mills, "The Architectural Works of Robert Mills," outline for an intended paper or book

"I have always deprecated the servile copying of the buildings of antiquity; we have the same principles and materials to work upon that the ancients had, and we should adapt these materials to the habits and customs of our people as they did to theirs."

Robert Mills, "The Progress of Architecture in Virginia," unfinished essay

"The popular idea that to design a building in Grecian taste is nothing more than to copy a Grecian building is altogether erroneous;—even the Greeks themselves never made two buildings alike. . . . If architects would oftener think as the Greeks thought, than to do as the Greeks did, our columnar architecture would possess a higher degree of originality and its character and expression would gradually conform to the local circumstances of the country and the republican spirit of its institutions."

Thomas U. Walter, lecture published in the Journal of The Franklin Institute, January 1841

"I say to our artists: Study your country's tastes and requirements, and make classic ground here for your art."

Robert Mills, "The Progress of Architecture in Virginia," unfinished essay

"Insist on yourself; never imitate."

Ralph Waldo Emerson, "Self-Reliance," 1841

"The obelisk form is peculiarly adapted to commemorate great transactions from its lofty character, great strength, and furnishing a fine surface for inscriptions. . . . There is a degree of lightness and beauty in it that affords a finer relief to the eye than can be obtained in the regular proportioned Column."

Letter from Mills to the Monument Commission

"The obelisk has to my eye a singular aptitude in its form and character to call attention to a spot memorable in its history. It says but one word. But it speaks loud. If I understand this voice, it says 'Here!'"

Horatio Greenough

"Mills is a wretched designer. He came to me too late to acquire principles of taste. He is a copyist, and is fit for nothing else. His Christian monument [in Baltimore] is an imitation of a design proposed for Lord Nelson. It is anything but a fit mausoleum for Washington. But he also has merit. He is an excellent man of detail, and a very snug contriver of domestic conveniences and will make a good deal of money. He wants that professional self respect which is the ruin of you and me, and therefore we shall go to the wall, while he will strut in the middle of the street."

Benjamin Latrobe to Maximilian Godefroy, October 10, 1814

Winning design for the Washington Monument at Baltimore, Robert Mills, 1814. Mills demonstrated his skill at architectural politics when he won the commission for the Baltimore monument despite late submission and a more elaborate design than allowed by the cost limits under the rules of the competition. He appealed to the jury for his selection as the only American-born and American-trained architect among the competitors. In a letter to the Board of Managers, he argued, "For the Honor of our country, my sincere wish is that it may not be said; to foreign genius and to foreign hands we are indebted for a Monument to perpetuate the glory of our beloved Chief."

Not surprisingly, costs required Mills's concept to be scaled down as development progressed. A simpler version of his columnar design was completed in 1819.

Winning design for the Washington Monument at Washington, D.C., Robert Mills, 1833. Mills's original design included an obelisk and pantheon with statues. The obelisk, which was to have the same proportions as obelisks of antiquity, was to rise to a height of ten times the width of its base. The base was to hold a tomb for Washington and statues of Revolutionary War heroes. On top of the entrance was to be an equestrian group with Washington driving a chariot.

Design for a monument to Washington, George Dance, 1800, commissioned by Benjamin West, an American painter, at the time he was President of the Royal Academy in London. Originally a 1790 Congressional resolution had called for a "marble monument . . . so designed as to commemorate the great events of [George Washington's] military and political life."

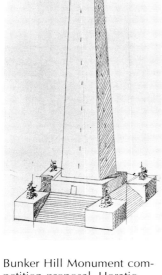

Bunker Hill Monument competition proposal, Horatio Greenough, Boston, Massachusetts, 1825. Greenough explained his choice of form: "I have made the choice of the obelisk as the most purely *monumental* form of structure. . . . The proportions of this obelisk are taken from one at Ancient Thebes."

Proposed design for a monument to Washington, Peter Force, 1837.

Patent Office, Robert Mills,
Washington, D.C., south
wing, shown on the letterhead
of patent letter as it came to
be integrated in the com-
pleted building. Robert Mills
supervised construction of this
wing, 1836–1840, and
vaulted the interiors. The
other three wings were completed 1850–1867.

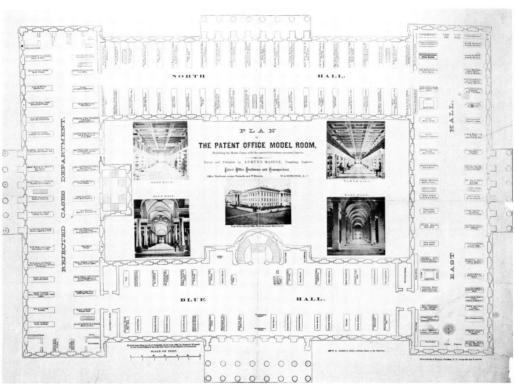

Plan of completed model
room of the Patent Office,
broadside by Edmund Mas-
son, 1861. The names of
exhibitions are indicated
on each of the model cases
drawn on the plan.

The double "floating staircase" in Mills's Patent Office, 1839.

"Twenty years *of my life have been spent in the Government service here, and my works there will prove my faithfulness to the interests of the Government. The buildings I have erected, compared with other Public buildings of a like character elsewhere, will show with what* economy *they have been constructed, costing but a* moiety *of other buildings of like dimensions. And tho' I have disbursed millions of dollars in such constructions, I have to* labor still for my bread. *Had I been unfaithful to my trust, I might have been wealthy at this day, in place of not having a dollar to call my own."*

Robert Mills, letter to friend, March 3, 1853

"*Great complaints being made, from time to time, by the members of congress, of the difficulty of hearing and speaking in the Hall of Representatives; and no satisfactory plan being settled upon, to remedy the defect, Mr. Mills took an opportunity, when on a visit to Washington, to lay before the House a plan of alteration and improvement of this hall, which would remedy, in a great degree, the evil complained of. He went into a scientific examination, at the same time, of the causes of the existing difficulties, grounded upon well-established principles in acoustics; and showed what the effect would be were these causes removed. The subject being referred to a select committee, they reported in favour of the plan proposed by Mr. Mills, and recommended an appropriation to be made to carry it into execution; which has since been effected under his supervision; and the present congress are now deriving the advantages of the alterations made, which have not disappointed public expectation, being acknowledged to be a decided improvement. Mr. M. is now engaged in the service of the general government, and resides at Washington."*

William Dunlap, History of the Rise and Progress of Arts of Design in the United States, *Volume 2, Part 1, 1834*

". . . *The author* [Mills] *has made it a rule never to consult books when he had to design a building. His considerations were,—first, the object of the building; second, the means appropriated for its construction; third, the situation it was to occupy; these served as guides in forming the outline of his plan. Books are useful to the student, but when he enters upon the practice of his profession, he should lay them aside and only consult them upon doubtful points, or in matters of detail or as mere studies, not to copy buildings from."*

Robert Mills, "The Architectural Works of Robert Mills," outline for an intended paper or book

"*Utility and economy will be found to have entered into most of the studies of the author, and little sacrificed to display; at the same time his endeavors were to produce as much harmony and beauty of arrangement as practicable. The principle assumed and acted upon was that beauty is founded upon order, and that convenience and utility were constituent parts."*

Robert Mills, "The Architectural Works of Robert Mills," outline for an intended paper or book

". . . *Robert Mills, Esq. . . . whose estimable character as a man, and widely-acknowledged skill as an architect induced President Jackson to confer upon him the appointment of architect for the general government. That he was not continued in that important position has been a misfortune to the country, as is shown by the defective buildings since erected."*

"Public Buildings in Washington," article in the Pottsville Emporium, *c. 1851-1855*

Barrel and groin-vaulted corridor, south wing of the General Post Office, Washington, D.C. Mills designed the building after a December 1836 fire destroyed the department's headquarters, the old Blodgett Hotel. The south section with two northward wings was completed by 1841–1842. The north section was added, 1855–1866, mostly under the direction of Thomas U. Walter.

U.S.Treasury Building, original design by Robert Mills, Washington, D.C., 1836–1842. The building at right is one of Hadfield's Executive Department buildings. Mills worked against difficult odds in designing this building; first, President Jackson, in a moment of pique, had selected the site, which resulted in the large structure's blocking the view from the Capitol to the White House. The building was also criticized for its selection of stone. Mills had recommended granite, but Congress insisted on the more economical freestone, which Mills said would wear less well. (By 1909, the columns showed signs of crumbling and had to be replaced with granite.) Finally, Mills's original design had called for a "building adequate for future accommodations," including several extensions to his original structure. Congress finally passed an appropriation for the requisite amount—on the day of Mills's death in 1855. Later extensions were completed by Ammi B. Young, Thomas U. Walter, and Alfred Mullett.

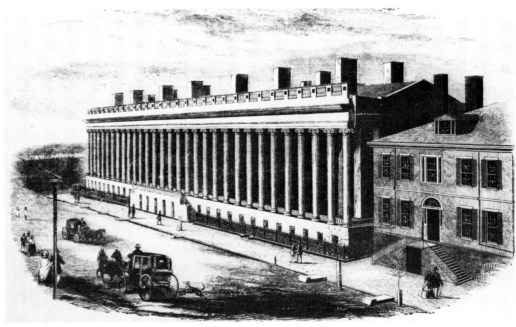

A law of 1807 appropriated money for erection in New Orleans of "a good and sufficient house" for customs collection in that port. This was the first allocation of funds for construction of the type of building that would later become part of the Treasury Department's "public buildings program": customhouses, courthouses, and post offices.

In 1817 the Secretary of the Treasury was authorized to construct more customhouses where needed. A scattering of smaller structures were built, but only four major projects were undertaken by 1850: a second replacement at New Orleans, and buildings at New York, Boston, and Charleston. According to an 1857 Treasury Department report, there were, with these four exceptions, "no very large appropriations" made in this building category until 1850.

The story of three successive customhouses in New Orleans provides a vignette of escalating prosperity and scale and costs. The 1807 appropriation for the first, modest customhouse was $20,000. The third customhouse was one of the largest federal structures in the country at the time it was built—and the fourteen interior marble columns cost $23,000 each.

John Frazee, by Asher B. Durand. Frazee, a sculptor, became "Architect and Superintendent" of the New York Customhouse in 1835. After nearly seven years of work and bureaucratic controversy, completion of the building was celebrated by a Congressional investigation, which promised to rehash past conflicts and delayed Frazee's remuneration. He obtained a post as a customs inspector. Frazee died in 1852, after contracting severe rheumatism. In 1859, his widow was finally awarded some money based on his claim for wages.

The Architect's Dream, painting by Thomas Cole, inscribed "Painted by T. Cole for I. Town, Archt., 1840." The architect Town reclines on folio volumes and contemplates his choices from the offerings of historical scholarship. In the background the pyramid of Cheops towers over a classical streetscape and a Gothic church. Although Town was said to dislike the painting, it expressed the approach of Town and Davis, the first professional architectural firm in the United States and the firm responsible for the New York Customhouse.

Bustling interior of the New York Customhouse in the heyday of its activities.

Detail, New York Customhouse, by John Frazee.

Longitudinal section, New York Customhouse. The exterior design is attributed to Ithiel Town and A. J. Davis; John Frazee is credited with most of its ornamentation. A contemporary writer observed that had Frazee been permitted to exercise his own judgment he "would have adopted a different order of architecture, and would have formed a design more appropriate to the business of a Custom House. But the foundation was already laid, and a large portion of the marble for the superstructure had been cut. He was therefore compelled to carry out, in all its essentials, the original design of the Parthenon."

"The style of Greek architecture as seen in the Greek temple . . . insists upon every feature of its original organization, loses its harmony if a note be dropped in the execution, and when so modified as to serve for a customhouse or a bank departs from its original beauty and propriety as widely as the crippled gelding of a hackney coach differs from the bounding and neighing wild horse of the desert. Even where, in the fervor of our faith in shapes, we have sternly adhered to the dictum of another age, and have actually succeeded in securing the entire exterior which echoes the forms of Athens, the pile stands a stranger among us! and receives a respect akin to what we should feel for a fellow citizen in the garb of Greece. It is a make-believe! It is not the real thing! We see the marble capitals; we trace the acanthus leaves of a celebrated model— incredulous odi! It is not a temple."

Horatio Greenough, "American Architecture," **The United States Magazine and Democratic Review,** *August 1843*

The third New Orleans Customhouse, designed by Alexander Thompson Wood, was begun after the second proved inadequate for the growing needs of the port. This was one of the largest federal structures in the country when it was built.

After a prolonged controversy about the site, construction began in 1848. Various delays—including protracted settling of the foundation and the Civil War—prevented completion until 1881. The building was used during the Civil War as a military prison.

Interior marble capital, third New Orleans Customhouse.

The so-called Marble Hall was the huge business room of the third New Orleans Customhouse. The size, the stained-glass-edged skylight, numerous relief carvings, and the black and white marble floor were a tribute to the importance of the port city and of the image of the federal government.

Customhouse, Astoria, Oregon, 1848, the first customhouse constructed by the federal government west of the
Rocky Mountains. The style
seems a very thin-diet version
of popular classical
elements—portico, columns,
pediment.

Customhouse, Ammi B.
Young, Boston, 1837–1847,
section. It was Young's success with this building that
commended him for further
Treasury Department work in
1851 and for the position of
Supervising Architect in 1853.
In 1915, the Government suc-
cumbed to the exigencies of
the urban real estate market
by surmounting this little temple with a high-rise tower.

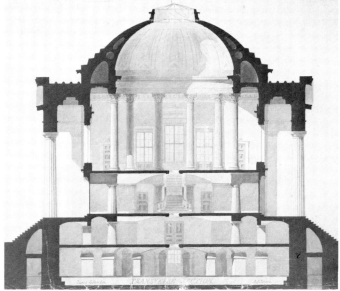

Gilded pine eagle on the
Salem Customhouse, which
was carved by Joseph True in
1826 and immortalized by
Nathaniel Hawthorne in *The
Scarlet Letter.*

Nathaniel Hawthorne, Surveyor of the Port, Salem, Massachusetts, 1846–1849. He was dismissed on June 8, 1849, on "superficial charges of fraud." Earlier, he had held the post of measurer at the Boston Customhouse.

Herman Melville, Inspector at the Customhouse in the Port of New York City, 1866–1885. He obtained the post through a friend. The salary was $4.00 per day. He resigned in 1885. Much earlier, he described a customs inspector's post as "a most inglorious one; indeed worse than driving geese to water."

"I again seize the public by the button, and talk of my three years' experience in a Custom House. . . . Over the entrance hovers an enormous specimen of the American eagle. . . . With the customary infirmity of temper that characterizes this unhappy fowl, she appears, by the fierceness of her beak and eye, and the general truculency of her attitude, to threaten mischief to the inoffensive community; and especially to warn all citizens, careful of their safety, against intruding on the premises which she overshadows with her wings. . . . The pavement round about . . . has grass enough growing in its chinks to show that it has not, of late days, been worn by any multitudinous resort of business. . . . The room itself is cobwebbed and dingy with old paint; its floor is strewn with gray sand, in a fashion that has elsewhere fallen into long disuse; and it is easy to conclude, from the general slovenliness of the place, that this is a sanctuary into which womankind, with her tools of magic, the broom and mop, has very infrequent access. . . . Neither the front nor the back entrance of the Custom House opens on the road to Paradise."

Nathaniel Hawthorne, "The Custom House" (Salem), introduction to The Scarlet Letter, *1850*

In 1794 and 1798, the United States undertook its so-called First and Second Systems, respectively, of harbor fortications in response to the threat of war with France. The forts in the First System were relatively crude installations with little or no overall rationale or inter-relation. The Second System included several substantial works, but these were dissimilar in design and did not form a cohesive defense unit. In 1816–1817 a board of professionals was assigned the task of creating a perma-nent and integrated network of harbor defenses, which became the Third System. Under various names and in various forms, such a body continued this function until World War II.

These fort systems were constructed under the supervision of the Corps of Engineers, which was Congressionally established in 1802. In the same act, the Corps was "constituted" as a military academy with headquarters at West Point, New York. Jonathan Williams,

View of the fort at Jamestown, drawn by John Hull, Richmond, 1657. Castillo de San Marcos, St. Augustine, Florida, 1672–1756.

The first settlers in the New World had sought footholds on the eastern perimeter of America where their first priority was defense. Some of these early forts, like Castillo de San Marcos, endured; others, like the fort at Jamestown, vanished without a trace. Castillo de San Marcos was more solidly built of limestone with outer walls 12 feet thick at the base. Today it is a national park site.

the first Chief of the Corps of Engineers, became the first Superintendent of the new Academy. Under the second Superintendent, Sylvanus Thayer, the Academy was reorganized from a strictly military to an engineering focus to prepare officers not only to build seacoast fortifications but also to conduct the explorations, surveys, and civil works needed to develop the nation's resources. Among Thayer's students were expedition leaders, Civil War generals, and three presidents.

Colonel Jonathan Williams, named first Chief of the Corps of Engineers and Superintendent of the Military Academy in 1802. A grandnephew of Benjamin Franklin, Williams founded the Military Philosophical Society, which included not only military personnel, but also noted scholars and scientists and the President of the United States. In translation, the Society's motto was: "Science in war is the guarantee of peace."

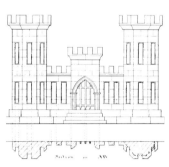

Corps of Engineers turreted castle insignia, design approved by Major Richard Delafield, Superintendent of the U.S. Military Academy, for wear by West Point cadets, 1839, and extended to all members of the Corps of Engineers, 1840. Several early forts built by the engineers were called "castle."

The Corps of Engineers button, used as early as 1814, was probably inspired by the works Colonel Jonathan Williams constructed to defend New York Harbor. The button portrays a masonry marine fort that is embrasured, casemated, and crenelated. The French motto, "Essayons," can be translated as "let us strive."

Castle Clinton, begun in New York Harbor in 1812 in response to the threat of war. (Castle Williams is in the distance.) The fort was not attacked, and in 1823 it was ceded to the city, which then leased it as a place of public entertainment, which was made into a "fanciful garden, tastefully ornamented with shrubs and flowers." The gunrooms were decorated with a panorama painted by "celebrated artists." The officers' quarters became a "saloon." Castle Garden, as it became known during this period, later served a number of other functions—opera house, immigration depot, and New York City Aquarium—until Castle Clinton National Monument was established in 1950.

American debut of "Swedish Nightingale" Jenny Lind at Castle Garden, 1850, attended by 6,000.

Joseph G. Totten, Chief of Army Engineers for 26 years until 1864. He achieved worldwide stature as a specialist in seacoast defenses. Because of his continuous and important involvement in building it, the Third System is sometimes called the Totten System.

Interior of Fort Sumter, buttressed with sand and cotton and its own fallen masonry, 1865. Photo by S. R. Seibert, one of the Confederate counterparts of Mathew Brady. Fort Sumter, one of the Third System of forts, was constructed to defend the harbor of Charleston, South Carolina, 1829–1860. Soon after April 12, 1861, when this five-sided masonry fort was bombarded by the Confederates, the nation was embroiled in the Civil War.

Fort Massachusetts, Ship Island, Mississippi. Construction began in 1859 but was interrupted by the Civil War. The Confederates held it until forced to evacuate by a Union naval blockade. The fort was later completed by the U.S. and used to house Confederate prisoners. In 1870, it was abandoned because its brick walls could not withstand a new type of cannon shell. In 1971 the fort became part of the Gulf Islands National Seashore.

The earliest American lighthouse was established at Boston in 1716. Colonial Americans, however, were not unanimous about the need for maritime safety, since seaside dwellers could profit—legally—from the business of scavenging wrecked ships. As in most profitable enterprises, illegal ventures developed, and there was looting by less finicky entrepreneurs, known as "moon cussers," who deliberately put up false beacons, or "Judas lanterns," to lure hapless ships to disaster on moonless and stormy nights.

But the leaders of the new nation valued the usefulness of lighthouses in safety, coastal defense, and law enforcement. The ninth bill of the first session of the First Congress in 1789 transferred ten colonial lighthouses to federal jurisdiction and assumed national responsibility for expanding aid to navigation. Despite strained economic circumstances Congress attested to its lofty maritime aspirations with generous appropriations for lighthouses. In 1800 the

United States had only 16 lighthouses. By mid-century there were 331 lighthouses and 42 lightships. Robert Mills authored a book entitled *American Pharos or Lighthouse Guide*.

In the case of lighthouses, the ubiquitous debate about the cost of design quality took an unusual turn: the administration in charge of lighthouses was accused of saving money at the potential expense of lives. Distressed by criticism of lighthouse service, Congress appointed a board of inquiry in 1851,

which found that many of the towers were poorly designed and constructed, the lamps inefficient, and the locations either too far apart or redundant. In 1852 Congress agreed to a total administrative overhaul and the creation of a nine-member Lighthouse Board composed of men with wide naval, engineering, and scientific experience. Under the new board, navigational aids, service, safety, and efficiency increased markedly. In 1939 the responsibilities of the Lighthouse Service passed to the Coast Guard.

Destruction of Minot's Ledge Lighthouse, Massachusetts Bay near Cohasset, 1851, engraving published in 1851. Between 1832 and 1841 there were 40 shipwrecks on this and nearby dangerous reefs. In 1843 federal officials decided a lighthouse was needed—an iron-pile lighthouse, which would offer less resistance to the waves than a stone tower. Construction work, begun in 1847, was conducted on calm days from a schooner. The light was first lighted January 1, 1850. The first keeper protested to Washington that the structure was unsafe. He resigned in October. After a few weeks and a terrific storm, his successor also reported the tower in danger. An investigatory committee, which examined the structure in a calm sea, decided that nothing should be done. In April 1851, after days of a battering storm, the weakened structure plunged into the sea. The two keepers lost their lives. A new granite tower was completed in 1860 and still stands today.

From the age of twelve until her death at the age of sixty-nine Ida Lewis lived in the Lime Rock Lighthouse, Newport, Rhode Island. After the death of her parents she became keeper of the light through a special act of Congress in 1789. She was renowned for her courageous rescues. Among her admiring visitors was President U. S. Grant. Her lighthouse is now a private yacht club.

"Whereas the taking away, removing, sinking or destroying the buoys may have very fatal results, be it therefore enacted:

"That if any person shall take away or remove, sink or destroy any of the buoys, he or they, on being adjudged guilty thereof . . . shall suffer death without benefit of clergy."

Virginia Legislature, 1774

Ship's letter, early version of a passport, verifying bearer's U.S. citizenship for passage "without any hinderance, seizure or molestation." Engraved by Edward Savage. Signed by President Thomas Jefferson and Secretary of State James Madison, September 8, 1804. Franklin Delano Roosevelt added his signature in 1940 at request of the document's owner.

Cape Henry Lighthouse, Virginia, 1791, first lighthouse built by the federal government, replaced by an iron structure in 1881. The older lighthouse and nearly all lights to the south of it suffered extensive damage during the Civil War when towers, as tactical targets, were burned and lenses either stolen or destroyed.

Bodie Island Lighthouse, on the outer banks of North Carolina, 1848. The bold striped dress of exterior walls aided seamen to distinguish between the many chartered lighthouses and thus verify their location along coastal waters. Distinguishing stripes were used on other lighthouses in diamond (Cape Lookout) and barber pole (Cape Hatteras) patterns.

Cape Hatteras Lighthouse, North Carolina, 1870. The present structure replaced an earlier lighthouse built in 1798, which was extensively damaged by Confederate forces to deprive Union ships of a vital beacon. It is the tallest lighthouse in the U.S. (208 feet) and still operates to guide ships in treacherous waters famed as "the graveyard of the Atlantic."

". . . In the early masonry lighthouses some of the best architecture of this country was to be found. The structures were simple and dignified, designed honestly to meet their purpose, and strikingly located. Such are the colonial and early federal lighthouses, as well as some of the massive and taller brick structures built in the fifties and sixties of the last century. Then lighthouse design became ornate, like other architecture in the United States, and the towers were over-decorated."

Commissioner of the Lighthouses George R. Putnam, 1937

Section, at several levels, of
the top of Cape Hatteras
Lighthouse, North Carolina.

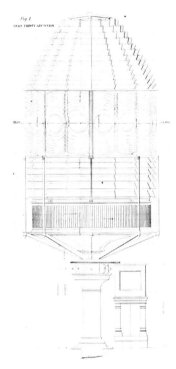

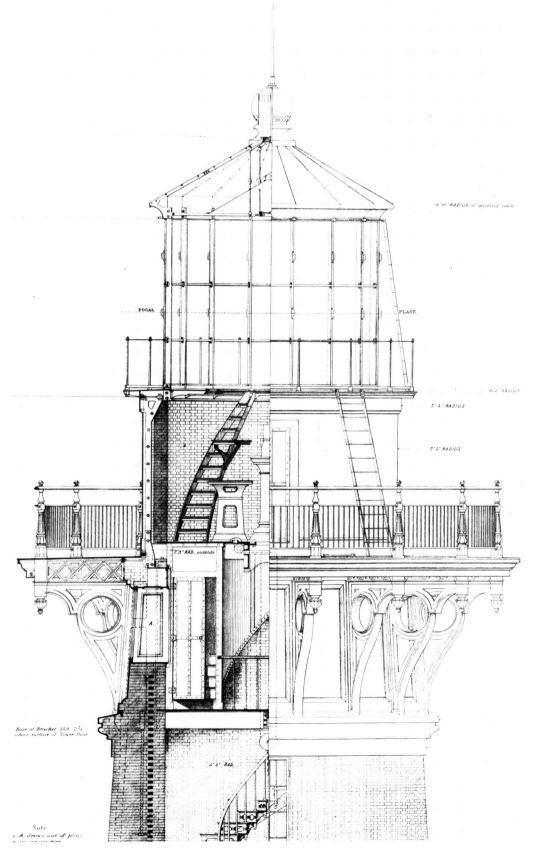

A first-order Fresnel lens,
named after its inventor Augustin Fresnel, who developed
it in the early 1820s. The lens
uses magnifying glasses and
prisms to intensify a light into
a powerful beacon. A clock-
work system rotates the lens to
achieve a flashing effect. The
"order" refers to size classification from the largest "first
order" to the smallest "sixth
order."

Stephen Pleasanton, the
General Superintendent of
Lighthouses, 1820–1852, resisted using this technological
innovation because it was expensive and probably, in part,
because his close advisor,
Winslow Lewis, held contracts
for supplying lighthouses with
the traditional reflector lights.
Congress mandated the use of
two lenses in 1838, and
Pleasanton said that their cost
was "nothing compared to the
beauty and excellence of the
light they afford." He nonetheless purchased only two
more over the ensuing decade—a triumph, perhaps, of
the designing abilities of a
government contractor.

Amelia Island Light, Fernandina, Florida, 1839.

"A storm in the fall or winter is the time to visit it [Cape Cod]; a light house or a fisherman's hut the true hotel. A man may stand there and put all America behind him."

Henry David Thoreau, **Cape Cod**

Proposal for Castle Hill Lighthouse, Newport, Rhode Island. Drawing by H. H. Richardson, 1885.

The federal government began acquiring hospitals under its first Medicare plan—a 1798 "act for the relief of sick and disabled seamen." The act was the forerunner of today's Public Health Service.

The role of the civilian merchant marine in the promotion of commerce and the national defense prompted Congress to set up a marine hospital fund financed by 20-cent deductions from seamen's monthly wages plus federal contributions. In the first forty years of the program, facilities were leased more often than built, and no more than three marine hospitals were ever in operation concurrently. The program operated through contracts with local institutions until abuses and profiteering resulted in a Congressional mandate to the Army to oversee new hospital construction.

As the nation grew and seamen plied the lakes and rivers, Congress was besieged with demands for more marine hospitals. Location of projects reflected Congressional influence on behalf of home districts which did not necessarily coincide with the locus of need. Sites selected often rendered the hospitals useless or undesirable: one was in a swamp, another near a blast furnace. New Orleans agitated 37 years for a marine hospital, but, when construction began in 1838, the project was located across the river from the city near a slaughterhouse. Completed in 1846, the hospital was in use for only 10 years because the Mississippi River inundated the site. Under the Army Engineers construction continued to be shoddy. The 1850s saw a return to the contracting system, but this did not bring a satisfactory result either and criticism mounted. By 1872 only 9 of the 31 marine hospitals established since 1798 were still in use.

While merchant seamen were the object of much solicitude, disabled servicemen faced an indifferent Congress. A tradition of antagonism to standing armies blinded Americans to the need for permanent health care facilities for military veterans. In 1811, the Navy proposed a wide-ranging health program, but the only result of this idea was construction in Philadelphia of an asylum (home) for disabled veterans in 1833. Similarly, the Army petitioned Congress unsuccessfully for more than 20 years for such a home. The plight of Mexican War veterans and the combined leadership of General Winfield Scott and Senator Jefferson Davis persuaded Congress to authorize the needed funds in 1851. The lobbying of Dorothea Dix resulted in an additional facility for military service veterans—an insane asylum at Washington, D.C. All three of these buildings are still standing.

Cover of Robert Mills's standard Design No. 2 for a marine hospital. Design No. 1 was for 100 patients. With the election of a "Westerner" (Jackson) as President in 1828, a clamor arose for Marine Fund hospitals on "Western" waters. A report of the Ohio General Assembly estimated that 43,000 seamen, "more than two-thirds of the number engaged in the maritime commerce of the Union," were exposed to the "insalubrious exhalations" of the banks of the Great Lakes and Ohio and Mississippi Rivers.

DESIGN

Nº· 2

FOR A

MARINE HOSPITAL

ON THE

WESTERN WATERS

to accommodate

50

PATIENTS.

"The poor rank and file, who have borne the brunt of the fight, drag home their shattered frames, only to lie down and die of poverty, or barely to support existence upon the charity of passers-by. This is . . . revolting to the sensibilities . . . of every man. . . . The establishment of institutions similar to . . . Les Invalides, in France, would go far to . . . remove some of the strongest objections to enlistment in our Army. If men knew that they would be taken care of, in case of disability in the service, there would be a much greater alacrity in joining our Army than exists at present."

From an article in the New Orleans Daily Delta, *March 12, 1848*

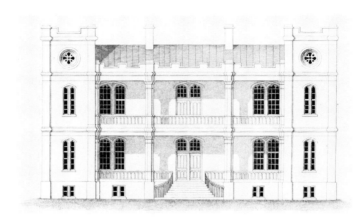

Facade of Mills's standard design, used, regardless of climate, for nearly all such structures from 1837 until 1872.

The marine hospitals designed by Mills's successor, Ammi B. Young, were characterized by open verandas and a style reminiscent of Italian villas.

" . . . True economy requires that we should either sink the marine hospitals, every one of them, or sell them. If there has been any one inexcusable, intolerable abuse in the public expenditure of this country it has been in this matter of building marine hospitals."

Senator Howe of Wisconsin in Senate debate, February 1870

U.S. Marine Hospital, Chelsea, Massachusetts, watercolor by Ann Little, 1830. When an 1849 report complained of the overcrowding of this 1804 structure a larger hospital was built (1857) using Robert Mills's "design for a marine hospital on the western waters."

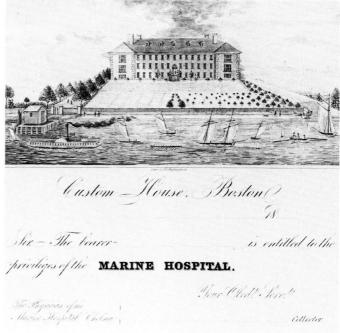

Form used to authorize hospital patients. Customs officers were local financial administrators of the marine hospital program.

"A home will be established here for the faithful tar who has been either worn out or maimed in fighting the battles of his country. A comfortable harbor will be secured where he may safely moor and ride out the ebb of life, free from cares and storms."

Commander William Bainbridge, Chairman, Board of Commissioners of the Navy Hospital at cornerstone ceremony for the asylum in 1827

The first U.S. Naval Asylum, James Strickland, Philadelphia, 1833. The asylum was the second American building to use cast iron columns.

Dorothea Dix, crusader for the mentally ill, in 1861 became "Superintendent for Female Nurses" for the Army. She declared that "no women under thirty need apply to serve in the government hospitals. All nurses are required to be plain looking women. Their dresses must be brown or black, with no bows, no curls, no jewelry, and no hoop-skirts." But by the time of the bloody defeat at Bull Run, she was asking only one question: "Are you ready to go to work?"

Soldiers' Home, Washington, D.C. Photo, 1904.

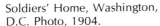

"The Government Hospital for the Insane" (now St. Elizabeth's), completed in 1855. It was intended for the insane of the Army, Navy, and the District of Columbia. Establishment of the hospital was a result of lobbying efforts of Dorothea Dix, who had hoped to persuade Congress to set aside five million acres in public land for facilities for the insane. From 1844 to 1846 she had traveled more than 10,000 miles visiting penitentiaries, jails, and almshouses, and had helped to found 32 state hospitals for the insane.

North Side   *Metropolitan Hotel*   *Penn. Ave. in 1843*   *South Side*

White House
↓

L'Enfant's plan for a federal city, like the Constitutional plan for a federal government, remained in the first decades only a statement of intention. The American people tended to ignore their central government, and the politicians, reflecting this mood, tended to avoid aggrandizement of their central enclave. Until 1834 there were only two major federal buildings in the capital city—the Capitol and the White House—and four minor ones. Until Congressional restrictions on the sale of liquor passed in 1835, the rotunda of the Capitol served as a peoples' hall for exhibits, marketing, and liquor sales.

Beginning with Mills's Treasury in 1836, however, some new large-scale buildings arose in the District—seemingly outpacing and outscaling the increase in government employment, since in 1851 there were only 1533 federal civilian employees in Washington. At least part of this new-found urge to build may have derived from some increased sense of the permanence and importance of the national government.

Washington, looking toward the White House on Pennsylvania Avenue from the west, as it appeared to the visiting Charles Dickens, 1843. Notations on this daguerrreotype were made in Mathew Brady's studio.

Pennsylvania Avenue cluttered with building materials for the new Treasury Building, c. 1836.

"Take the worst parts of the City Road and Pentonville, or the straggling outskirts of Paris. . . . Burn the whole down, built it up again in wood and plaster; widen it a little . . . ; put green blinds outside all the private houses, with a red curtain and a white one in every window; plough up all the roads; plant a great deal of coarse turf in every place where it ought not to be; erect three handsome buildings in stone and marble, anywhere, but the more entirely out of everybody's way the better; call one the Post Office, one the Patent Office, and one the Treasury; make it scorching hot in the morning, and freezing cold in the afternoon, with an occasional tornado of wind and dust; leave a brick-field without the bricks in all central places where a street may naturally be expected; and that's Washington. . . . It is sometimes called the City of Magnificent Distances, but it might with greater propriety be termed the City of Magnificent Intentions; for it is only on taking a bird's eye view of it from the top of the Capitol, that one can at all comprehend the vast designs of its projector, an aspiring Frenchman. Spacious avenues, that begin in nothing, and lead nowhere; streets, mile-long, that only want houses, roads and inhabitants; public buildings that need but a public to be complete; and ornaments of great thoroughfares, which only lack great thoroughfares to ornament—are its leading features. One might fancy the season over, and most of the houses gone out of town for ever with their masters."

Charles Dickens, American Notes, *1842*

"The wants of this people have called—imperatively called—the active and able men of the country to pursuits far removed from an investigation of the beautiful. . . . These minds have been engaged in laying the foundations, broad and deep, of a mighty empire. . . . The selection of this site, the ground plan of this city, show the outline of a master, and years must elapse ere any school which we can found will be capable of worthily filling it."

Horatio Greenough, "Aesthetics at Washington," The Travels, Observations, and Experience of a Yankee Stonecutter, *1852.*

"I was delighted with the whole aspect of Washington. . . . It has been laughed at by foreigners, and even by natives, because the original plan of the city was upon an enormous scale, and but a very small part of it has been as yet executed. But I confess I see nothing in the least degree ridiculous about it; the original design, which was as beautiful as it was extensive, has been in no way departed from, and all that has been done has been done well. . . . To a person who has been travelling much through the country, and marked the immense quantities of new manufactories, new canals, new rail-roads, new towns, and new cities, which are springing, as it were, from the earth in every part of it, the appearance of the metropolis rising gradually into life and splendour, is a spectacle of high historic interest."

Frances Trollope, Domestic Manners of the Americans, *1832*

"The town itself which, being a merely legislative metropolis, could never be very large, stretches and straddles between two distant points [Capitol and White House] trying in vain to grow into compactness."

Nathaniel P. Willis, American Scenery, *1841*

". . . With wheel-tracks meandering from the colonnade of the Treasury hard by, to the white marble [sic] columns and fronts of the Post Office and Patent Office, which faced each other in the distance, like white Greek temples in the abandoned gravel-pits of a deserted Syrian City."

Henry Adams, The Education of Henry Adams, *1906*

Robert Mills's Patent Office, daguerreotype by John Plumbe, 1846, which shows the impressive scale of this government temple amidst its surroundings. Plumbe was one of the founders of American photography and established the first chain of daguerreotype studios throughout the East. His particular method of photography was titled "Plumbetype." Plumbe is also reputed to be the author of the first plan for a transcontinental railroad, which was drawn up in 1836.

". . . I believe that the heterogeneous and chaotic character of these buildings and grounds arises from an ill-judged interference with technical design and arrangement on the part of men in authority, whether in the legislative or executive branches of government. Since our institutions carry with them, as a necessary consequence, a frequent change in the personnel of government, it is clear that if each succeeding wave of deputed authority is to leave the impress of its taste and its will upon the public structures, these must ere long be but a patchwork of as many whims, fancies, and artistic dogmas as have found favor in the eyes of the temporary occupants of place, unless some standard can be established which all will recognize—a consummation not now to be hoped for."

Horatio Greenough, "Aesthetics at Washington The Travels, Observations, and Experience of a Yankee Stonecutter, *1852*

"Setting aside, however, the question of economy, and looking at the question of propriety, can anything be more absurd than to expend millions upon noble pieces of masonry, and then to smear them with lead—thereby reducing them to a level with the meanest shingle palace? Stone among building materials, standing where gold stands among metals, to paint stone is like covering gold with tinfoil. So far has this been carried, that even in the Rotunda, where no conceivable motive could exist for the vandalism, the entire masonry has been painted, and that too of various tints, so that I will venture to affirm that many carry away the idea that the whole is but a piece of carpenter's work. The treatment of the Treasury buildings, where the granite basement has been painted of one color, the columns of a second, and the wall behind them

of a third, where even the lampposts have been daubed with divers tints, like a barber's pole, is noticed with priceless naivete in an important public document as a neat piece of work. What shall we say of the balustrades, where massive iron bars have been driven bodily into the columns, as though a column in a first class building, might be treated like a blind wall in the basest structure? and that, too, without a shadow of need. What shall we say of the iron railings that obtrude upon the eye about the blockings of the Patent Office, and veil with their inharmonious blackness the organization of that building? What of the one slender chimney of red brick, which peers over the broken profile of the marble Post Office? Will any adept in the science of construction explain why the gas light which is seen at the eastern entrance of the Capitol was made to hang with

so many feet of tiny pipe, and then secured by shabby wires driven into the columns? Would any person conversant with the proprieties of building tolerate such a slovenly arrangement in a private house? or in a private stable, if columns formed a feature of that stable? Do not such absurd and ignorant malpractices look as if a barbarous race had undertaken to enjoy the magnificence of a conquered people, and not know how to set about it?"

Horatio Greenough, "Aesthetics at Washington," The Travels, Observations, and Experience of a Yankee Stonecutter, *1852*

The General Post Office, daguerreotype by John Plumbe, 1846.

". . . The committee have been unable to separate the interest of the District from the interests of the United States. They regard it . . . as the creation of the Union for its own purposes. . . . And if this was the design, it is not easy to comprehend either the principle which would prevent the Government from a liberal appropriation of national resources to accomplish the object, or the policy which would confine the city to the means possessed by the inhabitants for its improvement."

Report of Senator Samuel Southard, 1835

"It [the General Post Office] is certainly a structure creditable to any city. The streets around it are all unfinished, and it is approached through seas of mud and sloughs of despond, which have been contrived, as I imagine, to lessen, if possible, the crowd of callers, and lighten in this way the overtasked officials within. . . . The official arrangements here for the public were so bad as to be absolutely barbarous . . . The distances of the city are very great, the means of transit through the city very limited, the dirt of the city unrivalled in depth and tenacity; and yet there is but one post office. Nor is there any established system of letter-carriers. To those who desire it, letters are brought out and delivered by carriers who charge a separate porterage for that service; but the rule is that letters shall be delivered from the window. . . . The purchase of stamps I found to be utterly impracticable. They were sold at a window in a corner, at which newspapers were also delivered, to which there was no regular ingress, and from which there was no egress. It would generally be deeply surrounded by a crowd of muddy soldiers, who would wait there patiently till time should enable them to approach the window. The delivery of letters was almost most tedious though in that there was a method. The aspirants stood in a long line, en cue, as we are told by Carlyle that the breadseekers used to approach the bakers' shops in Paris during the Revolution. This cue would sometimes project out into the street. The work inside was done very slowly. The clerk had not facility, by use of a desk or otherwise, for running through the letters under the initials denominated, but turned letter by letter through his hand. To one questioner out of ten would a letter be given. . . . A very trifling alteration in the management within would have remedied all the inconvenience."

Anthony Trollope, "North America," 1861–1862

Sheet music cover, 1851, showing the then 31 united states and the completed Capitol with the dome designed by Bulfinch. At the time, sewers drained into the canal in front of the Capitol, and at low tide it was an open marshy sewer. In contrast, according to an observer, "the grounds included within the walls of the Capitol . . . are ornamented with fountains, trees, and flowers. The grass plots are kept closely shorn, and present the most fascinating sights that could attract the eye within the range of artificial prospects."

General Andrew Jackson, by Clark Mills, 1853, the first equestrian statue in the country. It is located across from the White House in Lafayette Square.

". . . *The Vice-President's* [seat] *is slightly raised above the* [Senate chamber] *floor, and is canopied by crimson drapery, richly embossed, and held by the talons of an o'er hovering eagle, the chair is of morocco, and simple in its structure.* . . . *An emmence* [sic] *chandelier hangs in the midst, threatening the floor with destruction. The gallery opposite to the Vice-President's chair is mainly appropriated to ladies. It is very narrow and cramped, and when someone of the great Senatorial orators are to speak, no little confusion is occasioned thereby. Gentlemen going into the Senate Chamber are obliged to take off their hats. A man is employed, whose finger is constantly gesticulating to some absorbed visiter* [sic], *who, seeing no written rule to the contrary, keeps on his beaver. Printed cards stuck over the entrances, would be of great service.*"

P. Haas, Public Buildings and Architectural Ornaments of the Capital, *1839*

THE SEARCH FOR ORDER

3

"Westward the Course of Empire Takes Its Way" with McCormick Reapers in the Van, chromolithograph, n.d. Agricultural inventions hastened the cultivation of the nation as federal policies stimulated the westward movement of people. "The *untransacted* destiny of the American people," said William Gilpin in 1846, "is to subdue the continent—to rush over this vast field to the Pacific Ocean . . . to establish a new order in human affairs."

Construction of the Treasury Building, Washington, D.C., 1861. Begun in 1836 under the direction of Robert Mills, this building reached its current proportions in 1869. Over this period, Treasury employees in Washington increased from 372 to 2,650. Design and construction involved five major government architects: Robert Mills, Ammi B. Young, Isaiah Rogers, Thomas U. Walter, and Alfred Mullett.

By mid-century, the initial exuberance of nation building had given way to a more complex set of impulses and contradictions. Expansion became "Manifest Destiny," an expression coined in 1845 to title the American expansionist creed, with its curious mix of politics and geographical evangelism. But, while boundaries stretched westward, internal cleavages aligned ever more clearly along a north/south axis. Economically, agricultural and industrial revolutions took shape, machines in the American garden, dynamos in the virgin land. Socially, immigration and antislavery pressures made unity increasingly difficult.

Federal designs in American space reflected these transitions. The classical consensus in architecture gave way to a succession of other archaeological revivals. Land policy surrendered its ineffectual revenue emphasis to the desire for cheap land. The Army Corps of Engineers, denied an overall framework for their measuring and their construction, continued to respond to demand for specific projects. Federal designs on the land, like the Americans' consciousness, grew apace but lost coherence. In both architecture and in land policy, administrative reforms sought to bring rationality to growing confusion.

On the eve of the 1840 census report, a leading journal, *The United States Magazine and Democratic Review*, exultantly assessed half a century of measurable progress and found cause for celebration and for abundant optimism in the future. Destiny, the editors believed, was manifest in statistics as well as in geography.

"Without conquest or violence" the nation's original territory had been trebled. "What visions of fertility, population and power have thus been opened for the future, where free institutions and intelligent, moral, civilized beings are to supplant the savage, and illustrate all the benefits and glories of democratic principles from the Mississippi to the Pacific." The more than quadrupling of the national population was attributed to "a benign climate, with abundance of healthy food, with great exemption from the waste of wars, and perfect liberty in choice of business and place of settlement, so as to outstrip in early marriage, large families, fewer deaths, and rapid and permanent increase of population, almost every other nation on record. . . . The average duration of life has been so much increased here by temperance, abundance, liberty, medical science, &c. . . . In capacity for population and [productive] power hereafter, looking to her territory and her institutions it can hardly be deemed vanity, but is rather honest pride, to say we are evidently without a rival, much less a superior."

Such confidence in "our real advances in so short a period in all that is useful, practical and glorious" heralded the nation's age of Manifest Destiny. The lure of free land and imagined fortunes from fur and mineral wealth, the mythologies of empire and garden spurred the incessant drive to conquer and subdue the western spaces. New expressions entered the language—"self-made man," "almighty dollar," "to the victor belong the spoils." America's pursuit of its destiny assumed global proportions. Commodore Perry's expedition arrived in Japan; repeated forays were made into the frozen polar territories, exploring fifteen hundred miles of Antarctic coastline and incidentally contributing to the future U.S. role in the Pacific. A war with Mexico gave the United States another piece of real estate. Although the mood darkened after 1850 and the nation was blighted by civil war, the confidence in growth was never lost.

The pioneer and the axe and the tree stump entered the stock of images of American progress. And the Indian became the somber side of the dream. Measures to compensate the Indians for dispossession of their hunting grounds and freedom of mobility included annuities, reservations, land allotments, even proposals for separate statehood. Between 1778 and 1871 an estimated 370 treaties with Indians were signed and ratified by the federal government. In any balance of priorities, what the land could yield was the final weight in the scale and removal was the final outcome. From the administration of Jefferson to the Battle of Wounded Knee, Indian land titles progressively disappeared—at the conference table or on the battlefield—in front of advancing waves of settlement. In effect Indian land rights were recognized only in their forfeit.

With rapid growth and expansion the nation began to look different. In architecture, the tenets of classical symbolism began to yield to other archaeological motifs. In Washington a frontal assault on the federal tradition occurred when a Congressional building committee turned to twelfth-century Normandy for the style of the newest federal institution. The medieval castle of the Smithsonian Institution, a federally chartered entity, was completed in 1855. It was erected on the Mall amid similarly romantic landscaping, an antidote to the ordered mentality of the grid and the bare geometry of the preceding romantic-classical style.

Between 1820 and 1860 the nation's population more than tripled, from ten to thirty-one million. The scattering of these people over the landscape, combined with the patriotic boosterism typical of the times, created an immense and ever-increasing demand for physical manifestations of the federal presence. By 1853 the federal government was hard pressed to provide physical evidence of its expanding sovereignty as the nation spread rapidly across the continent. The government, which before 1850 had been inclined to house many of its activities in existing buildings, placed new emphasis on construction and in the process spawned a new bureaucracy to promote "more efficient management" of its undertakings. A new Office of Construction in the Treasury Department was headed first by an Army engineer officer, Captain Alexander H. Bowman. Under him, with the title of Supervising Architect, was appointed Ammi B. Young, who had assisted Robert Mills and had remained in the department after Mills's departure. Young was the first government appointee to be designated as 'Supervising Architect,' although the title was not legislatively established until 1864.

The new system under the fledgling office led to the centralization and standardization of government buildings to the extent that such structures as customhouses were often built in several cities from a single made-in-Washington plan, with only slight concession for differences in site, climate, or local needs and customs. Despite its emphasis on efficiency, the construction bureau's lines of control to the provinces were sometimes strained. Scandal, Congressional meddling, and gross inefficiency could delay completing construction for decades. A Congressional practice of legislating specifications promoted the fledgling iron industry, which was just developing a capability for producing structural components valued for their strength and their fireproofing potential. Paralleling such technological change were institutional changes in the ranks of those who applied it. Engineering and architecture emerged as distinct professions, each forming a separate organization in the 1850s.

Gaining one office to deal with the administrative pressures of national growth, the Treasury Department shed another office and supported the establishment of a new department. Since the beginning of the nation there had been efforts to organize a Home Department, but the lingering desire for a limited government and the opposition of states-rights proponents delayed acknowledgment of the growing confusion in the administration of domestic affairs, particularly in the development of the public lands. In 1849, at the request of Secretary of the Treasury Robert J. Walker, Congress finally established the Interior, or Home, Department, to take charge of the nation's internal affairs. Transferred to it were the General Land Office from the Treasury Department, the Patent Office from the State Department, and the Bureau of Indian Affairs and Pension Office from the War Department. Later responsibilities of the new department would result in the creation of such new Cabinet units as the Departments of Agriculture, Commerce, and Labor.

Congress also tried to order its control of expansion. Traditionally the legislators had debated and fixed far-reaching land policies when they were woefully short on facts and long on tall tales. Two-hundred-year-old hopes of finding a northwest passage to India persisted. And so powerful was the need of westward-moving settlers to think of the continental interior as a garden that often more credence was given to Daniel Boone fables, romantic landscape paintings, and the promotions of speculators than to reports of Army explorers who characterized the interior plains as the Great American Desert. It was a time when the public flocked to showings of enormous panorama paintings of the Mississippi River. Overheated advertising for one of these paintings was titled, *Description of Banvard's Panorama of the Mississippi River, Painted on Three Miles of Canvas, exhibiting a View of Country 1200 Miles in Length, extending from the Mouth of the Missouri River to the City of New Orleans, being by far the Largest Picture ever Executed by Man.* The Senate and House passed resolutions endorsing this spectacular as "a truly wonderful and magnificent production."

Into this dearth and confusion rode the Army Corps of Engineers. The scale of exploration had steadily changed. After the mountain men of the early years of the century came the official expeditions. By 1819 an expedition to Yellowstone under the topographical bureau of the Corps of Engineers had a thousand men in tow. In 1838 Congress established a separate Corps of Topographical Engineers.

In the theater of Manifest Destiny the Topographical Engineers came to center stage in a unique role, part scientific, part economic, part military, and very political, mixing geographical and military reconnaisance, often affecting war and diplomacy as well as settlement patterns. In one of the Corps's own historic accounts, published in

1966, the claim is made that western developments "were all accomplished by application of America's great power. That is the power of Engineering Character, Engineering Leadership, and Engineering Knowledge. All were employed to fulfill our destiny."

The singular achievements and ambivalent position of the Corps were dramatically demonstrated by the Pacific Railroad Surveys of the 1850s. For years, debate about a transcontinental route filled the records and overflowed the halls of Congress. When the politics of site selection reached a stalemate, Congress in 1853 consigned the decision to the objective evidence of science by launching four east-west expeditions along competing routes. A fifth expedition reconnoitered the Pacific coast. The expeditions were staffed with impressive complements of engineers, cartographers, topographers, surveyors, astronomers, geologists, botanists, zoologists, mineralogists, meteorologists, and artists.

When the reports were in, each expedition leader claimed his route feasible. Negative evidence was balanced with imaginative strategy—the southwestern party imported camels to cope with water shortage. The choice of route inevitably returned to the political arena, where it remained unresolved until after the Civil War, when parts of all the proposed routes were pieced together for the first transcontinental railroad line.

In their immediate intent of using science in the service of policy, the Pacific Railroad Surveys failed. But in the course of that failure more territory was explored and inventoried more completely and in less time than ever in human history. The monumental thirteen volumes of reports—costing twice as much as the surveys themselves—stirred enormous interest. When they were published they were widely discussed in newspapers, in magazines, and in Congress. From the volumes poured a chaotic mass of data, illustrations, observations, fulsome rhetoric—a cornucopia of riches beyond even the earliest European visions of a mythological land of abundance. New mapping of the trans-Mississippi West marked the culmination of six decades of effort to comprehend western geography. The last work in the West of the Topographical Engineers, before they were absorbed back into the Corps of Engineers, was to establish with the British the land boundary for the far Northwest. The space, then, was defined, although not yet fully conquered. It remained to fill it in, to come to terms with its other limits.

Before the next struggle with American space the nation was fragmented by the Civil War. As the war raged within what today is commuting distance of Washington, the iron framework for a new Capitol dome took shape. Finished in 1866, the dome was the crowning touch to all the previous building and rebuilding that had taken place in Washington since the turn of the century. The symbolic significance of the dome would be hard to estimate; its image has been emblazoned on everything from souvenir ashtrays to the mastheads of innumerable Congressmen's newsletters. To the embattled Abraham Lincoln, completion of the dome meant that the Union, though battered by divisive conflict, was structurally sound.

Vision of the New Eden, frontispiece from David A. Moore, *The Age of Progress,* 1856. Medieval spires appear above a classical palace in a luxuriant garden—a vision, like the Smithsonian building and grounds, quite different from the austere visual intentions of the nation's founders.

Envisioning "a suitable building of modest proportions . . . plain and durable, without unnecessary ornament," Congress in 1841 accepted a $500,000 bequest from James Smithson, an English scientist, "to found in Washington, under the name of the Smithsonian Institution, an establishment for the increase and diffusion of knowledge among men." This simple beginning became the focus for finding an appropriate style of national architecture. The resulting medieval castle, designed by James Renwick, was as wildly at variance with Jefferson's classical intentions as its new and romantic landscaping, by Andrew Jackson Downing, was with L'Enfant's.

The site chosen was part of "The Island," a portion of the city cut off by the unsightly Tiber Canal. Fifty years later, the *Washington Star* claimed that "the location of the building on the hitherto neglected Mall was the pioneer step in reclaiming . . . a section which had been up to that time about as unpromising as any portion of the District."

After Congress authorized construction, in 1846 Congressman Robert Dale Owen was appointed to head the Smithsonian Building Committee. Deliberations of the committee reflected an earlier Jeffersonian concern for an appropriate style for government architecture but in the context of the developing national interest in romantic architecture.

From 13 plans submitted in a design competition, two designs by James Renwick, one a decorated Gothic and the other Norman, were unanimously endorsed by the Building Committee. The latter was chosen because it was considered less ornate and less expensive, and, because of its irregularity, could more readily adapt to future expansion. Although first intended to be built in white marble, the building was finally executed in red-brown freestone.

From the beginning the building was plagued by construction delays and cost overruns. Renwick's design did not adequately comply with the competition program's stipulation that the building be fireproof, and during construction a conflagration consumed the entire central portion plus many valuable artifacts stored in it. The upper portions of the structure burned in 1865 and were rebuilt. Renwick's departures from the competition program provoked a published attack by losing competitors. In a pamphlet entitled *Animadversions on the Proceedings of the Regents of the Smithsonian Institution in Their Choice of an Architect, for Their Edifice at Washington: Founded on Observations Made During the Proceedings,* the losers alleged that Renwick's design was chosen even before all the entires were in; the designs were not exhibited publicly as stipulated; and Renwick's personal connections had secured favor for his design, which, the pamphlet claimed, did not follow the competition instructions.

Despite the professional controversy public consensus envisioned the Institution as a major center of scientific investigation. For enthusiastic Washingtonians the development of its proposed home was a dominant public topic.

Smithsonian Institution building, James Renwick, in a photo by H. G. Russell, June, 1862. A public holiday was proclaimed for the cornerstone laying ceremonies on May 1, 1847. Three military bands provided music for a mile-long procession of the D.C. militia, the local lodges of Masons, and assorted dignitaries. The Columbia Artillery fired a salute. The Masonic ceremonies took place in the presence of President Polk, the Cabinet, the diplomatic corps, city officials, and a huge crowd of citizens. The Grand Master of the Masons who performed the ceremony wore the apron presented to Washington by Lafayette and used the gavel employed by Washington when he laid the first cornerstone of the Capitol.

Title page from report of the Smithsonian Building Committee, 1849.

"The whole should be handsome, but plain and without unnecessary ornament. I believe that by going back to the pure Norman, with its Saxon arches and simple forms, you may produce something well suited to the purposes in view, and neither common place nor over expensive. I need not add a recommendation, that mere external appearance should, in all cases, be made to give way before convenience. My chief inducement to apply to you in preference to a regularly bred architect, is, that I know you will consult utility first, in the various internal arrangements and let architectural elegance follow, as a secondary, though not unimportant consideration."

Letter from Robert Dale Owen to David Owen, New Harmony, Indiana, August 15, 1845

"It affected everybody—day laborers, skilled artisans, merchants handling building supplies, people hoping for improvements in the city's appearance, and, above all, men eager to have the capital attain eminence in the American intellectual world."

Constance McLaughlin Green, Washington: Village and Capital, 1800–1878, 1962

". . . To combine solidity with architectural beauty and wholesome ventilation, and to satisfy at once true taste and stern economy by banishing useless embellishment, were aims always controlling and uppermost with the Regents."

From cornerstone address by George Dallas, Vice President of the United States and Chancellor of Board of Regents of Smithsonian, 1847

Proposed design for the
Smithsonian, Robert Mills,
1841.

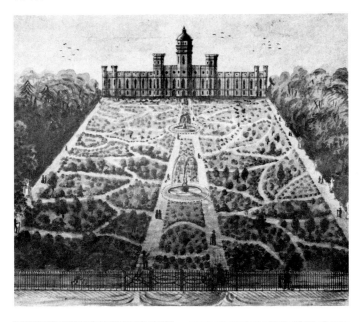

Renwick's Gothic proposal,
reminiscent of the architect's
design for St. Patrick's Cathedral in New York City.

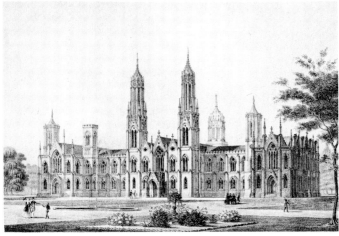

Joseph Henry, first Secretary
of the Smithsonian Institution,
who described the new building as "that monstrous cata-
falc" and complained of delays and mounting costs.

Representative Robert Dale
Owen, chairman of the Smithsonian Building Committee.

"Difficult as it is fully to convey by words, or even by aid of
the pencil, a distinct idea of the
feeling and principles which lie
at the base of each distinctive
style, I esteem myself fortunate,
in the present instance, in
being able to refer to an actual
example, at our Seat of Government, the architect of which
seems to me to have struck into
the right road, to have made a
step in advance, and to have
given us, in his design, not a
little of what may be fitting and
appropriate in any manner,
(should the genius of our country hereafter work such out,)
that shall deserve to be named
as a National Style of Architecture for America."

Robert Dale Owen, Hints on
Public Architecture, *report of
the Smithsonian Building Committee, 1849*

"Externally a Norman castle,
and it has cost a very large
sum. Unfortunately, architecture is frequently in antagonism
with science, and, too often,
when an architect gets his hand
into the purse of an establishment, everything else must
stand aside. Much trouble has
resulted from this building, it
has been a source of constant
anxiety and expense, the cost
having greatly exceeded the
original estimate."

*Joseph Henry, first Secretary of
the Smithsonian, quoted in*
Cosmos Club Bulletin, *February 1960*

Smithsonian, library, shown in a contemporary print.

"Suddenly . . . the dark form of the Smithsonian palace rose between me and the white Capitol and I stopped. Tower and battlement, and all that medieval confusion stamped itself on the halls of Congress, as ink on paper! It scared me. Was it a specter, or was I not another Rip Van Winkle who had slept too long. . . . I am not about to criticize the edifice. I have not quite recovered from my alarm. There is still a certain mystery about those towers and steep belfries that makes me uneasy. This is a practical land. They must be for something. Is no coup d'état lurking there?"

Horatio Greenough

Smithsonian, interior, from a nineteenth-century photo.

Smithsonian, interior view of window, south side.

The great Smithsonian fire of January 4, 1865, wood engraving by Philip Wharton in *Harper's Weekly*, February 11, 1865. The fire, caused by the faulty installation of a stovepipe, destroyed thousands of letters and papers, inventions, and the famed collection of Indian portraits by John Mix Stanley.

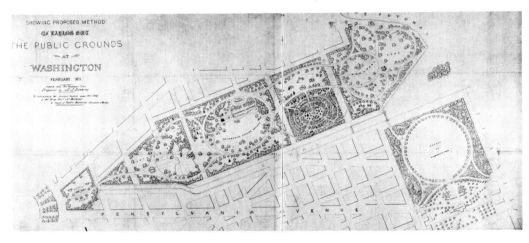

Deer on Downing's Mall. The Beaux-Arts style that would transform the Mall fifty years later would eliminate the cover for deer and other living creatures.

Landscape plan for the Mall and the Ellipse by Andrew Jackson Downing, 1851. Downing's scheme was executed only in the vicinity of the Smithsonian. It was intended, according to Downing, to be a rambling "pleasure grounds." "The straight lines and broad Avenues of the streets of Washington would be pleasantly relieved and contrasted by the beauty of curved lines and natural groups of trees. . . ." Today there is no remnant of Downing's work except a memorial vase designed by Calvert Vaux.

Prior to 1850 the Treasury met most of its space needs by purchasing buildings originally erected for other purposes. Thereafter, the tendency was almost exclusively toward construction by the government. By 1853 the Treasury Department owned 23 customhouses and 18 marine hospitals; another 15 customhouses were underway. The press of new construction—Congress authorized 16 additional buildings in 1854—led Secretary of Treasury James Guthrie to seek a means of "more efficient management." He created an Office, or "Bureau," of Construction, and Captain Alexander H. Bowman was detailed from the Corps of Engineers to be Engineer-in-Charge. Ammi B. Young, who had been hired to straighten out a scandal in Charleston, was given the title of Supervising Architect. Young was the first person actually to bear the title, although the position was not Congressionally established until 1864.

While Bowman and Young apparently worked well in tandem, their titles symbolized the evolving divergence of construction engineering and architecture as distinct professions. The first American engineering society was formed in 1852, and the American Institute of Architects in 1856. The appointment of an Army engineer as chief of the office reflects the Corps's general role in this era as the institutor of efficiency and rescuer of projects led astray by architects.

The Office of Construction began to centralize the Treasury's building activities and thus to replace the abused and cumbersome practice of local commissions awarding design contracts. Actual construction remained, in most cases, the responsibility of local superintendents, but now regulated by Bowman's chains of command and detailed requirements for systematic records and reports. The work load grew quickly; expenditures more than doubled from 1854 to 1856. Although demand for change in accommodations was most dramatic in gold rush country, the eastern cities also reflected the increased demand for government services. In 1857, Bowman noted, "the entire amount thus expended for the first *forty years* (for public buildings under the Secretary of the Treasury) did not exceed the amount expended during *the past fiscal year*." The Bureau employed, besides Bowman and Young, one clerk, six draftsmen, and one bookkeeper-draftsman. By 1913, the Supervising Architect's office numbered 253 employees in Washington and 103 in the field.

During his tenure as Supervising Architect (1853–1862), Ammi B. Young designed about seventy buildings. These structures tended to be smaller, in smaller, more widely scattered and remote locations than had earlier been the case. To deal with this design deluge, Young developed a series of standardized building types that allowed for minimal variation depending on region, function, and size. These buildings reflect the architecture profession's increasing departure from Jeffersonian classicism. Renaissance villas now appeared to house the federal presence.

The problem of standardization versus local variation plagued government architects ever thereafter. In 1884, for example, Mifflin Bell (like many of his predecessors and successors) proclaimed that "in the preparation of the designs of the various buildings I have endeavored to avoid monotony." He admitted, however, that this was "a difficult task to accomplish, in view of the fact that the uses to which the buildings are applied are so similar." Inadequate staffing and persistent busyness also militated against originality.

Young's departure from the Bureau in 1862 was in circumstances as politically chaotic as his arrival. A Congressional committee concluded that he was "not qualified" for his position "and should be removed." Among the Congressional accusations was extravagant expenditures in both the Charleston Customhouse and the extension of the Treasury in Washington. On the Treasury extension the committee cited a change in the capitals from granite to marble as well as overpaying for the marble itself. "We can conceive of no excuse for the supervising architect for such neglect of obvious duty to his employer—the government—in accepting a bid which was not in actual fact the lowest, by varying the size of stock after the bids had been received. The architect should have published a schedule to prevent such favoritism." Despite vocal supporters Secretary of the Treasury Chase wrote to Young in 1862: "Your services . . . are no longer required."

**Growth and the Begin-
nings of Bureaucracy**
100–101

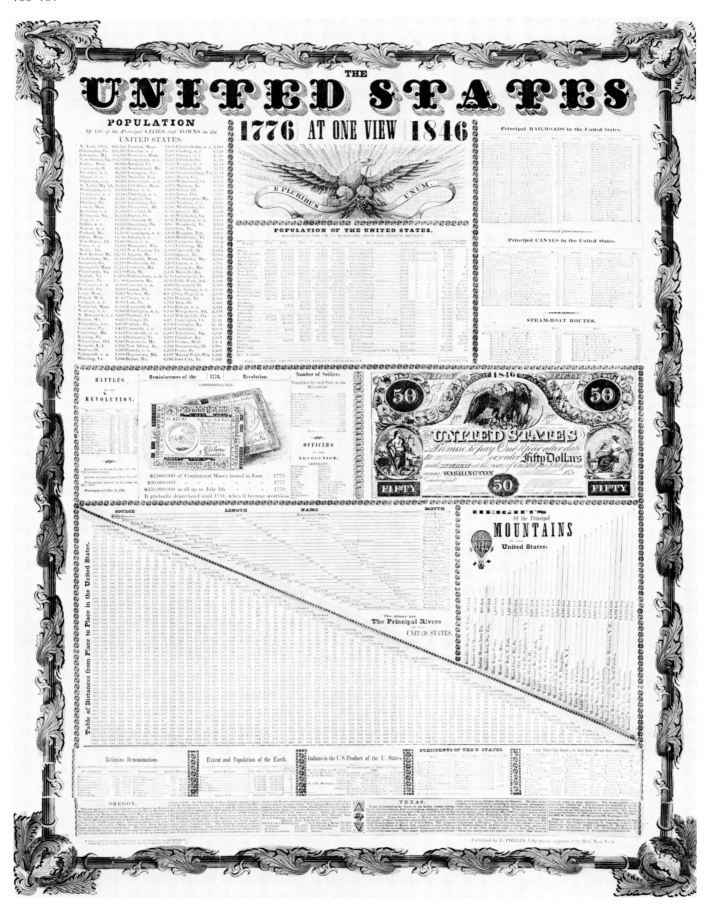

A glance at their progress (opposite) revealed to Americans in 1846 that their population had grown from almost four million in 1790 to over 17 million in 1840. Indians numbered 744,688, of whom over half then lived west of the Rocky Mountains. Maine, Vermont, and Massachusetts recorded no slaves, but one resided in New Hampshire, 5 in Rhode Island, 64 in Pennsylvania, 674 in New Jersey, 245,817 in North Carolina, 448,987 in Virginia, 3 each in Ohio and Indiana, 331 in Illinois, and 4,694 in the District of Columbia. Within the Union there were 2,487,113 slaves. (For purposes of determining representation in the House of Representatives 5 slaves counted as 3 whites.) Of the total population of the United States in 1840, 6,243 were counted on vessels—presumably at sea.

Customhouse and Post Office, Gridley Bryant, San Francisco, 1854–1856. Designed in Boston without regard for the local context of wooden architecture, this building was probably the first example of monumental federal architecture on the Pacific coast. It took the place of the hastily built frame structure that served the same purpose only seven years earlier. The discovery of gold in California was a particularly dramatic stimulus to local growth. San Franciscans numbered 850 in early 1849. They numbered 6,000 by the end of the year, double that a year later, and 34,776 in 1852.

Interior, New York Post Office, remodeled 1844 by Martin Thompson from the old Middle Dutch Church building (1727–1731). According to a local guidebook of the day, this post office in 1849 handled 40,000 letters and 120,000 newspapers daily. The post office was accommodated by this early example of adaptive use until 1875, when it moved to larger and grander quarters designed by Alfred Mullett.

Post Office, San Francisco, 1849, with a representative crowd of callers for mail and newspapers.

Growth and the Beginnings of Bureaucracy

Captain Alexander Hamilton Bowman, first engineer in charge of the Treasury Department's Office of Construction. Bowman was Superintendent of West Point, 1861–1864, and died in 1865.

Ammi Burnham Young (1798–1874) worked as an architect for the Treasury Department from 1842 to 1862 and became the chief architect of its new Office of Construction in 1853. When the profession rediscovered Young almost a century later, the editor of *The Federal Architect* magazine described his countenance as of "a gentleman who had that kindly, hard-boiled, wistful, shrewd, childlike, happy, faintly melancholy expression one usually associates with architects."

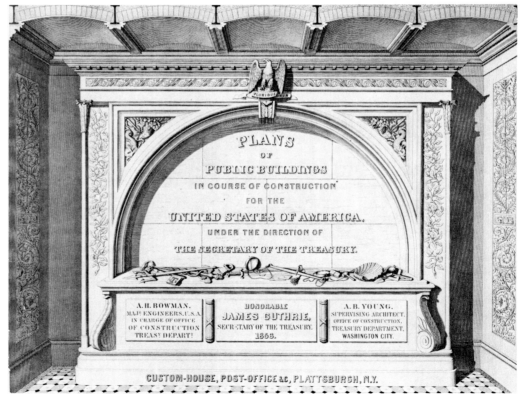

Frontispiece for designs in *Plans of Public Buildings in Course of Construction under the Direction of the Secretary of the Treasury*, a five-volume publication (1855–1856) that promoted and displayed the designs of the new Office of Construction.

This 1859 chart from the Treasury Department represented part of Bowman's campaign to develop a more judicious process for authorizing federal buildings. As history demonstrated and would continue to bear out, documentation of waste was no guarantee of its elimination.

Statement showing the places where custom-houses, court-houses, and post offices have been asked for but not authorized, the revenue collected at each, and cost of collection, for the fiscal year ending June 30, 1857, with the estimated cost of buildings.

Location.	Custom-houses.				Post offices.				Court-houses.	Aggregates.		Estimated cost of building and site.
	Revenue collected.	Expenditures.	Net income.	Excess of cost over revenue.	Revenue collected.	Expenditures.	Net income.	Excess of cost over revenue.	Number of days' session for the year ending December 31, 1856.	Total net income.	Total cost of collection over revenue.	
Machias, Me	$608 71	$2,605 72		$1,997 01	$798 11	$476 71	$321 40				$1,675 61	$20,000
Plymouth, Mass	395 12	3,216 04		2,820 92	2,090 36	1,099 44	990 92				1,830 00	20,000
Boston, Mass., P. O.					215,431 92	56,963 75	158,468 17		256	$158,468 17		1,000,000
Hartford, Conn., P. O.					23,604 46	7,675 39	15,929 07		52	15,929 07		150,000
Bridgeport, Conn	805 44	1,766 24		960 80	7,868 36	2,957 57	4,910 79			3,949 99		100,000
Rochester, N. Y*	128,722 48	6,549 23	$122,175 25		26,856 00	6,449 75	20,406 25		3	142,579 50		200,000
Sag Harbor, N. Y	723 72	635 72	88 00		1,448 27	720 12	728 15			816 15		20,000
Sackett's Harbor, N.Y.†	26,997 48	6,004 51	20,992 97		714 67	381 47	333 20			21,326 17		50,000
New York, N. Y	42,510,753 79	1,213,099 77	41,297,654 02		691,369 96	159,459 69	531,930 27		459	41,829,584 29		2,000,000
Albany, N. Y., C. H.					45,414 85	19,074 79	26,340 06		17	26,340 06		200,000
Brooklyn, N. Y., C. H.					22,255 49	4,735 00	17,520 49			17,520 49		1,000,000
Camden, N. J., C. H.	409 40	290 16	119 24		1,864 53	1,368 53	496 00			615 24		100,000
Trenton, N. J., C. H.					8,583 53	2,800 00	5,783 53		110	5,783 53		100,000
Jersey City, N. J., C.H.					7,717 01	2,800 00	4,917 01			4,917 01		100,000
Annapolis, Md., C. H.	180 75	929 20		748 45	2,360 65	1,191 29	1,169 36			420 91		50,000
Harrisburg, Pa., C.H.					23,724 26	8,583 31	15,140 95			15,140 95		500,000
Charleston, S. C., C. H.	441,100 78	58,263 41	382,837 37		43,006 18	10,587 00	32,419 18	113, including Columbus.	415,256 55		50,000
Greenville, S. C., C. H.					1,916 14	882 52	1,033 62			1,033 62		50,000
Macon, Ga., C. H.					8,938 91	3,361 17	5,577 74			5,577 74		50,000
Montgomery, Ala., C.H.					8,883 85	7,404 07	1,479 78		10	1,479 78		50,000
Vicksburg, Miss., C. H.	2,317 40	709 96	1,607 44		5,904 71	3,451 26	2,453 45			4,060 89		50,000
Paducah, Ky., C. H.‡	6,710 90	559 74	6,151 16		1,999 22	898 30	1,100 92			7,252 08		50,000
Tyler, Texas, C. H.					518 38	253 75	264 63		20	264 63		150,000
Columbus, Ohio, C. H.					14,671 18	10,446 53	4,224 65			4,224 65		50,000
Burlington, Iowa§	8,810 40	1,177 54	7,632 86		6,854 95	3,155 85	3,699 10		10	11,331 96		50,000
Iowa City, Iowa, C. H.					6,930 33	2,000 00	4,930 33		10	4,930 33		50,000
Keokuk, Iowa‖	11,390 90	862 46	10,528 44		7,287 63	3,470 24	3,817 39			14,345 83		50,000
Sioux City, Iowa, C. H.					1,098 83	585 64	513 19			513 19		50,000
New Albany, Ind., C. H.	2,141 10	382 53	1,758 57		4,837 94	2,000 00	2,837 94			4,596 51		50,000
Quincy, Ill	1,961 89	435 73	1,526 16		7,369 83	2,000 00	5,369 83			6,895 99		50,000
Alton, Ill	1,020 95	525 00	495 95		4,275 66	2,053 71	2,221 95			2,717 90		50,000
Peoria, Ill	210 20	363 60		153 40	8,512 69	3,585 26	4,927 43			4,927 43		50,000
St. Paul's, Minn					10,978 90	3,278 75	7,700 15			7,700 15		50,000
Total	43,145,261 41	1,298,376 56	41,853,565 43	6,680 58	1,226,107 76	336,150 86	889,950 90			42,740,500 76	3,505 61	6,560,000

* $122,033 40, amount of revenue from railroad iron in bond. † $26,883 90, amount of revenue from railroad iron in bond.
‡ $6,516 13, amount of revenue from railroad iron in bond. § $8,472 90, amount of revenue from railroad iron in bond.
‖ $10,323 50, amount of revenue from railroad iron in bond.

NOTE.—These estimates are such as would *be asked for*, judging by others for like places and purposes.

OFFICE OF CONSTRUCTION, *Treasury Department.*   A. H. BOWMAN, *Engineer in charge.*

Customhouse, Wheeling, West Virginia, 1856–1860. Cost, $96,600; cubic feet, 332,100; steam heat. Population of the town at the time of construction: 14,083.

Following the secession of Virginia from the Union in 1861 a convention of loyalists met in the Wheeling customhouse with the permission of the federal government. The West Virginia Declaration of Independence and Bill of Rights were adopted here, and the building became the temporary capitol. It is now used as the post office.

Customhouse and Post Office, Galena, Illinois, 1857–1858. Cost, $61,400; cubic feet, 130,000; hot water system. Population of the town at the time of construction was 7,500. At mid-century Galena was the largest and wealthiest town in Illinois. It was soon eclipsed by the railroad-stimulated growth of Chicago. By 1900 Galena's population had fallen to 5,005.

Customhouse in Georgetown in Washington, D.C., 1857–1858. Cost, $55,400; cubic feet, 130,000; steam heat.

Courthouse and Post Office, Windsor, Vermont, 1857–1858. Cost, $71,347.32; cubic feet, 281,000; heat supplied from a furnace and open fireplaces. Population of the town at the time of construction: 2,000.

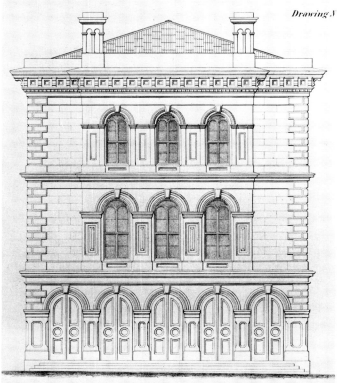

Drawing X

Typical unrendered elevation of one of the standard building types done by the Office of the Supervising Architect, 1855. Young frequently favored a Renaissance Revival style as a classical-related alternative to the waning Greek Revival. Versions of this Renaissance type appeared in several places, including Wheeling, West Virginia; Windsor, Vermont; and Oswego, New York.

The unsavory scandals and scandalous inefficiency connected with a new customhouse at Charleston, South Carolina, dramatized Washington's tenuous control over distant construction programs.

In November of 1849, the local commission with responsibility for the new customhouse advertised a design competition with a $300 prize for a structure 200 feet × 300 feet with "3 stories—first or basement story intended for the storage of heavy goods . . . of substantial and durable material . . . fireproof." By March of 1850, following a series of attempts to influence the selection, the commission chose a Gothic castle design by one E. C. Jones. The choice was vetoed in Washington, and the commission then adopted a plan, which incorporated what it regarded as the best aspects of four of the designs submitted.

The slighted Mr. Jones complained to the President of the United States and the Secretary of the Treasury that "the adoption of parts of the four leading Designs, namely the Ground plan of Mr. Norris—The Front Elevation of Mr. White—The Back Elevation of Mr. Hammerschold and the Portico and Dome of Mr. Jones was done simply to

conciliate the four architects and to neutralize the position of myself [sic] by having the unanimous vote of the Commissioners." Added to Jones's complaint were accusations of corruption and immorality—from purloining of building materials for a private residence to intoxicated workmen. Reportedly, there were even dark rumors of blackmail and murder. At least there was enough smoke to send the whole matter to the Secretary of the Treasury again.

In Washington, the plan was placed in the hands of Ammi B. Young, whom the Secretary of the Treasury had appointed as adviser on design matters after the dismissal of Robert Mills. Young ignored the combination plan and offered instead a design that resembled his earlier Boston customhouse design. Young's proposal was implemented.

But the building was not completed until 1879, thirty years after the first advertisement for its design. In the intervening time the project was alternately halted and resumed, praised and damned. It took 19 acts of Congress to appropriate necessary funds. Many of the original plans were lost or destroyed during the Civil War, and plans for the dome were scrapped afterward. Through the course

of construction nine Secretaries of the Treasury and seven Presidents held office.

One of the new authorizations in 1854 was for the first federal building in Texas, a combined customhouse, post office, and courthouse at Galveston. Unlike previous authorizations, which only directed the Treasury Secretary to erect "a suitable building" (within the authorized cost, of course), the 1854 act directed that the buildings be "of brick with fireproof floors, constructed of iron beams and brick work, iron roof, shutters, sills, &c." It also specified the three dimensions of the Galveston structure and required "a portico on two sides."

The detailed statutory language was probably a response to Treasury Secretary Guthrie's 1853 complaint about laws that left everything but cost to his discretion. The specifications no doubt originated in the Office of Construction, whose staff thus neatly told Congress what it should tell them to do.

The act's emphasis on ironwork reflected Guthrie's attempt to promote iron construction in order to stimulate the growth of

that fledgling industry and as a means of thwarting the nemesis of fire. Bowman claimed in 1856 that the office's use of wrought-iron beams and girders instead of groined arches was "wholly new." Between 1852 and 1857 the Treasury used 40 million pounds of iron in construction.

Dilatory tactics on the part of the Galveston building contractors, Cluskey & Moore, who hoped to increase their profits by substituting their own design for that drawn up by Young, forced two redesigns and consequent amendments (in 1857 and 1859) to the authorizing act. The originally mandated porticoes were, however, retained. (Clearly, Guthrie's effort to settle on a building's specifications by embalming them in law was not wholly successful.) A new contractor, working under the pressure of Texas's impending secession, improvised prefabrication techniques and rushed construction at the site to a conclusion in four months ending in March 1861. Within a day or two, Texas seceded and the Confederacy took over the building. As a result, one local historian wryly noted, "The first use the Government made of the new Custom-house was to throw shell into it in 1861."

Customhouse, Ammi B. Young, Charleston, South Carolina, 1853. By the time the building was completed in 1879 Young's proposed cupola was eliminated. The *Charleston Courier* of July 15, 1854, described the building then in construction as "Roman Corinthian." The structure would be "strictly fire proof throughout, the materials employed being granite, marble, and iron."

From the *Annual Report of the Secretary of the Treasury on the State of the Finances,* which included annual reports of the Office of Construction, 1854–1861, and after 1865 from the annual *Report of the Supervising Architect of the Treasury:*

1850

"The incumbrance upon the site selected for the custom-house at Charleston, South Carolina, has been removed, and no further delay in the erection of the building is anticipated."

1855

"The foundation of the front portico was retarded by a building which was on the ground it was to occupy."

1856

"The new custom-house in this city has not advanced as rapidly as could have been desired the past year. The superintendent attributes this to the delay in receiving the granite and marble as rapidly as it is required."

1857

"The new custom-house at Charleston, S.C. has not progressed as rapidly as was expected or could be desired."

1858

"The exterior of the new custom-house at Charleston, S.C., has not progressed as rapidly as I had hoped during the past year."

1859

". . . the work has progressed but slowly, and under great disadvantages [Congressional refusal to appropriate more funds]."

1861

"The superintendent at Charleston, Colonel E. B. White, was aiding the rebels at their forts during a period for which he claims pay from the general government, while the superintendents at Mobile and New Orleans, Captain Leadbetter and Major Beauregard are now prominent in attack upon the government. . . ."

1866

"This elaborate and costly marble building was scarcely injured by the bombardment, having been struck only 5 times during its continuance."

1871

"The resumption of work . . . has proved an undertaking of unusual difficulty, many of the plans having been destroyed during the war . . . the expenditures on this building prior to the war can be fitly characterized by the epithet of reckless extravagance, the workmanship, though fine, being apparently designed as a mere excuse for the expenditure of money."

1879

"This building has been occupied for some months, the interior decorations and the approaches having been completed since the last report."

1850 view of Charleston, South Carolina, shows that local residents then expected the new customhouse to be in the design of E. C. Jones. His Gothic castle appears in the background.

"If Messrs. Cluskey & Moore are depended on to erect your Custom House-Court House &c., I very much fear that the present generation will pass away before the building is complete! They lack two important requisites: viz. Means & Capacity."

F. H. Gibbon, a rival contractor, in a letter to Senator Sam Houston, 1859

"I have the honor again to call your attention to the growing variety of uses for which iron is most desirable in public buildings. Every new trial suggests new uses, and the opportunity thus given to stimulate . . . production . . . will not be neglected. . . ."

A. H. Bowman in Report of the Supervising Architect of the Treasury, 1859

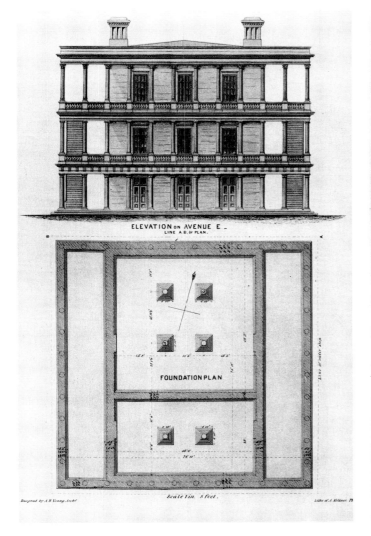

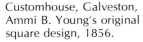

Customhouse, Galveston, Ammi B. Young's original square design, 1856.

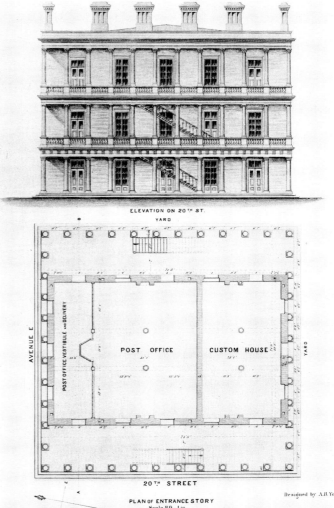

Customhouse, Galveston, Young's second design, a response to Congressional pressure brought to bear by the builders for a larger and more costly structure, lengthened the building by 23 feet. The Treasury agreed to enlarge its plans, but persuaded Congress to retain the original expenditure limit—thus leaving the builders in the lurch.

Customhouse, Galveston, working drawing of ironwork for Young's original design, using three different orders of capitals. Robert Mills, architect for public buildings in Washington, D.C., had been dismissed in part because of his preference for ornate (and expensive) Corinthian marble columns. The use of iron in these later designs allowed columns to be cast in any style with little difference in cost and with no attention to the availability of skilled craftsmen. Seventy years earlier Jefferson had chosen the Ionic style for the Richmond capitol because of the dearth of trained sculptors.

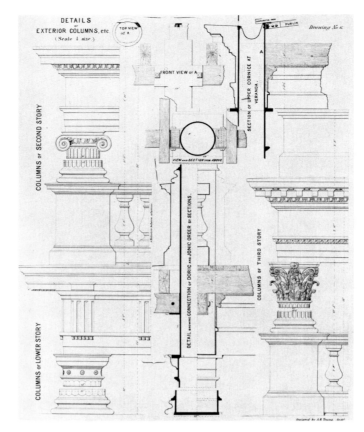

Customhouse, Galveston, as finally built and as restored for use as a U.S. District Courthouse in the 1960s in one of the federal government's first historic restorations. The building was dedicated for the first time in 1967; advent of the Civil War had precluded an official ceremony in 1861.

"Iron was used extensively in all buildings for decoration as well as construction. . . . On more than one occasion when fires swept through towns in which federal buildings were situated, the federal buildings were saved by the cast iron window shutters and the corrugated iron roofs. There was no wood or any form of construction on the exterior of the buildings which could contribute to a blaze. Interior staircases were cast iron, and the amount of ornamentation depended upon whether they were a main staircase in an entrance or merely a service staircase. Perhaps the most outrageous use of the material can be seen on the post office in Windsor, Vermont, where the cast iron 'coade stone' quoins around the doors and windows and at all four corners of the building blend in with the cornices. All are painted a stone color to contrast with the red brick."

Lawrence Wodehouse, Journal of the Society of Architectural Historians, December 1966

Lewis and Clark holding a council with the Indians, illustration from a journal published in 1811 by Patrick Gass, a member of the exploring party.

In the half century after the Lewis and Clark expedition, changes in mapping of the lands beyond the Mississippi dramatically revealed the rapid changes of population expansion and commercial development. The romance of exploration in the Lewis and Clark maps had yielded to the precise grid of property speculation.

To the Indians, there was other clear evidence of the white settlers' progress and of their intentions of staying in the Western lands. The sturdy forts they built were the antithesis of the mobile and vulnerable structures of hunting societies. Each new territorial capitol building further proclaimed the ambitions of the settlers.

Shortly after the purchase of the Louisiana Territory, the U.S. government established a string of forts in advance of the frontier settlement to act as a buffer between the Indians and the settlers. By 1845, on the eve of the Mexican War, there were 56 military posts, 11 forts, and the Jefferson Barracks west of the Mississippi. In 1849 administration of Indian affairs was transferred from the army to the newly created Department of the Interior. Assigning Indians to the reservations proved one thing; enforcing the assignment another, for such consolidation was often in conflict with the hunting culture of many tribes.

The real heyday of the frontier forts began in the 1840s and ended about 1880. In that time the United States annexed Texas, decided the ownership of Oregon, and acquired land as a result of the Mexican War. The acquisition of new lands, the westward expansion of the farmers and cattlemen, gold and silver rushes, and the development of transportation through trails, roads, canals, and finally the railroad brought masses of settlers in direct contact with Indians. To deal with the often violent results, the federal government had established, by 1869, 110 forts in the upper Missouri country alone.

With the gradual cessation of the Indian Wars in the late 1880s the federal government undertook the business of building white people's schools to "civilize" Indians. The most prevalent policy of assimilation of "savage" children was through education based on models devised by white educators—often in boarding schools deliberately far from Indian families. The job of designing and supervising construction of such facilities fell to the construction division of the Bureau of Indian Affairs—except for large projects, which were handled by the Supervising Architect or by the superintendents of various Indian agencies. Some smaller school buildings were constructed by Indians as part of a course of instruction. It was not until 1908 that Bureau of Indian Affairs Commissioner and educator Francis E. Leupp sought to relate classroom work and schoolhouse design to the outdoors and to the Indian way of life through the innovation of "outdoor" day schools for the Southwest.

Despite more humane approaches the Indians continued as charges of the state. Willa Cather later wrote of "the conquests of peace dearer bought than those of war."

Meeting of the United States Commissioners and Indians at Prairie du Chien, Wisconsin, September 1825, lithograph by James Otto Lewis.

"The several nations or tribes of nations, with whom we are connected, should not be molested or disturbed in the possession of such parts of our dominions and territories as, not having been ceded to, or purchased by us, are reserved to them, or any of them, as hunting grounds."

King George III, 1763

"The utmost good faith shall always be observed toward the Indians; their land and property shall never be taken from them without their consent; and in their property, rights and liberty they shall never be invaded or disturbed unless in just and lawful wars authorized by Congress; but laws founded in justice and humanity shall from time to time be made for preventing wrongs done to them, and for preserving peace and friendship with them."

Northwest Ordinance of 1787

". . . now reduced within limits too narrow for the hunter's state, humanity enjoins us to teach 'them agriculture and the domestic arts. . . ."

Thomas Jefferson, Second Inaugural Address, March 1805

"The hunter state can exist only in the vast uncultivated desert. It yields to the . . . greater force of civilized population; and, of right, it ought to yield, for the earth was given to mankind to support the greater number of which it is capable; and no tribe or people have a right to withhold from the wants of others, more than is necessary for their support and comfort."

President James Monroe, 1817

"A display of American power was essential to the success of treaty-making with the Indians. Usually, therefore, treaties were negotiated at a fort, where the Indian love of ceremonial could be gratified by a lavish military spectacle. The negotiations conducted at Prairie du Chien in 1829, for example, when the Winnebago bartered away their rights to the lead regions east of the Mississippi, were most impressive. 'The commissioners,' one of their number wrote later, 'sat on a raised bench, facing the Indian chiefs; on each side of them stood the officers of the army in full dresses, while the soldiers, in their best attire, appeared in bright array, on the sides of the council shade. The ladies belonging to the officers' families, and the best families in the Prairie were seated directly behind the commissioners, where they could see all that passed, and hear all that was said. Behind the principal Indian chiefs sat the common

people—first the men, then the women and children, to the number of thousands, who listened in breathless and death-like silence, to every word that was uttered. The spectacle was grand and morally sublime in the highest degree, to the nations of red men, who were present."

Caleb Atwater, Remarks Made on a Tour to Prairie du Chien, Thence to Washington City, in 1829, *1831*

"How sickening are the sentimental effusions upon the subject of the 'poor Indians'. . . . [T]he savage must ever recede before the man of civilization. . . . The square mile which furnishes game to a single family of hunters, will support a thousand families by agriculture and the mechanic arts, of which agriculture is the parent. . . . The savage who will not earn his subsistence, after the diminution of game, in the way that Providence prescribed, has the right of way upon the soil, and nothing more until the agriculturist appears for whom it was intended."

George Lepner in the Southern Literary Messenger, *1837*

Indians meet with government officials at Medicine Lodge Creek, Kansas, in 1867 and agree to move to a reservation. The deliberation was painted by U.S. Army Pvt. Herman Steiffel, who was present.

"The rapid progress of civilization upon this continent will not permit the lands which are required for cultivation to be surrendered to savage tribes for hunting. . . . Indeed, whatever may be the theory, the Government has always demanded the removal of the Indians when their lands were required for agricultural purposes . . . . although the consent of the Indians has been obtained in the form of treaties, it is well known that they have yielded to a necessity to which they could not resist. . . . . "

Secretary of the Interior Caleb B. Smith, 1862

"To whom does this land belong? I believe it belongs to me. If you ask me for a piece of land I would not give it. I cannot spare it, and I like it very much."

Chief Bear Rib of the Unkpapa Sioux at a treaty council, 1866

". . . A thin, scattering race of almost naked black children, these Goshoots [Indian tribes] are, who produce nothing at all, and have no villages, and no gatherings together into strictly defined tribal communities. . . . The Bushmen and our Goshoots are manifestly descended from the self-same gorilla, or kangaroo, or Norway rat, whichever Animal-Adam the Darwinians trace them to."

Mark Twain, Roughing It, 1872

". . . The Indians should be made as comfortable on, and uncomfortable off, their reservations as it was within the power of the Government to make them; that such of them as went right should be protected and fed, and such as went wrong should be harassed and scourged without intermission."

Commissioner of Indian Affairs Francis Walker, 1871–1873

"The agency boarding-school is the object lesson for the reservation. The new methods of thought and life there exemplified, while being wrought into the pupils, are watched by those outside. The parents visit the school, and the pupils take back into their homes new habits and ideas gained in the school room, sewing room, kitchen and farm."

Commissioner of Indian Affairs Hiram Price, Annual Report, 1881

"But so long as the American people now demand that Indians shall become white men within one generation, the Indian child must have other opportunities and come under other influences than reservations can offer. He must be compelled to adopt the English language, must be so placed that attendance at school shall be regular, and that vacations shall not be periods of retrogression, and must breathe the atmosphere of a civilized instead of a barbarous or semibarbarous community."

Commissioner of Indian Affairs Hiram Price, Annual Report, 1881

"If the Indian has been living in a certain way for untold centuries, I should not push him too rapidly into a new social order and a new method of doing things; I should prefer to let him grow into them of his own accord."

Commissioner of Indian Affairs Francis Leupp, "Back to Nature for the Indian," Charities and Commons, June 6, 1908

". . . If the supply of customhouses and pension agencies and agricultural experiment stations happened for the moment to be running short, he [a Congressman] would stir about to secure votes for an Indian school."

Commissioner of Indian Affairs Robert G. Valentine, Annual Report, 1910

Clark's 1809 map. St. Louis is marked in this segment of the map at the confluence of the Missouri and Mississippi Rivers.

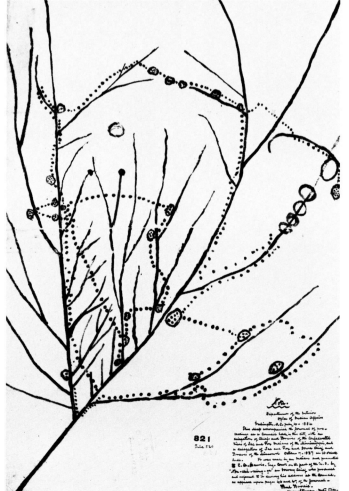

Indian map made during treaty negotiations in 1837. The small dots may represent a day's journey; the clusters of circled dots, the locations of friendly settlements. The lines depict water arteries, which were the easiest travel routes.

"... Just as it was the white man's way to assert himself in any landscape, to change it, make it over a little (at least to leave some mark or memorial of his sojourn), it was the Indian's way to pass through a country without disturbing anything...."—Willa Cather, *Death Comes for the Archbishop*, 1927.

"Although our country, vast in extent, is capable of supporting as dense a population as any other nation to the square mile, it is not probable it will be greater than seventy-five to the square mile. Leaving out 2,500,000 square miles for the deserts and cold, inhospitable regions of the extreme north, leaving a balance of eight millions of square miles, we will then have a population of seven hundred millions of inhabitants, speaking the same tongue, and living under one federal government, with internal trade in proportion to the wants of the people, presenting the grandest spectacle of national power and prosperity."

John H. Henry, 1868

"There is no compacted and consistent body of national law concerning the Territories. Acts have been passed, sections amended, overlapped, and repealed, and special features introduced to fit special cases. . . . Common people . . . cannot understand them; lawyers are paid for disagreeing on their meaning; and judges, when failing from its obscurity to ascertain what the law is, are compelled to decide what it ought to be."

Mason Brayman, Territorial Governor of Idaho, 1879

An 1853 map, part of the first geological survey of Missouri state. Compared with the 1809 map from the Lewis and Clark expedition, it represents a journey from mythology to real estate.

Colonel John J. Albert, chief of the Topographical Bureau, 1829–1861. In 1838 Congress made the bureau a separate Corps of Topographical Engineers, which served until 1861 as the public works department of westward expansion—providing the surveys, maps, roads, communications and defense vital for conquest and settlement. Its historic Pacific Railroad Surveys for a transcontinental route, which were published by Congress between 1855 and 1861, stirred wide public interest in the riches of the West.

Senator Thomas Hart Benton, a major voice for the westward expansionist policy that was justified by Manifest Destiny and one of the major backers of the exploits of the Topographical Engineers. Benton not only promoted the Pacific Railroad Surveys; he also supported privately sponsored expeditions when government expeditions showed evidence of leading to politically distasteful conclusions.

One of the enormous folding panoramas of seventy to one hundred miles of observed landscape, Pacific Railroad Surveys. These views were keyed to expedition maps with a system of symbols and descriptions.

Geographical cross section of the Grand Canyon, Pacific Railroad Surveys, 1857. Discovery of what was under the land turned the westward movement of white settlers into a tidal wave that engulfed the last resistance of the Indians. In contrast to this drawing were those made by the Prussian artist F. W. von Egloffstein, from the same expedition. His romantic drawings were the earliest first-hand scenic portrayals of the Canyon.

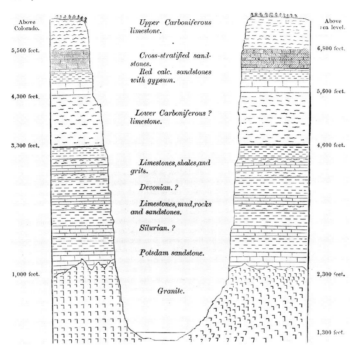

Above Colorado.		Upper Carboniferous limestone.		Above sea level.
5,500 feet.		Cross-stratified sandstones.		6,800 feet.
		Red calc. sandstones with gypsum.		
4,300 feet.		Lower Carboniferous ? limestone.		5,600 feet.
3,300 feet.		Limestones, shales, and grits.		4,600 feet.
		Devonian. ?		
		Limestones, mud, rocks and sandstones.		
		Silurian. ?		
1,000 feet.		Potsdam sandstone.		2,300 feet.
		Granite.		1,300 feet.

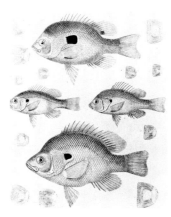

Examples of illustrations published in the reports of the Pacific Railroad Surveys. According to historian William Goetzman, from the expeditions' maps, plant and animal inventories, metereological data, geological and mineralogical surveys, and ethnological descriptions a ''whole new view of the continent emerged.'' That enriched view stimulated speculation and exploitation as well as settlement. After the Civil War photographs replaced artists' drawings in reports of federal surveys.

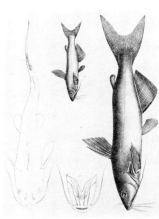

Fort Smith, Kansas, lithograph view, Pacific Railroad Surveys.

Fort Okinakane, Pacific Railroad Surveys, by John Mix Stanley, who became well known for a collection of his Indian portrayals at the Smithsonian. The collection was completely destroyed by fire. Artists commonly marched shoulder to shoulder with explorers and scientists in the development of the West.

Fort Union and Distribution of Goods to the Assinibones, Pacific Railroad Surveys, John Mix Stanley.

Fort Laramie, by nineteenth-century American artist Alfred J. Miller. Fort Laramie, one of the most famous Indian fighting forts, was originally a major western trading post owned by the American Fur Company. It was sold to the U.S. government in 1849.

Crossing the plains from St. Joseph, Missouri, to Boise, Idaho, photo taken in 1862.

A U.S. military post, late nineteenth century: Fort Yates ordnance storehouse and magazine. Placing the second level at a 45-degree angle with the first allowed defenders to fire in eight directions.

Reminiscences of
a Soldier's Wife

By
Ellen McGowan Biddle

Philadelphia
Press of J. B. Lippincott Company
1907

Life and amenities inside the Indian forts were spare. Ellen Biddle recalled her sojourn at Camp Halleck, Nevada, in about 1868: "It seemed to me while in the army, that the quartermasters were always using up scraps of paint; no two rooms were alike and each one uglier than the other. . . . Camp Halleck was but a two-company post; there was nothing, but an occasional ride over the sagebrush plains, to relieve the monotony of our life; had it not been for my children . . . who were hearty and thoroughly alive mentally and physically, I think I would have despaired. No one who has not lived an isolated life can appreciate what it is for a woman. The men had more interest in their lives, for when not scouting they had their 'companies' to look after, and when the morning duties were over they could swing a gun over their shoulders and go hunting, which is the greatest pleasure a man knows. . . . The Government at that time allowed no extra money to make the quarters comfortable, and I doubt if many of the discomforts we had were realised at Washington."

Navajo Indians under guard constructing a barracks building at Fort Sumner, New Mexico, 1864–1865. Secretary of War Lewis Cass, in his report to Congress in 1826, described the design policy for western forts: "The stockade works erected in the Indian country are important to overawe the Indians, and to restrain their perpetual disposition to war. . . . They command the great avenues of communication in to the country; they cover the whole frontier; they protect our citizens in the various employments required by their duties, public and private, and they produce a moral effect upon the Indians, which is visible and permanent. So long as they are maintained there can be no zealous cooperation between the Indians and any other power."

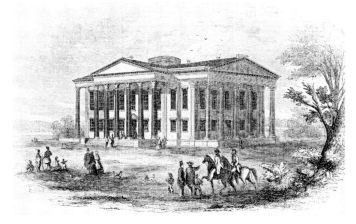

Territorial Capitol, Lecompton, Kansas, 1856. This large, elaborate stone building evidenced both traditional architectural influence and the optimistic ambitions of a territory that contained only a few thousand voters at the time of construction.

Congress usually gave $20,000 to the construction budget for a territorial capitol.

The location of an infant capital town generated tremendous interest, for there would be centered the location of important people, expanding trade, and rising land values. In style, Lecompton's 1856 structure would have been equally at home in settled New England, evidence of the urge to bring established, rather than new, institutions and forms to the new country.

Customhouse and Post Office, Alfred B. Mullett, Portland, Oregon, 1875, the first permanent federal building in the Northwest. Begun in 1869, it was a typically grand bow to local pride and aspiration. It was built for a town of 9,000 residents before the railroad arrived and before streets were paved.

American Progress, lithograph by George A. Crofutt, 1873, after John Gast's painting of 1872. The allegorical Columbia dispenses federal largesse as she conjures up railway and telegraph lines in the wake of fleeing Indians and buffalo, advancing settlers. In the last four decades of the century 400 million new acres came under cultivation and the land that could be cheaply turned into farms was gone.

Broadside, 1879.

Land office in Sedgwick County, Kansas, 1873. As early as 1818, according to Malcolm Rohrbough, sales of land at Huntsville, Tennessee, "inflamed the imagination of the most hardened speculator. They dismayed the district land officers charged with their execution and alternately delighted and terrified the administrators in Washington."

By 1882 a song popular in Kansas voiced the tribulations of some later landholders: ". . . For you'll find me out West in the County of Lane/Just a starvin' to death on my Government claim. . . ."

"We are a republic, and we wish to continue so; then multiply the class of freeholders; pass the public lands cheaply and easily into the hands of the People; sell for a reasonable price to those who are able to pay; and give without price to those who are not. I say give without price to those who are not able to pay; and that which is so given I consider as sold for the best of prices. . . . It brings a price above rubies—a race of virtuous and independent farmers, the true supporters of their country, and the stock from which its best defenders must be drawn."

Senator Thomas Hart Benton

Villa of Brale, Oklahoma territory, photo by Grabill, 1891.

Oklahoma City, four weeks old. At noon on April 22, 1889, Congress allowed land-hungry whites into the new lands of the Oklahoma Territory, lands formerly reserved for the Indians. Forty-five minutes later the town was surveyed and tents were pitched on the best lots. Two million acres were claimed in a few hours. Tents were followed by board shacks, and another western city was born.

Indian boys planting corn, St. Francis Mission, South Dakota, c. 1890. Intended as a humanitarian response to army and Department of the Interior policies, the Dawes Act of 1887 destroyed tribal autonomy, even on reservations, by providing 160 acres of land to each family head to cultivate.

From the beginning, Catch 22 was agriculture. Under Jefferson, Indian agents were instructed to convert Indians to farming or move them beyond the Mississippi. The Bureau of Indian Affairs was organized in 1834 to educate Indians to agriculture as a means of "domestication." If Indians refused agricultural conversion they were moved or exterminated. When they accepted agriculture, tribal culture was weakened. On less-than-fertile, cast-off land, "independent" farming insured dependent pauperism.

The Carlisle School, Pennsylvania, nineteenth century. The Bureau of Indian Affairs school was intended to be the cultural bridge between the tribal family and white society. Children were taken from their families, given haircuts, new clothes and Christian names, and made to attend boarding schools like the Carlisle School. Over the entrance of a school constructed for Indians in Fort Yukon, Alaska, was the inscription, "Speak Indian and Talk Alone/Speak English and Talk to the World."

Moqui Villages
Arizona March 1894

To the Washington Chiefs:

During the last two years strangers have looked over our lands with sky-glasses and made marks upon it, and we know but little of what this means. As we believe that you have no wish to disturb our possessions, we want to tell you something about this Hopi land.

None of us were asked that it should be measured into separate lots, and given to individuals for this would cause confusion.

The family, the dwelling house and the field are inseparable, because the woman is the heart of these, and they rest with her. Among us the family traces its kin from the mother, hence all its possessions are hers. The man builds the house but the woman is the owner, because she repairs and preserves it; the man cultivates the field, but he renders its harvests into the woman's keeping, because upon her it rests to prepare the food, and the surplus of stores for barter depends upon her thrift.

A man plants the fields of his wife, and the fields assigned to the children she bears, and informally he calls them his, although in fact they are not. Even of the field which he inherits from his mother, its harvest he may dispose of at will, but the field itself he may not.

He may permit his son to occupy it and gather its produce, but at the father's death the son may

a certain area around our lands, was proclaimed to be for our use, but the extent of this area is unknown to us, nor has any Agent, ever been able to point it out, for its boundaries have never been measured. We most earnestly desire to have one continuous boundary ring enclosing all the Tewa and all the Hopi lands, and that it shall be large enough to afford sustenance for our increasing flocks and herds. If such a scope can be confirmed to us by a paper from your hands, securing us forever against intrusion, all our people will be satisfied:

1) Há-yi of A'la. (Walpi)
2) Ho'-ni of Ica
3) Kwá-ná-ka of Pa'kab (Walpi)
4) Na-syûn-wé-ve of Ko-Kop (Walpi)
5) A-na-wi-ta (Pat-ki/Sitcomovi)
6) Intiwa of Ka-ra'-na (Walpi)
7) Tú-was-mi of Pa'Kab (Walpi)
8) Ha'-ni of Pi'-ba (Walpi)
9) Syûn-o-i-ti-wa of Ica-Kwai-na (Walpi)
10) Supela of Pat-ki (Walpi)
11) Kwá-tca-Kwa of Pá'-Ki (Walpi)
12) Tûni-ma of Ha'-ni (Sitcomovi)
13) Pa-la-Ka-Ka of Ku-lo̱n-to-wa

14) Kwá-la-Kwai of Kú-wa-tca'-n (Tewa)
15) Ka-nú of Pa'Kab-nyún (Walpi)
16)
17) Lo-ma-nak-cú of Tú-wa (Mú-coñ-ino)
    Pa-lûñ-au-úh of Ka'-la (Cipaulo)
18) Si-Kya-hon-ava of Katcina (Mú-coñ-ino)
19) Kwa-vi-o-ma of Cqú-wyo (Mú-coñ-ino)
20)
21) Ta-las-yau-ma of Pa'-túña (Mú-coñ-ino)
22) of Kwá-nú (Mú-coñ-ino)

Letter to "the Washington Chiefs" from the Moqui Villages, Arizona, protesting federal takeover of Indian lands, 1894, first and last pages.

Improvised Union field hospital at Fredericksburg, sketch by Thomas Nast for *Harper's Weekly*, December 27, 1862. Troops going into battle view the alarming conditions that await battle casualties. Beneath the table are amputated limbs. On the corner of the table is a bottle of whiskey— the only anesthetic available. Especially early in the war, many of the wounded did not survive the trip from such sites to more permanent hospitals.

When the Civil War broke out, the U.S. Army had no general hospital. Buildings, nurses, sick-diet kitchens, clothing, a readily available supply of medicines were all wanting. The War Department was ill equipped to cope with the situation because of overlapping bureau jurisdictions and an inefficient seniority system. Reportedly, there were two and one-half Union deaths from disease to each combat loss. On the Confederate side the ratio was three to one.

Determined that U.S. soldiers should profit from medical knowledge gained by the British in the Crimean War, a popular Unitarian minister and three doctors convinced Congress to establish a board of civilians to advise the Department on sanitary regulations in the camps. "A frail little man," Frederick Law Olmsted, arrived to run the United States Sanitary Commission, as the board was called. Possessing a genius for organization, Olmsted developed the commission into a large and powerful agency, which was to act as a gadfly in stinging the moribund War Department into more effective activity. Margaret Leech wrote, in her *Reveille in Washington*, that "theirs [the Commission's] were the plans for the new pavilion hospitals; theirs, the monographs which acquainted country practitioners in green sashes with hygiene and vaccination, with the treatment of dysentery and malaria and venereal diseases. They forced the necessity for camp sanitation on the Government's attention. Their barrels of potatoes and onions abated scurvy in many regiments. They equipped and staffed the hospital ships; and, later, built hospital cars, with swinging litters, kitchens and dispensaries."

One Sanitary Commission report to Congress suggested new ways to serve war veterans, including European programs like sheltered workers' villages and veterans' preference in employment. Out of this report came historic social welfare legislation that expanded the compensation of veterans from pensions and land grants to services. In 1865 Congress established a Board of Managers to provide and oversee a national military home for the relief of totally disabled veterans who could not function except in a sheltered society. Eleven total communities were created before they became part of a new Veterans Administration in 1930. Military fines and unclaimed death benefits were used for financing. Local communities competing for the favor of locations contributed land and additional money.

Frederick Law Olmsted, Sr., in the early 1860s when he resigned his position as designer and superintendent of New York's Central Park to become Executive Secretary of the Sanitary Commission.

The *Red Rover* was one of five ships reconditioned, equipped, and staffed as hospital ships by the Sanitary Commission. The design work was probably done by Frederick Law Olmsted, Sr.

Civil War wounded recuperating at a Washington, D.C., hospital, in a photo by Mathew Brady. At this kind of hospital, poet Walt Whitman helped care for the sick.

Sheet music cover, 1864. The huge Satterlee Hospital— 3,500 beds—was part of the pavilion hospital program.

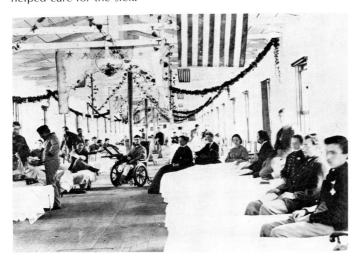

Mower U.S. General Hospital, Philadelphia, designed by John McArthur, Jr., the architect for the Quartermaster General's office in Philadelphia. The hospital covered 27 acres and had 3,600 beds in 50 wings that radiated from the central circular corridor. This "pavilion" pattern was a common response to contemporary concern with proper ventilation. (The Quartermaster General in this period was Montgomery C. Meigs, who later designed the Pension Building in Washington.)

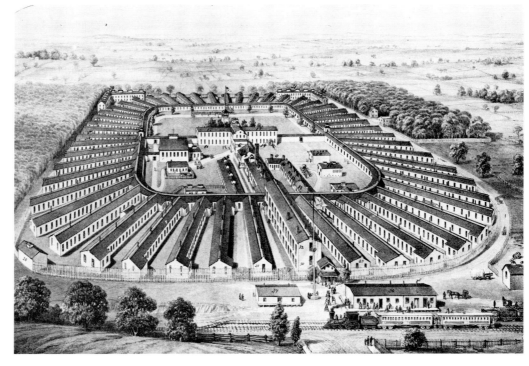

Confederate military prison at Andersonville, Georgia, notorious for its crowded, inhumane living conditions. Between March and August, 1864, the death rate rose from 300 to 3,000 per month. The 20-acre plot held nearly 32,000 Union soldiers.

National Military Home, Dayton, Ohio, 1867, the third and then the largest of eleven total communities created by Congress for the relief of totally disabled veterans. Experimental industrial shops were developed at the Dayton home by the Matron, Emma L. Miller, who was the first woman to receive a commission in the U.S. Army.

The consecration of the "Great National" military cemetery near Gettysburg on November 19, 1863, from *Frank Leslie's Illustrated Newspaper*, December 5, 1863. Eyewitness sketch by Joseph Becker. Left of the flagpole is the platform from which President Lincoln delivered the Gettysburg Address.

Entrance to the National Cemetery at Gettysburg. Photo by Mathew Brady.

East front of Capitol, with Bulfinch dome, c. 1846. Daguerreotype by John Plumbe.

Amid the strife of civil war, the continued push for completion of the Capitol dome symbolized Lincoln's determination to prevent complete dissolution of the Union. New legislative chambers, extending each wing of the Capitol building, had been completed by 1859 in accordance with Thomas U. Walter's scheme of 1851. However, construction of the dome dragged on because of piecemeal appropriations and exigencies of war. With the completion of the new dome in 1866, little remained of the original Thornton design.

The capital city itself was muddy, unfinished, and unhealthy. Soldiers died from wounds, both civilians and soldiers died from typhoid. In the summer of 1862 a smallpox epidemic hit the city, infecting even the President. Louisa May Alcott, who came to Washington as a nurse in 1862, wrote, "I was never ill before this time and never well afterwards."

At the end of four brutal years of war, the Capitol and the nation would never be the same.

Thomas U. Walter, painting in the Capitol by Francisco Pausas, 1925, after a photograph by Mathew Brady. Walter was appointed "Architect of the Capitol Extension" in 1851 based upon his successful design in a competition for enlargement of the Capitol. Montgomery C. Meigs was chief engineering consultant. A prominent Philadelphia architect and a student under William Strickland, Walter eclipsed Robert Mills and became the dominant architect in Washington until his dismissal from government service in 1865.

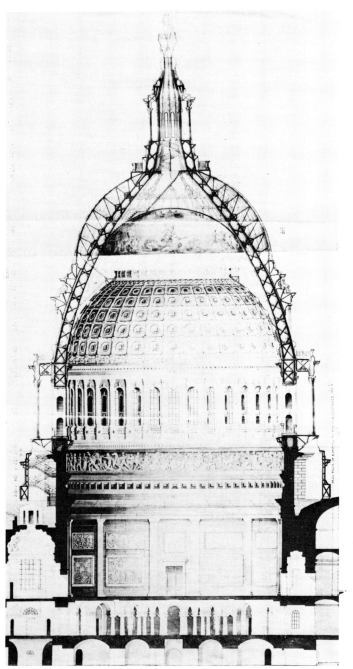

Section of the Capitol dome by Thomas U. Walter, 1859, reveals the use of iron trusses moldings, and frames. The drum of the dome was modeled after St. Peter's in Rome. The 36 Corinthian columns around the base represent the states of the Union at the time the dome was completed. The 13 columns of the lantern above the cap of the dome represent the original states.

"As a most honorable contrast to ever conflicting claims of private taste and whim to get utterance in the public works, I feel pleasure and pride in observing the course adopted by the architect [Thomas U. Walter] who has been honored with the task of adding the wings of the Capitol. That architect, trained in the severest school of ancient art, had he been called on for a new building would surely have attempted something very different from the actual Capitol. Called to enlarge it, he has sought to divest himself of every prepossession that would interfere with its harmony as a whole. He has approached his task with reverence. He has sought to keep company with his predecessor. This is not only honorable and just as regards Latrobe, but can take nothing from his own well-earned reputation."

Horatio Greenough, "Aesthetics at Washington," The Travels, Observations, and Experience of a Yankee Stonecutter, 1852

"The architecture of the exterior of the wings is designed to correspond in its principal features to that of the present building, and the disposition of the various parts is intended to present the appearance of one harmonious structure, and to impart dignity to the present building, rather than to interfere with its proportions, or detract from its grandeur and beauty."

Thomas U. Walter, Report of the Architect for the Extension of the Capitol, 1851

The new dome in an 1857 photo. During early planning of the dome the old Congressional library burned, and Walter decided to change the original wood design of dome and extensions to cast iron structures. The use of iron in the new House and Senate wings represented the most extensive American use of iron in a building erected up to that time.

"As in 1800 and 1850, so in 1860, the same rude colony was camped in the same forest, with the same unfinished Greek temples for workrooms, and sloughs for roads. The Government had an air of social instability and incompleteness that went far to support the right of secession in theory as in fact; but right or wrong, secession was likely to be easy where there was so little to secede from."

Henry Adams, The Education of Henry Adams, *1906*

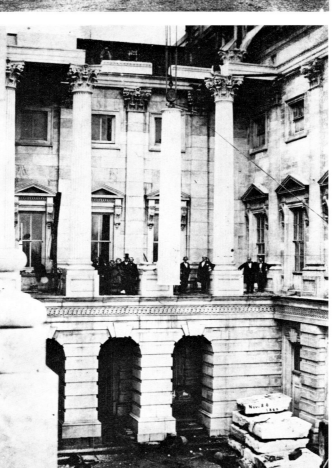

Hoisting a column for the Senate extension of the Capitol, November 26, 1860. Photo by Mathew Brady or assistant. Nearest to the suspended column is Jefferson Davis, who in three months (on February 18, 1861) would be inaugurated as President of the provisional government of the new Southern Confederacy of America at Montgomery, Alabama. At his inauguration other Corinthian columns and another dome, that of the state capitol, would serve as a backdrop. Beside Davis is Thomas U. Walter.

Inauguration of Abraham Lincoln, March 4, 1861.

"When the people see the dome rising it will be a sign that we intend the union to go on."

Abraham Lincoln

Hydrogen gas generators of the Union Army's "balloon corps" on the Mall in Washington. T. S. C. Lowe, chief of the Army Aeronautic Corps, sent observers aloft in tethered balloons to conduct "aerial reconnaissance" of Confederate encampments across the Potomac.

Lincoln ordering building of the dome to continue, 1863. Painting by Allyn Cox for House of Representatives wing of the Capitol, 1974.

Dome with Statue of Freedom and scaffolding. On December 2, 1863, a crowd assembled to watch the placing of "Freedom" on top of the lantern of the dome. At noon the 35-gun salute marked the completion of the Capitol's modern silhouette. The ceremonial fanfare was intended to provide inspiration for dispirited troops.

The Nation Continues

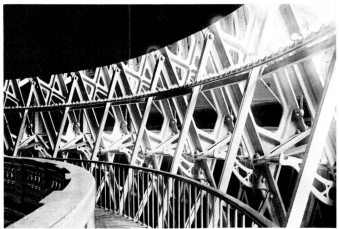

Structural work, interior of the dome of the Capitol. Under the dome the columns originally designed by Charles Bulfinch to carry his light wooden dome support the 8,909,200-pound weight of Walter's cast-iron structure.

Statue of Freedom, plaster model by Thomas Crawford in the Smithsonian. Shipped to a Washington foundry from Italy, Crawford's plaster model was cast in bronze by slave labor. The colossal figure required some changes, however. Senator Jefferson Davis of Mississippi noted that the figure wore a liberty cap of the kind worn by ancient Roman slaves who had been freed. He called this a provocation to the South. The harassed sculptor substituted a feathered eagle for the cap, and from the ground today Freedom on her high perch looks rather like an Indian with a disheveled war bonnet.

The body of Henry Wirz, commander of the infamous Confederate war prison at Andersonville, being lowered to the ground after his public hanging in 1865. Photo by Alexander Gardner.

Victory parade, Pennsylvania Avenue, 1865.

Sheet music cover, lithograph, 1865.

Constantino Brumidi, an Italian artist and refugee, was hired by Congress in 1855 to paint frescos for committee rooms of the House of Representatives. For twenty years he worked continually, drawing and painting for this commission. In between he worked on a three-year project for a fresco covering 4,664 square feet in the Capitol dome 180 feet above the floor. At a cost of $40,000, the dome fresco was the government's largest single art effort until the art programs of the 1930s.

Section of the dome frescoes by Brumidi, photographed while the paintings were still on an enormous easel. Photograph by Mathew Brady or Levin Handy.

"... The same purblind squeamishness which gazed without alarm at the lascivious Fandango awoke with a roar at the colossal nakedness of Washington's manly breast. This fact will show how easy it is to condemn what is intrinsically pure and innocent, to say the least; how difficult to repress what is clearly bad and vicious."

Horatio Greenough, "Aesthetics at Washington," The Travels, Observations, and Experience of a Yankee Stonecutter, 1852

Inside the dome, Capitol rotunda. Brumidi's frieze represents the discovery and settlement of the New World. Additions continuing the narrative were added in 1953. Brumidi, who said he wanted to live long enough "to make beautiful the one capitol on earth where there is liberty," died after a fall from scaffolding in the dome.

U.S. Capitol and Horatio Greenough's statue of Washington, ca. 1870. Originally intended to reside inside the Capitol, Greenough's statue, considered to be less than suitably clothed in its toga, was banished first to the grounds and at the turn of the century to the basement of the Smithsonian.

A rash of dome building in state capitals copied the new dome in Washington: Indiana state capitol, 1878–1888.

Illinois state capitol, 1868–1888.

THE EMBELLISHMENT OF PRIDE

4

Westward, the Monarch Capitol Makes Its Way, stereograph, John Carbutt, 1866. "The buffalo trail became the Indian trail, and this became the trader's 'trace'; the trails widened into roads, and the roads into turnpikes, and these in turn were transformed into railroads. . . . Thus civilization in America has followed the arteries made by geology, pouring an ever richer tide through them, until at last the slender paths of aboriginal intercourse have been broadened and interwoven into the complex mazes of modern commercial lines; the wilderness has been interpenetrated by lines of civilization growing ever more numerous. It is like the steady growth of a complex nervous system for the originally simple, inert continent. If one would understand why we are to-day one nation, rather than a collection of isolated states, he must study this economic and social consolidation of the country." (Frederick Jackson Turner, "The Significance of the Frontier in American History," 1893)

Construction of the Statue of
Liberty, Paris. Photo from *Album des Travaux de Con-
struction de la Statue Colos-
sale de la Liberté*, Paris, 1883,
a book of thirteen photos
taken by Reinharde Gontrand
et Cie., dedicated to Grand
Duke Vladimir of Russia.

The Civil War did not discourage what Mark Twain called "the drive and push and rush and struggle of the raging, tearing, booming nineteenth century." Together the industrial, agricultural, and transportation revolutions wreaked havoc with Jefferson's ideologically careful arrangements of American space and public architecture. A new way of life was being created.

In contrast to the forces of political disunion represented by the war, other events had the effect of welding the nation together geographically, economically, and culturally. In 1861, the year Confederates fired on Fort Sumter, the linkage of telegraph lines spanning the continent from east to west was completed with federal assistance. In 1862 federal land sales policies deferred to pioneers and speculators through the Homestead Act, which offered settlers free land from the public domain. The following year, the Morrill Act granted public lands to states for the purpose of endowing agricultural and mechanical colleges. In 1866 Congress endorsed the eight-hour day sought by the first national labor union. The 1870 census, for the first time, went beyond a simple head count to compile social and economic data. Federal patents protected inventions that increased agricultural and industrial productivity and accelerated the flow of commercial transactions. In 1865 a federal tax on state bank notes pushed financial institutions toward a uniform currency. The federal postal service grew to the largest in the world; cheap rates encouraged the world's largest circulation of newspapers in proportion to population. And in 1869 federal generosity helped complete the first transcontinental railroad.

The belief that the land was the basis of success continued to pervade both the American dream and public policy. With rapid industrial growth, however, the nation broadened its interest from the use of land for hunting and farming to the land as a source of minerals, lumber, and power—accessible through the use of new technologies. Reports of federal explorations still detailed the country's natural riches. But a new scientific precision in viewpoint, in language, and in documentation, dramatized by the use of photographs, helped Americans understand that the value of the land was not always in the eye of the beholder. In addition to huge gifts of public land, Congress also lavishly dispensed to the private sector mineral and timber resources from the public domain.

Throughout the second half of the nineteenth century federal policies were influenced more by markets than by political speeches. In the settlement of the western lands, official policy, said one Senator, was "declaratory of the custom of common law of the settlers." Far from the controls established in Washington, feverish settlement was accompanied by rampant speculation and fraud. And land abuse. Soil erosion and timber destruction were as characteristic of the westward movement as profits and boom towns and cowboys and the rhetoric of manifest destiny. Confused policies, misguided policies, lack of policies left a legacy of land ownership, land use, and land exhaustion that still plague the nation. Homesteading itself, which staked a parcel of land in a wager that the settler might stick it out for five years to gain ownership, was a short-term panacea for populating the wilderness, not a land policy. The intent to create a landowning, homeowning people had only temporary success. Within fifty years tenancy passed the fifty percent mark in many counties in which homesteads had prevailed in the 1870s.

At the core of the nineteenth century's transformations was America's romance with the machine, especially the train. "Consider how the spectacle of the machine on a virgin land must have struck the mind," wrote Leo Marx in *The Machine in the Garden*. "Like nothing ever seen under the sun, it appears when needed most: when the great west finally is open to massive settlement, when democracy is triumphant and gold is discovered in California, here—as if by design—comes a new power commensurate with the golden opportunity of all history. Is it any wonder that the prospect arouses awe and reverence?"

The 1876 Centennial celebration at Philadelphia focused the nation's bursting pride on its new technological toys and phenomenal progress. The world's largest steam engine generated the electrical power for the entire fair. A shiny, real-life train was displayed resplendent among potted palms. The machine was, indeed, in the garden, but few doubted then the happy future of technology. In contrast, the nation's anniversary a hundred years later would be marked by a nostalgia that cast aspersions on both the present and the future.

The engines of progress displayed at the Centennial were housed in buildings that gave little hint of the rapid technological strides that were being made in that period, which would eventually revolutionize both the practice and forms of architecture. This incongruity expressed a growing separation of aesthetic and technical standards. The day was past when architects could bridge all of society's building needs, and they less and less controlled even the fate of architecture. Instead the inventors of the telegraph, the elevator and the air brake, the political and industrial leaders who influenced the direction of public subsidies, were changing both the landscape and the architecture of America.

Past, too, was the consensus about classicism as the national style. The growth of historical knowledge in the nineteenth century, which had contributed first the classical and then medieval styles, opened all the periods of history to the designer's imagination. The style was styles. The mode of architecture, like that of the national temper, was possibility and change. Neither the static forms of the earlier classical revival nor those of the Modern Movement would have suited the general taste, which delighted in the accidents and variety of nature, in the metamorphoses of history, and in buildings as evolving forms expressive of freedom and discovery.

The architects of public buildings had long departed from Jefferson's appeal for modes "sufficiently chaste." The closest to an American model for the period was Henry Hobson Richardson's Allegheny County Courthouse in Pittsburgh. The towered-Romanesque style had a major influence on city halls, courthouses, and post offices.

From the drafting boards of the Supervising Architect's Office, however, flowed an amazing variety of stylistic elements: mansard roofs, towers, clusters of spires. The juxtaposition of styles was typical of the period, but the sometimes disjointed mix-and-match of federal architecture reflected a special characteristic of federal building—the long span from authorization to completion.

The growth of the federal government, which paralleled the nation's rapid industrial growth, provided the impetus for expansion of federal building. Between 1861 and 1871 the number of federal civilian employees increased from 36,672 to 51,020. By 1881 the total had doubled, and a decade later stood at 157,442. Although the number of federal employees in Washington trebled in the decade before 1871, they accounted for only 12 percent of the total. New mints, post offices, courthouses sprang up around the country, corroborating the statistical evidence that the federal business was widely dispersed.

By 1892 the total stock of the Supervising Architect's inventory had increased seventeen-fold over the 1853 stock of the Office of Construction. In 1901 *A History of Public Buildings under the Control of Treasury Department* presented the first public photographic inventory of the work of the office along with records of the often tortuous course of the public building process.

Each Supervising Architect struggled to order his growing bureaucracy and to leave the impress of his favorite style on the federal realm. Federal buildings no longer provided models for a foothold in the wilderness but rather embellished an ebullient nationalism. Despite the slings and arrows of outraged private architects, professional critics, Congress, and the courts, there is every indication that local pride was usually satisfied by the efforts of federal architects. Today's preservation efforts would seem finally to vindicate the popular sense of architectural occasion.

The postwar capital city itself, Henry Adams complained, was a "lovable" but "shabby" town. The dusty thoroughfares and primitive sewage system had barely withstood the ravages of wartime encampments, hospitals, and kindred temporary facilities. The increase in government employees made the construction of new public office space imperative. Although western growth had stimulated intermittent pressure to move the capital to a more central place, particularly to St. Louis, proponents of capital removal had failed to arouse sufficient interest. The decision by Congress in 1871 to build the State, War, and Navy Building was a clear sign that the issue was dead.

In the next two decades Washingtonians watched some marvels of monumental construction. A massive city improvement drive was carried out under a Congressionally appointed Board of Public Works. The federal domain itself included the immense, mansard-roofed State, War, and Navy building, briefly the world's largest office building. A new Library of Congress was the largest library in the world. Construction of the huge red-brick Pension Building acknowledged an expanded social welfare role for the federal government. It also marked a striking divergence from Washington's white marble ambience.

In an era of elaborate monuments as well as elaborate buildings the ultimate monument emerged simplicity itself. Robert Mills's tribute to George Washington in the capital city was finally completed in 1888. When it was finished, its wrought-iron supports formed the highest frame erected up to that time, more prophetic than most federal buildings of the use of new technology.

For the public architects and their colleagues who did business with them the entire period was marked by the kind of strife Latrobe had once called the "ruinous connection." The architects of the Library of Congress were, in fact, economically ruined by a prolonged legal struggle to get Congress to pay them. As is characteristic of public agencies that make massive expenditures, the Office of the Supervising Architect was often a center of controversy. One Supervising Architect, Alfred B. Mullett, was the subject of five investigations, a dismissal, and a court case. He committed suicide the year after he lost his case against the government. A successor was accused of graft.

Private architects insistently sought a piece of the public action. In 1892 the American Institute of Architects won passage of the Tarsney Act, which allowed, but did not require, the Treasury to acquire outside architectural services through competitions. The Treasury equivocated but eventually did select through competition some of the nation's best-known architects to design public buildings before the act was repealed in 1912.

Government subsidies for railroads directed the nature and the location of settlement and thus importantly influenced the location of new federal buildings. In one example, the first federal land grant for railroad development in 1850 had an astounding influence on a small settlement that had originally grown up around Fort Dearborn in Illinois. In 1851 the town did not have a single mile of track connecting with another city; by 1856 it was the largest railroad center in the nation and the site of extensive federal building. By the end of the century proud natives dubbed one of the city's intersections the "world's busiest street corner." "The sublimate of our entire experience," Bernard DeVoto has written, "was just this: here was a swamp and look! here is Chicago."

Some Americans, alarmed by the evidence of growth and its attendant plunder and by the portent of the recently published theories of Charles Darwin, warned of the need to plan against the exhaustion of the country's natural wealth and beauty. In 1872 Congress reserved the Yellowstone Valley as the first national park—after being assured by its House Committee on Public Lands that the area "is not susceptible of cultivation with any degree of certainty . . . the winters would be too severe for stock raising . . . and it is not probable that any mines or minerals of any value will ever be found there." In 1879 the United States Geological Survey was formed and the federal government began the first systematic cataloging of the public lands.

In his first inaugural address in 1801, Thomas Jefferson declared that America was ". . . a chosen country, with room enough for our descendants to the thousandth and thousandth generation." In 1890 the Superintendent of the Census reported that "there can hardly be said to be a frontier line." The "hither edge of free land" had receded and vanished. The federal government had owned a vast resource but had spent it to settle and develop a nation, relinquishing two-thirds of all the land of the continental United States in one of the greatest transfers of property in all history. For the government it was the easiest available subsidy to dispense in directing national growth. Expansion resulted in one huge nation, e *pluribus unum*, and one vast market—*caveat emptor*. With free land gone, growth and the spatial impact of federal policies would come to have new meanings.

The unfinished stump of Robert Mills's Washington Monument, 1854. Political turmoil and lack of funds halted construction until after the Civil War.

The grandiose architectural presence of government after the Civil War was reflected in equally grandiose expectations for public monuments. A rash of overwrought proposals appeared during the Centennial fever of the 1870s. Not surprisingly the still unfinished Washington Monument in the capital city became the likely subject for monumental imaginings. Memorializing the first president had earlier been attempted, amidst stormy debates, outside the capital city. Baltimore completed a classical column by Robert Mills in 1829. In Philadelphia and New York, Washington monuments never rose higher than a cornerstone. Of the many New York proposals, *Holden's Dollar Magazine*, of April 1848, lamented, "We have seen no design yet published which could be executed in much less than a hundred years." Finally New York unveiled a bronze equestrian statue of Washington in 1856.

In 1848 the cornerstone for Robert Mills's winning design for the Washington Monument for the nation's capital was laid in an elaborate Masonic ceremony, but construction was soon halted by lack of funds. In the 1850s the neglected stub survived the anti-Catholic ravages of the Know-Knothing American Party—activists who stole the building block donated by Pope Pius IX and dumped it into the Potomac, seized the Monument Society's offices and records, and even occupied the obelisk itself for a time. By the time of the Civil War, the truncated shaft rose only 150 feet above the Potomac marshes. And so it remained until 1876, when Congress appropriated funds for completion and put the Army Corps of Engineers in charge of the project.

Renewed interest in the monument stimulated an abundance of new proposals. But the commission to whom Congress had entrusted the monument's design settled on the simple obelisk of Mills's plan without his pantheon around its base. The monument was finished and finally opened to the public on October 9, 1888.

Broadside posted at polling places across the nation in 1860. Congress took over the project in 1876. The final cost was $1.3 million.

THE MEMORY
—OF—
GEORGE WASHINGTON.

EVERY true lover of his country will contribute something this day, in aid of the

Great National Monument
—TO—
WASHINGTON!

Have ready your donation, however small. The Contribution Box and the Ballot Box are this day side by side at every Poll in the United States.

The County in this State making the largest contribution in proportion to the number of votes cast, will be presented with an elegant three-quarter size MARBLE STATUE OF WASHINGTON, valued at $500.

CALIFORNIA, Nov. 6, 1860.

☞ Please put up this notice in the immediate vicinity of the Polls on election day, so that every voter can be ready with his contribution.

Washington National Sphinx.

Allegorical of Lofty Aspirations, Keen Foresight, Energy, Strength, Valor and Immortality.

Front Half Scale.

Proposal to replace Mills's monument, J. Goldsborough Bruff, 1873. Bruff said that he wanted four sphinxes "of collossal proportions, to be of bronze upon blocks of granite, suitably sculptured. Rendering it in true Egyptian style, I have nationalized it by the head and breast of our national bird. Such a figure is symbolic of keen, far sightedness, noble aspirations, energy, strength, courage and immortality. . . . Give to one of the sphinxes in lieu of the shield, a medallion of Washington, and to another one of Lafayette."

"Think of France with her noble and costly monuments to Napoleon; the Arc de Triomphe; the Column of Place Vendome and the Cenotaph. Think of Germany and her Valhalla, and her colossal Bavaria, etc. Florence, poor as she is, is now casing all the facade of her Duomo with splendid marbles, and everywhere erecting noble monuments to her great men. And is it possible that we can be content with a plain chimney to celebrate Washington?"

Letter to the Editor of American Architect and Building News, *January 11, 1879*

"But an obelisk . . . painfully built up out of small stones, and hollowed into a chimney up which patriots may crawl like ants, representing neither power of conception nor special skill of execution, but only dollars and days' work, seems to us altogether beneath the occasion."

American Architect and Building News, *July 5, 1876*

"I am aware that what is called
'advanced art' looks with scorn
on anything so simple and bald
as an obelisk.

". . . When I look around
and see what 'advanced art' has
done for us and done for itself
in the myriad soldiers' monuments which have been recently
erected, I fall back on the simple
shaft as at least not inferior to
any one of them in effect and as
free from anything tinsel or
tawdry."

Congressman Robert C. Win-
throp, 1878

Proposal for the Washington
Monument, Romanesque bell
tower design, John Frazar,
1879. This seven-storied
structure contained a statue of
Washington on horseback in
the niche at its base.

Proposal for the Washington
Monument, Gothic design
submitted by Mr. Hapgood,
an architectural student, 1879.
The American Architect and
Building News of March 15,
1879, described the design
thus: "Above, in the central
division of the shaft would be
bas-reliefs representing the
four sections of the country;
in the gable of one of these
panels could be placed the
arms of the Washington family. The base of the monument would be 27 feet above
the ground on a platform
around which would be
panels contributed by the 46
states and Territories, carved
with their respective arms."

"I understand . . . by embel-
lishment, THE INSTINCTIVE
EFFORT OF INFANT CIVILI-
ZATION TO DISGUISE ITS
INCOMPLETENESS EVEN
AS GOD'S COMPLETENESS
IS TO INFANT SCIENCE
DISGUISED."

Horatio Greenough, "Relative
and Independent Beauty," The
Travels, Observations, and
Experiences of a Yankee
Stonecutter, 1852

Membership certificate for the
Washington National Monu-
ment Society. Millard Fillmore
was President of the Society.
In the two ovals at the center
top of the certificate are the
proposed dimensions of the
obelisk.

"Inasmuch as the original design of the Washington Monument is unworthy of the spirit
of the architecture of an enlightened and civilized people, it
is

"Resolved by the American
Institute of Architects, assembled in Convention in Philadelphia:

"First, That the completion
of the said Monument on the
original plan, or upon the plan
now proposed for the same, is
to be deprecated.

"Second, That there be a
Committee of The American Institute of Architects to confer
with the Commission which
has been charged with the completion of the Monument, and
that the Committee be in-
structed to recommend that if it
be completed the Commission
shall, so far as in their power,
further the selection of some
different and suitable design to
which it may be made to
conform."

Proceedings, *AIA Convention,
1876*

"The present design was made
at a very undeveloped period in
our architecture, and does not
comport, unless by its bigness,
with either the dignity of its
aim, or the acquirements of
American architects, whose best
capabilities ought to be represented by it. If the best of our
architects could be got to offer
in competition designs for completing it, a wise selection from
them might give the country a
memorial of which it could rea-
sonably be proud, and one
which it might take up and finish with some enthusiasm."

American Architect and
Building News, *May 13, 1876*

Top of the stair and elevator shaft of the Washington Monument during construction. The wrought-iron columns that were the primary parts of the structure formed the highest frame erected up to that time.

Setting the capstone for the Washington Monument, December 6, 1884. President Chester Arthur and engineer Thomas Casey were present for the occasion amidst 60-mile-an-hour winds.

"Here is our public, the cultivated part of it, much occupied with every form of art, stirred, in fact, with more apparent enthusiasm for art than for anything else; the people at large blazing lately with ardor, not yet spent, to cover the land with monuments and seat up statues to all their perishable celebrities. . . ."

"The Washington Monument, and Mr. Story's Design," Atlantic Monthly, *1879*

Dedication of the Washington Monument, February 21, 1885. Photograph by Mathew Brady or assistant.

Alfred B. Mullett and Grand Edifices

Alfred B. Mullett and his wife, Pacific Pearl, in a portrait by Charles T. Bebber. Five months after his official appointment as Supervising Architect in 1866, Mullett married the daughter of a sea captain and shipowner of San Francisco. They had six children. The two eldest sons became architects and were in private practice with their father for five years before his death.

When Alfred B. Mullett was officially named Supervising Architect in 1866 he found the office ill equipped to handle the pressures of the architectural inundation that followed the Civil War. Files were few and incomplete; plans necessary for remodeling and repair were nonexistent; deeds for land were missing. Mullett completely reorganized the office, keeping in mind, as he reported to the Secretary of the Treasury in 1867, that his task was to design buildings "to the wants of the public service . . . peculiarities of locality, climate, material, and to the importance of the structure."

During his tenure as Supervising Architect Mullett designed a variety of structures in diverse but generally classical styles— from simple two-story post offices to enormous, multimillion-dollar buildings for America's fast-growing cities. He is best known for his six immense, richly decorated Second Empire edifices: customhouse/post office/courthouse combinations in Boston, Cincinnati, New York, Philadelphia, and St. Louis and the State, War, and Navy Building in Washington. Of these only the St. Louis and Washington buildings remain.

The State, War, and Navy Building, begun in 1871, was the first major federal construction undertaken in Washington after the Civil War. Its immense size characterized the dramatic growth in the federal establishment. In the preceding decade the civil service in Washington had nearly trebled in size, and the percentage of all government employees located in Washington doubled. Symbolically, this major building project ended the recurring debate about relocating the nation's capital in another city.

Stylistically, the building dramatized the government's shift away from the Greek Revival style. A new departmental building had been under consideration since 1838, when Robert Mills made the first of his three proposals. A competition in 1845 and drawings by Thomas U. Walter in 1853 again proposed a large building to replace the two George Hadfield structures that had been on the site since about

Headline from obituary for Mullett in *The Washington Post,* October 21, 1890. This and a story in the *Evening Star* are the major sources for accounts of his career. Mullet was born in Somerset County England, April 7, 1834. With his family he moved in 1845 to Ohio where he grew up and was educated. He traveled in Europe in the late 1850s. In 1863 he became an assistant to Supervising Architect Isaiah Rogers, a former partner in private practice. Although assuming the duties of Supervising Architect earlier, Mullett was officially appointed to the office on May 29, 1866, at an annual salary of $3,000. He resigned in 1874. He served on the Naval Yards Commission and, under Governor Shepherd, on the Board of Public Works for the District of Columbia.

A. B. MULLETT'S SUICIDE

The Well-known Architect Shoots Himself Through the Head.

DIED WITHIN SEVEN MINUTES

Financial Troubles and Despondency Caused by Ill Health Drove Him to the Act—He Designed the State, War, and Navy Department and Other Buildings.

1820. All of these designs were in the Greek Revival mode. Nothing came of these suggestions, and by the time the plight of the three foreign affairs departments again came into focus architectural fashions had changed as dramatically as the government's space needs. It would be fair to assume that not even the most enthusiastic prewar classicist had imagined a government building with over 900 columns.

The State, War, and Navy Building was designed in the Second Empire style that characterized Mul-

lett's major federal buildings. It took 17 years to complete. In the course of its construction the latest technological advances were incorporated, including electric lighting and the telephone, which became available after construction began but before completion. An agency whose sole purpose was to provide services for the new structure was set up in 1882. This agency eventually took on similar responsibilities for other buildings and is the ancestor of the building services function in the current

General Services Administration. In 1899 the women whose nightly chore it was to mop the nearly two miles of corridors conducted what may have been the first strike of federal employees. The incident occurred when their jobs were threatened with the introduction of mechanical scrubbers and they were set to polishing stairway balusters.

One measure of the growing importance of the Supervising Architect's role was the controversy that swirled around successive incumbents of that post.

The first, Ammi B. Young, was dismissed amid charges of extravagance and waste. Mullett himself was subjected to no less than five investigations, especially deriving from alleged graft and illegal profits made by the "Granite Ring," a politically influential group of companies that sold stone to the federal government. One scholar, Lawrence Wodehouse, concluded that Mullett "was as honest in his dealings as President Grant was in his leadership of the country, but both had unscrupulous subordinates."

Post Office and Customhouse, Alfred Mullett, St. Louis, 1873–1884. In the decade before 1870, the city's population had increased 93 percent to nearly 311,000. Yearly customs collections from heavy river traffic averaged $2 million. The times were still turbulent, and to protect the government's gold bullion Mullett designed a fortress.

Every door and window had sliding iron shutters with rifle ports. A 30-foot-deep moat with a 20-foot thick wall surrounded the building. A basement well and enormous ice boxes were provided in case of siege. Granite foundation walls are eight feet thick and exterior walls more than four feet thick. During construction 800 workmen toiled around the clock to prevent the surrounding streets from caving into the excavation pit.

Alfred B. Mullett and Grand Edifices

America at Peace and *America at War* by Daniel Chester French, detail from St. Louis federal building. Mullett's grand edifice, "an ornament to St. Louis commensurate with the dignity and importance of the city," cost $7 million instead of the estimated $4 million.

Post Office and Subtreasury, Alfred Mullett, Boston, 1868–1872. This postcard view shows the building as altered by Mullett's successor, an enthusiastic proponent of the Gothic. The structure served as a barrier against the spreading conflagration of the 1872 Boston fire, but was later demolished. In contrast, the French-empire-style city hall, by Arthur Gilman and Gridley Bryant, survived to be adapted to modern office use. Examples similar in style were James Renwick's Corcoran Gallery, the new city halls in Baltimore and Philadelphia, and the new state capitol in Albany. During his European trip Mullett may have seen the Parisian prototype—the Palais du Louvre.

Alfred B. Mullett and Grand Edifices
158–159

Courthouse and Post Office, Alfred Mullett, New York, 1869–1875. This building contained such modern facilities as loading bays and a pneumatic system that linked the building with other postal stations. But from the beginning it was attacked as an expensive eyesore. It cost $9 million and had a perimeter of one-fifth of a mile. During its demolition in 1939 some of the wrecking balls were shattered.

"Obviously, no expense was spared to give governmental dignity to federal structures. Interiors were composed of a wealth of richly textured materials. Courtrooms were usually situated on the third floor, within the height of the attic story under a tall mansard roof. The floors were carpeted in 'old gold and [were] very aesthetic.' The upholstery was leather, and fireplaces for ventilation were of rich marbles. Oak, black walnut, cherry, mahogany, and butternut were used in the millwork. Post office boxes were usually of brass. . . .

"Floors in the post office circulation areas were of marble and slate diagonal tiling, or black and white marble blocks. In office areas, black and white walnut strip floors were sometimes used."

Lawrence Wodehouse, *"Alfred B. Mullet and His French Style Government Buildings."* Journal of the Society of Architectural Historians, *March 1972*

Courthouse and Post Office, New York, 1930s photo by Berenice Abbott, WPA. A nineteenth-century critic feared that Mullett's well-built and massive buildings would endure as evidence for future generations to judge the profession and that earlier buildings such as Faneuil Hall and Old South Meetinghouse, being of poorer construction, would not last. Ironically, the smaller structures endured, and only two of Mullett's Second Empire grand edifices, in St. Louis and Washington, D.C., still stand. Until recently they, too, were threatened with demolition.

Alfred B. Mullett and Grand Edifices

State, War, and Navy Building, Alfred Mullett, Washington, D.C., photo c. 1890. At the time of its completion it was the largest office building in the world, containing 10 acres of floor space and 553 rooms. Although construction work began two days after the design was approved in 1871, the building was not completed until 1888.

Eventually the three departments outgrew even this spacious structure and moved on to other quarters. In 1949 the building became the Executive Office Building for agencies directly attached to the Office of the President. And the business of defense was conducted from the world's largest contemporary office building—the six-million-square-foot Pentagon.

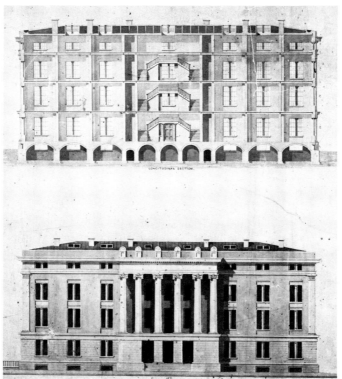

Competition for the State, War and Navy Building. One of William Strickland's drawings, 1845. Another classical design was proposed by Thomas U. Walter in 1870.

State, War, and Navy Building, one of eight spiraling cantilevered stairways.

Richard von Ezdorf, German-trained designer employed by the government for more than 47 years, was responsible for the rich baroque interiors and exterior details of Mullett's building.

State, War, and Navy Building, detail. Ezdorf designed this cast iron sculpture on the pediment at the top of the north wing's center pavilion.

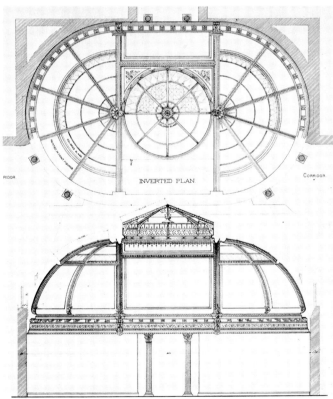

INVERTED PLAN

CORRIDOR

State, War, and Navy Building, detail. Ezdorf's structural designing skills are indicated in his drawing for the skylight and dome for the west wing stairway.

State, War, and Navy Building, bowspirit design for Navy Library. Though now called "cupids" these 800-pound sculptured lighting fixtures were adapted by Ezdorf from the figurehead of an old sailing ship.

The blank shield on the lower part of Ezdorf's gaslight chandelier was embossed according to the identity of the service branch using the room.

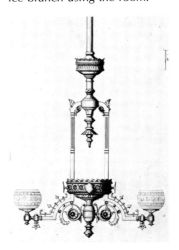

Each morning, the "time ball" on a galvanized iron flag pole atop the building was cranked up the pole and, at the signal from the Naval Observatory, was lowered down the pole—thus informing Washingtonians that it was noon. With the advent of radio and electric clocks the old landmark was eliminated.

The wreath-encircled anchor graced every doorknob in the Navy Department. Ezdorf designed doorknobs for State and War as well.

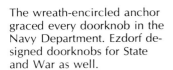

Paid Civilian Employment of the United States Government, 1861–1911

	Number of Employees
1816	4,847
1821	6,914
1831	11,491
1841	18,038
1851	26,274
1861	36,672
1871	51,020
1881	100,020
1891	157,442
1901	239,476
1911	395,905

Towns everywhere clamored for federally funded buildings as an indication of stature. And Congressmen obligingly served them up. For example, Memphis received a courthouse even though no federal courts were held there.

In the 1850s Capt. Alexander J. Bowman, Engineer-in-charge of the Treasury's Office of Construction, made indignant charts showing unneeded projects. He recommended finding some system "by which a more equal distribution may be made among the several states, and a just discrimination between the cities and towns for each state, based upon the actual need of such buildings."

Bowman's recommendations were ignored. His plea became a recurring, plaintive refrain of administrators, since new federal buildings catered not only to local pride but also to a real need to accommodate a larger civil service (see table). To some degree criticism of the Supervising Architect's Office and Congressional unwillingness to change it were the result of the office's role in the balancing act between the "need" for federal presence and the distribution of federal presents. In 1926 Congress finally genuflected in the direction of the executive by authorizing the practice of surveying "needs" prior to Congressional appropriation.

To order the phenomenal growth in America's communications needs, John Wanamaker, as Postmaster General from 1889 to 1893, introduced business practices of his famous store to the Post Office. As part of this effort he sponsored the first national inspection survey, achieved at very little cost to the government. Fully 2,200 postmasters volunteered their own time and expense to turn in responses to queries about distances of post offices from telegraph offices and savings banks, upkeep, and use of post offices for lounging. The reports, on over 45,000 post offices from urban edifices to lonely rural barns, were also accompanied by photographs and testimonial letters. Some reports were decorated with original, if homey, designs.

Whatever the process in Washington, new federal buildings were consistently well received in America's Peorias. And the design monotony that so affronted the critics' sensibilities had no reality to the residents of scattered towns where new post offices and courthouses were being planted. Indeed, to people in towns such as Dubuque, Iowa, and Astoria, Oregon, federal buildings represented the latest in architectural style and technology and, symbolically, membership in the Union.

Laying the cornerstone for the Chicago Courthouse and Post Office, June 24, 1874. This ill-fated building was caught in a changeover of architects and contradictory investigations into the soundness of construction materials and was not completed until 1880. It opened in 1880; sixteen years later it was demolished.

According to the *American Architect and Building News*, its beginning was hailed by local citizens: "... The cornerstone was laid with Masonic ceremonies; the day set apart for the formality was a public holiday in the city; and from that time forward the building attracted a great share of the attention of the people of Chicago, most of whom had previously been indifferent to what was being done on the Government Square...."

"*[The Post Office] is a source of boundless patronage to the executive, jobbing to Members of Congress and their friends and boundless abyss of public money.*"

Thomas Jefferson, letter to James Madison, 1796

"*... The building is beautiful and imposing, and the location is favorable and judicious but it is entirely too large for any wants, present or prospective of the city. The area for the Customs House and Post Office purposes, is four times as large as is necessary and involves additional useless expenses in lighting and heating besides its original extra cost. The size of the building and the materials were prescribed by Congress.*"

Letter from S. M. Clark, Acting Engineer in Charge of the Treasury Department, to the Secretary of the Treasury, regarding the Customhouse and Post Office in Portsmouth, New Hampshire, July 6, 1860

"*... The handsomest and best building in the Northern part of the state, and one very worthy of our young and growing city.*"

St. Lawrence Republican, *regarding the Customhouse and Post Office at Ogdensburg, New York, October 4, 1867*

"*... One of the handsomest buildings in this or any other country.*"

Springfield Republican, *regarding Customhouse at St. Paul, Minnesota, August 14, 1869*

Post Office, David G. Blythe, c. 1863. For many, the federal presence was symbolized by the post office, often housed in local make-do structures. By 1873 there were over 33,000 post offices in the U.S. Parcel post, railway mail cars and free mail delivery were the best received programs of the Lincoln administration for cities of more than 50,000.

Construction of the Detroit Courthouse and Post Office, circa 1891. The construction of a major federal building was a boost to local pride. It also boosted local business and employment. To encourage federal location some towns donated central sites to the government.

". . . A magnificent contribution to the architectural attractions of the city, and may justly be a source of pride to its inhabitants."

Illustrated Cincinnati, *regarding the Cincinnati Customhouse and Post Office, 1875*

"[Officials'] rooms are fitted up with a solid magnificence that is assurance of the liberality of the government and the Superintendent of Buildings."

New York Times, *regarding D.C. Post Office, January 21, 1900*

"It [the Post Office] is to the body politic what the veins and arteries are to the natural—carrying, conveying rapidly and regularly to the remotest parts of the system correct information of the operations of the Government, and bringing back to it the wishes and the feelings of the people."

Andrew Jackson, Message to Congress, 1829

Post Office and Customhouse, Alfred B. Mullett, Cairo, Illinois, 1872, postcard view, dated September 22, 1907. In 1872, the *Cairo Daily Bulletin* reported with pride the visit of the Supervising Architect to the newly opened courtroom on the top floor: "[It] is said to be the neatest courtroom in the U.S., such being the deliberately expressed opinion of Architect Mullett on his visit of inspection to the custom house when he surveyed with much satisfaction the entire building."

Design for a "U.S. P.O. Etc." from the 1888 annual report of the Supervising Architect. A parade of ethnic stereotypes in the foreground marvel at the splendor of the federal presence.

POST OFFICE AND CUSTOM HOUSE, CAIRO, ILL.

Design for a Courthouse and Post Office, Frankfort, Kentucky, 1884. The *Kentucky Yeoman* of February 5, 1884, reported that the Queen Anne style building was executed in stone after citizens objected to the use of brick and that "no pains will be spared to make it worthy of the State in which it is."

"The Federal Government, with liberality and wisdom, has determined upon the location in our midst of a building whose spacious dimensions will afford ample and appropriate accommodations for its officials, and whose architectural beauty [will] prove a handsome ornament to the city. We fully appreciate and are duly grateful that this evidence of national prosperity has been placed within our limits. To the able Senator and talented Representative through whose efforts and influence it was obtained . . . our most sincere thanks."

John L. Sneed, Acting Mayor, Frankfort, Kentucky, at cornerstone ceremonies for U.S. Courthouse and Post Office, February 4, 1884; quoted in **Kentucky Yeoman**, *February 5, 1884*

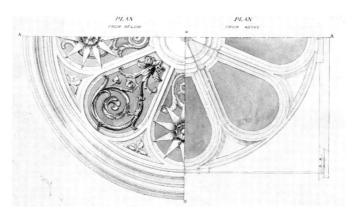

Interior, mint building, Alfred B. Mullett, San Francisco, as restored in the 1970s. The interiors of major federal buildings were remarkably consistent in their lavish display of materials. The extravagant use of detail and space so admired today were partly the result of Congressional pressures, which were seldom related to aesthetics.

Working drawing, details of ventilators, Courthouse and Post Office, Alfred B. Mullett, Springfield, Illinois, 1869.

PLAN FROM BELOW PLAN FROM ABOVE

"The first story is assigned entirely to the post-office. . . . These corridors and halls are wainscoted with marble, and have ornamented ceilings, enriched with gold and bronze, the floors throughout being of marble and terrazzo. . . . With the exception of the corridors, etc., the entire first floor is finished in quartered white oak with floors in hard wood. The marble wainscoting and floors are continued throughout the upper stories. The second story is devoted to the uses of the customs and internal-revenue services while the third floor is assigned to the circuit and district courts. . . . These rooms are in oak enriched by carving. On the fourth floor is the circuit court of appeals, the room for which is finished in marble and has a barrel vaulted ceiling with stained-glass panels admitting light from above. On this floor also is a law library finished in mahogany, with adorned ceiling which, like that in the court room, is partly of stained glass. . . ."

Description of the Courthouse and Customhouse, St. Paul, Minnesota, from the Treasury's History of Public Buildings, *1901*

". . . Probably one of the best buildings in the western country."

Daily State Journal, *Springfield, Illinois, regarding new Courthouse and Post Office, September 15, 1869*

Popular acclaim for federal towers took a favorite nineteenth century form—the picture postcard. The average gestation time for these buildings—from authorization to occupancy—was ten years.

Post Office and Courthouse, Detroit, Michigan, 1882–1897.

Courthouse and Post Office, Pittsburgh, Pennsylvania, 1881–1891, characterized in a government report as "modified Renaissance."

Post Office and Government Building, Jacksonville, Florida, 1886–1895.

Courthouse and Post Office, Dallas, Texas, 1882–1894.

Post Office, Buffalo, New York, 1896.

Courthouse and Post Office, Texarkana, located on line between Arkansas and Texas, 1888–1892.

Post Office and Courthouse, Baltimore, Maryland, 1882–1901.

Washington Inspecting the First Coins, engraving after an oil painting by John Dunsmore, 1914.

Another kind of federal presence followed the path of the unending American quest of gold.

Congress in 1792 declared it illegal for state or private mints to coin money, and established the first U.S. mint at Philadelphia, then the capital city. The first building erected for public use under the new constitutional government, the mint produced its first coins primarily by melting down foreign specie. In 1829 this structure was replaced by a larger one designed by William Strickland. However, nearly all of the gold minted there had to be shipped from mines in the South—a long, costly, and risky process.

Much of the ore and money ended up in the hands of highway robbers, and southern states awaiting return shipments from the mint often found themselves short of currency. In 1835 Congress finally agreed to establish branch mints at Charlotte, North Carolina; Dahlonga, Georgia; and New Orleans.

Fourteen years later the California gold rush was on, but those who struck it rich still found themselves "poor in money" and demanded closer mint facilities. While Congress dragged its feet, private mints sprang up, and business was transacted by barter and with a hodgepodge of English shillings, French louis d'ors, Dutch guilders, Indian rupees, and Mexican reals. After much prodding, Congress in 1852 authorized establishment of a branch mint at San Francisco. The mint was twice relocated in more efficient structures, the last of which still serves its original function.

In 1862 the government purchased for a branch in Denver a private mint that had been turning out "Pike's Peak" coins. Because of Indian raids, the Denver branch was restricted to assay activities for many years and was finally replaced by a mint that today conducts the bulk of U.S. minting activities. Carson City, Nevada, was given a branch mint in 1863—largely because of lobbying efforts of an aggressive city father and because ore sent to the San Francisco mint often wound up overseas at the expense of the U.S. Treasury. Philadelphia got its third mint building in 1901. The newest U.S. mint structure replaced this building in 1968.

A separate Bureau of Engraving was established at Washington in 1877 to print paper currency, a function up to that time performed—in several colors—by private bank note companies. Bills were not standardized until 1929, when a portrait series was inaugurated, including such little-seen faces as those of James Madison ($5,000 bill), Salmon P. Chase ($10,000 bill), and Woodrow Wilson, who adorned a $100,000 gold note.

Branch mint, Robert Mills, New Orleans, 1838. The federal government suspended coinage operations here from 1861 to 1878, but in 1861 Confederate governments used U.S. dies to mint $1,356,136.50. On June 7, 1862, after the Union recaptured the city, William B. Mumford was hanged from a beam adjusted between the two center columns of the front porch for taking down the Union flag over the building.

Returned Californians Waiting at the Mint, in *Gleason's Pictorial Drawing Room Companion,* July 19, 1851, which reported: "The morning after the arrival of the last Chagres steamer, some six or seven returned Californians were seen on the steps of the U.S. Mint, Philadelphia, at a very early hour, waiting for the Mint to open. Each one had his bag of gold dust and all seemed most impatiently awaiting the time when the doors should be thrown open. One or two seemed to be asleep, others are lying upon the steps—forming a characteristic scene that tells its own story. Our artist seized upon the occurrence as one of novel interest, and sketched it on the spot. It is by Devereaux."

Branch mint, Alfred B. Mullett, San Francisco, 1874, in the wake of the 1906 earthquake and fire. This was the second mint building in San Francisco. A private water supply system, installed only three weeks before the disaster, helped soldiers quench a seven-hour fire in the building, which served as the city bank in the ensuing days. Minting was transferred to another site in 1937. The building deteriorated until 1972, when it was restored to its 1874 appearance.

Abraham Curry, founder of Carson City, Nevada, and Territorial Prison Warden. He lobbied successfully for a mint in his town, then supervised its construction and became its first superintendent.

Branch mint, Alfred B. Mullett, Carson City, Nevada, 1870, now the Nevada State Museum. Mullett's first design for the federal government was done in a style associated with college architecture of the time. An 1881 observer described the style as "Pict." Stone for the walls came from the quarries of the Nevada State Prison. According to the building's historian, Howard Hickson, "It was a good mint, but died, smothered by a dark cloak of politics, the Thirty Years War on Silver, and recurring bullion shortages."

"*The unit and uniformity of the currency, together with its stability which have thus been secured, make this banking reform of perhaps equal value with the abolition of slavery, produced also by the war. A national bill now circulates, without question, and at par, from Maine to Oregon, and the industry of the country is no longer subject to the annoyance and loss which were formerly the inevitable accompaniments of the insecure, unstable and irresponsible currency furnished by the banks of ten years ago. Such a reform as this is one of the most influential in producing the unity of our national life. . . .*"

Salmon P. Chase, Secretary of the Treasury, 1872

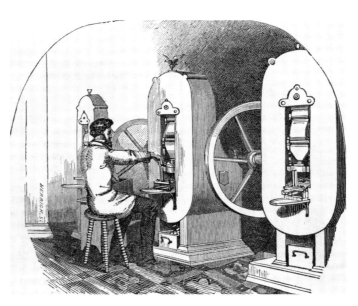

Carson City Mint, coin presses.

Assay Office, Sitka, Alaska Territory, 1840. *A History of Public Buildings,* published by the U.S. government in 1901, recorded: "This old log building was constructed by the Russians about 1840 and is located on Lincoln street. It is one-story, 52 by 30 feet, and was originally used as a public bath. From 1867 to 1871 it was used as a laundry by the American soldiers stationed at Sitka; then for a short time as a public native school by Rev. Sheldon Jackson, and now is occupied as an assay office."

"The chief tavern in the town was the building believed to afford the best security, and an apartment adjoining the barroom was made a depository of the treasure of the United States. Immediate access from the bar-room to the depository was shut off by closing the door of communication, and, as further security, the partition-wall was lined with boards; but as the glass lights in the communicating door were left uncovered, in order that the keeper of the public treasure might, when in the bar-room, see into his own apartment, a determined burglar, could, in a few minutes, have forced his way in.

"The entrance into the depository was through a back passage under a stairway. Every person who attempted to enter had to stoop till he was almost double, and then he found his further progress obstructed by a grated door, fastened by an iron chain in such a way that it could not be opened except by main force, or with the consent of the subtreasurer. . . . [There was] an iron safe, in which the depositary kept his gold and so much silver as he could. . . . Around this apartment ran a low gallery, constructed by the depositary expressly that, in case of attack, he might, if in danger of being overpowered below, retire above, and shower down upon his assailants stones, bottles and other missiles of this kind, of which he had provided an abundant store. He slept in this room, and guns, pistols, and pikes completed his assortment of weapons, offensive and defensive."

U.S. Treasury Department, Report of the Secretary of the Treasury on the State of the Finances for the Year Ending June 30, 1854

Columbia reveals the fruits of her progress to an admiring world in this page from a commemorative journal of the fair. In the distance is the main exhibition building.

Certificate of capital stock, issued by the Centennial Board of Finance.

"What better method of celebrating our Country's birth to freedom than a grand exhibition which shall contain the BEST THAT WE CAN DO?" So wrote the chairman of the Centennial Exposition of 1876. A series of spectacular international fairs encouraged backers of the Centennial to look upon it as a dramatic way for the still developing nation to impress the international community.

After years of pressure, Congress in 1871 set up a Centennial Commission to organize the exposition, which was to be held on 450 acres of Fairmount Park, in Philadelphia. The United States was not to be held responsible for any debts incurred by the exposition, and a separate Centennial Board of Finance was authorized to issue capital stock intended for purchase by the various states. Thirty-eight nations agreed to participate.

The year began with an elaborate New Year's Eve celebration. Carpenters' Hall was lit up with gas jets spelling *The Nation's Birthplace*. Fireworks illuminated the sky with portrayals of the founding fathers. But enthusiasm for the nation's birthday party outran the dollars before opening day; stock for the exposition was undersubscribed. Reluctantly Congress came up with last-minute aid to complete construction so the exhibition could open on schedule.

On May 10 the crowds surged through 106 gates to watch the opening ceremonies, to hear the speeches, to listen to "The Centennial Inauguration March," commissioned from Richard Wagner. By closing day, November 10, the total attendance at the Centennial was a record-breaking 9,910,966. Organizers of future fairs would be influenced by the festive plan of large and small pavilions in a park, by the efficient transportation service, and the faultless management. But the nation's bursting pride was not focused on the plan or on the picturesque architecture. It was focused on its new technological toys and phenomenal progress. The exhibition's promoters and 31,000 exhibitors strained to impress the international community with the newest, the biggest, and the best the nation's industry and technology had to offer.

The fair abounded in faith in the future. The nation's anniversary celebration a hundred years later would seem a curious contrast with its insistent emphasis on the past, its melancholy silence on the future.

Centennial Exposition, United States Government Building. The building covered 4½ acres and was divided among the Departments of War, Navy, Treasury, and Interior and the Smithsonian Institution.

"In a more distant retrospect it [the Centennial] becomes an event in its own right. With great clarity and sureness it manifested the spirit which in the decades to come was to remake the national environment. Here in Fairmount Park, within topographically defined limits, was a characteristically American organization of space: the interaction between landscape and architecture, the areas with specialized functions, the emphasis on the linear process; here also was displayed the principle of regulated flow—of energy, of materials, of people. The whole world could see and wonder at the qualities of Americans: their indifference to history, their delight in organizing space and time and labor, their eagerness to acquire new ideas, their abundant creativity. It is from this event, all but forgotten by most of us, that we can well date the birth of a new relationship between the American people and their landscape."

J. B. Jackson, American Space: The Centennial Years, 1865–1876, 1972

"When the Centennial Exhibition was projected, many Congressmen declared that we had nothing to show to the foreign nations. They were probably thinking of Raphaels and Praxiteles. Perhaps we had not such as these, but we had a nation to show."

General Joseph R. Hawley, President of the Centennial Commission

United States Government Building, interior. Exhibits were designed to "illustrate the functions and administrative faculties of the Government in time of peace, and its resources as a war power." Collections of the Smithsonian occupied more than 40 percent of the space. The remainder was occupied by the Patent Office, the War Department, the Navy Department, and the Treasury Department. Here, too, was displayed the pride of the Supervising Architect's Office, photos and drawings representative of a range of sizes and styles in federal facilities.

Historical Monument of the American Republic, oil, 9 feet by 13 feet, Erastus Salisbury Field, 1876, probably started in response to the competition for a central building at the Centennial Exposition. Imperial columned towers, connected by steel suspension bridges, bear symbolic inscriptions, busts, statues, and reliefs from episodes of American history.

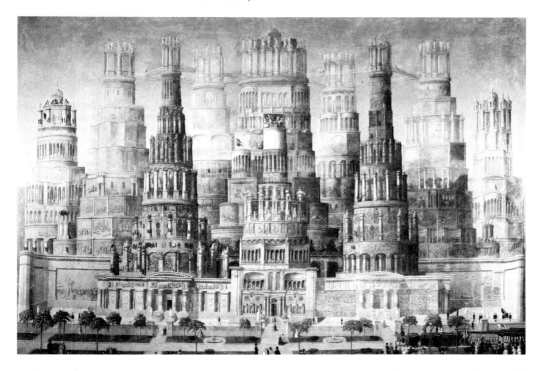

Centennial Exposition, Women's Pavilion, which was erected "to show what has been effected in the past by the brains and hands of women and to prove there are higher aims and nobler ends than can be obtained by devotion to the needle." Among the exhibitors at the Centennial were more than 75 women who had or would obtain patents. The attention to women's achievements was a tribute to the growing strength of the suffragette movement.

Centennial Exposition, arm of the Statue of Liberty on display.

Visitors marveled at the giant Corliss engine, the biggest steam engine in the world at the time. From its place of honor in the 14-acre array of mechanical exhibits in Machinery Hall, it generated the electrical power for the entire fair.

Centennial Exposition, Indian exhibit, produced jointly by the Smithsonian and the Department of Interior. Before the fair opened explorers had been dispatched to collect artifacts. Among the collection were painted canoes and carved totem poles from Alaska. At the last moment Congress balked at appropriating money to finance the scheme of bringing some Indians to the Centennial. If they came it was as tourists.

United States National Museum, Adolph Cluss, Washington, D.C., 1880, built to receive the overflow of exhibits from the Centennial. Finished in a record-breaking 15 months, the building incorporated new advances in American technology. It was also the least expensive permanent government building to date. Its four-square exterior symmetry allowed all the elements to be duplicated at least four times. The maze of roof shapes and angles elicited one description of its style as ''bastard Swiss bellringer.''

For the Bicentennial, the building, now called the Arts and Industries Building, was restored to its original vigorous Victorian interior as a setting for a partly reassembled and partly recreated Centennial exhibit.

United States National Museum, one of the main halls. The public got its first view of the interior of the new building at the inaugural ball of President James A. Garfield on March 4, 1881, shown here. The festive occasion was attended by 5,000 people. According to the next day's *Washington Evening Star,* the building resembled ''a crystal palace. The contrast between the whiteness of the electric lights in the rotunda and dome and the yellowness of the thousands of gas burners elsewhere produced a very fine effect as seen through the many windows. None of the numerous scenic effects of the day or evening surpassed this.''

Brick walls and piers were faced with plaster applied to resemble stone and decorated with stenciled patterns in red, yellow, blue, and green. Later, the wood floors were replaced with colorful geometric-patterned encaustic tile and black and white marble squares. The building's exterior was made equally colorful by the use of red, buff, and blue bricks.

Flood on Pennsylvania Avenue, 1889, caused by an inadequate storm sewer system.

During the Civil War years Washington experienced its first wartime inundation and its population more than tripled. By the time Lee surrendered to Grant, the remains of hospitals and encampments and the results of hard use had obscured even the city's magnificent intentions. Dusty thoroughfares became bogs of mud after every rain. The primitive sewage system was a menace to health and an affront to sensitivities.

The continued growth of the federal government, reflecting the nationalistic concerns of the postwar era, formed the economic basis for a much needed physical transformation of the city in the remainder of the century. In the 1860s the number of local

federal civilian employees tripled in an increase that had taken three decades in the antebellum era. The District share of all federal employees doubled during the decade and then continued to increase through the end of the century. By 1901 federal employment in the District was nearly 13 times what it had been in 1861. Little wonder that the "happy village" of 1868 had disappeared when Henry Adams returned in 1892.

In 1871 Congress created a Board of Public Works under a new territorial form of government. Alexander Robey Shepherd, a speculator and developer, gained control of the

Board. "Openly, courageously, and with dictatorship abandon," he embarked on a vast municipal improvement program. Not everyone was pleased with the results. Zina May Pierce wrote in the *Atlantic Monthly* in 1873, "DEVASTATION, indeed, is the only word than can express much of the work of the present regime. . . ." The villain, she said, was masculine lack of sensibility, and "one may judge here how much the palaces and public places of Europe probably owe to the taste and aspiration of the royal ladies who inhabit and delight in them; since men are alone responsible for everything in this draggletail metropolis."

By 1880 new suburban areas were being developed. In 1878 it was reported that 119 "electric speaking telephones" had been installed in government offices. The first electric light appeared in 1881; the first electric streetcar in 1888. In 1895 the comparatively tranquil local scene was briefly disrupted by "Coxey's Army" of 300 unemployed workers who marched from Ohio to Washington to "petition the Government for a redress of grievances."

By 1900 the Washington of John Randolph—who had declared that "a Washington pedestrian should provide himself with an overcoat, a duster, a pair of rubber shoes and a fan"—had given way to a large, albeit sleepy, modern city.

Alexander Shepherd, head of
the District of Columbia
Board of Public Works, 1871–
1874, and Governor of the
Territory, 1873–1874. "With
czarlike zeal, he tore up the
tracks of the railroad which
crossed Pennsylvania Avenue
at the foot of Capitol Hill. . . .

"Before the dew was off the
grass in the morning, he supervised the tearing down of
the old Northern Liberties
Market House. . . .

"One Saturday night, he
nearly buried the depot of the
Baltimore and Ohio Railroad
. . . by building up the street
preparatory to grading and
surfacing it." (George Roth-
well Brown, *Washington: A
Not Too Serious History*,
1930).

Inauguration of President
Cleveland, March 4, 1885.
Here, crowds on the grounds
south of the White House
view display of fireworks.
*Frank Leslie's Illustrated
Newspaper* of March 14,
1885, described "the Mam-
moth set-piece, representing
the national capitol, with portraits and other emblems, furnished by the Unexcelled Fire
works Co., of New York."

State dinner at the White
House. Mark Twain and
Charles Dudley Warner have
a character in *The Gilded Age*
describe a meal there with
some disdain: "the President's
table is well enough—for a
man on a salary—but I am
surprised about the wines. I
should think they were manu-
factured in the New York
Customs House." There was
more than glitter and graft in
Washington of "the gilded
age." There were shantytowns
and disease and death. There
were also good music, theater, and lectures.

Snapshot from one of the earliest hand-held cameras.

"The established grades of the streets were changed, some filled up and others cut down, often leaving houses perched up on banks twenty feet above the street, while others were covered nearly to their roofs. Not unfrequently, buildings had their foundations so injured that they were in danger of falling, and then the owners were notified that they must render them safe within 30 days, or they would be pulled down at their expense! . . .

"It was a daily occurrence for citizens to leave their houses as usual in the morning, and when they returned at evening to find the sidewalks and curbs, which not unfrequently had but recently [been] laid anew, at their own expense, all torn up and carted away! They would be charged for new, while this same material would often be put down opposite another's property, and he be made to pay for it at the price of new. They tore down the old market by force, and they tore up the tracks of both steam and street railways by force! It is safe to say that no American city ever witnessed such high-handed proceedings as were carried on in the National Capital during the reign of the Board of Public Works."

E. E. Barton, Historical and Commercial Sketches of Washington and Environs, 1884

National Cemetery, Arlington, 1870. This lithograph notes: "White Graves 9666, Colored Graves 1120, In Vault 2111, Exhumed Graves 262. Total Graves 16159."

Dead letter office, General Post Office, Washington, D.C., 1880.

"But the marvel of marvels is, why, when the Capitol Extension was planned twenty-five years ago, and men had seen plainly where, contrary to the original expectation, the city had built itself, that occasion was not seized for making the grand facade on the west instead of on the east front, and of placing the statue of the dome facing in the same direction; for now the Goddess of Liberty looks as if, shrugging her shoulders at the hap-hazard city behind her,—nay, at the 'great sloven continent' itself,—she were gazing regretfully toward the ocean across which she had floated hither, and were vainly wishing herself safe back in the 'tight little island' of respectabilities and proprieties that gave her birth. . . .

"The grand facade of the Capitol, especially since the Presidential inaugurations take place from its central porch, ought to be on the west; and until that is accomplished, every other interest of the building should be put aside, excepting only such as relate to the convenience of the Congress itself. More room is even now imperatively demanded, but there is no reason why it should not be gained as well on the west as on the east, while every argument of beauty and fitness—since our whole continent lies to the westward, as well as the city itself—is in favor of spending our millions on the former."

Zina May Pierce, Atlantic Monthly, 1873

"Washington is a beautiful city in proportion as you see less of it."

Henry Adams

Pennsylvania Avenue with electric streetcars, c. 1895.

"In ten years from the time the Board of Public Works began its improvements, the city was transformed. The streets were covered with an almost noiseless, smooth pavement. Fifty thousand shade-trees had been planted; the old rows of wooden, barrack-like houses had given place to dwellings of graceful, ornate architecture; blocks of fine business buildings lined Pennsylvania Avenue and the other prominent thoroughfares; blossoming gardens and luxuriant parks were to be seen on all sides; the squares and circles were adorned with the statues of heroes, and bordered with costly and palatial mansions; splendid school-houses, churches, market buildings, newspaper offices had been erected. The water-works and sewer system were unequalled in the country. Washington had risen fresh and beautiful, like the Uranian Venus, from stagnation and decay."

Joseph West Moore, Picturesque Washington: Pen and Pencil Sketches, 1883

The bureaucracy required to administer the pension programs for U.S. war veterans found a home in a grand, red-brick structure designed by General Montgomery Meigs and built in Washington between 1882 and 1885. Because it did not conform to Washington's norm of white classical buildings, the Pension Building, with its fifteen million bricks arranged vaguely in the form of an Italian Renaissance palace, was not universally acclaimed. General Sherman was reported to have complained, "It's too bad the damn thing is fireproof." One observer, commenting on the size of the central court, reportedly said ". . . nothing short of an inaugural ball or a thunderstorm could possibly fill the immense void." Undaunted, twentieth-century administrators filled the grand space with desks and fluorescent lights.

U.S. Army Engineer General Montgomery C. Meigs. Called to Washington in 1852 to design and oversee construction of public works projects and buildings, then-Captain Montgomery Meigs was to develop strong grievances against unscrupulous contractors who cheated laborers and government alike. By 1856 the contractors had successfully pressured Congress into prohibiting army officers from supervising any form of construction other than military, and an amendment passed specifically barring Meigs from the Washington Aqueduct Project. Meigs was banished to Fort Jefferson in Tortugas, Florida. He was reinstated under Lincoln and subsequently rose to the rank of Quartermaster General. Besides the Pension Building, Meigs played a role in the construction of the Capitol dome, the Smithsonian Arts and Industries Building, and the Washington aqueduct system.

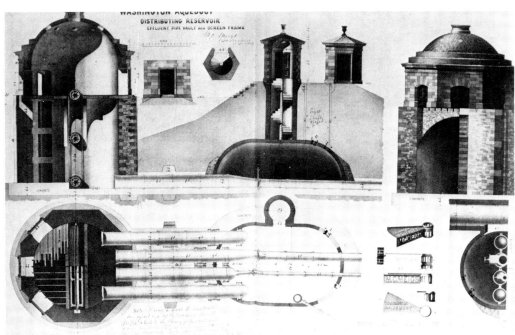

Washington Aqueduct, watercolor by Montgomery Meigs, 1857.

Pension Building, Montgomery Meigs, Washington, D.C., 1885. The materials used in the building and its technical design attributes reflect Meigs's engineering background and an innovative approach. In an effort to reduce summer heat in the building, Meigs introduced double-glazed windows with separated panes. He also achieved an unusually high ratio of office space, nearly 80 percent, by eliminating corridors and using galleries around the courtyard instead. The General Accounting Office took over the building in 1926. Today it houses the Superior Court of the District of Columbia. It is being considered for the home of a proposed Smithsonian addition, the National Museum of the Building Arts.

Pension Building under construction, 1883. Within the courtyard of the building these huge columns rose 75 feet to the roof. They were each constructed of 55,000 bricks but were painted to resemble Siena marble. The courtyard was covered by a clerestory with vertically placed glass to light the courtyard without letting in as much heat as horizontal or sloping glass.

Section of a terra-cotta frieze, a three-foot-tall band which extends 1,200 feet around the exterior between the first and second floors. Meigs said that the frieze, done by the Bohemian-born sculptor Casper Buberl, "alludes to the origins of the Bureau for whose use the building is intended." The frieze depicts various aspects of the Union Army experience.

Commissioner's office in the Pension Building, as shown on a nineteenth-century stereopticon slide.

Center court, Pension Building, in a photo taken at President William Howard Taft's inaugural ball, 1909, to which 18,000 people thronged. Meigs had wanted the Pension Building to accommodate receptions and parties which hitherto had not had appropriate space in Washington. Inaugural balls were also held in the center court for Benjamin Harrison, Grover Cleveland, William McKinley, and Theodore Roosevelt. Reportedly in these earlier days purchase of a ticket was the only requirement for admission and crowds grew from 9,000 for Cleveland's ball to 18,000 for Taft's. Later, the court was sectioned into offices.

Congress Builds Itself a Library
188–189

Library of Congress, Smith-meyer and Pelz, Washington, D.C., 1897.

Three-quarters of a century after its founding in 1800 the Library of Congress, housed in the Capitol, had grown phenomenally—from a catalog collection of less than a thousand volumes and nine maps to millions of items, including engravings and musical scores. In 1870 the copyright law was revised to require that two copies of every publication in the United States be deposited in the library, which so outgrew its space that books were jammed under tables.

After ruling out proposals such as honeycombing the Capitol dome with books, Congress fastened on the idea for a grand new national library that would rival the great libraries of Europe. A competition held in 1873 was won by John L. Smithmeyer and Paul J. Pelz, who submitted an Italian Renaissance design. (Pelz was later to claim that he was sole architect.) It was not until

1886 that Congress appropriated money for construction of the building, which was to be supervised by a commission. From the inception of the project and throughout what was to become the stormy saga of its completion, Congressmen continually changed their minds about style and location of the building. They demanded several times that the architects redesign the library, then refused to pay them for their work.

In 1888 the commission was abolished and the Army Chief of Engineers, Thomas Lincoln Casey, became supervisor. In 1892 Casey's 28-year-old son, Edward, a New York architect, replaced Pelz and supervised some 50 sculptors and fresco painters in completing the lavish interior of the library. The building was finally occupied in 1897. When it was completed, it was the largest library in the world. The final design recalled the Paris Opéra, one of Europe's most elaborate Beaux-Arts structures.

John L. Smithmeyer and Paul J. Pelz. Congress refused to pay the architects what was owed them for repeated changes in plans. The long struggle with Congress marred Smithmeyer's reputation irrevocably until he could get no further clients. He died destitute, and Pelz, who also received neither just compensation nor credit, had to borrow money to bury his partner.

Congress Builds Itself a Library

From 1874 to 1886 Smithmeyer and Pelz, at the request of various library committees, submitted drawings for different locations. Among the new designs the ill-fated architects made to try to please Congress were (a) Victorian, (b) French Renaissance, (c) Modern Renaissance, and (d) German Renaissance—so called.

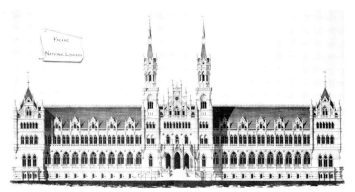

Library of Congress competition, first prize. Smithmeyer and Pelz defeated 26 competitors, including former Architect of the Capitol Thomas U. Walter.

Opéra, Charles Garnier, Paris,
1874, a postcard view photographed before automobiles
and traffic lights entered the
scene.

Library of Congress, Main
Reading Room, architectural
center of the library and the
center of the reference service
to the public. The octagon is
richly decorated with brown
marble from Tennessee and
yellow marble from Siena,
Italy.

Thomas Lincoln Casey, chief of the Army Corps of Engineers, sketch (based on a photograph) which appeared in *Harper's Weekly* in 1884. General Casey was in charge of the library's construction until his death in 1896. He was well known for his work on the Washington Monument and the State, War, and Navy Building.

Edward Pearce Casey, General Casey's son. At the age of 28 he replaced architect Pelz in the supervision of the sculptors and fresco painters who did the interior work for the library.

Dome, Library of Congress. The dome and the flame of the torch were originally covered with 23-carat gold leaf. The 15-foot-high torch was designed by Edward Pearce Casey.

Scaffold designed by Bernard R. Green, superintendent of construction of the library, for decorating the interior of the dome of the main reading room. The collar painting on the dome, by Edwin Blashfield, represents the painter's idea of the evolution of western civilization. Germany is a printer who has the face of General Casey; England, an actress, with the face of Ellen Terry, holding a book of Shakespeare's plays. The face of France, Emancipation, is that of the artist's wife.

From the ethnological collections of the Smithsonian, Curator Otis T. Mason made plaster models of "savage and barbarous peoples" for the sculptors to make the 33 keystones that ornament windows on the main floor of the library.

Stone carvers working in the Library of Congress. *Frank Leslie's Weekly* commented in 1894 that Americans should give thanks "for what the functionaries at Washington have given us, for be it said that these works on and within the Congressional Library will start American sculpture upon a new plane, and mark a new era in plastic art in the western hemisphere."

*"That false idea of grandeur
which consists mainly in hoisting a building up from a reasonable level off the ground,
mainly in order to secure for it
a monstrous flight of steps
which must be surmounted before the main door can be
reached. . . ."*
*Russell Sturgis, on the main
entrance of the Library of Congress, 1898*

Library of Congress, main
entrance

Schoolchildren visiting the Library of Congress, 1899. Photograph by Frances Benjamin Thompson, who is known for her pictures of the capital city of this period.

Wedgwood plate, 1900. On the back with the hallmark is printed: "It stands today the largest, most imposing, most sumptuous and most costly Library Building in the world."

Work of the Office of the Supervising Architect reflected the nineteenth-century concern with historical knowledge, a concern that inevitably caused the dominant classicism to be unseated as one historical style succeeded, overlapped, and mingled with another.

The long span from authorization to completion of major federal buildings allowed each Supervising Architect to "correct" the designs of his predecessor. Alfred Mullett redesigned some of the rooflines of Ammi B. Young. He also proposed but did not carry out his favorite mansard-style topping for Robert Mills's General Post Office in Washington. Mullett's design still embodied classicism, albeit on a new massive scale and often in a French interpretation. His departure in 1874 marked the end of the nineteenth-century conviction that, whatever the adaptation, the sources of federal architecture should be classical. To Mullett's distress, his successor, William Potter, was an ardent Gothicist who rearranged some of the Second Empire rooflines to reflect the popular Gothic fashion. Potter was soon followed by James Hill, who, during his tenure from 1876 to 1884, favored red-brick rectangular buildings topped by romantic clock towers.

Towers, in fact, became quite the fashion for public buildings. Henry Hobson Richardson's neo-Romanesque style, competing with the Gothic for public favor, was especially popular in the tower edition. His Allegheny County Courthouse in Pittsburgh stimulated a rash of towered city halls and courthouses across the country. In an era of otherwise low buildings, a government tower became as easy to spot from a distance as the traditional church spires.

As the century ended, Supervising Architects increasingly scrambled their historical allusions—Dutch, Queen Anne, Et Cetera. For public buildings the battle of the eaves would continue into the next century, coming perhaps full circle when John Russell Pope suggested reforming the roofline on Mullett's State, War, and Navy Building—into a re-revived classical mode to match Robert Mills's nearby Treasury.

Heads of Office of the Supervising Architect

Robert Mills (title, Federal Architect)	1836–1842
Ammi B. Young (Architectural Advisor)	1842–1852
Ammi B. Young (Supervising Architect)	1852–1862
Isaiah Rogers (Supervising Architect)	1862–1865
A. B. Mullett (Supervising Architect)	1865–1874
W. A. Potter (Supervising Architect)	1874–1877
James B. Hill (Supervising Architect)	1877–1883
M. E. Bell (Supervising Architect)	1884–1886
Will A. Freret (Supervising Architect)	1887–1888
James H. Windrim (Supervising Architect)	1889–1890
W. J. Edbrooke (Supervising Architect)	1891–1892
Jeremiah O'Rourke (Supervising Architect)	1893–1894
William Martin Aiken (Supervising Architect)	1895–1896
James Knox Taylor (Supervising Architect)	1897–1912
Oscar Wenderoth (Supervising Architect)	1913–1914
James A. Wetmore (Acting Supervising Architect)	1915–1933
Louis A. Simon (Supervising Architect)	1933–1939

Battle of the Eaves
196–197

Three designs for a Courthouse and Post Office, Detroit, Michigan, 1883, 1887, and 1888.

Courthouse and Post Office, Detroit, Michigan, as completed in 1897.

Customhouse and Post Office, Cincinnati, Ohio. The first version, as begun by Mullett, and, shown in the second illustration, as finally completed by Supervising Architect W. A. Potter. The steeply angled roofline topped by wrought-iron railings represented a federal version of the Gothic fashion.

Post Office, Washington, D.C., 1891–1899. Supervising Architect W. J. Edbrooke's building was criticized by a Senator of the time as "a cross between a cathedral and a cotton mill." Another critic called it "an unfortunate production" that would "require dynamiting before it can be brought into harmony with its surroundings." In 1901 Cass Gilbert said, "Its undue height and excessive prominence exemplify what should be avoided irrespective of its bad design." In the 1930s it blocked the completion of the grand scheme for the Federal Triangle. In 1963 a federal official called the still officially friendless structure "a monster Gothic derelict abandoned at midpoint on the most important avenue of the nation." In the 1970s politics and styles entered yet another mode and admirers rallied to the defense. The facade was cleaned and a competition staged for its adaptive reuse.

Appraisers' Warehouse, Philadelphia, 1871, an example of
the functional—and plainer—
federal structures of the Mullett era.

Customhouse and Post Office,
Des Moines, Iowa. The original two-story structure by
Mullett was completed in
1871. An additional story and
an extension were completed
in 1885. Supervising Architect
Hill's clock tower stuck on
Mullett's classical base was a
kind of seriatim eclecticism.

Appraisers' Warehouse, W. J.
Edbrooke, New York, 1899.
Without the fashionable tur-
rets and towers of the sym-
bolic government presence,
this building closely resembles
Edbrooke's D.C. Post Office. It
also resembles Richardson's
Marshall Field Warehouse and
Louis Sullivan's Auditorium in
Chicago.

Cover design, *American Architect and Building News*, which began publication in 1876. The magazine was an insistent voice in the debates about federal architecture. Under the editorship of an American member of the Pre-Raphaelite Brotherhood, it could find little to praise in Mullett's classically inspired designs and little to fault in Potter's Gothic work. For the most part the magazine harped incessantly on the poor quality of federal work—an aesthetic position consistent with the magazine's strong support of the American Institute of Architects' effort to have public work contracted to private architects.

Battle of the Eaves

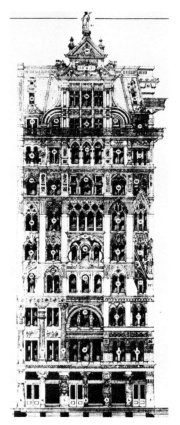

Proposal for the American Institute of Architects Building, John Moser, New York, 1884. Moser said his design was "an embodiment of the history of our art . . . where every epoch in architectural history shall be represented by details from the best examples now obtainable, following each other in regular and orderly sequence."

H. H. Richardson, as he posed for photographers in his home, which reflected his fascination with things medieval. His tower buildings were popular models for federal archi-tects. His popularity with the profession was evident in the appearance of five of his buildings in the top ten of a poll conducted by the *American Architect and Building News* in 1885.

Post Office and Courthouse, Quincy, Illinois, 1883–1887. European styles adopted for post offices and other government buildings in this period were national or regional as well as historical, as shown by this French chateau and the following two examples from Clarksville, Tennessee, and Paterson, New Jersey.

Drawing of the Paterson, New Jersey, Post Office, 1899, by Oscar Wenderoth, who later became a Supervising Architect. The style was characterized as "Dutch."

Post Office, Clarksville, Tennessee, 1891–1898, a Germanic Romanesque example.

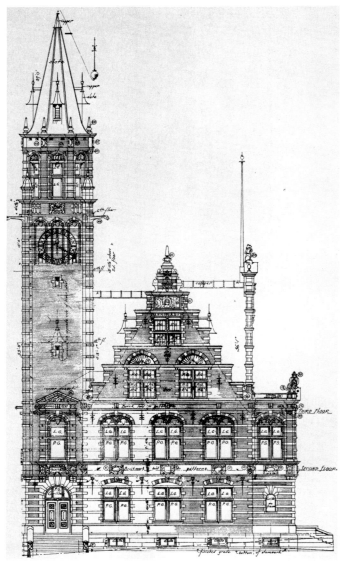

A ''fold-out'' tower from the
Report of the Supervising Architect of the Treasury, 1895.

Courthouse and Post Office,
St. Paul, Minnesota. The
building was occupied by
1900 but a not-unusual delay
in appropriations delayed
completion of the tower until
1909. The building was transferred to the local community
for adaptive reuse in the
1960s.

By 1892 the Office of the Supervising Architect controlled an inventory of 297 buildings with 95 more in the process of completion —compared with the 1853 stock of 23 buildings inventoried by the Office of Construction. Construction was plagued by piecemeal appropriations, contractors' delays, cost overruns, materials shortages, investigations, political pressures, criticism from professional architects, and even yellow fever. According to the *American Architect and Building News* in 1894, "The average time of completion of large private structures is 29 months. Of government buildings it is 96 months. . . ." Both the building and administrative processes have proved remarkably impervious to technological change: In 1971 the Administrator of the General Services Administration testified, "Right now, it takes us as long as seven years to construct a building private industry can construct in two or two and one-half years."

In its early years following the Civil War, the American Institute of Architects continually expressed opposition to the widely used method of selecting architects through design competitions. In 1893, the New York chapter refused in a body to enter an important competition. As Chief of Construction for the Columbian Exposition, Daniel Burnham refused to consider any method of competition to select designs. An American Institute of Architects President said that competition was "a sorry subject for architects. It burns the fingers of those who meddle with it. . . ."

But as early as 1876 the Institute was also actively promoting legislation to initiate competitive selections of architects for federal projects. All civil federal buildings at the time were being designed by the staff architects of the Supervising Architect's Office. Competitions offered a means of getting private architects in on this work although the justification was an argument that the efficiency and quality of work in the Supervising Architect's Office were not up to the standards maintained in private architectural offices.

In 1893 the American Institute of Architects (AIA), which then represented less than 20 percent of the country's practicing architects, won passage of the Tarsney Act. The act allowed, but did not require, the Treasury to acquire

Interior, Supervising Architect's Office, photo taken in 1891, when the office had 148 employees.

outside architectural services through competitions. The Treasury claimed that the law's provisions were vague and did not rush to use the new authority.

AIA members assumed that a new post office for Buffalo, New York, would occasion the first Tarsney competition. When a Buffalo paper in early 1894 published the Supervising Architect's design for the building, the AIA protested and an acrimonious exchange of letters ensued. The increasingly heated correspondence ended when Secretary of Treasury John G. Carlisle wrote AIA President Daniel

Burnham: "Your very offensive and ungentlemanly letter of the 9th instant is just received, and you are informed that this Department will have no further correspondence with you upon the subject to which it relates, or any other subject." Thereafter, agitation for implementation of the Tarsney Act was often accompanied by criticism of the Supervising Architect for failing to adopt the Beaux-Arts style made popular at the 1893 Chicago Fair.

With the change of presidential administrations in 1897, Lyman J. Gage, who had been president of the Columbian Exposition, became Secretary of the

Treasury. He immediately put the Tarsney Act into operation and issued regulations, which required the appointment of three or four outside architects to act as a jury for each competition. In the following fifteen years some 35 buildings were designed under the act's provisions. Some of the best-known architects were chosen, including McKim, Mead and White, Albert Kahn, Cass Gilbert, and Daniel Burnham.

In 1911 a Congressional committee recommended repeal of the Tarsney Act, concluding that the cost of employing private architects exceeded that of similar services performed by the Supervising Architect.

The committee's report and hearing record also indicate its members' suspicions that jury appointments, invitations to compete, and awards of commissions were biased in favor of AIA members. In 1912, despite by then strong support from the Secretary of the Treasury, Congress repealed the Tarsney Act.

Whether or not the Act was "democratic" in intent or operation, it found favor only during years of Republican control of government.

"Good Architecture be
_____! Secretary Carlisle has decided that designs for government buildings shall be turned out by machinery as heretofore." Cartoon printed in *Life*, April 12, 1894, supporting the AIA's contention that design competitions would improve government architecture. The robed figure is Treasury Secretary John G. Carlisle. The gnome beside him is labeled "Supervising Architect." At Carlisle's feet is a fallen muse.

· LIFE ·

GOOD ARCHITECTURE BE _____!

SECRETARY CARLISLE HAS DECIDED THAT DESIGNS FOR GOVERNMENT BUILDINGS SHALL BE TURNED OUT BY MACHINERY AS HERETOFORE.

Design for the Post Office,
Buffalo, New York, prepared
by the Office of the Supervising Architect, Jeremiah
O'Rourke, 1894. Release of
this design to the Buffalo press
incensed the leadership of the
American Institute of Architects and precipitated a
heated correspondence with
the Treasury. Adding insult to
injury, the Supervising Architect displayed the design on
the frontispiece of his annual
report of 1893.

Alfred B. Mullett

"The occurrences of this evening render it necessary for me to resign the Office Supervising Architect of this Department. . . . My health as you know is broken down. I am consequently nervous and perhaps more irritable than I am aware of. You are also aware that I consider the salary so inadequate that the office is of no value except so far as it affords an opportunity for making a reputation."

Letter of resignation, November 21, 1874

William Potter

"Experience has shown that it is difficult, if not impossible, to separate the Office of Supervising Architect from political control to a greater or lesser degree. . . . And, furthermore, the objects for which the buildings erected in this office are constructed are, with very slight exceptions, so nearly alike that the difficulty, the impossibility of endowing them with variety and individuality must be apparent."

Proceedings, *AIA Convention*, November 17–19, 1875

"The office is no sinecure by any means; and I doubt whether you could get a capable architect, in good practice, to give up his office for the post. It needs to be made more distinctively artistic, and many of the mere routine duties lopped from it."

Upon his resignation, 1876

James B. Hill

"The issues were undefined, and irrelevant evidence grew in proportion, to cloud the judgements and poison the minds of both the committee and the public, to whom it sat with open doors. . . . I was compelled to suffer through more than two months of unbroken and uninterrupted insult."

Letter to Secretary of the Treasury, 1883

Mifflin E. Bell

". . . The office labors under great difficulties in being unable to offer rates of pay sufficient to secure and retain in the service of the Government architects and draughtsmen competent to perform the work satisfactorily."

Report of the Supervising Architect, *1884*

"In the two years I have occupied the office I have had to transact its business with four different Secretaries of the Treasury. . . . All of these officers have as much as is possible for them to attend to in the transaction of other business of the Treasury Department, and in consequence of this condition, the Supervising Architect's recommendations are frequently called in question by designing and scheming contractors, who have no other interest than their personal profit and who appeal to you or your assistants simply because you or they have no expert knowledge of the subject at issue."

Report of the Supervising Architect, *1885*

James H. Windrim

"Attention is respectfully asked to the fact that the present draughting room of the office is inadequate in size and poorly lighted; frequent absence of the draughtsmen is occasioned by opthalmia."

Report of the Supervising Architect, *1889*

W. J. Edbrooke

"I am of the opinion that much of the comments and criticisms of the work and business of this office could be prevented if the reports and estimates made from this office were allowed, where necessity required, to properly affect the legislation relating to public buildings."

Report of the Supervising Architect, *1891*

Jeremiah O'Rourke

". . . The only reason for the slow progress of these works is the want of a technical force adequate to the demands on the office."

Letter to the Chairman, Committee on Public Buildings and Grounds, U.S. Senate, January 13, 1894

J. M. Carrère

"The work itself is scattered over the entire United States, and is absolutely beyond the reach of any one man excepting by proxy, and practically beyond his control. . . . The present condition of the work is in such a disorganized state, that it would take the best part of any man's time to organize the work itself, irrespective of the department. The accumulated waste of money is beyond belief. The department, in the main, seems well organized though cumbersome. . . . The tenure of the office is controlled either by civil service rules or by political influence, and with this state of affairs the Office of Supervising Architect, legally, is mainly that of a clerk of the department, appointed by the Secretary of the Treasury, and though his responsibility is supposed to cover all of the above work, his authority is absolutely dependent on the Secretary of the Treasury, and much of it is divided with heads of departments.
"My examination of the office and its possibilities convinces me that the underlying principle upon which it is based is radically wrong, and that it is beyond the power of any one man to make a success of it. The system, not the man, should be changed."

Letter to the Secretary of the Treasury declining the offer of the job of Supervising Architect, *1895*

Secretary of the Treasury Franklin MacVeagh

"The repeal of the Tarsney Act was received with great regret by the Treasury Department, and by great numbers of people who are especially interested in the art and fitness of government buildings. . . . To my mind it is absurd to believe that any single architectural office, whether a government office or any other, ought to design every one of the large number of Government buildings turned out annually, when those buildings are charged with a mission of architectural education to every part of the country. . . . And no architect's office, such as this or any other, should be thrown in upon itself or should be taken out of constant association and competition with all the other successful architects and architectural offices."

Secretary of the Treasury, Annual Report on the State of the Finances, *1912*

THE AGGRANDIZEMENT OF POWER 5

A member of the Pioneer Automobile Party in his Toledo car at the rim of the Grand Canyon, Arizona; photograph by Aultman, c. 1902. ''But each man and each woman of you I lead upon a knoll . . . pointing to landscapes of continents and the public road.'' (Walt Whitman)

Triumphal arch, by McKim,
Mead and White, World's Columbian Exposition, Chicago,
1893. According to Vincent
Scully, the Roman-style arches
at the fair were decorated
with Indians instead of the
barbarian slaves of antiquity.

In 1905, when Henry James returned to America after a twenty-year absence, he remarked on ". . . the will to grow—everywhere written large, and to grow at no matter what or to whose expense." By the turn of the century America's industrial revolution had caused a rapid accumulation of great wealth; dynamos were generating electric power by 1890; and a well-developed railroad system facilitated the high level of commerce and industry.

If the close of the frontier in 1890 officially ended expansion across the continent, it did not end expansive aspirations and actions—nor expansive words. "A nation like ours," President Theodore Roosevelt said, "with the unique position of fronting at once on the Atlantic and the Pacific, a nation forced by the mere fact of destiny to play a great, a mighty, a masterful part in the world, cannot afford to neglect its navy. . . ."

Actually, the Navy had not been neglected. It had become clear long before this that Manifest Destiny was not to stop at the water's edge. After 1866 a modern fleet began to undergird a more widespread American presence in the Western Hemisphere and off Asian coasts. Early in 1898 the sinking of the battleship *Maine* off the coast of Cuba ignited the Spanish-American War. One legacy for the United States was an important naval base in the Philippines. Another base was acquired with the annexation of Hawaii in 1900.

This foreign adventuring also had domestic, architectural consequences. As befitted the rising prestige and power of the Navy, a 200-acre expansion of the Naval Academy at Annapolis began. An ambitious expansion and rebuilding program was also undertaken at the U.S. Military Academy at West Point. The cornerstone of the Army War College was laid in 1903.

With its new territories in Cuba and the Philippines after the war of 1898, the United States turned to finishing a canal, begun by France in 1881, to join the Pacific and Caribbean. While Congress debated, Roosevelt and his Secretary of State jumped into the fray between companies and countries to seize a controlling American interest. The administration's complicity in a Panamanian revolt against Colombia and a display of gunboat diplomacy gave the United States a six-mile right of way for a canal across the Isthmus of Panama—perhaps the first and last time the United States created a country in order to carry through a building project. Roosevelt demanded ex post facto approval from Congress in language remarkably similar to that used by Jefferson after the opportune purchase of the Louisiana Territory: "If I had followed traditional conservative methods I should have submitted a dignified state paper of probably 200 pages to Congress and the debate would be going on yet; but I took the Canal Zone and let Congress debate; and while the debate goes on the canal does also."

The increasing affluence and power of the United States was in few ways more visibly expressed than in its architecture. Although skyscrapers began appearing in American cities after 1884 it was the World's Columbian Exposition in Chicago in 1893 that offered Americans a model for what their growing cities might become, what their growing affluence might buy.

Visitors to the White City were dazzled by opulent buildings—plastered and white-washed and brilliantly illuminated—surrounding a graceful reflecting pool. The unifying style of the major buildings was that of the so-called Beaux-Arts, popular at the time in France, where the art of civic embellishment was identified with the Ecole des Beaux-Arts and its preference for monumentality, symmetrical plans, and richly orna-mented classical forms. The Beaux-Arts approach was grounded in the support of in-stitutional values through recognizable architectural symbols—in this case, classical.

For Americans accustomed to living on perpetually unfinished streets, the tidy, ele-gantly landscaped boulevards of the fair provided a compelling new concept. The fair's image of a well-planned ensemble of buildings generated enthusiasm for a new scheme for aggrandizing the nation's capital, and gave birth to the City Beautiful movement, which established the favored pattern for urban development for several decades. The fair's planning emphasis would stimulate a generation of civic planners like Lewis Mumford, Clarence Stein, and Walter Burley Griffin.

Outside the fairgrounds Chicago architects were trying to reconcile the growing sepa-ration between architecture and engineering by designing forms thought to be more compatible with function. "Progress before Precedent" was the slogan coined by the Architectural League of America, founded in Chicago in 1899. But after the 1893 fair, the Beaux-Arts neoclassical forms and their predominantly eastern architects eclipsed the sterner Chicago school in popularity. In 1895 the American Academy in Rome was founded for students of exceptional promise to study Roman antecedents. In 1905 Congress blessed the Academy with government incorporation. As far as federal building was concerned the Supervising Architect declared officially for White City classicism in 1901.

Some protested against the lemming-rush to the Beaux-Arts style and the rigid appli-cation by American students of principles learned in Paris. The culture represented by the White City, Louis Sullivan wrote, was "snobbish and alien to the land . . . when what the world needs is . . . a moral standard that is plain, valid and livable." In fact, however, the fair and its progeny remarkably mirrored the national disposition for aggrandizement.

A giant redwood erected by the Interior Department in the Federal Building reversed the symbolism of the 1876 Centennial. Now the garden was in the machine. In the face of an unprecedented level of consumption and the official pronouncement that the frontier had vanished, the nation was cautioned to inventory its resources. Re-ports from government expeditions on the arid lands of the Southwest had officially ended the founding fathers' supposition of equal value for equal size and suggested that water, not the sky, marked the limits of western growth. That the federal government might even be able to remove those limits was the assumption behind the creation of the Bureau of Reclamation in 1902, a momentous Congressional decision eventually leading to a federal role in power generation and flood control that made possible the subsequent development of much of the arid West.

No longer comforted, however, by Jefferson's belief that there would be land for expansion "to the thousandth and thousandth generation," a small but influential group of national leaders perceived the widespread use, abuse, and misuse of free and cheap land and sought to put the brakes on wastrel practices. The conservation movement which resulted grew out of a diversity of national needs and under the stimulus of men with widely varied priorities.

Theodore Roosevelt's White House Conference of Governors, called in 1908, led to the appointment of the National Conservation Commission. Its 1909 report to Congress—the first comprehensive inventory of the land, water, forest, and mineral resources of the United States—advocated "wise and beneficial uses" of those resources. In a 1901 message to Congress Roosevelt had been blunter: "Forest protection is not an end in itself; it is a means to increase and sustain the resources of our country and the industries which depend upon them. The preservation of our forests is an imperative business necessity."

In 1906 Roosevelt signed the Antiquities Act, which made it possible to set aside from the public domain, through Presidential proclamation, scientific and historic areas as national monuments. Nine national parks, then a uniquely American institution, had been designated by the time the National Park Service was created in the Interior Department in 1916. In 1896, with the first Pollution Control Act, the Corps of Engineers assumed responsibility for keeping the nation's waterways free of contaminants.

Most leaders of the conservation movement advocated the "rational" use of natural resources. They belonged to an era and usually to a class that greatly prized efficiency. Expertise and professionalism were attaining recognition. It was an era of time-motion studies and specialization in the industrial process. Homemakers became aware that they practiced a domestic "science." Federal officials were enthusiastic about the possibilities of applying scientific principles to resource development. The debate on natural resources often pitted the advocates of "wise use" of the land against preservationists who were primarily interested in saving the landscape and wildlife and believed that almost any development defeated these goals.

Other forces were even more radically changing the physical character of America. Between 1790 and 1890 the urban population had multiplied dramatically faster than the total population. Roosevelt, like many Americans, believed the growth of cities threatened the stability of social life in the United States. To review rural conditions and recommend improvements in rural life, Roosevelt appointed the Country Life Commission in 1908.

But popular journalists who, like Horatio Alger, urged the country boy to head for the city to "strive and succeed," had a more accurate view of reality. The urban trend was not to be stemmed in this or any other period that Roosevelt or his contemporaries could foresee. And its impact on government services, and thus on federal stimulus to development, was profound.

A kind of reciprocal action was taking place, for example, in the development of cities and towns and the expansion of the postal service. Communities hurried to meet the Post Office's requirements for the paving and naming of streets and the numbering of houses and buildings. The department, meanwhile, strained to provide service to mushrooming towns. Rural free delivery provided a strong stimulus for the development of country roads, at the same time contributing to the deterioration of small villages centered on postal stations.

Nothing, however, compared with the automobile as a stimulus for development of cities, towns, or rural areas. As early as 1891 an alliance of cyclists and farmers had begun agitating for good roads. A complex of pressures, formed with the assistance of federal officials and given added impetus by rising automobile registrations, led to passage in 1916 of the landmark Federal Aid Highway Act.

The impact of the automobile was not limited to highways—how and where they were built. It seemed to overshadow other technologies. In New York and other cities, for instance, the Post Office had installed miles of underground pneumatic tubes for mail delivery in core areas. Although these had been used successfully in European cities, the conduits were abandoned when the department opted for motor delivery of mail in all areas.

Viewed in isolation, that decision could hardly be assigned any substantial measure of blame for the congestion that came to frustrate movement in Manhattan and Chicago and hundreds of other cities. It was, however, a part in the cumulatively large, irreversible series of federal commitments to the automobile, made over the next half century, which would have a dramatic and lasting affect on architecture and the use of space.

The new century brought a marked increase in work in the Supervising Architect's Office. In 1899, the Office had responsibility for construction or management of 399 buildings; by 1912, the number was 1,126. By 1916 the Secretary of the Treasury noted that the number of federal buildings was "being increased at the rate of a new building every fourth day in the year." Rising costs and delays that resulted from this building boom revived interest in the notion of standardized design—a concept that had never been far from center stage of federal architecture. A Treasury Department standardization order in 1915 was in part a defense against charges of fiscal extravagance. Also, the resort to what were thought of as business methods of increasing efficiency was typical of Progressive era reforms; in this sense, establishing a classification system for standard building types and locations derived from the same mentality as the parallel promotion of efficiency and "wise use" doctrines in the development of natural resources.

While architects sketched plans that would give the capital an image to match the nation's increasing power and the White House an elegance to match the power by then accrued to the Presidency, prisonlike tenements were proliferating in the older cities. The growing literature on problems of social reform and photographs of inhuman housing conditions had little apparent effect on the architects of the period and were unnoticed by architecture journals. The federal government's concern at the new Ellis Island facilities for welcoming aliens to America did not extend beyond the official disembarkation. No federal agencies addressed the festering problems of tenements in cities that received the new arrivals. "The professional architects of the generation 1885 to 1912," wrote historians John Burchard and Albert Bush-Brown, "failed to read the future. They created for their profession the reputation of being a luxury, something less than engineering or medicine or law, a reputation it still sometimes has if not enjoys."

With the exception of Ellis Island and prisons only one other building type emerged in this period to herald a twentieth-century expansion of the government's social welfare role. World War I also plunged the government—although only briefly—into the construction of public housing for workers in war-related industry. Some prominent architects and planners like Frederick Law Olmsted, Jr., saw the new agencies Congress established to oversee the effort as "first steps toward a new age of social reconstruction." But the Armistice and the "Red scare" that followed it ended these experiments. The next and immensely larger expansion of the government's social responsibilities awaited a devastating economic depression that would generate pressures for federal assistance from all segments of American society.

In its most conspicuous national institutional image, at least, the Beaux-Arts style adorned the architecture of a prideful and confident nation, returning federal architecture to the classical traditions that had been briefly interrupted by the eclectic forays of the Victorian era. For the next half century some form of classicism would dominate official architecture. The grand new proposal for Washington, authored by a distinguished group chaired by Daniel Burnham, who disdained "little plans," reflected the monumentality of L'Enfant's plan but focused it on the Mall area, ignoring his larger vision of a monumental city for government and citizens alike. Through successive controversies over matters great and small, Burnham's group and their successors planted modern monumental Washington on the fertile soil L'Enfant had provided. Thereafter, the 1902 plan was the ideal toward which federal architecture would strive. In the turmoil of political realities, it was a haven, a refuge, the federal government's magnificent, massive, marble version of a "clean, well-lighted place." At the end of World War I victorious American troops paraded in Washington, passing back into their new world "normalcy" under a great arch reminiscent of the Beaux-Arts arch of the 1893 Chicago exposition and of the distant arches of the Roman empire.

Lithograph invitation poster to the World's Columbian Exposition, Chicago, 1893. Despite Uncle Sam's gesture here, Congress appropriated money to support the fair reluctantly. Eventually the federal government gave $1.5 million, which included funds for the Federal Building and the Women's Building.

Authorized by Congress in 1890, the World's Columbian Commission nurtured the fifteenth international fair into full flower at Chicago in 1893. As chief of construction, Daniel Burnham led a team of well-known architects and artists in developing the extravagantly neoclassical atmosphere in which bloomed an exotic "White City."

To this White City, which celebrated the four hundredth anniversary of Columbus's discovery of America, the federal government contributed two structures: the Government Building and a Women's Building. The former, designed by the Supervising Architect, housed exhibits from the Departments of Treasury, Agriculture, War, Navy, State, and Interior. Among other things, it contained a "courting scene and a covey of chickens which is natural to the last degree." In the rotunda, the Interior Department erected a 30-foot-high section of a 23-foot-wide California redwood that had been carried eastward on 10 railroad boxcars and hollowed out to form two exhibit rooms connected by a spiral staircase.

The Women's Building was the result of a design competition sponsored by a Board of Lady Managers, authorized by Congress in a time of growing feminist activism. The goal of the Board, according to its president, Bertha Honore Palmer, was to organize an exhibit that would "clear away misconceptions as to the value of inventions and industries of women" and that would "present a complete picture of the condition of women in every country of the world . . . particularly of those women who are bread winners." Louise Bethune, who in 1888 had become the first woman member of the AIA, refused to participate because, she said, "competition is an evil" and gender restriction the "most objectionable form" of competition. The $1,000 first prize and the commission was awarded to Sophia Hayden, who a year earlier had become the first woman to graduate from the architecture school of the Massachusetts Institute of Technology. In May of 1893, Palmer dedicated the building to "an elevated womanhood."

Elsewhere, visitors marveled at the architectural self-images of the American states: Iowa came draped in Early French Renaissance, Indiana in French Gothic, Arkansas in French Rococo; and the New York Pavilion was an exact replica of a Medici villa. Among the state buildings were references to early America, including Mt. Vernon for Virginia and the tower of Independence Hall for Pennsylvania. Along the dazzling "Midway," fair goers were confronted by a bizarre conglomeration of everything from Samoan and Eskimo villages to the Blarney Castle, the Ruins of Yucatan and a Malayan palace called "The Bungalow of the Sultan of Johore."

Within the "Stormy, husky, brawling City of the Big Shoulders" and in the midst of a gathering economic depression, the Beaux-Arts fair was, literally and figuratively, a whitewash job. But it was an enormously influential one—and the vision of white monumental buildings in a strictly ordered environment would stimulate the imagination of Americans for decades to come and be most nearly recreated in the nation's capital. It would also underwrite the influence of academically trained architects.

From the Chicago fair to World War I a plethora of fairs celebrated national pride and confidence. These Beaux-Arts ensembles included federal buildings, which were clothed in the prevailing style. State governments often chose to recall the symbolic images of the beginning of the Republic. A Pan American Exposition at Buffalo, New York, in 1901 was marked by violence; President McKinley was assassinated when he attended this fair. A curious historic footnote is added by an article in *World's Week* magazine of August 1901, which claimed, "There is nothing at Buffalo in which the mass of visitors seem to be more interested than the big and little guns of the ordnance exhibits."

The Panama Pacific Exposition at San Francisco, where nearly 700,000 viewed a working model of the Panama Canal, was the last of the monumental scenic displays of plaster architecture.

"If the people . . . actually knew what was good when they saw it, they would some day talk about Hunt and Richardson, La Farge and St. Gaudens, Burnham and McKim, and Stanford White when their politicians and millionaires were otherwise forgotten. . . . Chicago asked in 1893 . . . the question whether the American people knew where they were driving. Adams answered, for one, that he did not know, but would try to find out . . . ; he decided that the American people probably knew no more than he did; but that they might still be driving or drifting unconsciously to some point in thought . . . and that possibly . . . this point might be fixed. Chicago was the first expression of American thought as a unity; one must start there."

Henry Adams, The Education of Henry Adams, 1906

". . . These conditions cannot be reproduced except in another World's Fair, and not literally even there. Men bring not back the mastodon, nor we those times. It is, however, the architects who do not know these things with whom we have so largely to reckon."

Montgomery Schuyler, "Last Words about the World's Fair," Architectural Record, January–March 1894

"You will see by the way that I filled out the blank crop report that my crop was almost a total failure which was caused by two very destructive Hail Storms; . . . Secretary P. M. Rusk, I have a request to make of you if it is in your power. . . . will you be so kind as to see that I get a complimentary ticket for me and wife to attend the World's Fair to be held in Chicago Illinoise in the year of 1893, and oblige."

Letter from W. H. Sipherd, an Iowa farmer, to Secretary of Agriculture Jeremiah M. Rusk, n.d.

The Court of Honor, World's Columbian Exposition. Its buildings were designed by the Burnham team in Renaissance classical style and executed in plaster on temporary whitewashed frameworks. The artificial landscape on 600 acres along Lake Michigan was designed by Frederick Law Olmsted, the creator of New York's Central Park. "The whole is better than any of its parts and greater than all of its parts, and its effect is one and indivisible," wrote critic Montgomery Schuyler in 1894. "The landscape plan is the key to the pictorial success of the Fair as a whole."

The Court of Honor at night. Buildings were highlighted by one of the largest displays of electricity assembled up to that time. Reportedly the electric bill was the fair commission's third highest bill. The building in the center is the Administration Building, designed by Richard Morris Hunt. In an 1893 *History of the Columbian Exposition*, William E. Cameron wrote: "By popular verdict this magnificent structure has been pronounced the gem and crown of the Exposition palaces. Although this building is small . . . the universal verdict is that it constitutes one of the noblest achievements of modern architecture."

Government Building, Office of the Supervising Architect, World's Columbian Exposition. The *American Architect and Building News* of April 7, 1894, was one of its severest critics: "One of the most conspicuous examples of the lack in artistic, and we might go further and say educated feeling was shown at the World's Columbian Exposition where the Government building, although more expensively erected, and possibly better constructed than the other buildings, was a source of mortification to those who felt pride in having their country show to advantage. The dome and pavilions of the building were wanting in good proportion, the details were crude, and not appropriate, and to complete the disagreeable impression produced, a pall was thrown over one's feelings by painting the dome black, and the building a disagreeable grey on the exterior."

". . . The Government building is a rude and crude and ignorant compilation of features that are not good in themselves, and upon the relations of which no pains whatever appear to have been spent. . . . If there be any doubt in the minds of the Senators as to the propriety of passing that measure [Tarsney Act] the doubt would be dissipated by a pilgrimage to Chicago, and by a comparison there found between the conditions of official and the conditions of unofficial architecture in these United States.."

"*Architectural Aberrations,*" Architectural Record, January–March 1893

"*In their place, at the Fair, these classic buildings were all that could be demanded. . . . Form and function, ornament and design, have no inherent relation, one with the other, when the mood of the architect is merely playful: there is no use in discussing the anatomy of architecture when its only aim is fancy dress. As a mask, as a caprice, the classic orders are as justifiable as the icing on a birthday cake: they divert the eye without damaging the structure that they conceal. Unfortunately, the architecture of the Renaissance has a tendency to imitate the haughty queen who advised the commons to eat cake. Logically, it demands that a Wall Street clerk shall live like a Lombardy prince, that a factory should be subordinated to esthetic contemplation; and since these things are impossible, it permits 'mere building' to become illiterate and vulgar below the* standards of the most debased vernacular. Correct in proportion, elegant in detail, courteous in relation to each other, the buildings of the World's Fair were, nevertheless, only the simulacra of a living architecture: they were the concentrated expression of an age which sought to produce 'values' rather than 'goods.'"

Lewis Mumford, Sticks and Stones, 1924

Sophia Hayden Bennett, who at 22 was called to Chicago to supervise the construction of her winning design for the Women's Building. The following year she designed her last building—again commissioned by women—though she lived past eighty.

Women's Building, Sophia Hayden, World's Columbian Exposition. The architect said of her design that the "details . . . are modelled after classic and Italian Renaissance types, and on account of the comparative small size and scale of the building, are more delicate and refined than those of the other main structures of the Fair." The *American Architect and Building News* carped, "As a woman's work it 'goes' of course; fortunately it was conceived in the proper vein and does not make a discordant note: it is simply weak and commonplace." The article went on to call the roof garden "'a hen coop'— for petticoated hens, old and young."

"Even more important than the discovery of Columbus, which we are gathered together to celebrate, is the fact that the General Government has just discovered woman."

Bertha Honore Palmer, President of the Board of Lady Managers, remarks at Exposition dedication, from Madeleine B. Stern, We the Women: Career Firsts in Nineteenth-Century America, *1975*

"Golden Door," Transportation Building, Louis Sullivan, World's Columbian Exposition. A commissioner of the Union Centrale des Arts Décoratifs of Paris praised the richly decorated warehouse-style building as "truly original" and having "the special merit of recalling no European building." Blue, yellow, dark green, and red-orange and low-relief ornament enlivened the flat surfaces of Sullivan's showpiece, a colorful exception to the surrounding "snowy palaces, vast and beautiful."

"The Fair is going to have a great influence in our country. The American people have seen the 'Classics' on a grand scale for the first time. . . . I can see all America constructed along the lines of the Fair, in noble, dignified, Classic style. The great men of the day all feel that way about it—all of them."

Daniel Burnham to Frank Lloyd Wright, recounted in Wright's An Autobiography, 1932

"'Frank,' he [Daniel Burnham] said, 'the Fair should have shown you that Sullivan and Richardson are well enough in their way, but their way won't prevail—architecture is going the other way.'

"'But, it is essentially the uncreative way . . . isn't it?'

"'Uncreative?—What do you mean uncreative? What can be more beautiful than the classic lines and proportions of Greek architecture? That architecture will never be surpassed. We should be taught by it and accept its rules. . . .'

"'I know. Yes—I know, Uncle Dan, you may be quite right but somehow it just strikes on my heart like—jail.'"

Exchange between Frank Lloyd Wright and Daniel Burnham, recounted in Wright's An Autobiography, 1932

"The damage wrought by the World's Fair will last for half a century from its date, if not longer. It has penetrated deep into the constitution of the American mind, effecting there lesions significant of dementia."

Louis Sullivan, Autobiography of an Idea, 1924

The Chicago fair's architects, artists, and officials, May 1891. Left to right: D. H. Burnham, George B. Post, M. B. Pickett, Henry Van Brunt, Francis D. Millet, Maitland Armstrong, Colonel Edward Rice, Augustus Saint-Gaudens, Henry Sargent Codman, George W. Maynard, Charles F. McKim, E. R. Graham, Dion Geraldine. In his *Autobiography*, Burnham recalled, "All day long Saint-Gaudens had been sitting in a corner never opening his mouth and scarcely moving. He came over to me, and taking both my hands said, 'Look here, old fellow, do you realize that this is the greatest meeting of artists since the fifteenth century!'" The concept of a group of artists working cooperatively to produce a coherent plan carried over from this 1893 experience to the collaborative Plan for Washington of 1902—produced by the so-called McMillan Commission—in which Burnham, McKim, and Saint Gaudens were again influential participants.

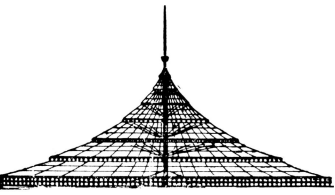

A plan (not carried out) to put all the Columbian Exposition exhibits under one roof. The Chicago *Tribune* of March 9, 1890, reported the designer's aspirations: "Chicago can outrival Paris in a truly American way. It can build the biggest building ever built, one four times larger than any Exposition building of the past. And, by constructing it without any inside columns it can produce, by the aid of electric lights, vistas of a magnificence never before dreamed of. Think of it—193⅔ acres under one roof and the whole interior open to the eye!"

Tennessee Centennial Exposition, Nashville, Tennessee,
1897. A recreated Parthenon
was a popular attraction at
this fair and at the 1915 San
Francisco fair.

U.S. Government Building, Office of the Supervising Architect, for the Trans-Mississippi International Exposition, Omaha, Nebraska, 1898.

Negro Building, Jamestown Exposition, 1907. According to the official guide book of the exposition, "The building was designed by W. Sydney Pittman, a graduate of Tuskegee and Drexel Institutes and at present an architect in Washington. The United States Government bore the major portion of the expenses entailed by this exhibit and the building was erected under the Government's auspices. The architect of this building was the first negro whose design had ever been accepted by the Government. All work on the structure was done by negroes, the contractors were negroes and so were the workmen. Dedicatory remarks predicted: 'The showing that we will make in this building will startle the world, it will astonish those who are unfamiliar with the true condition of the Negro and it will be stimulating to our race.'" The guide book account agreed: "He was entirely right. . . . The unprejudiced observer could see what had been done during the forty-two years that had elapsed since slavery was abolished and could not fail to predict hopefully for the future. . . . Many intelligent, thoughtful, purposeful white men visited the exhibit and were deeply impressed."

Louisiana Purchase Exposition, St. Louis, 1904, view. Temporary plaster buildings in a garden were in the White City tradition of the Chicago fair. At St. Louis nearly 20 million people also saw amazing displays of electric light, a powered dirigible flight, and the first demonstration of the dial phone.

U.S. Government Building, Office of the Supervising Architect, Lewis and Clark Centennial Exposition, Portland, Oregon, 1905.

United States Building, Paris Exposition, 1900. The Turkish pavilion is to the left. Of the twenty-three official pavilions, only the American one was not done in a distinctively native style. It was a copy of the Roman Pantheon. The French *L'Illustration* of August 4, 1900, commented, "No, the art of Richardson, Burnham, or Root could not appear sufficiently consecrated, official, pompous, triumphant, or imperial." The same observer also attended the nightly receptions at the pavilion where the "diamonds of the American women, the beauty of their shoulders, and splendor of their complexions made one pardon the banality and empty pomp of the decor."

"I have seen tonight the great-est revelation of beauty that was ever seen on this earth. I may say this meaning it liter-ally and with full regard for all that is known of ancient art and architecture and all that the modern world has hereto-fore seen of glory and grandeur. I have seen beauty that will give the world new standards of art, and a joy in loveliness never before reached. That is what I have seen."

Edwin Markham at the first lighting of the Panama Pacific Exposition, 1915

"This festive and ephemeral na-ture of exposition architecture tends to loosen the bands of re-straint which should be felt in designing permanent struc-tures."

Commissioner of the Louisiana Purchase Exposition, 1904

Demolition of the plaster arch of the "Court of the Universe," Panama Pacific Exposition. Most of the build-ings were ephemeral and van-ished with the crowds after fairs closed.

The crew of the battleship *Olympia*, led by John Philip Sousa's band, march triumphantly through New York to celebrate the end of the war between Spain and the United States, 1899. Over the arch appeared: "To the glory of the American Navy and in greeting to our Admiral a grateful city relying on their valor has built this arch, 1899."

At the outbreak of "the splendid little war" the *Washington Post* observed the nation's growing appetite for empire:

"A new consciousness seems to have come upon us —the consciousness of strength —and with it a new appetite, the yearning to show our strength. . . .

"Ambition, interest, land hunger, pride, the mere joy of fighting, whatever it may be, we are animated by a new sensation. We are face to face with a strange destiny.

"The taste of Empire is in the mouth of the people even as the taste of blood in the jungle. It means an Imperial policy, the Republic, renascent, taking her place with the armed nations."

With the late-nineteenth-century American concern for enlarged and reorganized military services, attention inevitably also focused on the academies that trained officers, including West Point, Annapolis, and the National War College. Rebuilding programs for these institutions were particularly interesting for their emphasis on master planning, an approach popularized by the 1893 Chicago fair.

The Annapolis campus had changed little since its inception in 1845 when the Navy accepted Fort Severn from the Army. (The circular fort was then being used as a gymnasium.) In order to improve the training of officers in the steel and steam technologies, a review board recommended a complete rebuilding program, including "a permanent sanitary sewerage system."

Ernest Flagg, a New York architect, was chosen to replan the 200-acre campus where the Severn River flowed into Chesapeake Bay. Construction began in 1899, while in Congress some members demanded a competition and a more careful review of the academy's requirements. Controversy over the academy abated, and construction continued to completion. And the academy, which in 1886 had graduated 25, was transformed into another brass factory, producing 350 officers at the 1907 commencement exercises. In 1909 the old Fort Severn was demolished; by then, except for monuments, the colonial-scale red-brick campus had been completely replaced by "educational palaces" in a grand Beaux-Arts ensemble.

In 1902 the War Department held a competition for a rebuilding program at West Point. The jurors included two officers and architects George B. Post and Cass Gilbert. Ralph Adams Cram, of the winning firm of Cram, Goodhue, and Ferguson, explained in his autobiography that "opinion at 'the Point' was sharply divided as to style." The Gothic tradition, according to Cram, was "held in high honour" by most officials, but two recent West Point buildings designed by McKim, Mead and White in the "specifically Renaissance style" presented an alternative. Cram et al.— whose Gothic predilections were well known— were included among the nine invited competitors in order that the "'battle of the styles' should be well balanced." Daniel Burnham submitted an uncompromising neoclassical design.

The Cram, Goodhue, and Ferguson designs dominated the Point campus, but the firm did not complete its work because of a disagreement over fees. The dispute brewed for thirty years without definitive outcome except to confirm for Cram the wisdom of advice for those who had won government competitions. He wrote an account of "the West Point affair," he said,

". . . . to show how wise and accurate in their diagnosis were those who, when by a miracle we won the great competition, had little to say except 'Beware!'"

Stanford White, of McKim, Mead and White, designed the new buildings at the Army War College in Washington, D.C. So as not to impede the view of the new college, White located the white-columned officers' houses to the side of the entrance gate. According to historian Constance McLaughlin Green, "The day he [White] discovered that the War Department had refused to tear down the obstructing old arsenal buildings and the grim four-square red brick prison in which the conspirators involved in Lincoln's assassination had been hanged, the outraged architect turned on his heel and never again set foot on the grounds."

U.S. Naval Academy, 1908.

The diploma of the United States Naval Academy, showing the small scale of the old Annapolis buildings. Fort Severn is in the background.

"It seems to have been the policy of the Government to build [at Annapolis] in the poorest way, and to place the buildings wherever there was a vacant place, with absolutely no regard to the convenient and economical working of the institution. . . . In the scheme of rebuilding, it has been the endeavor to place every building in the location best adapted to it—where it will fit in most advantageously for the routine work of the institution, and most harmoniously from the artistic standpoint."

Ernest Flagg, *"The New Naval Academy,"* Metropolitan Magazine, *February 1905*

Noon formation at the U.S. Naval Academy, exhibiting the grand, symmetrical sweep of Ernest Flagg's Beaux-Arts planning.

"The new home of the Naval Academy will be quite as notable architecturally as from other standpoints. The entire plan was evolved by Mr. Ernest Flagg of New York, and is accounted his architectural masterpiece. There are, of course, a considerable number of buildings, and these have been arranged in an elaborate group plan, designed not only to facilitate the operations of the institution, but also to present an ensemble at once harmonious, imposing and artistic . . . and the liberal space available for this setting, combined with the massive character of construction, stone being used almost exclusively, has produced a series of educational palaces which are triumphs of utility and beauty."

Metropolitan Magazine, *February 1905*

Design accepted for improvements of West Point, Cram, Goodhue, and Ferguson, architects.

CHAPEL HOTEL STABLES · HOTEL · CADET HEADQUARTERS · OLD ACADEMIC BIG FUTURE BLDG POST OFFICE · GATE WAY · NEW ACADEMIC BLDG POST HEADQUARTERS RESTAURANT · OLD RAILWAY LIBERTY STATION GATEWAY · POWER RIDING FERRY OFFICERS CULLUM HOUSE HALL STATION MESS MEMORIAL · BACHELOR OFFICERS QUARTERS · BATTERY

GATEWAY POST OFFICE RAILWAY STA. · PRIVATE BLDG · POWER HOUSE · FUTURE BLDG · CADET HOSPITAL · POST HEADQU · CADET HEADQU · CHAPEL RIDING CONSERVATORY HALL NEW ACADEMY BLDG · GYMNASIUM · OFFICERS MESS · CULLUM MEMORIAL · BACHELORS OFFICERS QUARTERS

"We were warned that, intentionally or not, the relations of the Government with architects had usually resulted either in breaking their hearts or their bank accounts. We discounted all this, however—for were we not dealing with the War Department, rather than with the Treasury or with Congress directly? Besides, we were young and this was our first Government job. We became more wise in later years."

Ralph Adams Cram, My Life in Architecture, 1936

West Point, 1945.

The nave of the chapel at West Point. This edifice and two of the cadet barracks were credited by Cram as the "individual and exclusive creation" of Bertram Goodhue. Cram designed the post headquarters, the riding hall, and the power plant. The two men worked together on all other buildings.

National War College Building, Stanford White, Washington, D.C. 1903. Although the red brick and white trim recalled colonial details, the scale and siting of this building and nearby officers' quarters were in the Beaux-Arts manner. Architect Stanford White placed the building at the tip of a point where the Anacostia River would serve as a backdrop and an unimpeded half-mile of lawn along the channel would provide a grand approach.

In his annual report of 1901, Supervising Architect James Knox Taylor announced the official return to "the classic style of architecture." The new mint in Philadelphia, he wrote, was "an illustration of the new departure in Government architecture . . . in-

comparably the best structure thus far erected by the Treasury Department." Consistent with the popular institutional style of the day, this meant Beaux-Arts design and not the austere lectures of Jeffersonian classicism.

The nonsymbolic buildings, like Edbrooke's 1890s Appraisers' Warehouse in New York, continued to reflect the new tendency toward the practical forms of the Modern Movement.

The exemplar of the dichotomy between symbolic and workaday architecture was the work of Cass Gilbert, who not only designed buildings for state and federal government but also was a major force in a new Beaux-Arts plan for Washington.

U.S. Mint, Philadelphia, 1898.

Post Office and Courthouse,
Henry Ives Cobb, Chicago,
1905, built under Tarsney Act
provisions. Replacement for
the short-lived Mullett-Potter
hybrid of the preceding period, this building would be
demolished in 1966 to make
way for a steel and glass complex designed by Mies van
der Rohe.

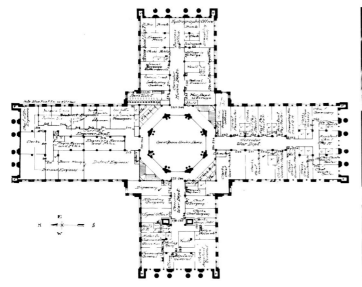

Post Office and Courthouse,
Chicago, fifth floor plan, in
the symmetrical arrangement
favored by the Beaux-Arts
school.

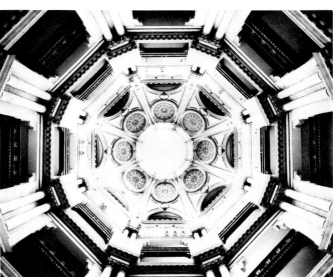

Post Office and Courthouse,
Chicago, interior of dome.

Customhouse, Cass Gilbert, New York, 1901–1907, a seven-story Beaux-Arts testimonial to the prosperity, importance, and permanence of the Port of New York. It contains one-fourth as many cubic feet as the Empire State Building. The customhouse was commissioned through a Tarsney Act design competition won by Cass Gilbert in 1899. Gilbert's appointment was delayed, reportedly because a Senator was incensed by the failure of the accepted design to incorporate a dome.

Cass Gilbert, 1859–1934. The ideal for a public building, according to Gilbert, was that it should inspire "just pride in the state, and [be] an education to oncoming generations to see these things, imponderable elements of life and character, set before the people for their enjoyment and betterment. The educational value above is worth to the state far more than it cost—it supplements the education furnished by the public schools and university [and] is a symbol of the civilization, culture and ideals of our country."

"The Custom House (New York) is a tamed mountain, a sort of Eastern mesa, and although it wears a correct Beaux Arts dress and is adorned with correct neo-Renaissance statuary, something about it seems to go straight back into prehistory; glimpsed at twilight or in the early morning, it looks as if an unknown race of giants might have quarried it up in great chunks out of the living rock of Manhattan Island."

Brendan Gill, essay for exhibit catalog, The U.S. Custom House on Bowling Green, *1976*

Customhouse, New York, details.

"The art of architecture is divided against itself. The architect resents the engineer as a barbarian; the engineer makes light of the architect as a dilettante. It is difficult to deny that each is largely in the right. The artistic insensibility of the modern engineer is not more fatal to architectural progress than the artistic irrelevancy of the modern architect. In general, engineering is at least progressive, while architecture is at most stationary."

Montgomery Schuyler, Butterfield Lecture, Union College, Schenectady, New York, March 9, 1894, published in Architectural Record, *July–September 1894*

Interior, Post Office and Courthouse, James Knox Taylor, San Francisco, 1905. In 1960, the chief Judge of the Court was instrumental in reversing a plan for relocating the court in new quarters.

"Uncle Sam has adopted Beaux Arts and we need good architects to carry it out."

Charles McKim, quoted in Charles Moore, The Life and Times of Charles Follen McKim, *1929*

"It is only since the Renaissance, and in Europe and America, that classic forms have been used as an envelope of constructions not classic, and that the attempt to develop building into architecture has been abandoned in favor of the attempt to cover and conceal building with architecture."

Montgomery Schuyler, Butterfield Lecture, Union College, Schenectady, New York, March 9, 1894, published in Architectural Record, *July–September 1894*

"The Department, after mature consideration of the subject, finally decided to adopt the classic style of architecture for all buildings as far as it was practicable to do so, and it is believed that this style is best suited for Government buildings. The experience of centuries has demonstrated that no form of architecture is so pleasing to the great mass of mankind as the classic, or some modified form of the classic, and it is hoped that the present policy may be followed in the future, in order that the public buildings of the United States may become distinctive in their character."

Report of the Supervising Architect of the Treasury, 1901

"Our Federal Government is the largest builder of buildings ever known in the world—and its building enterprises are to be far more important still; and the fact that it builds in every part of our great country gives it an unexampled influence upon the architectural art of the entire people. It cannot avoid affecting in a pronounced degree the architectural taste, knowledge, and enjoyment of the nation. . . . The Government, therefore, enjoys in its building operations a tremendous opportunity for good in the judgment of all who regard architecture as one of the important factors of the higher civilization."

Secretary of the Treasury, Annual Report on the State of the Finances, *1912*

Ammi B. Young's Boston Customhouse (1837–1847) with a 1915 skyscraper plunked down atop it, a rather peculiar resolution of the symbolism/utility quandary.

Post Office, McKim, Mead and White, New York, 1913. Although housed in classical forms, its postal services took advantage of contemporary technology. Abandoning the use of an extensive system of underground pneumatic tubes, the Post Office Department opted for motor delivery of mail in New York and other core city areas. Over the columns is engraved: "Neither snow, nor rain, nor heat, nor gloom of night stays these couriers from the swift completion of their appointed rounds."

U.S. Army Supply Base, Cass
Gilbert, Brooklyn, c. 1918.
Designed without symbolic
pretensions, the great gray
concrete buildings lacked,
Cass Gilbert wrote, any
"trickets, gewgaws and patterns and . . . fictitious cor-
kels. . . . The logic forbids
such intentions."

Legislative Building, Manila,
the Philippines, the backdrop
here for the inauguration of
President Manuel Quezon,
December 1936. Construction
of this grand reminder of the
U.S. presence, like the Panama Canal, was an outgrowth
of the Spanish-American War.
In 1905 the Philippine Commission invited Daniel Burnham to submit a plan for a
summer capital.

The second decade of the twentieth century was a particularly trying one for the executors of federal building policies. Underlying the various controversies that plagued federal architecture in this and nearly every other period was the question of what constitutes a "need" for public building, especially in small communities. Was the decision to build "dictated by local reason"—as Treasury Secretary William McAdoo discreetly said in 1916—or was it required by "government business"

or the "convenience of the people"? This was the so-called pork barrel issue.

The terrific pressure in Congress for more federal presents, especially post offices, around the nation led to adoption in 1902 of the first so-called omnibus public buildings law, which provided for increased limit of cost on over 60 buildings, and authorized approximately 150 new projects. Previously, separate bills had usually been passed for

each new project. The omnibus approach, which was continued in subsequent Congresses, facilitated the log-rolling process so vital to effective use of the pork barrel. Prior to this date, legislation had but rarely authorized more than three projects at a time.

The omnibus buildings legislation brought allegations of waste from the Treasury and cries of "pork barrel" from the press. The Treasury's reaction—to put an

annual ceiling on the dollars for contracted buildings—resulted in an attack by Congress on the Supervising Architect's office. In 1911, the Supervising Architect's work force was cut by about 15 percent and output fell by 20 percent despite a considerable backlog of authorizations.

In 1913, Congress created a Public Buildings Commission to make recommendations concerning prompt completion of buildings, standardized

Supervising Architect's Office, 1914.

procedures, and the issue of how to determine need for buildings. Chaired by McAdoo, it offered an opportunity to work out the disagreements between the executive and legislative branches over buildings policy, but only four of the seven members agreed to the whole report. The Commission recommended that buildings previously authorized be erected, but that "a board of estimates and property" be established to review the need for each proposed new building and that stand-

ardized design be rigorously implemented. In short, the commission made a number of useful recommendations but passed the buck on the specifics of reform. Back at the Treasury, McAdoo established a classification system for standard building types and locations as a departmental defense against charges of extravagance.

Still the pork barrel controversy raged. In February and March, 1916, the *AIA Journal* published articles by Charles Harris

Whitaker on "Our Stupid and Blundering National Policy of Providing Public Buildings." Whitaker blasted the government for renting too much and building too little at Washington and for building too much and renting too little in small towns across the country.

The attacks prompted Representative Frank Clark, Chairman of the House Committee on Public Buildings and Grounds, to take the House floor to rebut the "storm of ridicule

and abuse." He denied that the omnibus bills were a matter of "'you tickle me and I'll tickle you'," and he laid the blame for extravagance and especially for delay at the door of the Treasury Department's Supervising Architect's Office. Clark noted that no public building legislation had been enacted since 1913. Despite his eloquent declarations, the next omnibus bill did not pass until 1926.

Federal Building, Brunner and Tryon, Cleveland, Ohio, 1905, the result of a Tarsney Act design competition. Although it was a typical federal building for a large, early-twentieth-century city, similar buildings could be found in smaller cities of the same period. The Cleveland building was intended to be an element in a new civic plan, and architect Brunner was appointed to serve on the plan commission—along with architects Daniel Burnham and John Carrère. In 1900 the population was 381,768.

"The building operations of the Government outside of Washington, D.C. are found to be as follows:

"State Department: No outside buildings.

"Treasury Department: Post offices, customhouses, United States courthouses, Public Health Service quarantine stations and marine hospitals, mints, assay offices, subtreasuries, appraisers' stores and barge offices, immigration stations for the Department of Labor, now constructed under the Supervising Architect's Office, and life saving stations, now constructed by the Life Saving Service.

"War Department: Garrisoned posts, 168; arsenals, 12 (total value of arsenals, $12,125,177.96); coast defenses, 28; West Point.

"Department of Justice: Three United States penitentiaries, 6 courthouses in Alaska, 1 courthouse and jail in Alaska, 10 jails in Alaska, 2 jails in Oklahoma, 2 detention hospitals in Alaska.

"Post Office Department: Buildings constructed and maintained by the Treasury Department.

"Department of the Navy: Stations, coaling stations, barracks, hospitals, naval proving grounds, etc., including Annapolis; value of buildings and dry docks, $69,304,390.

"Department of the Interior: Indian Service, 5,100 buildings, value $10,845,374.48; Glacier National Park, 25 buildings, value $8,710; Bureau of Education: Alaska school service, 76 buildings, aggregate cost $256,068.22; Bureau of Mines, two buildings, cost of one $7,366.48; other turned over by the War Department. Hot Springs Reservation, six buildings, cost $110,359.28; total, $11,227,878.46.

"Department of Agriculture: Weather Bureau, 64 buildings; Bureau of Animal Industry, three animal quarantine stations; Forest Service, 1,200 cabins; Morgan horse farm in Vermont; two experiment stations in Maryland.

"Department of Commerce: Seventy residences, 39 fish hatcheries, 5 laboratories, 100 miscellaneous buildings.

"Department of Labor: Seven immigration stations, constructed by the Treasury."

From *Report of the Public Buildings Commission,* 1914.

U.S. Government Building Florence, Alabama, 1918, housing the Post Office, Courthouse, Recruiting Office, and Corps of Engineers. In 1910 the population of Florence was 6,689.

Federal Building, Cheyenne, Wyoming, 1906. Grand buildings in small cities were a tribute to the power of Congress over the Supervising Architect's analysis of need. Much of the extravagant use of detail and space so admired today were the result of Congressional pressures, which were seldom related to aesthetics. The population of Cheyenne in 1900 was 14,087.

"Standardization is the hope of the layman and the despair of the architect."

Report of the Public Buildings Commission, *1914*

"There are a half dozen places in my district where Federal buildings are being erected or have recently been constructed at a cost to the Government far in excess of the actual needs of the communities where they are located. Take Uvalde, my home town, for instance. We are putting up a post-office down there at a cost of $60,000.00, when a $5,000.00 building would be entirely adequate for our needs. This is mighty bad business for Uncle Sam, and I'll admit it; but the other fellows in Congress have been doing it for a long time and I can't make them quit. Now we Democrats are in charge of the House and I'll tell you right now, every time one of these Yankees gets a ham I'm going to get a hog."

Representative James A. Garner of Texas, speech reported in Metropolitan Magazine, *February 1916*

"He [the country boy] sees very little of the blessings of government beyond the post office and the rural carrier, and if I had the power I would erect for every presidential post office through the broad domain of the Republic a Government building representative of the sovereignty and the glory of this great country. From Maine to California and from the Great Lakes to the Gulf, in every town of sufficient importance to have the President name the postmaster, I would erect a suitable but not extravagant building, and from its apex the Stars and Stripes, proud emblem of the glory of the Republic, should forever wave an inspiration to the youth of the land. Suppose here

and there it should be a little more expensive in dollars and cents to own a building than it is to rent. Is it worth nothing to inspire patriotism and love of country in the hearts and minds of the youth of the country? No youth or citizen ever looked upon a Federal building in which the business of his country was being conducted but that he became a better American."

Representative Frank Clark of Florida, Chairman of the House Committee on Public Buildings and Grounds, Congressional Record, *January 17, 1916*

"I am convinced that methods pursued by the Congress for the past 15 years of providing Federal buildings through so-called omnibus public-building bills have resulted in the construction of many public buildings in small towns and localities where they are not needed, and at a cost which is clearly unjustified by any actual requirements of the communities in which they are erected. The conclusion is irresistible that authorizations for public buildings in these small communities are too frequently dictated by local reasons and without regard to the best interests of the Government.

"In the past two decades the Congress has authorized and appropriated approximately $180,000,000 for public buildings, and the major part of this great sum has been expended on costly structures in small localities where neither the Government business nor the convenience of the people justified their construction, and while the initial cost of these buildings represents a large waste of public funds, this is not the worst of it. The most serious aspect is this: The annual operation and maintenance of these buildings impose on the Treasury a permanent and constantly increasing burden."

Secretary of the Treasury William McAdoo, Annual Report on the State of the Finances, *1916*

"And, Mr. Speaker, I want to say here that the post-office building of the future should be essentially a workshop. It should be constructed with a view to utility and comfort rather than with a view to outside architectural beauty. The truth of the whole business is that the waste and extravagance of the past is chargeable directly to the fact that the esthetic dreamers who have been in the Supervising Architect's Office have sacrificed the utility of the building and the comfort of the workers therein to the gimcracks and curly cues of architecture. [Laughter and applause.] Mr. Speaker, I venture to say that with a common-sense system of standardization and a competent, level-headed architect with executive ability in charge of the Supervising Architect's Office we can effect a saving of at least 40 per cent in the building operations of the Government, have more and better buildings, and catch up with the work in less than three years. . . . It is absolutely nonsensical to tell me that a post-office building suitable for a certain-sized town in New Hampshire would not be equally suitable for the same-sized town in Rhode Island, or that a post-office building for a certain-sized town in Mississippi would not be equally suitable for a town of like size in Louisiana. A plan of this kind would save to the Government annually a large sum in the drafting of new plans, to say nothing of the immense saving in the matter of time."

Representative Frank Clark of Florida, Chairman of the House Committee on Public Buildings and Grounds, Congressional Record, *January 17, 1916*

While Washington was a far cry from the embryo capital of 1800—the 1893 Baedecker guide called the city "one of the most beautiful in the United States"—the central Washington of 1900 had not yet taken on the overwhelming white marble image that Americans now associate with it. The Washington of official architecture was, as Henry James observed, essentially a "background" city. Most improvements—like the sanitary system and a Centennial proposal for a shopping street bridge across the Potomac—were for the benefit of the residents. Many of the spaces L'Enfant had left were still waiting "for that aggrandizement and embellishment which the increase of the wealth of the Nation will permit it to pursue at any period, however remote."

Celebration of the District's centennial in 1900 renewed interest in L'Enfant's original grand conceptions and the potential of visible expression in the nation's capital of the power and dignity of government. Combining with the grandiose dreams of the "city beautiful" movement—to which, in turn, Washington planning provided a major impetus —this interest resulted in several plans for central Washington prior to the historic McMillan Commission planning proposals of 1902. A particularly ambitious and popular proposal by hardware merchant Franklin Webster Smith was fittingly entitled, "The Aggrandizement of Washington." It was published by Congress in 1900. At the December 1900 AIA convention, plans for Washington were presented by Cass Gilbert, Paul J. Pelz of Library of Congress fame, and others.

A major renovation brought the President's House to a state of palatial splendor. In 1902, following a decade of proposals, President Theodore Roosevelt secured Congressional approval of funds and hired Charles McKim to rehabilitate the century-old structure and to provide more office, residence, and entertainment space. "I am a simple man," Roosevelt reportedly said to McKim, "and I want simplicity in the White House. I don't want extravagance." "Certainly," McKim answered, "but you must realize that simplicity is expensive. Pine can be sawed and gilded quite cheaply, but plain surfaces must be thoroughly made."

The building also received a new official designation when Roosevelt adopted "The White House" to replace the "Executive Mansion" label given to it by Madison in 1818.

Between 1895 and 1897, nineteen artists were commissioned to do 112 murals in the Library of Congress. A similar program of mural painting was undertaken in the Capitol from 1901 to 1905. A contemporary critic waxed eloquent at "the spirit of art and labor" he viewed in the Library effort. "It was something as it must have been in Florence or Venice in the Renaissance," he said. On the Capitol grounds a memorial to Ulysses S. Grant was the occasion for a design competition. The winner set a record for size and exuberance.

Meanwhile slums grew within sight of the Capitol itself.

From the District of Columbia Centennial Program, 1900.

Rendering "gratuitously made
by Mr. Bertram G. Goodhue,
of Boston, architect" to illustrate *The Aggrandizement of
Washington, D.C.*, published
in 1900 as a Senate docu-
ment.

Design for a National Pavilion
to contain restaurants, open-
air and covered; halls; apartments; and a roof garden.
From *The Aggrandizement of
Washington, D.C.*

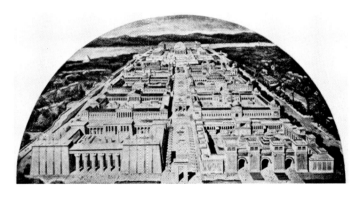

"Washington itself mean-
while—the Washington always,
I premise, of the rank outsider
—had struck me from the first
as presenting two distinct faces;
the more obvious of which was
the public and official, the
monumental, with features all
more or less majestically playing the great administrative,
or, as we nowadays put it, Imperial part. This clustered, yet
at the same time oddly scattered, city, a general impression
of high granite steps, of light
grey corniced colonnades, rather
harmoniously low, contending
for effect with slaty mansard
roofs and masses of iron ex-
crescence, a general impression
of somewhat vague, empty,
sketchy fundamentals, however
expectant, however spacious,
overweighted by a single Dome
and overaccented by a single
Shaft—this loose congregation
of values seemed, strangely, a
matter disconnected and remote,
though remaining in its way
portentous and bristling all in-
coherently at the back of the
scene. The back of the scene,
indeed, to one's quite primary
sense, might have been but an
immense painted, yet unfinished cloth, hung there to a
confessedly provisional end and
marked with the queerness,
among many queernesses, of
looking always the same;
painted once for all in clear,
bright, fresh tones, but never
emerging from its flatness. . . .
The foreground was a different
thing, a thing that, ever so
quaintly, seemed to represent
the force really in possession;
though consisting but of a
small company of people engaged perpetually in conversation and (always, I repeat, for
the rank outsider) singularly
destitute of conspicuous marks
or badges. This little society
easily became, for the detached
visitor, the city itself, the national capital and the greater
part of the story; and that,
ever, in spite of the comparatively scant intensity of its political permeation. . . . The
charming company of the foreground then, which referred itself so little to the sketchy back-
scene, the monstrous Dome and
Shaft, figments of the upper
air, the pale colonnades and
mere myriad-windowed Buildings, was the second of the two
faces, and the more one lived
with it the more, up to a certain point, one lived away from
the first. In time, and after per-
ceiving how it was what it so
agreeably was, came the recognition of common ground; the
recognition that, in spite of
strange passages of the national
life, liable possibly to recur,
during which the President
himself was scarce thought to
be in society, the particular
precious character that one had
apprehended could never have
ripened without a general consensus. One had put one's finger on it when one had seen
disengage itself from many an-
omalies, from not a few droller-
ies, the superior, the quite
majestic fact of the city of Conversation pure and simple, and
positively of the only specimen,
of any such intensity, in the
world."

Henry James of his visit to
Washington, The American
Scene, 1905

One of three designs for expansion of the White House. The structure in the foreground is a greenhouse by Mrs. Benjamin Harrison's architect, Fred D. Owen.

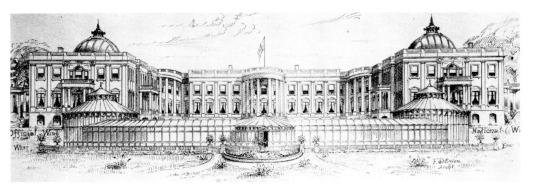

The White House with proposed additions, Arthur Dillon, 1896. This plan for expansion, conceived during the Cleveland administration, would have continued the basic style of the existing structure.

Plan for expansion of the White House conceived during the McKinley administration by Colonel Theodore A. Bingham, Superintendent of Public Buildings and Grounds. In 1902 McKim, Mead and White added an Executive wing to the White House, removing the noisy business of the Presidency from the First Family's living quarters. During the Truman administration, the entire interior of the White House was gutted and rebuilt. A complex of offices and other facilities now flank Hoban's original 170-foot by 85-foot structure, of which only the exterior walls and some woodwork remain.

The White House, Theodore Roosevelt's State Dining Room, decorated by McKim, Mead and White, 1902, to return it to the style of Jefferson's time. The Roosevelts disposed of much of the old furniture that did not harmonize with the neoclassical order of the McKim renovation. A sideboard presented by a temperance society, for example, found its way to a saloon. This outraged Representative John Wesley Gaines of Tennessee, and he complained bitterly to the House about such outrages upon items of historic and sentimental value. Representative Cannon, in bemused rebuttal to this and all compulsive preservationists, recalled that an early First Lady, "a gracious woman and incomparable housewife," had hung the family wash in the unfurnished East Room. "The wash was extensive. The room was large. So she had to use a long and valuable clothes-line." Striking a dramatic pose, Cannon asked, "Where, where, sir, I ask you, where is that clothes-line now?"

"If great Government buildings are to be scattered about the country, if a boulevard is to traverse the National Capital, if the future buildings for the Government are to be effectively placed in this beautiful city, if the White House, in which we all take such pleasure and pride, needs to be increased in size, we want each and all of these works carried out by the best artistic skill that the country can produce, and by nothing less efficient. Nor are we alone in this wish. So far as I have observed, the public aspires to even better things than our best talent produces. They want the very best. Now that architecture is a matter of active interest to great numbers of people in all parts of the country, it ought to be possible to bring to life again the admirable artistic spirit which one hundred years ago planned the city of Washington and built its earlier and best monuments."

Robert S. Peabody, President of the AIA, at the AIA Convention of 1900

"I am living in a house that has been made beautiful by Mr. McKim. It is a house to which you can invite any foreigner from any country, however artistic, and feel it is a worthy executive mansion for a great nation like this, combining dignity and simplicity, and reflecting in all its lines . . . the dignity and simplicity of the art of Mr. McKim."

President William Howard Taft, 1909

"The plans . . . for remodeling of the White House presented in 1900, were prepared under the directions of an aesthetically minded mistress of the executive mansion. They were extravagant and destructive of historic values; they would have made the President's House . . . into a cross between a railway-station and an exposition building. The American Institute of Architects condemned them vigorously. But the real veto came when Mrs. McKinley told Senator Allison (chairman of the Committee on Appropriations) that 'she didn't propose to have any hammering in the White House while she occupied it.'"

Charles Moore, "Theodore Roosevelt's Service to the National Capital," Architecture, *October 1919*

*"In the mud and scum of things,
There alway, alway something sings."*

The Ideal Rising Above Neglected Conditions; the Washington Monument in Contrast to the Dump Heap Where People are Finding Food.

[Photo by Weller]

(322)

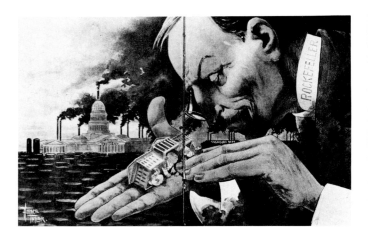

The Verdict, Horace Taylor, January 22, 1900. Oil magnate Rockefeller thinks, "What a funny little government" in Taylor's cartoon commentary on the tight control of the business trusts on Washington.

Page from *Neglected Neighbors*, a 1909 muckraking study of the Washington slums by Charles Weller, which was in stark contrast to the ebullient aggrandizement of official Washington. In 1901 the Associated Charities and the Central Relief Agency, speaking also for Washington's churches, begged the Parks Commission "in formulating plans for the systematic beautification of our city to give especial consideration to its poorer neighborhoods."

At a national conference in 1910 speakers pointed out that city planners everywhere, captured by a "superficial quest for beauty" had paid too little attention to overcrowding in vital residential areas; consequently "from a social and hygienic standpoint" a community might continue to be undesireable "though outwardly it may be 'the city beautiful.'"

Proposal for a summer White House for President Woodrow Wilson, Jacques J. B. Benedict, 1915, Mount Falcon, Colorado. Reportedly Wilson rejected the design as too extravagant for him.

The Aggrandizement of Washington

Horatio Greenough's statue of George Washington being moved, November 21, 1908. Originally placed in the Capitol rotunda in 1841, the statue was first moved to the east grounds because of the public's objection to Washington's state of undress. On November 21, 1908, the statue was once again transferred from the grounds to the Smithsonian Institution, and the base became the cornerstone of the Capitol power plant.

"Washington to-day, the Washington whose centennial Congress will appropriately celebrate during the month of December, bears no more relation to 'the Federal City' founded by the first President than the blue lump of clay does to the flashing diamond. . . . The lump of clay has been ground on the wheel of time and polished by the hand of progress, until its glistening facets make it the centre of that imperial diadem of cities,—the pride of the New World, the admiration of the Old. . . .

". . . On the map it is South; in manners and thought and ideas it is of the North, yet still bearing the mark of its birth. Its climate in summer is tropical. . . .

"In Washington, more interesting than White House or Capitol, attractive as they may be, are the men whose roofs they shadow. . . . Washington is the paradise of woman: there she holds greater sway than anywhere else; there she wields greater influence than falls to the lot of her sisters elsewhere . . . woman rules, because in Washington everything revolves around the social centre, and society and politics are inseparably interwoven. . . . Washington is the paradise of the poor man with brains. . . . In no other capital in the world, in hardly any other city, does money mean so little as it does in the capital of democracy."

A. Maurice Low, "Washington: The City of Leisure," Atlantic Monthly, December 1900

General Ulysses S. Grant
Memorial, one of the competition models and winning design. In 1901 Congress authorized a design competition
for the memorial. The jury,
which included sculptors
Daniel Chester French and
Augustus Saint-Gaudens,
chose a design by sculptor
Henry Merwin Shrady from
among submissions by
twenty-three sculptors. The
losers protested the award to
an unknown, but on a retrial
the commission was again
awarded to Shrady, who devoted the following twenty
years to completing the work,
the largest ever commissioned
by Congress to that time.
President Roosevelt and others
protested placing the memorial on the Ellipse, believing
that it would impede the view
of the Potomac from the
White House. The location
was moved to the east end of
the Mall; the resulting disrup-
tion aroused the superintendent of the nearby Botanic
Garden to protest in court the
removal of large trees. The
22½-foot-high marble superstructure was finally erected
in 1909, but the massive
bronze statue grouping was
not completely finished until
1922.

Grant Memorial competition
design by Warren, Wetmore,
and Morgan. All the losing
entries were in a similar
Beaux-Arts temple style. James
A. Wetmore was Supervising
Architect from 1915 to 1933.

The business of government was entering the age of the administrative state. By 1910 there was one federal employee per 237 people of the total population, compared with one per 502 people in 1880. This was the largest proportional change in the nation's history to date. The ratio had changed to one federal employee per 120 people by 1940, and in 1970 was one per 69, a figure that does not reflect the proliferation of government business through contracts.

Treasury cash room, c. 1906

White House offices, c. 1906. To today's viewers, photographs suggest that the White House staff was barely at the beginning of its modern expansion.

Directly out of the planning for the capital's centennial came recommendations for improvements in the central area of Washington. Senator James McMillan, Chairman of the Senate District Committee, tried to secure an appropriation for a special commission to undertake a plan for the area. Powerful "Uncle Joe" Cannon, who in 1903 would become Speaker of the House of Representatives, opposed the whole idea. According to the then Secretary of the AIA, Glenn Brown, Cannon regarded public expenditures "on anything of an artistic character a raid on Treasury." So from the House McMillan could only obtain approval for the Corps of Engineers to prepare a plan. (Since 1867 the Corps had had jurisdiction over most of the federal lands in the city.)

To secure funds for an independent professional commission, McMillan resorted to a parliamentary circumvention. He obtained a Senate resolution that allowed the District Committee to get professional advice for "plans for the development and improvement of the entire park system" of the city. The project was to be paid for out of the Committee's contingent fund.

McMillan selected his "Senate Parks Commission"—Daniel Burnham, Charles McKim, Frederick Law Olmsted, Jr., and Augustus Saint-Gaudens—a coterie at once august and talented. In spring 1901, they traveled together to study the public buildings and spaces of the great European cities and the ideas of their architects and planners. The result was a grand scheme, reworked from the original L'Enfant plan, that the commission presented to the public in the form of a grand exhibit. Reaction was largely favorable, with the striking exception of Speaker Cannon's supporters. To architects and to the public, the plans prepared by Colonel Theodore A. Bingham of the Corps of Engineers paled by comparison.

Having gone around Cannon to obtain the plan, McMillan faced the frustration of his hope of having Congress adopt the plan as a guideline for future development. Despite McMillan's death in 1902 and Cannon's continuing opposition, however, the McMillan Commission plan—by virtue of its grand vision and its expression of currently fashionable taste—became a revered model of Washington planning.

The AIA and others lobbied for a permanent agency that would act as executor of the plan. After one false start and considerable controversy, an act of 1910 provided for a Commission of Fine Arts with jurisdiction over "statues, fountains, and monuments" in the District of Columbia. This restricted mandate and its exclusion of issues relating to the Capitol and Library of Congress reflected

Congressional antipathy toward what one Representative called "a class of men that do not know anything about law, and respect it less when it interferes with what they believe to be the artistic line . . . ." With a foot in the door, however, the tastemakers gradually maneuvered their way into the inner sanctums: a series of executive orders, based on a clause in the legislation that said the commission "shall also advise generally upon questions of art" upon request of President or Congress, gave the body review jurisdiction over federal buildings, public grounds, and other design matters. The membership of the commission—Burnham, Olmsted, Cass Gilbert, Daniel French, Francis Millet, Thomas Hastings, and Charles Moore—guaranteed its commitment to the styles and assumptions of the 1902 plan. As it became reality, official architecture moved from background to foreground and abetted the decline of commercial vitality in the capital city's downtown.

Senator James McMillan, Chairman of the Senate Committee of the District of Columbia. He said of the plan that "the task is indeed a stupendous one; it is much greater than one generation can hope to accomplish."

In January 1902, the Parks Commission mounted an elaborate display of models, photographs, renderings, and bird's-eye perspectives for the public at the Corcoran Gallery of Art. Before the opening Charles McKim spent half the night on a stepladder putting the finishing touches on the 197 exhibits, which included some remarkable photographs taken by Olmsted of examples of European park planning.

"I have no hesitation in declaring . . . that it has always been my invariable opinion, and remains still to be so, that no departure from the engraved plan of the city ought to be allowed, unless imperious necessity should require it, or some great public good is to be promoted thereby."

George Washington to William Thornton, June 1, 1799

President Theodore Roosevelt being shown the Parks Commission's plans. According to Charles Moore, McMillan's political secretary for eleven years, the President was "interested, curious, at first critical and then, as the great consistent scheme dawned on him, highly appreciative."

"Hitherto our public improvements have had no definite scheme including the entire system and making each feature harmonious with all the rest. Now, however, we appear to have done with the haphazard and fitful and to have started on a scheme that time cannot render obsolete. The exhibition at the Corcoran Gallery of Art is tangible proof of good work accomplished and a bright promise of great results to follow."

Washington Post *editorial, January 16, 1902*

"Uncle Joe" Cannon, the "hardboiled hayseed." At an AIA dinner in 1905 he said, "I may preach [about economy in building]; but when you come and criticise and talk about 'sky line,' somehow or other you get the people with you."

"We can have nothing but praise for the magnificent scheme of Messrs. Burnham, McKim, Olmsted and St. Gaudens. Their part in the making of a beautiful city has been so well done that they already deserve to be ranked with L'Enfant in the gratitude of Washingtonians and of all Americans who wish to be justified of their pride in the Capital."

Montgomery Schuyler in Architectural Record, *May 1902*

"It was a sad day for the city of Washington and all the people of the country interested in the welfare of the National capital when Charles F. McKim was sent to Paris to be educated at the Ecole des Beaux Arts."

Washington Evening Star, *January 14, 1908*

Caricature coat of arms of the Senate Parks Commission, 1901, by A. M. Githens.

Charles Follen McKim.

"Uncle Dan" Burnham.

". . . When you get through with your work on the other side and come home ready to build, you will find opportunities awaiting you that no other country has offered in modern times. . . . The scale is Roman and it will have to be sustained. . . . Enough has been done to assure the development of the future City of Washington along the lines of School 'projects.' . . . The best of it is that Uncle Sam is now proud of what is being done and is going to demand the very best that millions can purchase."

Charles McKim, letter to Laurence Grant White, then finishing his studies at the Ecole des Beaux-Arts

". . . Whenever hereafter a public building is provided for and erected, it should be erected in accordance with a carefully thought-out plan adopted long before, and . . . it should be not only beautiful in itself, but fitting in its relations to the whole scheme of the public buildings, the parks and the drives of the District."

President Theodore Roosevelt, address at AIA dinner, 1905

". . . The so-called Park Commission propose to mutilate the L'Enfant Grand Vista plan by placing a great square barn in Lafayette Square for an executive office building, thereby utterly destroying the 16th Street from the White House to the heights at the city boundary.

"This structure will not only hide the fine view on 16th street, but will require the destruction of the noble old trees in Lafayette Square, and the removal of [the statue of Andrew] Jackson to some more obscure position; probably to the swamp in the Botanic Garden, to keep company with Gen. Grant in the degraded position assigned to him by the so-called Park Commission. . . .

Washington Evening Star, January 14, 1908

"President Roosevelt disposed of the matter [the fate of Pennsylvania Railroad station on the Mall] by ordering the immediate and speedy demolition of the building. Before official Washington rubbed its eyes open, the big stick had done its work. No such high-handed proceeding had occurred since Boss Shepherd, having lured the District of Columbia judges to a clambake down the Potomac, had the North Liberties Market . . . torn down while those injunction-powers were beyond reach. The 'temporary' army and navy factory-office buildings, which intrude their huge and ugly bulk up to the very steps of the Lincoln Memorial, await the advent of another constructive destroyer."

Charles Moore, "Theodore Roosevelt's Service to the National Capital," Architecture, *October 1919*

". . . The members of the Commission of 1901 were . . . definitely garden-minded. So we have this all-too-human situation: L'Enfant, when the site of Washington was a forest, dreamed of the Mall as a fashionable Parisian avenue, while the Commission of 1901, with a big city spreading all about them, dreamed of the Mall as a quiet sanctuary from the city's noise and bustle. . . .

"The word automobile does not occur in the commission's report. The nearest I can find is 'spirited horse.' . . .

"Yes, these pictures in the 1901 report, showing the Mall as it was intended to appear in 1940 or 1950, are worth study. Let us consider the view of the Mall at Fourteenth Street. Lawns undulate, the parklike drives look at least twenty feet wide, and the Monument floats in the background. And then, giving "needed life" to the charming scene, we discover:
"1 horse, pulling a dogcart
1 man, driving same
1 shepherd
1 flock of sheep!"

Elbert Peets, The Sunday Sun Magazine, *Baltimore, March 3, 1935*

View of the Mall looking east from the Washington Monument, 1906, showing nineteenth-century plantings.

While debate proceeded, from 1902 to 1910, over whether and how to implement the Parks Commission plan, several buildings were completed in central Washington. In controversies about siting, the architects established the inviolability of the 1902 plan. Their first victory was achieved in 1910, even before the plan was finished, when Alexander J. Cassatt, President of the Pennsylvania Railroad and brother of the painter Mary Cassatt, gave up his plan to construct a new station on the Mall and agreed to a site north of the Capitol (upper left of photo). The Senate and House office buildings (which flank the Capitol and Library of Congress in the north-south axis of monumental buildings at the photo's background) were also sited in harmony with the Plan. The National Museum (the domed structure at the left) established the northern line of the Mall and the new Department of Agriculture Building established the southern. The latter had existed for many years in two parts—wings built separately in the hope of forcing Congress to appropriate more for the central portion (lower right). Originally, the building was to stand closer to the center of the sacred Mall, but it was beaten back by Parks Commission forces.

Rendering of a model of the Parks Commission's proposals for the Washington Monument, the Monument Gardens, and the Mall.

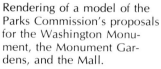

". . . It was little wonder that civic leaders in other communities soon began to think of duplicating the Washington effort in attempts to beautify their own cities. The seed of discontent with the ugliness of American cities had already been sown at the Chicago World's Fair of 1893. This seemed the time to cultivate the idea of the city beautiful throughout urban America, with the apparently vigorous growth of Washington as an example of what might be achieved by skillful planning and hard work.

"This emphasis on civic beauty coincided with a more general reform movement in the nation's cities. . . ."

John Reps, Monumental Washington: The Planning and Development of the Capital Center, 1967

The reality of Mall development included cutting down the tree growth from the nineteen century and was loudly protested in a local newspaper. Above, new trees line up like soldiers for the Parks Commission Plan.

Commission of Fine Arts, 1920. Charles Moore is seated second from left.

"As to the character of the new buildings the lesson of the past again suffices. The Capitol, the White House, the Treasury, and the Department of the Interior . . . set standards not to be improved, because they express adequately the simplicity, dignity, and power of the Government.

"This commission therefore advises that the same ideas of good order and convenience which were the guiding principles in early days be followed in future buildings, and also that the precedents established by the chief structures of the earliest days determine the architectural styles for a new building. The commission has confidence in making this latter recommendation, because the style selected by the founders is the universal architectural language for the expression of ideas of permanency, dignity, and grandeur."

Letter from the Commission of Fine Arts, District of Columbia, to the Public Buildings Commission, 1916

The *Washington Evening Star,* January 14, 1908, cartoon by Berryman. The *Star,* which had originally supported the 1902 plan, blasted the "McKim people" when they later advocated a site for the Grant Memorial that would require "the destruction of all the noble shade trees in the People's Park from the Capitol to the river to make way for a sixteen-hundred-foot wide track of desolation as bare and as hot as the Desert of Sahara." The cartoon depicts a "group of tree butchers and nature butchers . . . on their way with axes to make a 'clean sweep' as they proclaim of all the grand old trees on the Mall. . . . Architect McKim . . . is blowing a big horn—his own. He also has a big head. . . ."

Lincoln Memorial, U.S. five-dollar bill.

Perhaps the most important of the early fights over building under the 1902 plan was about the location of the Lincoln Memorial. As finally situated—in what was a triumph for the Fine Arts Commission—the Memorial formed the axis of the proposed Mall and thus seemed to insure that other pieces of Washington architecture would be fitted to the picture presented in the 1902 plan.

Congress had authorized a Lincoln Memorial Association in 1867, but nothing came of it. In 1902 another commission was formed. One proposal it received, in 1909, was from Representative James McCleary, who—after a trip to Europe to review similar projects—suggested a 72-mile-long, 200-foot-wide highway from Washington to Gettysburg. Others proposed various sites around the District of Columbia for an appropriate edifice. The Burnham group and adherents of the 1902 plan plumped for the site at the west end of the Capitol–Washington Monument axis in the Potomac Park area that had been reclaimed from marshy swamp in the late nineteenth century. Speaker Cannon, carrying on his crusade against the 1902 plan, warned that the "malarial ague" from the former swamp's mosquitoes would shake any structure there to pieces. Years of debate ended in 1912 with a decision in favor of the Potomac Park site and with approval of Henry Bacon's plan for the memorial.

The Memorial was dedicated on Decoration Day, 1922. Dr. Robert Moten, president of the Tuskegee Institute, was invited to speak at the unveiling of the Daniel Chester French statue of the Great Emancipator. Moten was relegated to a special section —one reserved for blacks, across a road from the white audience.

The Lincoln Memorial, 1923.

"Here [Lincoln Memorial], building remains subservient to sculpture, but appropriately provides a resonating void for the statue, a platform for illuminating it, a colonnade that crowns it as a laurel. . . . The monumentality of the Lincoln Memorial is a matter of composition, refinement and sculptural art, not of Greek and Roman forms, and, alas for architecture, it may owe most of its final quality to the text of the Gettysburg Address cooperating with the statue. But this may be a compliment to Bacon's architecture if he sensed, as architects never do today, that sometimes architecture should act mostly in a supporting role."

John Burchard and Albert Bush-Brown, The Architecture of America, *1961*

"There is no good reason for mixing up architecture with literature. The Gettysburg speech is beautifully phrased, but that does not make it architecture. People read it and get their heads all muddled up with recollections of school readers and Decoration Day blaze-of-glories. The realities of architecture and sculpture mean nothing to senses floating away on the dear, familiar clouds of sentimental memory. . . .

"The interior of the Lincoln Memorial is like a play written by a preacher. It was shaped by ideas, but its essential dramatic symbolism has not been fused with its architectural form. It is a series of speeches rather than a beautiful dance that has the power to draw crowds of men into its overpowering rhythm."

Elbert Peets, The American Mercury, *June 1925*

"Down the middle of the road let there be a greensward forty or fifty feet wide, a well kept lawn looking like a beautiful green carpet of velvet. To lend variety to this central line of beauty, here and there flower gardens and other decorative features could be introduced. At intervals could be erected fountains and other monumental embellishments that might be appropriate.

"On each side of this central line of beauty let there be a smooth roadway forty or fifty feet wide. . . .

"Outside of these driveways could be double-tracked electric railways, occupying a width of twenty feet each and separated from the driveways by hedges. . . .

"Bordering 'The Lincoln Road' on each side there should be a row or rows of stately trees, the rows broken at points where could be obtained fine views of mountain or valley or river. . . . If it were possible to consult Abraham Lincoln himself as to the character of memorial that would be most pleasing to him, can any one doubt what his answer would be?"

James T. McCleary, "What Shall the Lincoln Memorial Be?" (proposal for a memorial highway), The American Review of Reviews, *September 1908*

View of pyramid with Doric porticos, from the series of charcoal sketches of Lincoln Memorial proposals by John Russell Pope, March 1912. Sketch attributed to Rockwell Kent.

View of ziggurat topped with a colossal statue, from the series of charcoal sketches of Lincoln Memorial proposals by John Russell Pope, March 1912. Sketch attributed to Rockwell Kent.

AIA pageant at the Lincoln Memorial honoring architect Henry Bacon, 1923. In an article in the *AIA Journal*, Harry F. Cunningham wrote: "... Beauty had sent her spirit to sit with us, and she had cast her Mantle over and around about us. ... Little shivers still run up and down my spine every time I think of it. ... Everything was smooth and still and fairy like. ... At one stage in the dream a portly gentleman appeared. ... came out of the dream and was discovered to be Mr. Taft, the Chief Justice of the Supreme Court. ... The usher ... informed the Chief Justice that he was expected to come 'in a burst of Glory'—'No,' said Mr. Taft, 'I came in a Dodge.'"

"So long as I live I'll never let a memorial to Abraham Lincoln be erected in that God damned swamp."

Representative Joseph Cannon to Elihu Root

"I have been in many fights, some I have lost—many I have won—it may have been better if I had lost more. I am pleased I lost the one against the Lincoln Memorial."

Representative Joseph Cannon to Glenn Davis, 1915

"With the transition from republican to imperial Rome, numerous monuments were erected to the Divine Caesar. Within a much shorter time than marked the growth of the imperial tradition in America, a similar edification of patriotic memories took place.

"... In the Lincoln Memorial ... one feels not the living beauty of our American past, but the mortuary air of archaeology. The America that Lincoln was bred in, the homespun and humane and humorous America that he wished to preserve, has nothing in common with the sedulously classic monument that was erected to his memory. Who lives in that shrine, I wonder—Lincoln, or the men who conceived it: the leader who beheld the mournful victory of the Civil War, or the generation that took pleasure in the mean triumph of the Spanish-American exploit, and placed the imperial standard in the Philippines and the Caribbean?"

Lewis Mumford, Sticks & Stones, *1924*

"The Lincoln Memorial ... is a neoclassic temple, combining a Grecian Doric order with an attic in a design of such excellence that perhaps only Frank Lloyd Wright has fully succeeded in despising it."

Walter C. Kidney, The Architecture of Choice: Eclecticism in America, 1890–1930, *1974*

The Lincoln Memorial under
construction.

Robert Lincoln, son of Abraham Lincoln snapped while
attending the dedication exercises at the Lincoln Memorial.

French's sculpture of Lincoln
inside the Memorial.

French's Lincoln, detail.

Marian Anderson Singing on the Steps of the Lincoln Memorial, Easter Sunday, April 9, 1939, mural by Mitchell Jameson in the Department of the Interior.

Actor James Stewart in front of the inscription at the Lincoln Memorial, from the movie "Mr. Smith Goes to Washington."

In the decade from 1881 to 1890, the flow of immigrants into the United States swelled to reach 5,246,613, nearly twice the total for any previous intercensal decade. When the rate slowed in the next ten years, observers concluded that immigration was waning. This perception was influenced, perhaps, by the well-publicized end of the frontier. If there was no longer a "hither edge of free land," then America could no longer be the "land of opportunity." But it was not so. The flood tide of the "new" immigration from eastern and southern Europe surged again until it was cut off at the source by World War I and then blocked out by restrictive U.S. legislation.

The port of debarkation for most immigrants in this era was New York. From 1855 to 1890, New York State ushered the aliens into America through Castle Garden, a coastal fort built during the War of 1812. Following an investigation of charges of inefficiency and abuse at Castle Garden, the federal government terminated its contract with the state as of April 18, 1890. The new Federal Bureau of Immigration made Ellis Island its site of operations, but during two years of construction there, immigrants were herded through the cramped Barge Office on Manhattan.

The first Ellis Island station, with its picturesque towers and blue-slate roof, opened in 1892. It was compared by *Harper's Weekly* with "a latter-day watering place hotel." The main building itself was larger than the original island, which had been doubled by landfill. The Ellis Island buildings, made of pine, burned to the ground on June 14, 1897, without loss of life, and the Barge Office was reopened.

A competition was held—among the first under the Tarsney Act—and a contract for a new Ellis Island building was awarded to the New York firm of Boring and Tilton in August 1898. Complete fireproofing was emphasized for the new building; inside the brick exterior were concrete floors, iron railings, iron beds. By December 17, 1900, the new station was ready for use. The *New York Times* described the immigration station as carefully planned and well designed. Unfortunately, Boring and Tilton's design was meant to accommodate no more than the 500,000 newcomers per year that official estimates projected. The facilities soon were hopelessly overcrowded when the tide of immigrants rose unexpectedly. During World War II interned German families and others considered aliens were held on Ellis Island, a few as late as 1947.

Mulberry Street, New York, photo by Jacob A. Riis, early 1890s. Photographs by Riis and other muckrakers exposed the deplorable conditions in city slums that received the new immigrants.

Riis had this to say of slum accommodations: "I do not marvel much at the showing of the Ailden Tenement House Committee that one in five of the children in the rear tenement into which the sunlight never comes was killed by the house. It seemed strange, rather, that any survived."

"As a pilgrim father that missed th' first boats, I must raise my Claryon voice again' th' invasion iv this fair land be th' paupers an' anarchists iv effete Europe. Ye bet I must—because I'm here first."

Mr. Dooley (Peter Finley Dunne)

VOL. 17 NO. 440 · MARCH 22 1890 · PRICE 10 CENTS

Judge

ENTERED AT THE POST OFFICE AT NEW YORK AS SECOND-CLASS MATTER. · COPYRIGHT 1890 BY THE JUDGE PUBLISHING CO.

THE PROPOSED EMIGRANT DUMPING SITE.

STATUE OF LIBERTY—"Mr. Windom, if you are going to make this island a garbage heap, I am going back to France."

On a cover of *Judge* magazine from 1890 the Statue of Liberty assumes a less than welcoming stance for the immigrants being dumped at her feet. The U.S. Treasury, the Capitol, and a legislator form the skyline.

The Only Thing They Fear, John Tinney McCutcheon, 1929. The super-patriotism of World War I and fears of Bolshevism engendered the notorious "Palmer raids," which began on January 1, 1920, when Attorney General A. Mitchell Palmer authorized the arrest and deportation of foreign nationals considered to have questionable political and social values.

Ellis Island, the original pine
structure, which was opened
in 1892 and burned to the
ground in 1897.

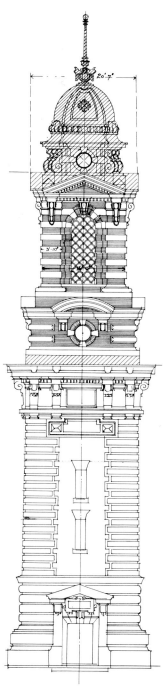

Ellis Island, main building,
Boring and Tilton, 1898–
1900.

Ellis Island, main building, architects' drawing, ink on
linen, 1899.

Commissioner William Williams conducting President Taft on a tour of Ellis Island. Williams, a young Wall Street lawyer, was appointed in April 1902 as Commissioner of Ellis Island. This appointment was part of a more general effort by President Roosevelt to eradicate corruption in the Bureau of Immigration. Williams crushed the graft and abusive practices on the island. By August, *Leslie's Weekly* said that "the aliens are now treated in the main quite as considerately as would be crowds of like size and character in the heart of the city."

Ellis Island, Main Hall, c. 1910. This enormous waiting and processing room held 5,000 people. It was 200 feet long and 100 feet wide, with a 56-foot-high vaulted ceiling. For many newcomers it was the largest room they had ever seen.

Immigrants were tagged and numbered, 240 at a time, and were then processed, which included medical inspection and various interrogations and tests. Though every effort was made to process new arrivals quickly, they frequently had to spend the night. There were accommodations for 600 sleepers, as well as food, baths (which accommodated 200 at a time), and a laundry.

Slovak women, winter 1907,
Ellis Island.

Christmas dinner at Ellis Island for Bulgarian and Bohemian newcomers. c. 1907.

Wilson's Inauguration Day parade on Pennsylvania Avenue, 1917. The tower of W. J. Edbrooke's 1899 post office appears in the background.

World War I saw the arrival of the tank and the airplane. But it was primarily a war of attrition that depended on the productive capacities of the nations involved and their ability to deliver the goods to the front.

At the beginning of 1917, the Corps of Engineers consisted of 2,500 men. By November 1918, 300,000 men were in the Corps. In less than two years, these new men had been trained at bases established in France. Courses were Bridging, Camouflage, Flash and Sound Ranging, Mining, Topography, and Searchlight.

During their overseas wartime assignment the Engineers constructed 6,000 feet of docks, provided space for 280,000 hospital beds, and erected 16,000 barracks. The Corps built roads, bridges, and railroad supply lines. They were responsible for water supply and electrical service. They designed and constructed machine-gun emplacements, turrets, and observation posts. Many construction projects reflected the advent of the airplane as a tactical

weapon: the art of camouflage, for instance, required new attention, and the Corps enlisted the services of an American artist who had lived in Paris for several years.

The Great War also forced the government into the unprecedented business of constructing housing—a new role justified legally under the war powers enumerated in the Constitution. Hundreds of thousands of workers in war-related industries had poured into areas that did not have facilities to house them, with the result that many returned home or

were underproductive. Congress only reluctantly responded to this acute shortage a year after the war had started by authorizing two agencies to improve access to factories, to upgrade existing housing, and to construct new housing. A little over half of the 360,000 workers and their families served by these agencies gained access to war industries through improved transportation rather than new housing.

Frederick Law Olmsted, Jr., came to Washington to work with builder Otto Eidlitz on emergency construction of industrial

President Woodrow Wilson asks Congress to declare war against Germany, April 1917.

housing. A Camp Planning section was set up in the War Department to handle projects at army stations. A new executive agency, the U.S. Housing Corporation, was assigned the job of providing new housing at industrial sites. Olmsted managed its Town Planning Division. Prominent architects, landscape architects, and engineers came to work for his division and for another executive organization, the Emergency Fleet Corporation, set up under the U.S. Shipping Board to oversee accommodation of in-creased numbers of shipyard workers within communities. Unlike the Housing Corporation, the Emergency Fleet Corporation carried out its mandate through construction loans to shipbuilding companies. However, the agency's regulations were so strict that companies were, practically speaking, government agencies.

Many of the prominent architects and planners in key posts in the American war-housing agencies saw their task as the beginning of a new social age. They were influenced by "garden city" planning of war housing in Great Britain, where attempts were made not only to provide pleasant housing for workers, but also to create entire planned communities.

The Armistice brought an end to the housing experiments, although projects that were well along were allowed to proceed to completion. In the Red Scare atmosphere of the postwar years, Congress launched an antagonistic investigation of the "socialist" ideas embodied in public construction by the Housing Corporation. The homes subsidized by the Emergency Fleet Corporation remained in the hands of the private shipbuilding companies or people to whom these companies sold them. However, the Housing Corporation, rather than selling off the homes to "speculators," continued to rent the dwellings it had constructed until they could be sold directly to homeowners. "It has been well said," wrote Secretary of Labor James J. Davis, "that home ownership is the most effective antidote for Bolshevism." The agency was finally liquidated in 1945.

The classic image of Uncle Sam appeared on this 1917 recruiting poster by artist James Montgomery Flagg. It is believed to be a self-portrait of Flagg.

Human Statue of Liberty, Camp Dodge, Iowa, 1918. Photographer Arthur Mole took the picture from the top of a 60-foot wooden tower he built. To obtain perspective from this height the area laid out allowed base to shoulder, 150 feet; right arm, 340 feet; right thumb, 35 feet; torch and flame combined, 980 feet. The number of men in the various parts: flame of torch, 1,200 men; torch, 2,800; right arm, 1,200; body, head, and balance of figure, 2,000. Mole traveled from base to base composing living photos, including flags, shields, portraits, and the Liberty Bell. Soldiers were instructed what to wear and where to stand within taped outlines. The photographs took only a few days to set up; arranging men and actual shooting seldom took more than an hour.

Hospital base in Gironde, France, 1918. During the war the Corps of Engineers provided facilities for 280,000 beds overseas. After the war ended, the Corps helped rebuild the French road system, bridges, and public utilities.

Engineers replacing masonry bridge at Grandpré, France. Hundreds of bridges of all types were built in the drive across France, some of them literally overnight.

A Housing Corporation development under construction in Waterbury, Connecticut.

Layout of Atlantic Heights, in Portsmouth, New Hampshire, built under contract with the Emergency Fleet Corporation. The influence of the British "new towns" idea is evident here in the curvilinear streets, the emphasis on open space, and the small-town ambience.

James Marston Fitch, in *American Building: The Historical Forces That Shaped It,* observed of the war housing program that "these few concrete examples were important out of all proportion to their size. They were widely published, criticized, admired. They had the salutary effect of shifting the architect's attention from esthetic abstractions to social reality."

"Apart from the immediate accommodation of war workers, the significance of the federal war-housing program was threefold. For one thing, the federal government, for the first time in American history, accepted responsibility for maintaining the standards and supply of working-class housing, thus establishing a precedent for the more elaborate and continuous federal housing program of the 1930s. More importantly, the construction and sanitary standards, the aesthetic and social ideals that guided the program resulted in housing contrasting sharply with the ordinary working-class accommodations provided by the speculative commercial builder; moreover, the architectural and planning directors of the two housing agencies regarded the individual house as part of a total community, thus contributing to the development of city planning in this country. Finally, the federal housing program sparked a debate on the role of government in housing which, if not productive of immediate results, was productive of ideas."

Roy Lubove, "Homes and 'A Few Well Placed Fruit Trees': An Object Lesson in Federal Housing," Social Research, *1960*

U.S. SHIPPING BOARD
EMERGENCY FLEET CORPORATION

WAR WORKER

The "handsome, strong, cloth service flag" that the Chairman of the Shipping Board sent to Emergency Fleet Corporation workers with six months of experience in the yards who sent him letters describing their experiences and offering suggestions for improvement. Forty responses claimed that some workers were loafing. Twenty complained about health and safety matters. Eighty asked to be released from the draft.

A ZR-3 dirigible and Navy landing crew at Lakehurst, New Jersey, October 15, 1924. Hangars housing these early airships were among the largest structures in the world at the time they were built. In style they resembled the first aircraft hangars built by the U.S. military in 1918.

Victory parade passes under a temporary arch on Pennsylvania Avenue, Washington, D.C., September 1919.

STARVED CLASSICISM

6

Hoover Dam, originally named Boulder Dam, Bureau of Reclamation, Colorado, 1933, part of the federal government's elemental transformation of the arid west. To meet the housing needs of 5,000 isolated workers the Bureau also planned, built, and administered a new town complete with parks, paved and lighted streets, schools, and churches. The Bureau maintained ownership and management of "Clean Green Boulder City," Nevada, until 1960.

"What do we want with this vast worthless area—this region of savages and wild beasts, of deserts, of shifting sands and whirlwinds of dust, of cactus and prairie dogs? To what use could we ever hope to put these great deserts . . . ?" (Daniel Webster, 1854)

U.S. Mint, San Francisco, 1937. Terra-cotta reproductions of United States coins, inserted in the upper part of each of the piers between the windows, provide the barest ornament—in contrast to the richly decorated mint erected at San Francisco during Alfred Mullett's tenure as Supervising Architect.

By the 1920s the federal role in transforming the American environment was assuming immense proportions and implications. Massive dams, extensive highway systems, multitudinous new buildings pervaded the land. The antecedents were nineteenth century, but the scale of endeavor was new, reflecting the burgeoning growth of the administrative state. The facelessness of this massed power recalled scholar H. P. L'Orange's description of the change between the early and later Roman Empire: "... the new 'block-style' in art emerged contemporary with the formation of massive structures in the state and community, and ... in both contexts the traditional individualization and articulation of the various elements were gradually reduced or disappeared altogether."

To its already deep involvement in highway construction, the federal government added its support to the infant air industry in the form of safety aids to navigation and contracts to carry U.S. mail. Out of these modest beginnings would grow the extensive government aid for airport construction and subsidy of air transportation that would contribute to the decline of railroads much as the support of the rail industry had once affected the fate of water transportation. In the resulting spatial reorientation, city growth would be freed from dependence on rail and water transportation arteries, and the effective distances of the nation would shrink dramatically.

Growth was also freed of dependence on local water supply as the Bureau of Reclamation continued to transform the topography and productivity of arid lands and to transmit the power generated from the vast energy stored behind the concrete walls of its massive dams. At the time of its construction, Boulder, later Hoover, Dam was the world's highest dam and its construction contract the largest ever awarded by the federal government. The Bureau's Grand Coulee Dam became the largest concrete structure in the world; and, measured by volume, Fort Peck Dam is still the largest dam in the world. Equally awesome were the building activities of the Corps of Engineers, extended into major flood control work by 1917 legislation. After it was called to respond to the devastating Mississippi River floods of the 1920s, the Corps's levee building reached the scale of the largest earth moving project in human history.

Twenty-four years of research and design by federal engineers and geologists preceded passage of the Boulder Canyon Project in 1928, which was representative of the multipurpose ambitions of the Bureau of Reclamation. The harnessing and diversion of the Colorado River involved seven states and Mexico to achieve a new level of control over the natural environment. The Boulder Canyon Project not only provided the reclamation goals of flood and siltation control, water storage and irrigation; it also generated unheard of amounts of hydroelectric power. The Southwest would not just have farms; it would have twentieth-century electric farms, city lights, and the industries that cheap power would make possible.

The water supply versus wilderness dispute of the pre–World War I period continued, and a new issue emerged. Throughout the 1920s the intensified involvement of the federal government in resource development raised serious questions about the propriety of translating public investment into private profit. The Teapot Dome scandal, involving the leasing of public lands for oil exploration, represented one extreme of the issue in the abuse of the public resource/private gain system. The wartime Muscle Shoals complex, including government-built nitrate plants and Wilson Dam, represented the other extreme, with proposals for straightforward public enterprise. Farmers, led by the Chairman of the Committee on Agriculture, Senator George Norris of Nebraska, urged public completion of the dam; private utilities fought against government control; and millionaire Henry Ford offered to lease the whole project.

Although river basin planning held forth the promise of regional economic and social well-being through water control and development, the attempts to convert Wilson Dam and the wartime plants at Muscle Shoals to peacetime use under public ownership were unsuccessful throughout the 1920s. In 1931 President Herbert Hoover vetoed a Norris-sponsored bill for public ownership with the admonition, "That is not liberalism, it is degeneration." With the massive economic privations of the 1930s, crisis overtook debate, and the Muscle Shoals facilities became part of the publicly owned system of the new Tennessee Valley Authority.

Nor, in the 1920s, was the nation eager to spend public dollars for constructing new buildings. Between 1913 and 1926 Congress authorized no new spending for public buildings. Meanwhile, in 1920 the Treasury reported a "wonderful growth in the public business" and a resulting rent bill for federal office space of $20 million in 1923.

Two Public Buildings Commissions—one for the District of Columbia and the other for the rest of the country—reported to Congress by the end of the War with recommendations for a revamped building program that would base building location and size decisions on "business considerations" rather than Congressional logrolling. The 1926 Public Buildings Act ordered the Treasury Department to implement the "business considerations" policy—a response, after nearly 75 years, to Alexander Bowman's protests over unneeded projects in the 1850s.

Responding to Treasury and Post Office Department reports of space requirements, the Hoover Administration and Congress increased funding for the program in 1928 and, under the impetus of the Depression, again in 1930 and 1931. The final figure stood at over $700 million. In 1933, the program was placed under the planning authority of the New Deal's Public Works Administration. Congressional pork barrel had been traded for Executive pump-priming, and "business considerations" moved back into the shadows of public building policy.

Bought with this money were some 1,300 new buildings. The federal presence was manifested architecturally in 1,085 communities that had not previously "owned" a federal building. The stock of buildings under Treasury Department control—the major, general-use federal structures—was nearly doubled. In terms of establishing the image of the United States government, this program was the most important undertaken since the first few decades under the Constitution.

It was to those early years of federal building that the officials in charge turned in their search for an architectural style. Time after time, they proclaimed their adherence to the classical, claiming it was either historically correct or uniquely expressive of democratic values, or both. The style held such great sway that even huge dams were draped in classical raiment.

The actual building designs, however, reflected other influences as well. One was the increased scale of government and society. Not only did the buildings take up more ground and air space, but they now often housed collections of seemingly indistinguishable government bureaus rather than a few, discrete public offices. The name "Federal Building" began to be used in place of "Post Office, Courthouse, and Customhouse." To draw a further comparison with H. P. L'Orange's description of architecture in the later Roman Empire: ". . . buildings lose their organic corporality, the clear articulation of their parts, and the functional relationships among them; they are gradually dissolved into a system of plain, simple walls . . . the traditional decor, friezes and architectural ornament, is absorbed more or less completely by the massive wall. . . ."

The other major influence was the emergence in the twenties and thirties of the "modern" or "international" style of architecture. This movement's early rallying cries, "ornament is crime" and "less is more," alienated the Beaux-Arts-trained architects who dominated the profession in America as well as in Europe. But its view of buildings as space-enclosing envelopes fit in well with the functional needs of mass organizations for interchangeable work areas. "Modern" architects expressed this interior requirement and the new technologies of construction in exterior surfaces that were thin, flat, continuous, and unembellished.

The "traditionalists"—including the period's leadership and rank and file in the Supervising Architect's Office—rejected the arguments of the modernist manifestoes in part, it seems, out of an unwillingness to change—but also, in part, out of a genuine belief that the modernist vocabulary failed to take account of the symbolic role of a building's design. The debate over the modernist challenge dominated discussions of public architecture through World War II and well into the postwar period.

It was not until the late 1950s that the government would begin encouraging overtly "modern" design. But beginning early in the thirties, modernists' ideas were infiltrating traditionalists' drafting rooms. Undifferentiated work spaces—though not the interpenetrating, asymmetrical volumes characteristic of the modern movement—appeared early in ground plans for the new public building program. Slightly later, but more gradually, the facades became simplified, their classical ornaments turning angular and disappearing into the masonry, their walls becoming more planar and their window openings shallow and anonymous. What resulted was a gaunt, underfed, "starved" classicism, denoted as much by white masonry and the rhythm of wall and window as by vestigial columns. Today, it is this starved classicism, rather than the correct Roman forms advocated by Jefferson, the Greek temples of Robert Mills, or the ebullient Beaux-Arts style of the early 1900s, that most Americans think of when they think of federal architecture at all.

Borglum at work. To bring the
sculpture to its present state
required these preliminary
models, hundreds of sketches,
another set of model heads
each five feet tall for transfer-
ring measurements to full
scale more easily, and fifteen
years of labor by Borglum and
his team of engineers. Borglum received about
$170,000 for this major work
of his life.

The sculpting of four gi-
gantic presidential heads
into a granite cliff in South
Dakota's Black Hills would
never have begun in 1927
without the passionate tenacity of sculptor John
Gutzon de la Mothe Bor-
glum. The project would
just as surely never have
been completed in 1941
without being financed by
the federal government.
The Mt. Rushmore monu-
ments, originally promoted
piecemeal by South Da-
kota Chambers of Com-
merce, eventually became
a million-dollar national
shrine, 85 percent paid for
by Congressional appro-
priation.

Gutzon Borglum took
every opportunity to pro-
mote his efforts and pulled
publicity stunts to gain
support for "America's
Shrine for Political De-
mocracy." When President
Coolidge was vacationing
in the Black Hills in 1927
and considering a visit to
Rushmore, Borglum flew
in low over the western

White House and dropped
a wreath of flowers on the
lawn. Coolidge dedicated
the monument later in the
summer at the commence-
ment of drilling and of-
fered Washington's
support.

Mt. Rushmore, in Bor-
glum's eyes, would immor-
talize America's "empire
builders," the Presidents
most responsible for the
"creation, preservation
and expansion of the
Union." When several
questioned the wisdom of
enshrining President Roo-
sevelt so soon after his
death, Borglum countered
that T. R. was "preemi-
nently an all-American
President," representing
the "restless Anglo-Saxon
spirit that made the ocean-
to-ocean republic" inevi-
table.

Others considered but not
chosen for an equal place
in the Dakota sun include
various western heroes,
Calvin Coolidge, Susan B.
Anthony, and F. D. R.

The sculptor directing work on the Lincoln face. The faces were carved to the scale of men 465 feet tall. From chin to top each head is about 60 feet. Each nose is 20 feet long and each mouth 18 feet wide, and the eyes are 11 feet across. Borglum believed, "A monument's dimensions should be determined by the importance to civilization of the event commemorated."

"How long will it last, and why did we make it large? We made it large so that it would be as large as the mountain and last as long as the mountain. The mountain has been there forty million years, geologists tell us, and it wears down at the rate of an inch in a hundred thousand years, so your children's children and their children on, and the peoples of the world, will find here on this mountaintop the story of . . . the unspoiled American dream."

Gutzon Borglum, speaking to an assembly of Boy Scouts in 1937

"In early human monuments, as the Pyramids, it was required that they should be enduring, and the expression of their import was sought solely in magnitude. It is but natural that the symbol to express greatness which first presented itself to the mind of man should be physical magnitude. Modern architects are still somewhat possessed by an art superstition of this kind."

Leopold Eidlitz, The Nature and Function of Art, *1881*

Mt. Rushmore, work in
progress.

*Disturbing Results of Sculptor
Gutzon Borglum's Newspaper
Campaigns: A View of the
Rocky Mountains, etc.,* Liberty
Magazine, October 22, 1927.
Borglum stirred up equal parts
of enthusiasm and controversy
in the press wherever he
went. He was dismissed from
work on the huge Confederate
Generals of Stone Mountain,
Georgia, after demanding too
much money, and Atlantans
wrote furious letters of warning to South Dakota. When
first shown Mt. Rushmore,
Borglum quickly sketched
where Washington and Lin-
coln might fit, then pointed to
another peak and said he
would do Teddy Roosevelt on
horseback over there, which
inspired this cartoon.

In April 1932, *The Federal Architect* magazine published the results of a poll "to find out what the architectural profession thought of itself." None of the twenty-six well-known architects and firms who responded showed any proclivity for the "modern." The Lincoln Memorial topped the poll. In the first nine places, the only "modern" representatives, in the view of the magazine editors, were the Empire State Building, the Nebraska Capitol, and the Chicago Daily News Building. "We are . . . pleased," the magazine commented, "that the modern selections were of the calm and restrained type, designed as architecture and not merely for the purpose of being different and advanced." In fact, the buildings the editors labeled "modern" do not now appear to have been in the mainstream of the Modern Movement at all, nor were they embraced by the modernists at the time.

Rhetoric, compromise, and inconsistency were typical of the battle that raged between the modernists and traditionalists in the post–World War I era. In the public sector the conflict was further complicated by a concern for public image, which weighted the results in favor of tradition. Synthesis of modern and traditional and symbolic produced a classicism diluted in all these intents, overscaled to serve a growing bureaucracy, and unreadable as a commonly understood architectural lecture on public virtues. Indeed, to in-

sure survival of the vestigal message of an earlier classicism, the old virtues were now incised as words in the new building stones and portrayed in literally instructive art.

The adoption of starved classicism as an official style coincided with the creation of a new kind of federal presence—cemeteries on foreign soil. Created by Congress in 1923, the American Battle Monuments Commission erected memorials at eight military cemeteries already established in Europe by the War Department and placed monuments on the battlefields as well. General Pershing was appointed first chairman of the commission; he named Paul Cret its architectural consultant. Cret, whose work is more fully discussed in the next section, served until his death in 1945 and designed several of the World War I memorials. In 1945 the firm of Harbeson, Hough, Livingston & Larson replaced Cret as architectural consultants to the Commission.

Postcards of the period display the new federal buildings, which fashioned a pervasive modern image of federal architecture. Although Washington acquired several starved-classical buildings during the 1920s and 1930s, the city's existing architectural ambience seemed to draw most designers toward a more ornamental solution. Away from the capital, designs for federal buildings crossed over to the more austere end of the classical spectrum. Shown here, from top, are post offices in Minneapolis, Minnesota; and Waterbury, Connecticut; Norfolk, Virginia; and Manchester, New Hampshire.

Belief in the appropriateness of the "classical" for federal buildings was so strong during this period that some nonconforming buildings from earlier eras were eyed as heathens ripe for conversion. The Memphis, Tennessee, Post Office, Courthouse, and Customhouse was remodeled in the new style, as shown in these photos from *The Federal Architect* magazine, July 1932. Most of the older buildings were viewed as heretics, though, and were condemned to death by demolition.

"The reason for the unimaginative dullness of most public buildings has been due to irrelevant political influences, to a complete lack of taste upon the part of members of representative bodies, to the conservative leanings of most public administrators, to the application of the aesthetic canons of the genteel tradition by fine art commissions, and to the bitter fact that public architecture cannot rise higher than the unfortunate state of the art itself. The great majority of public buildings have been characterized by a dusty formalism and routine flatulence: our worst architectural failing of all is a sentimental pretentiousness, and in public buildings this is carried to its extreme point and there canonized."

Frederick Gutheim, "The Quality of Public Works," Magazine of Art, April 1934

Page Two   The FEDERAL ARCHITECT   *July, 1932*

UNITED STATES POST OFFICE, COURT HOUSE AND CUSTOM HOUSE,
MEMPHIS, TENN.
Office of Supervising Architect, Architects

The building pictured above was the result of a remodelling of the structure below. The arches of the old building fixed the motif for the first story treatment and set the spacing of the columns above. The structural columns and the construction generally of the old building was retained and extended. The excellent effect of the completed building as compared with the uninspiring original shows the possibilities of good earnest architecture.

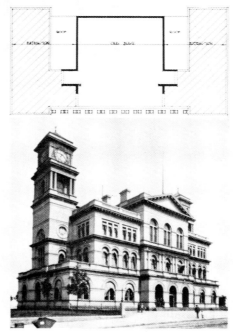

Twentieth-Century Gladiators

288–289

In 1917, the Fine Arts Commission's annual report displayed a "suggestion" to remodel Alfred Mullett's mansard-roofed State, War, and Navy Building to resemble the Treasury Department on the other side of the White House. The sketch was prepared by Commission member John Russell Pope. The same year, Waddy B. Wood came up with a similar, but more detailed plan (bottom illustration). The Treasury sponsored the Wood proposal in 1929 and Congress authorized funding in 1930, but rescinded it when estimates of renovation costs started to increase.

Sketch for remodeling the State, War, and Navy Building, John Russell Pope.

Sketch for remodeling the State, War, and Navy Building, Waddy B. Wood.

Wilson Dam, built during World War I, showing concrete housing for the machinery designed to imitate classical masonry and columns. Completely masked was the real structural material—steel.

Twentieth-Century Gladiators

"The fault with the extreme Traditionalist is that he is preoccupied with his vocabulary rather than his thought. The fault with the extreme Modernist . . . is that he has made a new dictionary with about nine words in it. . . . Until these two sets of fellows admit this major fault in each case, they are drifting along toward nowhere."

The Federal Architect, *July 1939*

"We find in the architectural world a bevy of independent thinkers, who cavort adventurously in this new modern field, having cast aside all the stuffy garments of tradition and precedent.

"We find the uncomfortable BVD's of Vignola hanging on the nearby fence. The blue garters of Prentice are kicked out of sight. The nicely pressed trousers of the Italian Renaissance and the silk shirt of the Grand Prix lay abandoned on the ground where contented cows pause over them.

"All is free and untrammeled, in this valley of Utopia. There are no styles, no rules, no restrictions. You dance your own architectural design. The garlands with which you deck yourselves may be roses or thistles or inner tubes or buttercups, or dried discs of the field or any other thing your mind picks on as a new idea in decoration."

The Federal Architect, *1933*

Can Modern Architecture Be Good

THE germ of Modern Architecture is with us. Quarantining at the respective state borders has been of no avail. Spraying with strong solutions has failed. The deadly germ, propagating like the Japanese beetle in obscene profusion, has leaped all geographical boundaries, thrived heartily upon all poisons set out to destroy it. It is too strong to combat. Rather, we must accept it.

The problem of the Government architect and all other architects is to study this germ carefully and decide how much of it is malevolent and how much benevolent.

There is no doubt that there is a great deal of the bad boy about this Moderne. There is a great deal of thumb-nosing at the past. There is a great deal of it that is in the spirit of exciting sabotage, prompted by the Hallowe'en idea of window-breaking and gate-stealing.

That is the spirit that actuates the generation in which we live. The world is just a trifle bored with itself. It is anxious to rise up and chuck the old stuff—just because it is tired of it. That applies not only to architecture, but to all the outward and visible signs—to clothes, to manners, to books, to music. The intent is to jazz it up.

But it is well to remember that the very forces that favor now the revolution in architecture will doubtless turn against it. The public, greeting it now as something new and as a relief, will turn from it when it ceases to be new and seek relief in something else. Then only so much of the modern as is sound will live. The rest will be ready for the dynamite.

Hartford County Building
Paul P. Crèt
Smith and Bassette
Associated Architects

Advertisements from *The Federal Architect*, October 1930. In the debate over architectural style, labels became confusing. As these ads illustrate, "classical" could mean any design fairly directly borrowing a historical style, even if the style was Italian renaissance; "moderne" was often applied approvingly by the traditionalists to examples of starved classicism that would never have been embraced by the modernists.

"Architecture has now gone into a conventional era. It has taken on a set of purification rules. . . . It looks back upon the excesses of McKim and Carrère and Bacon with hanging head, and dedicates itself to total abstinence. . . .

"The present purification will go on for a while, a long while, and then—

"About the end of the century you will find the young architects gathering round and they will be saying, 'Did you fellows ever look into the fine inspired thing they did about the beginning of the century? None of this sterilized stuff we have been doing with plain walls and chopped-out ornament and only one style allowed. Those pre-contemporary guys were free as air. They let their imagination wave. They could work in any style they pleased, and they used columns—you know, round things.'"

The Federal Architect, *July 1937*

"The cultural influences in our country are like the floo-floo bird. I am referring to the peculiar and especial bird who always flew backward. To keep the wind out of its eyes? No. Just because it didn't give a darn where it was going, but just had to see where it had been.

"Now, in the floo-floo bird you have the true symbol of our government architecture, too, and in consequence how discredited American culture stands in the present time! . . . No, we can have nothing by way of official Government until the thing is at least ten years in the past. What can Government do with an advanced idea? If it is still a controversial idea, and any good idea must be so, can Government touch it without its eye on at least the next election? . . . Why should Government ever be entrusted to build buildings? Inevitably buildings are for tomorrow. That is the last thing Government should be expected or allowed to do because in entrusting building to Government, we must go 10 or 100 years backward instead of 10 years ahead into the future."

Frank Lloyd Wright, address to the Association of Federal Architects, October 25, 1938

Oisne-Aisne World War I cemetery; Ardennes World War II cemetery. The site plans of these overseas cemeteries follow Beaux-Arts principles of symmetry and axial orientation. Their architecture traces the development of twentieth-century classical style: from the ornamental Beaux-Arts, through starved classicism, to the gaunt government monumental of the post–World War II period. As the Ardennes monument shows, sculpture takes a similar course to a severely stylized end.

"Conspicuous and expensive discomfort is, to most people, the equivalent of beauty in public buildings; to others beauty is discovered only in the archaic and the obsolete, especially the imported obsolete; and still others habitually lend their judgment in aesthetics to those whose 'taste' they emulate or to those who are supposed to be informed and wise in such matters. All of these are apt to be friends of neo-classic architecture."

Joseph Hudnut, Dean of the Harvard School of Architecture, "Twilight of the Gods," Magazine of Art, *August 1937*

". . . I doubt if I have seen the democratic virtues, liberty, equality, fraternity, expressed in architecture—unless it be in Cape Cod cottages—and certainly the authorities in this matter are far from agreement. Thomas Jefferson, for example, who may be presumed to know something about democracy, crowned our newborn government with the dome of the Pantheon . . . William Morris, equally an authority, proposed as democratic expression a revived medievalism . . . and I know an architect in Wisconsin who, in a torrent of exposition, has discovered the very essence of democracy in his own romantic genius. [This reference is to Frank Lloyd Wright.] I should not be surprised if our democratic architecture, assuming that we ever have such a thing, will be the most chaotic and perverse of all architectures."

Joseph Hudnut, Architecture and the Spirit of Man, *1949*

U.S. Courthouse, Cass Gilbert and Cass Gilbert, Jr., New York, 1936. The classical mode merges with the high rise imperative.

State Capitol, Bertram Goodhue, Lincoln, Nebraska, designed 1920, completed 1932. Goodhue won a competition with this design. Although initially described by some observers as "Gothic," the Capitol was embraced by classicists as a paradigm of modern monumentality. There soon appeared a bumper crop of municipal centers and state and federal courthouses in the tower-with-flanking-wings formula—a modern derivation of the dome-with-wings model of the U.S. Capitol. The Nebraska Capitol is noted for its rich application of symbolic art and sculpture, which includes Greek mythological allusions as well as western American motifs of corn, wheat, bison, sunflowers, and Indians.

Detail of pier, Memorial
Bridge, Washington, D.C.,
1926–1932.

"A Government Office Building for a Metropolis," William
Adams Delano, 1932. Delano
was a member of the Board of
Architectural Consultants, and
his stolid New York firm designed the Post Office Department building for the Federal
Triangle in Washington. The
early 1930s were banner
years for Delano, so perhaps
it is not so surprising that they
produced this fanciful study.
Delano commented on his
resolution of symbolic image
and modernism: "I feel that it
contains all the elements of
great architecture. It shows
freedom from restraint; it displays none of the narrow
provincialism which characterizes the work of the architects of Greece, Italy, France,
and even our own Colonial
Period. It is free from all prejudices, inhibitions, fallacies,
and traditions which throughout the ages have done so
much to cramp architecture
and bring it into disrepute. It
has form, mass, and move-
ment. The plan expresses the
elevation and the elevation
the plan. Both are simple and
straightforward and display
those qualities of Nationalism,
Fundamentalism, Functional-
ism, and Space-enclosurism
so rarely found and so much
to be desired in the best
architecture."

Paul Cret, Modern Beaux-Artiste

Paul Philippe Cret landed in the U.S. in 1903, joining other Ecole des Beaux-Arts graduates recruited to teach at American architectural schools in the wake of the popular Chicago fair of 1893. In a thirty-four-year career at the University of Pennsylvania, Cret had many future federal architects as students. But his pivotal importance to federal architecture lies in the example and influence of his public building designs.

Cret believed in the creative possibilities of designing within traditionally set limits and took issue with what he felt to be the modernists' insistence on newness for its own sake. At the same time, he approved of the modernists' emphasis on the value "of restraint, . . . of designing volumes instead of merely decorating surfaces, . . . of empty surfaces as an element of composition." This design philosophy was translated into vertical strips of windows and unornamented, planar walls and columns on a flow of Cret-designed monuments and public buildings in the 1920s and 1930s, setting both the trend and the standard for "starved classicism." Demonstrating the peaceful coexistence of classical with modern on the exterior, the interiors of Cret's buildings adhered to Beaux-Arts traditions of axiality and grand public entrance and circulation spaces.

His influence was amplified by his service on numerous architectural juries and public commissions, including the national Commission of Fine Arts and the American Battle Monuments Commission.

Paul Cret, by Theo B. White, 1919.

Book plate drawn by Cret.

Folger Shakespeare Library, Paul Cret, Washington, D.C., 1932. Privately funded, the library occupies a prominent site across from the Capitol. It was the first example of Cret's mature "starved classicism" and caught the eye of the profession and the fancy of Washington.

Federal Reserve Bank, Paul Cret, Philadelphia, 1931–1935, entrance detail.

Paul Cret, Modern Beaux-Artiste

296–297

Federal Reserve Board Building, Paul Cret, Washington, 1937. To be architect of this building, Cret won a 1935 competition restricted to "traditionalists." Like the Ecole des Beaux-Arts where he studied, Cret placed great stock in architectural competitions. He entered twenty-three of them in the U.S. and placed first in seven.

Stair hall gallery, Federal Reserve Board Building.

Charcoal drawing by Paul Cret showing a detail from a bronze balustrade, Federal Reserve Board Building.

American Battle Monuments
insignia, designed by Paul
Cret.

National Naval Medical Center, Paul Cret, Bethesda, Maryland, 1940 (with F. W. Southworth, Navy architect). Referring to this naval hospital, Cret philosophized that his buildings were "never better than when there is a whole lot of nature and only a pinch of architecture."

"I unfortunately lack the strong faith of the modernists in the 'functionality' of their architecture. Looking at it with a critical eye, I cannot see in it anything but the age-old method which consists in being logical, truthful and functional in design as long as it is convenient, and being decidedly less so when certain aesthetic results are wanted. . . .

"Those who have tried to develop good taste in students, know how impossible the task is if you cannot refer to the traditionally accepted masterpieces of the past . . . all this talk of return to primitive naiveté is the most unsufferable of affectations. It is as unbecoming to us, heirs to an old civilization, as affected baby-talk is to an overripe person. . . . we must no more be hypnotized by the desire to be original than by the complex to be archaeologically correct."

Paul Cret, *"Ten Years of Modernism," The Federal Archi-*tect, *July 1933*

Château-Thierry monument,
Paul Cret, Château-Thierry,
France, shown at its dedication, October 7, 1937.

Late in 1927, a group of government architects in Washington founded the Association of Federal Architects, hoping it would encourage an exchange of ideas among the various construction agencies, enhance design and technical standards, and boost the morale of architectural civil servants. Louis A. Simon, Supervising Architect of the Treasury, served as the organization's first president.

Throughout the Depression years and on into World War II, the AFA held dinners featuring guest speakers like Frank Lloyd Wright, Eliel Saarinen, Richard Neutra, and assorted government officials. It also sponsored a series of lectures on building materials, several design competitions, an occasional social outing, and an annual exhibition at which awards were bestowed not only for the best agency exhibit and individual on-the-job efforts, but also for watercolors and other artworks done by Association members in their spare time. Membership, which peaked in the late 1930s at about 350, was by invitation and included nonarchitects whose duties were related to building.

In July 1930, the AFA published the first issue of a quarterly magazine, *The Federal Architect*, to show, it said, "those in the Government service and those outside of it, if they are interested, the progress of work on the Federal building program." The magazine concentrated its coverage on the traditional part of that program carried out by the cabinet departments, and gave scant attention to the New Deal alphabet agencies. Edited and designed by Edwin Bateman Morris, of the Supervising Architect's Office, and his wife, *The Federal Architect* also carried accounts of the AFA's activities, inspection trips to far-flung federal building projects, and architecture outside the government.

From Morris's pen there flowed a stream of front pages in which he carried on wry, thoughtful combat against "modern" architecture and the demands from private architects that government architects surrender their design function. Mixed in with these columns were others, sprightly and whimsical, in which Morris observed the passing Depression, the labors of the government architect, and the demise of "small town" Washington (and the pedestrian and then the parking space).

Morris put out a final issue in 1946, unable any longer to sustain the magazine with his own funds, as he had many times in the past. The issue was dedicated to Paul Cret, Morris's teacher at the University of Pennsylvania and the man whose work best embodied Morris's ideal of "the Moderne traditionalized, the Traditional modernized."

Late in the year, the magazine was revived under new editorship that promised neither to "praise nor condemn" developments in federal architecture, the design of which by then was almost exclusively in private hands. The magazine and the AFA appear to have faded away within a year.

Postmaster General James Farley with Edwin Bateman Morris (left) at a 1939 AFA dinner commemorating the 103rd anniversary of the Supervising Architect's Office. (AFA traced the Office to Robert Mills's appointment as Architect of Public Buildings.) Morris was president of the AFA for several years and, with help from his wife, edited, designed, and published *The Federal Architect* from its inception until 1946, often drawing on personal funds to keep it going. He also led a successful campaign to erect a monument over Robert Mills's grave in the Congressional Cemetery in Washington. Morris joined the Supervising Architect's Office in 1908, becoming a top assistant before retiring in 1942. One of his ten published novels—*The Narrow Street*—was made into both silent and talking film versions.

Cover of the first issue of the magazine. For the next five years, the center silhouette was a prominent feature of each cover.

Cover for October 1946, displaying the seal of the AFA. Under new editorship, only a few issues came out under this cover before the magazine folded.

Federal Architects Unite

The FEDERAL ARCHITECT

JULY, 1930

Published by
THE ASSOCIATION OF FEDERAL ARCHITECTS

WASHINGTON, D.C.

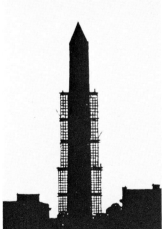

In February 1937, the AFA held a "smoker" at a suburban Washington country club with Eliel Saarinen as the guest speaker. Saarinen urged the government architects not to follow stylistic traditions blindly. William P. O'Hare, of the Supervising Architect's Office, supplied these sketches for *The Federal Architect*'s article on the occasion.

Sketches made at the Saarinen meeting by our artist Wm. P. O'Hare

"Let's see now. Accomplishment Number 1: [the AFA] has built up a contact between the architectural agencies of the Government. . . . Accomplishment 4: It has striven to take the word smug out of Government Architects' contemplation of their own work and out of private architects' criticism of that work. Accomplishment 5: It publishes a magazine which whatever may be said of it is at least perennial.

"As we look on that list, it seems rather humble and meagre in print. But those things point to one thing and that is the existence of a pride of the Government architects in their own work. The Association may have had something to do with that. . . . At any rate there is far more esprit de corps, far more interest, far more earnestness, far more architecture in the Government offices today than there was twenty-seven years ago when we first marched with our carpet-bag into the Supervising Architect's Office."

The Federal Architect, *October 1935*

The Federal Architect observed that architects acquired much of their knowledge about building materials from printed advertising. In 1939, the AFA sponsored an Exhibition of Advertising Pages at which awards were given to promote "a goal of making the advertising pages of technical magazines as helpful in an educational way as the text pages." Some advertisers in The Federal Architect went to great lengths to reach this goal; others scarcely heeded it. But nearly all took pains to publicize their products' use in federal building projects.

"It is the most comforting thing about being in Uncle Sam's architectural service. To the men in that service, the buildings erected are nearly human. These men long to be there and lay a hand on their products, and get an affectionate response therefrom. When one of them goes through a town without looking for the Post Office, it will be a sign that architecture has dried up and withered away."

The Federal Architect, October 1934

Shortly after the outbreak of World War II, the AFA and a ceramic company sponsored a competition for the interior design of a bomb shelter done in tile. These submissions were published in *The Federal Architect*, January–March 1942.

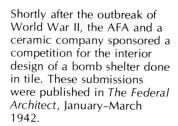

President Franklin Delano Roosevelt speaking at the dedication of the new post office, Rhinebeck, New York, May 1, 1939. Present among the President's guests were Crown Prince Frederik and Crown Princess Ingrid of Denmark and Iceland, and two Cabinet Secretaries.

According to the dedication program the building was "an authentic reproduction of the first house of any consequence built in Rhinebeck, having been erected in 1700 by Hendrick Kip on a patent from the Dutch government. All of the stone used in the construction of this new building was taken from the ruins of the original house and from the adjacent Beekman lands."

Like many citizens the President took a prideful interest in his local federal buildings. Unlike most citizens, however, he could choose the architectural style. He favored the style of the Dutch fieldstone farmhouses of upper New York state for the Rhinebeck Post Office, a post office he dedicated in 1940 in his native Hyde Park, and for the Franklin D. Roosevelt Library.

Local Pride

304–305

Moving the old Federal Building, St. Cloud, Minnesota. The city of St. Cloud had decided that the old Federal Building, which was to be replaced by a new one on the same site, would make a suitable city hall.

"Here it comes. This is a view taken down St. Germain Street during the moving maneuver. The street is 60 feet wide from curb to curb, and the building 48 feet, which with careful manipulation gave ample clearance. The structure weighed 2500 tons and was said to be the largest vehicle which has traversed these streets. The manufacture of souvenirs by placing pennies on the rails to be flattened out became a matter of interest to the citizens."—*The Federal Architect*, July 1937

"The parade, including the American Legion, Legion Band, Legion Auxiliary, city officials, school children, Girl Scouts, Sea Scouts, Boy Scouts, and the high-school band is scheduled to start promptly at 9 a.m. from the gymnasium. . . .
Upon completion of the ceremonies at the cemetery, the entire parade is to march to the new post office, where a joint program begins at 10 o'clock. The public is invited to inspect the post office from 1 to 4 o'clock."

Notice of Memorial Day dedication of the Post Office, Mayville, Wisconsin, in Trade and Farm News, *1940*

"Evidence that the Federal government has done an exceptional thing for Wichita is now daily before the eyes of the people of this community. That evidence is the beauty of the new Federal building, far enough along now to show that the structure is one of those superlative architectural achievements rare in a world always aiming at beauty in building but seldom attaining it.

"Those who designed the Post Office and Court House for Wichita have not committed a single sin against simplicity. Only those ornaments which would give stress to that simplicity were indulged. Every inclination to delirium in decoration was summarily ditched in the architect's office down in Washington, and entire reliance placed in the incomparable charm found only in straight lines kept in symmetrical proportion.

"As a symbol of the majesty of the law and as an implement of the vastly important business of ready intercommunication, the edifice is to enter deeply into the future life of the citizens of Wichita but neither as symbol nor as implement will the building have as great an effect on this people as from the daily subtle impact of its beauty upon their civic consciousness in confirmation of a persistent popular belief that in the art of architecture things really can be done right."

Editorial, "A Thing of Beauty," The Wichita Eagle, Wichita, Kansas, June 21, 1931, reprinted in The Federal Architect, July 1931

"Now that the facade of the new post office on South Main street is complete, residents have been able to note with great satisfaction the look of it. It would be a little difficult to determine its exact style, but from the architectural standpoint of disposition of masses and weights, the use of straight lines over windows and larger spaces, instead of curves, it can probably be determined as classic, yet still, without the grim pillars, it is not a familiar type. It rises only a little distance in the air but covers a large area of ground. The dark gray stone, the uncompromising right angles, the deep insets, give it an appearance of tremendous solidity, and that appearance is preserved by confining the small amount of ornament to certain cuttings of the surface in low relief. Classic with a flavor of Egyptian. As one looks, he knows instinctively that it is a massive and enduring sample of the builders' art. There is a serious and simple indication about its lines. And it is a style of which nobody can ever grow tired, a style which in itself is entitled to remain for many years and which, let us hope, may be allowed to remain. The good sense of older European countries of letting buildings stand which have beauty, we have not yet acquired. Many things of merit have been erected in this country, and then afterward have been torn to pieces. One cannot look at the new erection with any other thought except that of permanence, and the idea of its destruction is hard to entertain in any circumstances. It is attractive, substantial, worthy and dignified as an addition to our architectural store in the valley and a graceful reminder also that the three most recent buildings of large extent in this city have been such as to stir gratification and rouse the pride of the community."

Wilkes-Barre Times-Leader, reprinted in The Federal Architect, October 1934

"Excitement here is running
   high;
Just listen and I'll tell you
   why.
We're leaving this old haunted
   stand,
For a new building far more
   grand.
"The pulpit preaches to the
   pew,
'Behold old things will be as
   new.'
When we depart from this old
   shell,
'Twill be as entering heaven
   from h——l.
"Adieu! Farewell to thee, old
   barn,
We'll have a place to keep us
   warm
Whenever wintry winds do
   blow,
And streets are filled with ice
   and snow.
"When Summer's Sun was
   shining down,
On city streets and fields so
   brown,
Our skylights caught the glow-
   ing blaze,
And magnified it forty ways.
"We've seen this building out
   and in.
We're waiting, eager to begin
Our first day's work within its
   walls.
Its lobby built like marble
   halls—
"Inspires in us the will to do,
And once again our pledge
   renew,
To serve our public with a pride
Which in this place we ne'er
   can hide.
"Our City's pride enhanced
   will be
By this grand pile of masonry.
Erected on its Plaza site,
'A cloud by day, a fire by
   night.'
"A guide to those who still
   must roam,
A boon to those who stay at
   home.
Inanimate though it may be,
It lives and breathes for you
   and me."

"The Old Postoffice and the New," written by George A. Barker, veteran postal clerk, for the move into the new St. Louis Post Office, 1937

Local Pride

'"Well, Sir, I see by the papers that some thirteen or a dozen post office buildings are to be erected in and around sundry and several locations. I think I'm safe in saying that Pocomoke has one to sell at a bargain price, small payments and long time notes. There will be no extra charge for the pip-jimmie (spelling not guaranteed) on the roof nor the large supply of water still on hand in the cellar. They can have the flag pole and I'll advise 'em to hitch the ropes to the building, haul it up a little further out of the ground, and block it up with mine props before throwing it open for the rush of mail. . . .

'"I see that our sister town, Snow Hill, wants one and seems in a fair way to get it. You know, in some localities where tragedies have been caused by collisions of automobiles and railway trains, the people have erected raised platforms and placed the smashed up cars on top of 'em, as a warning for other motorists who might come that way.

'"Now, before the good people of our county seat allow the first stone to be laid in their proposed structure, I'd advise 'em to drive solemnly by the Pocomoke pile and—take warning. If they want something that resembles a goods box, turned upside down, and a joint of stove pipe looking toward the skies, why all O.K., get our blue prints. But, otherwise, get something else.'"

Worcester (Mass.) Democrat and the Ledger-Enterprise, n.d., reprinted in The Federal Architect, July 1938

Fort Wingate, New Mexico, 1906. Regional styles influenced construction work of the Quartermasters, even in an earlier, less affluent era.

Classicism was the dominant but not the only theme in federal architecture between the wars. Log-cabin and stone-house construction were favored in the national forests and parks. A few federal projects displayed the new art deco style, born of the 1925 exposition of decorative arts in Paris and stimulated by the interest of industrial designers in an aesthetics of the machine and motion, or what came to be known as streamlining.

But the major deviation appeared in hospital and army quarters, where regionalism exerted a temporizing influence on construction work. Regional and colonial period motifs found their way into the work of the Construction Division of the Army's Quartermaster Corps and the Construction Service of the new Veterans Administration, established by Congress in 1930 as an umbrella agency for all veterans' programs.

In the mid-1920s public outcry over the postwar degeneration of army posts prompted Congress to finance a new look. Quartermaster General B. Frank Cheatham hired civilian city planners to provide "a deviation from the set type of military posts" and placed the architectural staff under officers formerly associated with the architectural firms of Cass Gilbert and McKim, Mead and White. New hospitals, theaters, and living quarters replaced deteriorating buildings as staff architects of the Construction Division produced flexible designs for different regions—"Colonial" for the Atlantic seaboard, "French Provincial" for the Gulf states, and "Spanish Mission" for the Southwest. Trees and shrubs were planted; garden clubs were founded on almost every post; and a committee of women, headed by the Quartermaster General's wife, advised on the decor of family quarters. Building activities for the Quartermasters burgeoned with their enlistment in Depression projects. In late 1941, however, the Construction Division was consolidated with the Corps of Engineers.

In contrast, World War II expanded the Veterans Administration to one of the major construction branches of the U.S. government. The Construction Service of the VA, a descendant of the post-World War I Veterans Bureau, built medical complexes, which, in their scale, dormitory functions, and architectural style, resembled college campuses. While regional styles appeared in appropriate areas, a collegiate colonial look of columns, red brick, and white trim was more generally associated with VA hospitals. Eventually these styles developed a pared-down appearance for a kind of "starved colonialism."

"Architectural treatment of the exteriors is carefully studied and every effort is made to have the buildings in harmony with the traditions of the locality. With respect to the latter, the Technical Division [Veterans Administration] has been unusually fortunate in having architects among its personnel who have practiced their profession in every part of this country and are, therefore, thoroughly conversant with the appropriate type of architecture and local conditions affecting building construction, such as climate, soil conditions and availability of materials.

The Federal Architect, *October 1944*

The Wright Brothers Memorial at Kitty Hawk, designed and built by the Construction Division, Quartermaster Corps. It is located on a dune kept from shifting by planting grass that grows on sand.

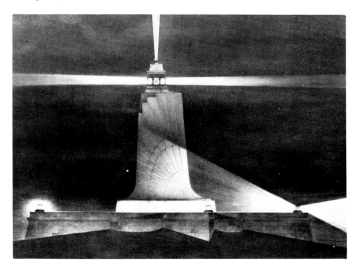

Headquarters Building, Hamilton Field, California, 1934. *The Federal Architect* of April 1935 reported of a similar photograph: "A delegation from San Rafael, glowing with health and energy, brought the picture into the Supervising Architect's Office to show a Government architectural agency how to design a California building, forgetting for the moment that the building was designed by a Government architectural agency."

Post Chapel, Randolph Field, Texas.

Hospital, Veterans Administration, Lyons, New Jersey, 1930, in one of the most popular styles for VA facilities.

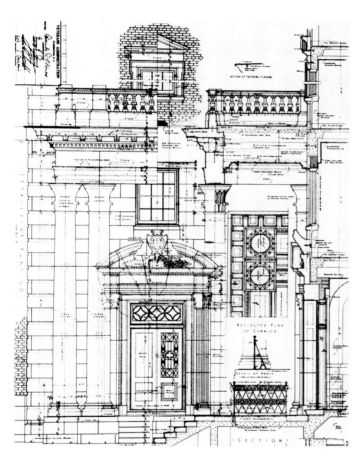

Scale detail, Bath, New York, Veterans Hospital by Construction Service, Veterans Administration. Drawing, 1936.

Hospital, Veterans Administration, Albuquerque, New Mexico, 1932. *The Federal Architect* of October 1932 reported that "it was felt that the atmosphere of . . . picturesque pueblos was so definitely associated with the country of New Mexico in particular that in perpetuating it with modern building materials a lasting monument to the aborigines of America might be erected."

Nearly all the plans produced for the 1900 District of Columbia Centennial staked out the triangular tract of land between Pennsylvania Avenue and the Mall for public buildings and monuments. The Senate Parks Commission set it aside as a D.C. municipal buildings precinct.

In 1917, the Public Buildings Commission (PBC) claimed the triangle for new federal department headquarters, which the Senate Parks Commission had wanted to array around Lafayette Square, across the street from the White House. In the 1926–1928 public buildings acts, Congress ratified the PBC plans for "the Federal Triangle."

There were some in Washington who hoped the government would disperse its new buildings throughout the city, decentralizing Washington's business and employment centers. L'Enfant had unsuccessfully proposed a similar development approach to George Washington in 1791. The idea fared no better this time around: the PBC and the Treasury decided that efficiency and economy would be better served by concentrating agencies in one area. Moreover, they believed a Triangle development would "reclaim" the notoriously ramshackle south side of Pennsylvania Avenue.

Only after the advent of the Depression, however, did these considerations of efficiency and socioeconomic improvement become prominent in official

The Federal Triangle, looking west, 1936. The base of the Triangle is formed by the Department of Commerce Building, which, when completed in 1932, was the largest monumental building ever erected by the federal government. In length it exceeds both the U.S. Capitol and the British Houses of Parliament. Its length also exceeds the height of the Chrysler Building in New York. *The Federal Architect* prophesied in April 1937, "When the old Postoffice crumbles into dust, they will complete the circular plaza." But it refused to crumble, despite efforts as recent as those of the 1964 Pennsylvania Avenue Plan. The D.C. Municipal Building, completed only in 1908 in exemplary Beaux-Arts form, also withstood the Architectural Consultants' plans for its demise.

pronouncements; until then, proponents emphasized the project's aesthetic values. As early as 1896, the Supervising Architect suggested placing all major government buildings on Pennsylvania Avenue, to create "an effect hardly attainable in any other capital of the world." The PBC talked about "the need for a great single architectural composition." Citing Baron Haussmann's grand nineteenth-century plan for Paris (a plan noted for its ruthless execution as much as its aesthetic attainment), the Treasury promised that its Triangle development would similarly "place Washington in the forefront of the architecturally beautiful cities of the world" and set an example "for the country as a whole in the matter of planning." Noted civic planner Elbert Peets suggested that a statue of L'Enfant "be set up in the remaining corner of the square that marks the midpoint of Pennsylvania Avenue. Let the sainted hero of American civic art be shown facing toward the Department of Justice Building, violently tearing out his hair."

To those who advocated the emerging "modern" style, the Treasury replied that in Washington the "early builders . . . set a very definite stamp" on the style of federal buildings, "a tradition which may not be lightly disregarded . . . [a] national inheritance . . . that the United States Government should cherish." The buildings would be neoclassical, as the PBC and the national Commission of Fine Arts had urged.

Following a precedent of the 1893 fair, Treasury Secretary Andrew Mellon appointed a "Board of Architectural Consultants" to coordinate planning and design. In the Public Buildings Acts of 1926 and 1930, Congress authorized the Treasury—for the first time since the 1912 repeal of the Tarsney Act—to contract with private architects. Under this authority, Mellon appointed Edward H. Bennett, a former partner of Daniel Burnham, chairman of the advisory board consisting of five other private architects, and Louis Simon, the Supervising Architect. Mellon coaxed the private architects to serve by confidentially promising them the design commissions for the individual Triangle buildings.

The classical–French Renaissance facade of the Post Office Department building, suggested by the Place Vendôme in Paris, forms a semicircular end for the Great Plaza. The plaza was to have been landscaped, but was soon overgrown with automobiles, not plants, as seen in this 1935 photograph. The interior courtyards, which give the Triangle its honeycombed effect from the air, did not live up to the promises made for them. Most were soon taken up by automobile parking and loading docks. An aluminum fountain installed in the Justice Department courtyard attracted few building employees until Attorney General Robert F. Kennedy had picnic tables installed in the early 1960s. The courtyards saw their most intensive use, however, in 1969 as troop staging areas during a large anti-Vietnam war demonstration.

"Shadow" of the Department of Justice Building on the Acropolis, from *The Federal Architect*, July 1932. From this and other overwhelming "shadow" comparisons, the editors concluded: "The feeling that arises in us is . . . one of awe and trepidation at the size of our modern projects and centers of civilization. The fear arises that these may be too big and far-reaching, like our business and economic structure, which periodically collapses, as at present."

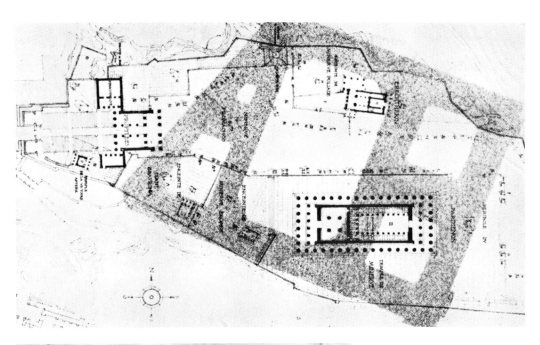

Although the masonry facades hewed to the neoclassical orthodoxy, "modern" heresies crept into some appurtenances. Here, 20-foot-high aluminum doors at the Department of Justice. The "roaring lions typify watchfulness and strength."

"The building erected in co-operation with Secretary of Commerce Hoover, the Great Engineer, simply threw to the winds all the achievements of modern engineering in order to make itself over into a Roman-Renaissance palace. The fact that the monumental cubical shape imposed upon the building from outside forced the great majority of the employees to work in offices opening on any one of six small, ugly, and poorly ventilated interior courts, was apparently of no concern to the men in charge. . . .

". . . $100,000,000 of taxpayers' money is being used, not to provide the modern, efficient, stripped-for-action office buildings which every federal department has been needing so badly, but to provide a parade of monumental structures that are copies of French palaces when they are not reconstructions of pagan temples."

William Harlan Hale, "The Grandeur That Is Washington," Harper's Monthly Magazine, April 1934

"At a time when the mechanism of banking . . . was comparatively simple, Robert Mills screened the offices of the Treasury Department with Doric peristyles, a symbol of governmental dignity; it was only after several miles of such dignities had been hung on the walls of the Departments of Justice, of Commerce, of Labor, and of Agriculture, that architects observed the terrific burden which such an untractable vocabulary of form imposed on the complicated and varied machinery within. Nor does the grouping of such buildings, or their relation to the scheme of government or to the city acknowledge to any important degree their part in an organic whole. The buildings of the Triangle dance their eternal minuet about the graceful plazas and like the courtiers at Versailles take no note of the clamor of the great city sprawled out about them. . . . No genuine dignity is attained. All sense of a convincing unity vanishes in the Triangle as soon as one has apprehended the movement of life behind these elegant facades and the palpable dissonance between use and expression which they embody."

Joseph Hudnut, "Twilight of the Gods," Magazine of Art, August 1937

Arcade of the Post Office Department.

"The Triangle wipes out a large patch of the L'Enfant plan, substituting not merely a different plan but a different type of planning so that, whatever may be said in its favor, it destroys the stylistic unity of the Washington design. At the same time the national officials and planners effect a gorgeous exhibition of self-deception—for I think they are quite sincere about it—by interminably lauding L'Enfant. The mental mechanics of the situation might seem to permit only one explanation, that the planners have never looked at L'Enfant's plan. The self-deception theory, however, is more plausible, for we Americans have to an extraordinary degree the power to entertain in our minds diametrically opposed ideas. A trained capacity for dutiful self-deception sustains our religion, our politics, and our patriotism. Why should it not also enter into our art, particularly here at Washington, the busiest market for this kind of thought, in all its branches?"

Elbert Peets, "Washington," in Werner Hegemann et al., City Planning and Housing, *1937*

"The kind of building best adapted to the needs of the Government is the modern office-type structure, designed with due regard to the safety, health, and comfort of the people who are to use it. To embark upon a program of building Greek temples for housing the Government departments is both foolish and unnecessary. These buildings are exceedingly expensive and wasteful of space."

D.C. Public Buildings Commission, 1922

"Buildings constructed in prominent locations would necessarily be of a classical design and entirely in keeping with the ideas of enhancing the beauty of the national capital and yet be of a practical and economic type."

D.C. Public Buildings Commission, 1924–1925

"[The Triangle will be] an architectural composite that will be a distinctive product of the early twentieth century, depicting the revival of classic architecture for the use of modern business demands."

D.C. Public Buildings Commission, 1927

"Finally, the Federal Triangle separated the government from the city of Washington. Pennsylvania Avenue became a barrier between the massive government buildings on the south and the edge of the city's downtown area on the north. As time passed, the office and commercial core of the city shifted away from the Avenue to the northwest area of the city."

The Pennsylvania Avenue Plan, 1974

Federal Triangle, details.

"It is the translation of rhetoric into stone—a feat often fatal to the rhetoric, always fatal to the stone."

Horatio Greenough, "Aesthetics at Washington," The Travels, Observations, and Experience of a Yankee Stonecutter, *1852*

"Inscriptions are a great temptation to architects. There are few members of our great profession who can take them or let them alone. . . .

"The flaw in the architect's reasoning is that he considers an inscription as a decoration, an appeal to the eye: whereas it is a literary matter, an appeal to the mind and the emotions. . . .

"Most of the inscriptions devised or selected by architects are picked with a thought to their architectural appearance only. They have the requisite number of letters but there, so frequently, the merit of the inscription ends. Too often, its sentiment and its sound value have the flat triteness of a Fourth of July political oration and unintentionally, the inscription therefore is a painful insult to the intelligence of the public reading it.

"When an inscription becomes an absolute necessity we believe there should be some fund set aside for payment to a competent authority to select or compose it. But, generally, under the head of 'Advice to architects about to call for an inscription,' we believe the proper reply is 'Don't.'

The Federal Architect, *October 1933*

The program for the Triangle included a generous outlay for sculpture. Executed were friezes, pediment panels, high and low reliefs, and free-standing statues relevant to each building's function and more or less in tune with its style. Designing and modeling were done in an aircraft hangar at the Presidio of San Francisco in 1934–1935.

Inscriptions on the facades provided additional lessons in history, democratic principles, and the contributions of each agency's work to the progress of civilization.

Man Controlling Trade, Federal Trade Commission, Michael Lantz, representing man (symbolic of the FTC) restraining a horse (symbolic of monopolies). The design was chosen in a 1938 competition of 494 entries.

Post-World War I Washington, as both foreground and background, was impressed as never before on the national consciousness through news photos and movies of the day. The stage set itself was approaching a reality envisioned in 1902 by the Senate Parks Commission.

While the Federal Triangle was taking shape, projects were materializing in other parts of central Washington that would contribute substantially to the city's twentieth-century Beaux-Arts image. Construction followed the dictates of the 1902 Plan faithfully enough, in fact, that the editors of *The Federal Architect* entitled their April 1937 issue, "Washington Completed."

The Senate Parks Commission had complained that the Capitol grounds were not "framed" in the appropriate monumental trappings. Accordingly, during the 1930s, Union Station Plaza and the adjacent Capitol grounds were treated to a neo-Baroque landscaping, a fourth side was added to the Senate office building, and a new Botanic Garden, Library of Congress annex, House office building, and Supreme Court building were completed.

The Mall was cleared of World War I "temporaries" and the remains of its Victorian gardens and pathways to make way for linear, tree-lined drives. The two side wings of the Department of Agriculture, built twenty years before, were connected by a central structure, and a massive office annex was immediately tacked on behind. The Bureau of Engraving and Printing, the Federal Reserve Board,

and the Interior Department all moved into new headquarters.

A municipal center was begun north of Pennsylvania Avenue, near the National Archives. The Arlington Memorial Bridge, spanning the Potomac River at the Lincoln Memorial, was completed in 1932, its design, by the firm of McKim, Mead and White, nearly identical to one of Charles McKim's drawings published in the 1902 Plan.

In planning Washington, L'Enfant had intended major development to take place first east of the Capitol building. Early disastrous real estate speculation there had refocused development to the northwest, around the White House. The Senate Parks Commission ignored the area. In 1931, the National Capital Park and Planning Commission proposed turning East Capitol Street, leading from the front of the Capitol east to the Anacostia River, into an "Avenue of the States," with a major, ceremonial "Independence Square" at its midpoint. A Beaux-Arts competition was held to solicit designs, but neither this nor a similar scheme proposed in 1941 received funding. The Robert F. Kennedy sports stadium was, however, later located at the street's terminus with the river, as suggested in both plans.

This frenzied activity attracted wide—and overwhelmingly favorable—publicity. Art critics occasionally lampooned the capital's "Romanization," but it was not until late in the decade, when plans were announced for the Jefferson Memorial, the capstone to the 1902 Plan, that this opposition hardened.

Cover of *The Federal Architect*, April 1937.

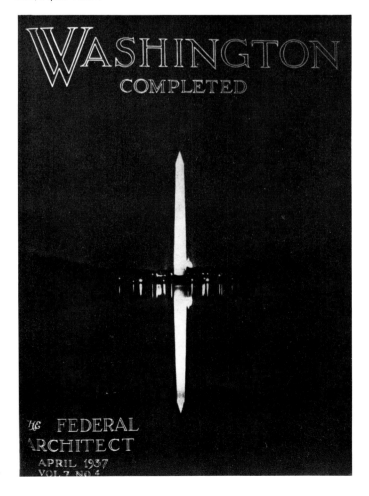

Some of the FEDERAL BUILDINGS in Washington D.C. in which *Plastoid* PUTTY has been used

Department of Agriculture, aerial view. The Gridiron annex (foreground), completed in 1934 and encompassing forty acres of floor space, was referred to by Secretary of Agriculture Henry Wallace, "in dirt farmer language," as the "south forty." It was designed in the Supervising Architect's Office by Edwin Bateman Morris, editor of *The Federal Architect*. Paul Cret's heating plant, at bottom right, provided heat for 77 government buildings.

Advertisement from *The Federal Architect* portrays the twentieth-century image of classicism, which overwhelmed the earlier forms advocated by Jefferson and Mills.

Repair of Washington Monument, 1934, to carry out repainting and cleaning of the entire shaft. The U.S. Commission of Fine Arts observed in its 1936 *Twelfth Report*: "In the early 1930's, the Senate Parks Commission's plan for monumental treatment of the Washington Monument grounds was revived. Uncertain soil conditions under the obelisk called the wisdom of cutting into its supporting hillside into doubt." In November 1932, the Fine Arts Commission rejected a compromise scheme: "It is better to wait a quarter of a century rather than resort to any compromise plan. Public taste is of slow growth. When the Mall shall be completed . . . public taste will call imperatively for the treatment of the Washington Monument grounds as the gem for which the other parts are but a setting. Time is not the essence of this problem."

IF MEMBERS OF THE HOUSE DRESSED TO FIT THEIR SURROUNDINGS

ATTIRE SUGGESTED FOR UNITED STATES SENATORS

Cartoons in *Vanity Fair*, October 1931. *Vanity Fair* reported that "... slowly and surely, under the eye of the Fine Arts Commission, Washington is having its face lifted and is blossoming into a conglomeration of Roman architecture, lacking only triumphal arches and a Coliseum to rival the ancient city of the Tiber. Millions have been spent, are being spent, will be spent, to convert the capital of a nation of structural steel, super-power and mass-production into a cluster of memorial marbles, crowded with columns, plastered with pilasters, permeated with pediments and acanthus, peristyles and other architectural survivals of the age of masonry and slave-labor."

"... Symbolism and romance are inescapable elements in architecture. They are highly desirable elements also, provided one does not pay too dearly for them. The price at Washington is colossal. To attain a 'perfect harmony' of classic form, to create a stupendous symbol of the power and permanence of the Federal Authority, to satisfy a romantic sensibility towards that quality of form which is established by the Early Republic (as if scale and magnitude had nothing to do with the quality of form!), we deprive the Federal City ... of that sense of a heroic past which is the true source of dignity in cities. ... To these I might add the incalculable burden imposed upon the practical operation of the business of government. ..."

Joseph Hudnut, "Twilight of the Gods," Magazine of Art, August 1937

"In 1939, the PBA [Public Buildings Administration], on the advice of the President and Congress, created this simplified structure [Federal Office Building No. 1] as a new method of meeting the pressing office space problem in Washington. The thought was to provide a building which could be allocated to any Government agency, temporary or permanent, which had a particularly pressing space problem at any given time."

Federal Works Agency, Second Annual Report, 1941

"Another project that failed to materialize was the conception of Senator Theodore G. Bilbo of Mississippi, chairman of the Committee on the District of Columbia: 'As a citizen of the wealthiest and most powerful republic on earth ... I am ashamed of the old, dilapidated, dirty Capitol Building in Washington. For convenience, comfort, and sanitation, the Pearl River County (Miss.) courthouse has got it beat forty ways from Sunday.' Bilbo proposed a new Capitol, east of the present one and down the street from the Supreme Court building. He estimated the cost at $250 million and said he believed he could get the railroads to pay for it by threatening to filibuster a bill that they very much wanted to see pass."

Washington Evening Star, September 30, 1945

*Bargain Day in Washington—
If the Craze for Government
Property Continues*, Ellison
Hoover, printed in *Life*, March
6, 1924. When the Teapot
Dome scandal broke, cartoon-
ist Hoover portrayed this
move of Washington's sym-
bolic architecture to characterize the sell-out of public
integrity.

"Sometimes we wish they
would get Washington city finished. A person can't tell where
it is going to break out next.
He drives down a street and
hasn't much more than got out
of the block before they have it
torn up ready for pipe-burial.

"The District of Columbia is
the earthquake centre of the
world. There are faults and fis-
sures everywhere. When a man
walks along the street, suddenly
it opens up, when one foot is
on one side and the other on
the other, and down in the
crevice between his legs are fellows taking up iron pipe and
laying aluminum pipe.

"Covering insurance is being
written against automobiles
falling down crevices that
weren't there in the morning
and develop contrary to anybody's expectation before night
fall.

"There are special employees
whose duty it is to patrol the
streets and report to the District Building when new sewer
and gas excavation breaks out
and begins to spread.

"Reserves of police and fire-
men are then rushed at once to
the spot to surround it and keep
the disaster within bounds.

"Last week in the block in
front of the Bureau of Engraving and Printing several trucks
with steel teeth that attack concrete broke loose, tearing up a
quarter of mile of paving before
the cavalry arrived from Fort
Myer.

"Authorities are keeping in
touch with the situation, but
there is no disguising the fact
that it is serious. No prediction
can be made as to when or
where these seismic disturb-
ances may occur.

"The Red Cross and the
Coast Guard were working
twenty-four hours a day for a
full week succoring starving
citizens in the Mall who were
entirely surrounded by excava-
tions and street improvement
projects, and were rescued only
after intense hardship by improvised breeches-buoys.

"The courage of the citizens
is marvelous. Workers kiss their
wives good-bye in the morning,
knowing it is an even chance
they will, by eve, be lying stark
beside a water pipe in an un-
foreseen excavation.

'Traffic engineers and town
planners tell us that such dis-
turbances, in the same manner
as the chestnut blight and the
Japanese beetle, run their
course. It seems that eventually
benevolent germs attack the excavation bacilli and exterminate
them.

"May it come soon."

The Federal Architect, October 1934

Supreme Court, Cass Gilbert, 1935.

"The monuments of Egypt and of Greece are sublime as expressions of their power and their feeling. The modern nation that appropriates them displays only wealth in so doing. . . . If from what has been thus far said it shall have appeared that we regard the Greek masters as aught less than the true apostles of correct taste in building, we have been misunderstood. We believe firmly and fully that they can teach us; but let us learn principles, not copy shapes; let us imitate them like men, and not ape them like monkeys."

Horatio Greenough, "American Architecture," The United States Magazine and Democratic Review, *August 1843*

"This concentration of monuments, memorials, museums, and endless department office buildings in the central area of the city is destroying the city, as a work of art and as a social entity, in the process of glorifying the capital—or perhaps more accurately the government. People who have no sense of the beauty of large spatial organizations, people who do not love the life of a city and who do not see that snobbishness—even though it be official snobbishness—is fatal to civic art, people who cannot distinguish between art and splurge, obviously cannot see how far we are getting from L'Enfant's conception. For he dreamed, not of a beautiful court of honor, but of a beautiful city."

Elbert Peets, "Washington," in Werner Hegemann et al., City Planning and Housing, *1937*

View of Washington, c. 1938, photo by Theodor Horydczak, whose idyllic photographs of Washington are still used on postcards.

Pantheon, Rome.

Through years of Republican rule in Washington, Representative John J. Boylan, a Tammany Hall Democrat, had futilely crusaded for an official monument to the nation's third President and first Democrat. In 1935, the Democratic Congress obligingly named Boylan chairman of a Thomas Jefferson Memorial Commission.

John Russell Pope, whose "well-nourished" classical work was represented in Washington by several landmark buildings, including the just-finished National Archives, was named erchitectural adviser to the Commission, and, a short time later, architect for the memorial itself.

Pope designed a marble Pantheon while the Commission chose a site on the Tidal Basin, forming a Mall cross-axis with the White House. Both site and design conformed to the 1902 Plan. The 1902 Plan

had not, however, specified a subject for the memorial; Pope, in fact, had once prepared a similar design for a proposed memorial to Theodore Roosevelt on this site. The Commission of Fine Arts found fault with minor aspects of Pope's design and rejected it. It took over a year, ten revisions, a vote of the Congress, intervention by Pope's by-then widow, and an appeal to the President to secure approval for a design nearly identical to Pope's original.

Meanwhile, in the architectural community, the débate quickly escalated— in magazine articles, letters to editors, and meetings of the League for Progress in Architecture— into a bitter exchange between modernists and traditionalists. (The two camps agreed only that there should have been a competition to select the architect.)

Marquis Childs, writing in the April 1937 issue of the *Magazine of Art*, observed the "profound irony in the selection of a monument of imperial splendor to hallow the memory of a man who was a free spirit, a free thinker. . . ." When traditionalists pointed out that Jefferson had favored the classical himself, modernists countered that Jefferson was but a "modern" architect in his day, in revolt against the entrenched Baroque style. Some modernists suggested that a living memorial, an auditorium or arena, would be more Jeffersonian in spirit—an idea perhaps prompted by the rainy 1937 presidential inaugural. Others ridiculed the site plan because it would impede automobile traffic and cited traffic congestion in the Triangle area as proof of the traditionalists' blindness to this modern design requisite.

Pope borrowed again from the Pantheon in designing the National Gallery of

Art. Sketches were published early in 1937, but debate over the design was subdued, probably because of the unquestioned value of the art collection that Andrew Mellon donated to the nation along with the building. Edward Bruce, chief of the Treasury Department's Section of Fine Arts and a modernist, suspended his gratitude long enough to call the Gallery "that pink marble whore-house."

Of greatest concern to native Washingtonians was potential damage, from construction of Jefferson's temple, to the Tidal Basin, and especially its Japanese cherry trees. This concern stirred up the most militant protest: on the day in 1939 that excavation finally started, a group of women chained to the trees confronted the construction crew. Most of the trees were saved, only to become strange victims of war—after Pearl Harbor, they were referred to simply as cherry trees.

Jefferson Memorial, John Russell Pope, 1934–1943. The rotunda is virtually a duplicate of a design by Pope for the Henry E. Huntington Mausoleum at San Marino, California.

"Buildings modeled on those of ancient Rome are not necessarily un-American. The founding fathers believed that they were creating a government similar to the Roman republic . . . Not only did they style our chief governmental building the 'Capitol,' after the Capitolium, a famous Roman temple of Jupiter; they even referred to a sluggish stream at the foot of Capitol Hill as Tiber Creek."

Charles H. Probert, letter to the editor of the Washington Post, February 26, 1937

"The undersigned desire to protest against the carrying out of this scheme for the following reasons:

"1. The proposed design is completely inappropriate as a memorial to Thomas Jefferson. The proposed design could equally well serve, by a simple change in the inscription, as a memorial to Theodore Roosevelt, Edgar Allan Poe or the Supreme Court. In fact, one rather suspects it has. . . .

"The memorial should be one that will, by its nature, be a memorial to Jefferson instead of to the architect and the Commission. Washington is sorely in need of mass recreational areas, public gathering places or other projects for popular use. . . .

"[Signed]
Catherine Bauer
Henry S. Churchill
Carl Feiss
Talbot Faulkner Hamlin
Joseph Hudnut
William Lescaze
Lewis Mumford
William Zorach."

Letter to the editor of The New Republic, April 7, 1937, from noted modernist architects and critics of the day

Proposal for Theodore Roosevelt Memorial, John Russell Pope, for the site that was finally used for Pope's Jefferson Memorial.

Interior, Jefferson Memorial, in a scene from the movie "Born Yesterday," Columbia Pictures, 1950.

"The question why there was no competition for the design had been raised. But the answer appears to be perfectly obvious when one examines, even cursorily, the original of the memorial. . . . The new buildings of the past seven years have been judiciously parceled out among a small coterie. Surely there are many architects whose ideas and point of view are more nearly related to the present. What Jefferson would want would be public buildings designed by men interested solely in the art of architecture and undistracted by the art of wire-pulling."

Marquis W. Childs, "Mr. Pope's Memorial," Magazine of Art, *April 1937*

"That Congress should assist the immortality of Thomas Jefferson by the reconstruction of a temple once dedicated to the seven gods of Rome is a project which, objectively considered, is surely one of the most fantastic in the history of architecture. The Classic Revival, itself the most fantastic of architectural fashions—which sought to confine a modern world in the strict fabrics of the Greek temple and the Roman bath—is to be brought to a climax in a Pantheon not only larger and more splendid than any of the four hundred Pantheons which have hitherto enlivened that movement but one which embodies the essential creed of classicism with a hyperorthodoxy so exacting as scarcely to admit the heresy of an original line; and this at a time when architecture throughout the world is being swept triumphantly into new and magnificent modes of expression."

Joseph Hudnut, "Twilight of the Gods," Magazine of Art, *August 1937*

"I am very sympathetic with the effort to end the 'petrified forest' of columns in Washington, but I feel, in view of Jefferson's own strong feeling about the classic, that the Jefferson Memorial is not the place to begin. Let us carry out the proposal for the Memorial . . . and then let us turn to the task of infusing the architecture of Washington henceforth with modern character."

Fiske Kimball, Member, Thomas Jefferson Memorial Commission, and Director, Philadelphia Museum of Art, in a letter to the Magazine of Art, *May 1938*

National Gallery of Art, 1941.

Interior, National Gallery of Art.

"The Museum has long been convinced that architects for government buildings must be chosen by the democratic method of open, anonymous competition if American official architecture is ever to get out of its long-accustomed rut. A competition for a National Gallery of Art might have resulted in something more lively than the costly mummy which now faces the Mall."

Philip L. Goodwin, preface to Museum of Modern Art exhibit catalog, Built in USA, 1944

As the renewed public buildings program got underway, the Supervising Architect's Office expanded to keep pace, growing from a 1929 force of 432 to nearly 750 in 1932. At the same time, private architects, too busy in the 1920s construction boom to pay attention to the federal program, developed a keen interest in its fortunes. Nearly half the country's architectural firms failed in the first year of the Depression, and the 5,000 remaining averaged a quarter of their 1928 income. Twenty-five hundred architects applied for jobs in the Supervising Architect's Office in 1932. The private architects' assault on the federal worklode generally took a different angle, however.

Led by the American Institute of Architects, they demanded that the actual design tasks be contracted out to private firms. Barely concealing their economic distress behind arguments that the government's own design production was inferior, more costly, too time-consuming, and antithetical to the principles of free enterprise, they won an ever-increasing share of the work.

The Public Buildings Acts of 1926 and 1930 authorized—but did not require —the Treasury Department to hire private architects. The Hoover administration, categorically refuting the AIA arguments, used the authority sparingly. (It is difficult to judge now which side had the best of the cost and time disputes, and it is equally difficult to award design laurels: both private and public architects turned out competent starved-classical buildings.) The Roosevelt administration was more receptive.

The New Deal held other traumas for the Supervising Architect's Office. With the pump-priming policy still being debated and the buildings program suspended in 1933, the staff was furloughed four days a month. Then, with the pump activated, full and part-time "consultants" were variously hired, laid off, and rehired to cope with the fluctuating work load, and morale suffered. In a Treasury Department reorganization, the office lost its independent status as well as its quarters in the Treasury building, and became part of the "Public Buildings Branch" in a "Procurement Division." In 1939, in an overall New Deal administrative retrenchment, it was merged with the buildings management arm of the Park Service to become the Public Buildings Administration (PBA) within the Federal Works Agency. In this incarnation, the title of Supervising Architect vanished and administrators and engineers gained ascendancy over architects in the buildings bureaucracy.

Under this 1939 arrangement, some architectural supervision was delegated to regional offices for the first time, following a precedent set in a series of regional design competitions. Early in 1938, a group composed mostly of modernist architects, but including Paul Cret, formed a National Competitions Committee to advocate the use of open (any and all invited) competitions to select private architects for federal projects. (The Committee was an outgrowth of the modernist League for Architectural Progress, which had protested the Jefferson Memorial architect selection and neoclassical design.) Just twenty-five years removed from its strong support for the Tarsney Act competitions, the AIA offered only grudging support—and only for limited competitions at that.

For several years previous, the Treasury's Section of Painting and Sculpture had used competitions in its program to embellish federal building interiors. Drawing on this experience, in mid-1938, the Supervising Architect organized a competition offering ten prizes for designs suitable for small post offices, part of a late-1930s effort at standardized design. Ten more competitions were announced, open only to architects in each of ten newly drawn regions, for design of larger buildings in designated cities. The competitions drew over two thousand entries. First-place awards went to noncommittal starved-classical designs, but modern designs garnered some lower honors. Excluded from these competitions, survivors of the Supervising Architect's Office held one among themselves in 1939 and selected 12 designs for small post offices.

As war preparations accelerated, the Navy and Army established a system for direct selection of private architects that closely followed AIA recommendations. Selection criteria stressed a firm's past experience and credentials and did not solicit design proposals for the project at hand. This system was generally adopted throughout the government and is essentially the one used today; design competitions were not revived after the war.

During the war, the Public Buildings Administration designed and built temporary office buildings and housing for defense workers. Little new work for public buildings was authorized after the war, and the architectural branch atrophied. In 1948, the Hoover Commission, noting that the federal government had become "the most gigantic business on earth," recommended creation of a single agency to provide housekeeping services for the executive branch of government. A year later, the General Services Administration (GSA) was formed and the PBA (later to be named the Public Buildings Service) was folded into it. Since its inception, GSA has relied on private architects exclusively to perform all but its most minor design work.

Louis A. Simon, Supervising Architect, 1933–1939. Simon graduated from M.I.T. in 1891, joined the Supervising Architect's Office in 1896, and from 1905 to 1933 was superintendent of the architectural section. Since the office was presided over from 1915 to 1933 by "Judge" James Wetmore, who, being a lawyer, was designated only the Acting Supervising Architect, Simon determined the office's architectural directions throughout the starved-classical period. A well-respected and conservative designer, he was decorous in manner, too, and required his staff to wear coats and ties even at the drawing board.

"We believe that the country is entitled to the services of the best architectural talent available, and that the concentration of so large a volume of work as the present appropriations provide, into the hands of a single Government bureau, must inevitably tend to produce stereotyped, mediocre and uninspiring results . . . ."
Resolution of the Board of Directors of the AIA at the 1931 Convention, in American Architect, June 1931

"The ethics of the profession has certainly taken a jolt when the architects of the country on letterheads of their A.I.A. Chapters blacken without investigation the work of other architects' offices with the naive and frank admission that it is for the purpose of getting architectural commissions for themselves.

"The Federal Architectural offices are weaned and reared on criticism. If they use material A, delegations appear to lambaste them for not using material B. Or vice versa. If they face the building north, a newspaper crusade develops because it was not faced south. Or vice versa. The bitter attacks of private architects are, therefore, merely the regular order. . . . But—one could have wished that architects would have stood by architects."
The Federal Architect, April 1931

"We read in the April American Architect a well-printed article on the question of Government work and private architects, which courteously labels the Supervising Architect's office as Russian and un-American."
The Federal Architect, April 1931

"Maintaining of architectural offices by the Government to design public buildings is fundamentally wrong in principle because it places the Government in direct competition with private business, contrary to the aims and ideals upon which the Government of the United States is based."
Excerpt from sample petition urged on readers by the editor, American Architect, May 1931

"It was with no great feeling of joy that . . . we saw the good old Supervising Architect's Office, the oldest architectural office in the country . . . buried without flag or volley in the Procurement Division . . . .

"From a purely professional point of view, it is perhaps unfortunate that architecture should be submerged under the purchasing of coal and typewriters, necessary and important though those operations may be.

"This eclipsing of government architecture has not been discouraged by the attitude of the American Institute of Architects, who have spread abroad the fact that they are not interested in good architecture unless they design it themselves."
The Federal Architect, October 1933

"The Federal policy of designing in Washington its own post-offices and other public buildings still remains the chief topic of conversation wherever architects gather. . . . One architect, whose taste is impeccable, said that he had taken the article we published in the June issue showing recent government buildings throughout the United States, had covered up all credit lines, and had then proceeded to grade the various buildings from A to F. . . . It was found . . . that the buildings designed by the Treasury Department had a higher rating than those designed by private architects. . . . there were no A ratings in the Treasury Department's work, nor any F's. In a word, the government-designed architecture maintained a higher, if not an especially brilliant, standard."
Architecture, October 1934

"The Federal Warehouse, to which the Supervising Architect's Office is to move, is somewhat distant from the seething marts of trade . . . and can be reached by boat on the Potomac River, by ox cart, and in other ways."
The Federal Architect, January 1934

In a last burst of beleaguered pride, the reorganized, renamed, and displaced incumbents of the Supervising Architect's office enlisted muralist Harold Weston to decorate the lobby of their outpost in the Federal Warehouse, renamed the Procurement Building. In a series of twenty-two murals Weston portrayed the program of construction undertaken by the Treasury Department's Procurement Division. One wall of the lobby depicted architecture activities, and another wall treated the construction activities of the supply branch of the division. Six separate panels over the elevator entrances traced stages in modern construction through different types of buildings erected around the country by the Procurement Division.

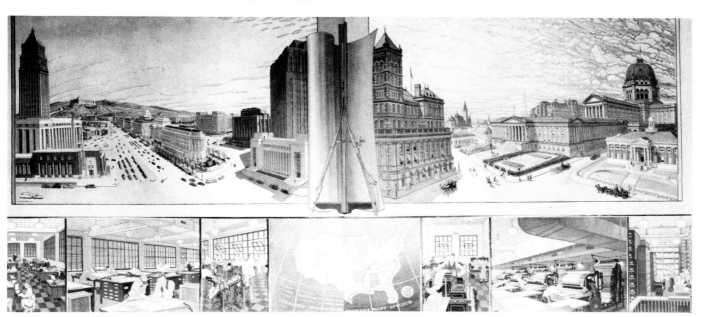

Mural portraying the activities of the architectural branch of the Procurement Division, lobby of the Procurement Building, south end wall, Harold Weston, 1937. Symbols of architecture are depicted in the center, including a scroll of paper, a T-square, and a bow pen. The large scene on the left represents a montage of contemporary work completed between 1933 and 1937, including the tower of the New York City Courthouse, the Federal Triangle, and, on the highest hilltop, the San Francisco Mint. On the large right panel is a montage of historic work of government architects, including Robert Mills's Treasury and Alfred Mullett's State, War, and Navy Building.

The Venerable Office
330–331

Mural panel, Harold Weston: stone-brick-tile (in the finishing process of one of many post offices built throughout the nation, probably a New England location shown here).

Mural panel, Harold Weston: creating the building plans—drafting room.

Mural panel, Harold Weston: blueprinting. In 1936 the blueprinting room at Procurement turned out more blueprints than any other establishment in the world—working twenty-four hours a day on a high-speed press.

Mural panel, Harold Weston: central heating.

Starved classicism found a home in countries of diverse ideologies, resulting in a "government international" style that flourished in the midst of the polemical storm over the better-known International Style propounded by Bauhaus architects and Le Corbusier.

Government International picked up stray trappings of indigenous culture, reflected more or less influence from the Modern Movement—depending on where and when it erupted—and was received with official praise for its political correctness in every manifestation. In Eastern European countries and the Soviet Union, the style seems to have staved off the modernists longer than anywhere else.

Symbols, like styles, were also international. The eagle and sticks bundled about an axe, or fasces, the ancient Roman symbols of state power, appeared in the modern industrial states, indifferent to the niceties of ideology.

Japan: National Diet, Tokyo, 1920s.

"No quality in architecture is more treacherous than symbolism. . . . Architectural symbols . . . can lose their command over our hearts with every change of knowledge or vision, with every shifting of prejudice or self-interest. The art of the Classic Revival . . . can be as readily despised as the art of Napoleon, as admired as the art of Jefferson. To Napoleon and to Jefferson, moreover, this art stood for sharply opposed ideals, since to Napoleon the classic was a symbol of political absolutism and to Jefferson a symbol of the resolute republicanism of early Rome. It is one of the intriguing qualities of classicism that it can be reinvented with the special desires of each era."

Joseph Hudnut, "Twilight of the Gods," Magazine of Art, *August 1937*

Germany: Sculpture outside
the Olympic Stadium, Berlin,
1936. Government sculpture,
like buildings, showed international similarities.

Germany: House of German
Art, Munich, 1934, pictured
on the cover of a book about
Nazi building programs published in the U.S. by the Nazi
government in 1940. The
cover of the 1939 report of
the U.S. Public Works Administration, "America Builds,"
(see page 347) stressed employment and production over
architecture.

A NATION BUILDS

"... The classical formula has
been a recurrent architectural
motif in Germany, and it is
never more appropriate than
when it is used to symbolize an
ideal or serve as a monument to
one. But contemporary German
classicism is no mere imitation
of the temple motif. It has made
a harmonious correlation between Hellenic serenity and the
austere simplicity of modern
functional architecture."

German Library of Information,
A Nation Builds, 1940

Germany: Chancellory, Albert
Speer, Berlin, reminiscent of
Paul Cret's Federal Reserve
Board in Washington.

"The Party Buildings at Nuremberg designed by Professor
Albert Speer have introduced a
new idea into the history of architecture. Impressive as they
may be in themselves, as symbolic monuments dedicated to
ideals of unity and a disciplined
social order, they only achieve
their true intention when they
are adorned with flags and
filled with the massed thousands who meet at Nuremberg
for the Party Conventions."

German Library of Information,
A Nation Builds, 1940

"In every European country,
and in America too, the thirties
saw a resurgence of interest in
monumental styles for which
modified neoclassical forms were
employed. . . . What differen-
tiates the development of Nazi
architecture . . . is the degree
of ideological significance attached to it by the Nazi leaders
and the intensity of the political
propaganda which surrounded
it. These characteristics of Nazi
architecture can only be understood in the light of the fierce
political controversies over architecture which took place
during the Weimar period. That
the architectural policy of the
Nazi regime emerged out of this
background determined both the
general character of its architectural program and its political
significance. Thus, although
the political involvement of architecture reached its height in
Germany under Hitler, it began
in 1918."

Barbara Miller Lane, Architecture and Politics in Ger-
many, 1918-1945, 1968

Switzerland: League of Nations, c. 1935. This design was executed after a winning competition design by Le Corbusier was rejected by the League's head diplomats.

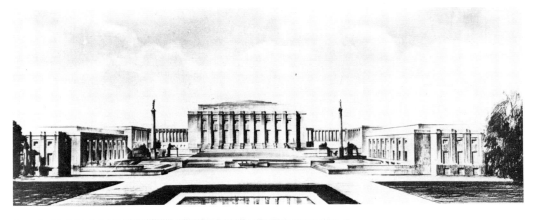

England: Proposed design for a government office building, London, 1939.

"We consider that proletarian architecture should develop through the application of dialectical materialism in both theory and practice.

"We are for the dialectical utilization by architecture of all that science can offer. . . .

"We are for a proletarian class architecture, for technico-formal unity in architecture, for a vigorous architecture which through the will of the masses promotes organization in the struggle and on the job."

Manifesto of V.O.P.R.A. (All-Russian Association of Proletarian Architects), an antimodern group, 1929

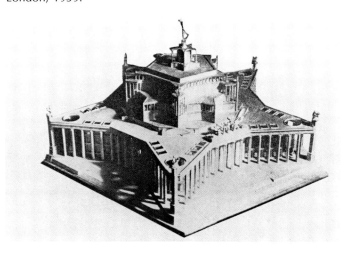

Soviet Union: Central Red Army Theatre, Moscow, 1940 (model). In plan the five-pointed star almost describes a pentagon.

Edward Bruce, chief of Treasury's Section of Fine Arts. In May 1938, Bruce elaborated on his expectations for the Smithsonian competition, which the Section sponsored: "My idea is something genuinely simple and beautiful— no classical columns of any kind. . . . What I would like to see is a one story building with a beautiful garden and suitable courts where people would enjoy coming to."

For the second time in less than 100 years, a competition for a Smithsonian Institution building produced a design that broke sharply with the prevailing federal style. The father/son/son-in-law team of Eliel and Eero Saarinen and Robert Swanson won the 1939 competition for a Smithsonian Gallery of Art with a project unmistakably "modern." As with James Renwick's romantic Norman castle, it would be some twenty years before the mainstream of federal architecture would follow the course it set. The Saarinens were not to share Renwick's satisfaction in seeing the project built, however.

The Gallery was the idea of Edward Bruce, head of the Section of Fine Arts in the Treasury Department's Public Buildings Branch. For six years, Bruce's Section had been conducting competitions to select muralists and sculptors for federal buildings, and

Bruce saw the need for a gallery dedicated to contemporary American artists to counterbalance the "mausoleum for dead masters," as he called the new National Gallery of Art. Working with Frederic A. Delano, the President's uncle and chairman of the National Capital Park and Planning Commission, Bruce persuaded Congress to provide a building site on the Mall and $40,000 to conduct a design competition, but Congress balked at funding construction and left that to private means.

Architect selection and critical reaction to the design presented almost a mirror image of the Jefferson Memorial experience. The competition jury was packed in favor of modernists: Delano as chairman, Walter Gropius, founder of the Bauhaus and Harvard professor, and George Howe, prominent American modern architect, constituted a majority of votes. Joseph Hudnut, Dean of Harvard's

School of Architecture, served as professional adviser to the jury, and a member of the Museum of Modern Art architecture staff served as technical adviser. Out of 1,408 entries the jury picked ten finalists before declaring the winners. Modernist Percival Goodman placed second.

Now it was the traditionalists' turn to protest. The Commission of Fine Arts announced that it would reject the Saarinen design—and any other with a "similar flavor of modernism"—when submitted. Supervising Architect Louis Simon, Bruce's nominal boss, complained that the museum would mar the impression he had been working to create in Washington. Modernists rallied to the design. Hudnut argued that it had a classical feeling in its own

way, and that, counting the Egyptian Washington monument, Georgian White House, Doric Lincoln Memorial, and Imperial Roman Jefferson Memorial, there were nineteen different architectural styles already facing the Mall. The Museum of Modern Art in New York had an exhibit of the competition designs.

Difficulty in raising private money, a government reorganization that put the Section of Fine Arts in limbo, and then the pressures of war mobilization combined to stop the gallery project. In 1958, the Mall site was reassigned to the Smithsonian's Air and Space Museum. But just up the Mall, in 1974, the Smithsonian opened the Hirshhorn Museum, dedicated to international modern art and designed in a brutal modernism by then not unusual to federal projects.

View of the Mall facade, model of the Saarinens' winning design for the Smithsonian competition.

View of the Saarinen model from the rear.

"That an impeccable jury should have chosen—for Washington—a building without the usual Roman draperies is not only a tribute to their courage and honesty, but gives, at long last, some hope that the Capital may show three dimensional evidence of its existence in the twentieth century."

"The great virtue of the winning design . . . is that it shows that the monumental tradition of Washington can be given appropriate expression, and new vitality, within the framework of modern architecture."

Architectural Forum, *July 1939*

Smithsonian competition, design by Paul Cret, one of the ten finalists. The classicism of the Mall facade has nearly "starved" to death; the south elevation is completely "modern."

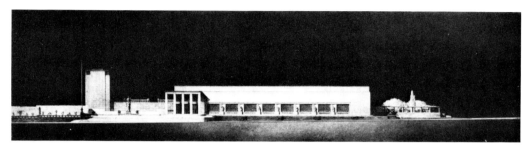

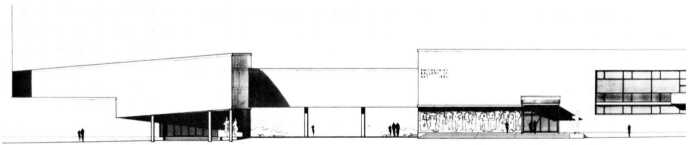

Smithsonian competition, final design of Robert W. Kennedy and Eliot F. Noyes, which received one of eight third prizes. Another third-prize winner was Edward Durell Stone, who was chosen twenty years later to design the Kennedy Center for the Performing Arts. Second place was won by Percival Goodman.

"This award marks the first time since the days of Thomas Jefferson that the architect for an important building in the Nation's Capital has been selected by open competition."

Architectural Forum, July 1939

"The vague institutionalism of contemporary public architecture is a hesitant style, lost in the land between what was and what is to be. When the will to build is reborn, the city will probably take its theme from Eero Saarinen's unbuilt design for the Smithsonian Gallery of Art, or other buildings that give opportunity to the genius of our times."

Frederick Gutheim, Potomac, 1949

THE LEGACIES OF CRISIS

7

Dust storm, South Dakota, 1934. On May 11, 1934, an immense dust storm moved 300 million tons of soil from the Great Plains, tearing topsoil off some fields to the depth of a plow. Dust was sighted and tasted in New York and Washington. Reportedly, it hung above ships 200 miles at sea.

"The soil is the one indestructible, immutable asset that cannot be exhausted, that cannot be used up." (U.S. Bureau of Soils, 1909)

Bonus Marchers stage a protest vigil on the Capitol lawn, 1932, part of an army of 20,000 jobless World War I veterans who came to Washington in an unsuccessful effort to collect their benefits in advance. Skirmishes with police led to a drastic official response: On July 28 federal troops burned the temporary demonstration encampments and with bayonets, tanks, and tear gas, drove veterans from the city.

Across the nation farmers' uprisings, hunger marches, and the shantytowns of the dispossessed, called Hoovervilles, were symptoms of deepening economic depression. In January 1933 Franklin Delano Roosevelt assumed the presidency. Abroad, governments were toppling and armies were on the move as depression fueled the conflicts that would erupt in World War II.

"The dawn came, but no day. In the gray sky a red sun appeared, a dim red circle that gave a little light, like dusk; and that day advanced, the dusk slipped back toward darkness, and the wind cried and whimpered over the fallen corn." So John Steinbeck described the great dust storm of 1934. The nation, in the grip of an historic economic depression, was experiencing another dramatic reminder that its abundant resources were not limitless. In a few years it would confront the crisis of World War II. The sweeping mobilizations required to meet these emergencies would radically change the nature of government, the business of federal building, and the American landscape.

By 1933 more than 13 million workers were unemployed; more than a thousand homes were being foreclosed every day; cities were going bankrupt. Floods, drought, and dust storms were exacerbating the already deplorable plight of farm workers. "Soils which have been built steadily for 20,000 years since the last ice age," wrote Stuart Chase in 1936, "now in a single century lose the benefits of several thousand years of accumulation. More than 300 million acres—one-sixth of the country—is gone, going or beginning to go."

Presidential doubts of the 1920s about government's constitutional responsibility became the certainties of the 1930s. "It is common sense," said President Franklin Delano Roosevelt, "to take a method and try it. If it fails, admit it frankly and try another. But above all, try something."

Under the economic stress of the Depression the government began or expanded programs that affected the nation's physical development. Reforestation, grazing control, rural electrification, flood control were attempts to secure the physical basis of the nation. The Omnibus Flood Control Act of 1936, for instance, accelerated the Corps of Engineers' program of dam building and channelization of rivers and authorized the yeoman efforts of the Soil Conservation Service, which helped ameliorate the destructive farming practices, begun in colonial times, that led to the dust bowl. The Engineers' continual improvement of river channels and flood control works benefited barge transportation and salvaged valley land for development. An army of jobless young men were enlisted in a Civilian Conservation Corps and a battle to preserve the nation's natural resources. "Emerging," wrote historian Arthur Schlesinger, Jr., "were the lineaments of a new land."

The fact that all these programs provided a substantial number of jobs was a major factor in Congressional support of them during the Depression. But they were also favored as traditional "pork barrel projects" in the context of an unquestioned national

commitment to growth-as-good. It was not until that growth dramatized the finiteness
of natural resources and the limits of federal magic in generating resources that the
negative side of federal development programs would be considered.

At high tide the New Deal was trying many things. To stimulate the economy, a new
Public Works Administration (PWA) was directing billions of dollars into loans and
grants to federal, state, and municipal agencies for construction of projects "of public
benefit" and pioneering in urban construction that in later decades would be addressed more ambitiously by the federal government. Through the PWA the federal
government for the first time was also clearing city slums and constructing the first
peacetime low-cost public housing, an effort that ended when the National Housing
Act of 1937 shifted the federal role to one of lender and subsidizer and relinquished
the building role to local housing authorities.

The new Tennessee Valley Authority was redeveloping one of the most depressed
areas of the country in the single demonstration of federal regional planning. The new
Subsistence Homestead Administration was attempting to entice city dwellers back to
the land by building planned communities in rural areas. The new Resettlement
Administration was providing shelters to house migrant workers and building suburban greenbelt communities for low-cost housing in a small-town environment just
outside city job markets.

The number and variety of structures built under these programs greatly expanded the
federal repertoire. The results were often architecturally unremarkable, particularly in
those programs that gave first priority to speeding increased opportunities for employment. In contrast, the Resettlement Administration's social innovations attracted able
design and planning professionals to government staff positions; the challenges of
need and real economy elicited, in their best projects, solutions that emphasized fitting design to the present rather than fitting the present into the designs of other periods. The symbolism in all the New Deal buildings, however, lay in the very fact of
their existence, their evident commitment to the shift of government from neutral ar-
biter to social welfare activist.

For all their seeming pragmatism, New Dealers shared a vision that was part of a continuing American dream—clean, white, green, and preferably fenced. Their ideal
America included formerly unrepresented minorities like industrial laborers, farmers,
and particular ethnic groups but slum dwellers and blacks were still not included in
the deal. Nor were the most deprived rural people, the southern tenant farmers. M. L.
Wilson, head of the subsistence homestead efforts, said that his program was "a middle class movement for selected people, not the top, not the dregs."

As historian William E. Leuchtenburg wrote, the New Dealers "had their Heavenly City: the greenbelt town, clean, green, and white, with children playing in light, airy, spacious schools; the government project at Longview, Washington [a subsistence homestead community], with small houses, each of different design, colored roofs, and gardens of flowers and vegetables, the Mormon villages of Utah that M. L. Wilson kept in his mind's eye—immaculate farmsteads on broad, rectangular streets; most of all, the Tennessee Valley, with its model town of Norris, the tall transmission towers, the white dams, the glistening wire strands, the valley where 'a vision of villages and clean small factories has been growing into the minds of thoughtful men.' Scandinavia was their model abroad . . . because it represented the 'middle way' of happy accommodation of public and private institutions the New Deal sought to achieve. 'Why,' inquired Brandeis, 'should anyone want to go to Russia when one can go to Denmark?'"

The rural idyll promoted by many New Deal programs was one facet of hope in a time of adversity. In contrast was the vision of a high-technology, utopian future presented by the big fairs of the 1930s. Here, exhibits prosletyzed for a triumvirate of industry, science, and good design as the means to resolve the ills of society. A sleek, pseudoscientific architecture fashionably collaborated with the message.

Outside the fairgrounds and outside the Roosevelt administration's propensity for a simpler past, the nation was learning the ominous statistics of urban life. By 1935 one-fifth of all the employable persons on relief were in the ten largest cities. The employment-oriented crises of depression dramatized a statistical reality: America was becoming a predominantly metropolitan nation, whatever its small-town dreams. To alleviate economic distress quickly, the federal government had to deal directly with cities, bypassing the traditional administrative hierarchy of nation-state-local contacts—a far-reaching change for the development of American government.

And for the first time since the attempts at national planning of the early 1800s the federal government sponsored an effort to set national planning priorities. In 1934 Roosevelt appointed an interdepartmental National Resources Board to coordinate federal planning activities and to recommend yearly to the President and Congress "a priority of projects in the national plan." The Board pioneered in national research on and analyses of social and economic issues, studies which would become a commonplace in the 1960s, albeit without any national priority framework. As it viewed the American scene, the board investigated technological advances, land use, population change, and regionalism. Its public policy proposals and its studies of the social, economic, and political implications of planning were of unprecedented national scope. During its ten-year existence, and through three name changes and three reorganizations, the board emerged as the federal government's most urban agency. Its comprehensive investigation into the role of cities in the national economy was the first federal study of urban problems. Its report *Our Cities* was prophetic: "Surely in the long run the nation's destiny will be profoundly affected by the cities which have two-thirds of its population and its wealth."

The threat of national planning to the Corps of Engineers' interest in local rivers and harbors projects and the Congressional interest in local patronage guaranteed the board's end. In 1943 Congress voted the National Resources Planning Board out of existence. The board's attention to the city in a national context was replaced by the emerging federal concern for the city as a place to subsidize the building of houses. "The difference was crucial," wrote historian Mark Gelfand, "the consequences [were] momentous."

Although the New Deal proved that it could alleviate some of the more painful and apparent results of economic crisis, it never proved that it could achieve prosperity in peacetime. As late as 1941, unemployment, although substantially lowered from 1933, was still high. World War II, not domestic social programs, eliminated joblessness.

Mobilization for war blurred peacetime niceties of design and planning. Some New Deal programs, like the WPA arts projects and the greenbelt towns, were dismantled. Others, like the TVA, went to war. Wartime pressures produced engineering innovations, feats of construction by the Corps of Engineers, like the Alcan Highway and the Burma Road, and the contemporary image of some of the huge war industry plants. The results were also apparent in egg-crate temporaries on the Mall of the nation's capital, loyalty oaths, and the dusty streets and barren structures of the Japanese detention camps.

The end of the successive crises of depression and war would not mark any return to precrisis conditions. Instead the administrative state of a modern industrial nation would convert its unparalleled wartime industrial capacity to peacetime consumerism. It would also try to order its plethora of domestic programs, its far-flung overseas commitments—the acquisitions of crisis. And the often unruly, red-tape-cutting administration of the crisis eras would be replaced by the administration of "normalcy," with its inevitable emphasis on constraints instead of possibilities.

Particularly hard hit by the Depression were the construction trades and related industries. To stimulate recovery, Congress in June 1933 created a Public Works Administration (PWA), which was authorized to disburse money to both federal and nonfederal agencies for construction projects of public benefit. State and local applicants could seek grants of up to 45 percent and loans of up to 70 percent of project cost; federal agencies could apply for grants of up to 100 percent. Although the PWA required that certain standards of design and construction be met before a project was given approval, attention to specifically architectural review was cursory.

President Roosevelt chose Secretary of the Interior Harold L. Ickes to head the new agency. Ickes spent money so carefully that his agency never fulfilled its promise as a pump-priming device, but the impact of PWA on public works building was considerable, especially in retarding physical deterioration in cities, where employment needs were most pressing. Historian Arthur Schlesinger, Jr., wrote that the PWA "left behind, as Ickes so passionately wished, a splendidly improved national estate."

Responding to the first national housing surveys, which found one-third of all dwellings substandard, Congress also in 1933 authorized the PWA to use federal money for an attack on the slums. The Constitution's general welfare clause provided the legal sanction. Ickes soon abandoned the subsidy approach of other PWA programs as ineffective for serving the ill-housed, and, in a move unprecedented in peacetime, he put the government into the business of constructing urban housing. The PWA selected the sites, acquired the land, determined what projects should be built, built them, owned them, and operated them.

The PWA's slum clearance was shortlived; a court ruled that the federal government could not use its power of eminent domain to acquire land for local housing projects. Fearful of the Supreme Court's antagonism to other New Deal Programs, the administration at the last minute withdrew from a high court test of the PWA's housing program. By the time the Supreme Court's decisions began to favor the New Deal, housing reformers had succeeded in pushing through Congress the 1937 Wagner-Steagall Housing Act, which created a public housing corporation to make loans and pay subsidies to local public housing authorities. Thereafter the federal government retreated into the role of lender and spender, relinquishing its building role to local government. The stubborn pattern of limited federal power, briefly breached in 1934, eventually became firmly re-entrenched in the growing power of autonomous local interests.

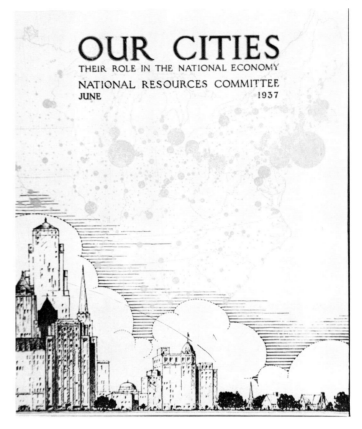

Our Cities, cover of the Report of the Urbanism Committee to the National Resources Committee, June 1937, the first federal study of urban problems. The interdepartmental planning committee evolved out of an earlier planning board initiated by Ickes in PWA to encourage regional, state and local planning and to devise a national scheme for public works development. The advisory board of the National Resources Committee included cabinet-level departmental secretaries from the departments of the Interior, War, Agriculture, Commerce, and Labor as well as the administrator of the Works Progress Administration; Frederic A. Delano, uncle of the President and former chairman of the National Capital Park and Planning Commission; Charles E. Merriam, public administration authority, political science professor at the University of Chicago, and earlier vice-chairman of President Hoover's Research Committee on Social Trends; Henry S. Dennison; and Beardsley Ruml. Among its staff members was a young economist, John Kenneth Galbraith.

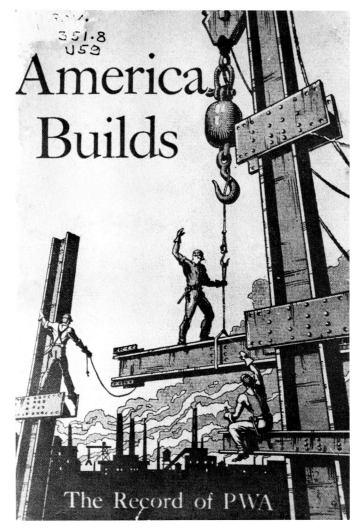

"Cities will probably, unless present trends are reversed by large-scale rehabilitation of the blighted areas, continue to increase in density of population at the periphery and to decrease at the center."

Our Cities, *National Resources Committee, 1937*

"It may well be that the future of our civilization will in large measure depend not upon man's ability to escape from the city but upon his ability to master and use the forces that move and control it. It is doubtful whether without the city we can hope to enjoy the plane of living that contemporary civilization makes possible. The central problem of national life in regard to cities is a problem of creating those conditions that are required to make cities livable for human beings in a machine age."

Our Cities, *National Resources Committee, 1937*

Cover of *America Builds: The Record of the PWA*, 1939. Between 1933 and 1939 the PWA helped in the construction of about 70 percent of the nation's new educational facilities; 65 percent of its courthouses and city halls; 65 percent of its sewage disposal plants; 35 percent of its hospitals and public health facilities; and 10 percent of all roads, bridges, subways, and similar engineering structures. PWA projects and the industries providing for the projects employed billions of man-hours of labor.

Chart from *America Builds: The Record of the PWA*. Between 1929 and 1932, private construction had taken a plunge from $7.5 billion to $1.5 billion; industrial construction, from $949 million to $74 million. Building by financially strapped state and local governments was nearly nil. Among the architecture profession, four thousand firms failed, and the average annual volume among the remaining five thousand declined to a fourth of the 1928 level. According to John Burchard and Albert Bush-Brown, "the total cost of all buildings directed by architects plunged from three and a half billion dollars to half a billion."

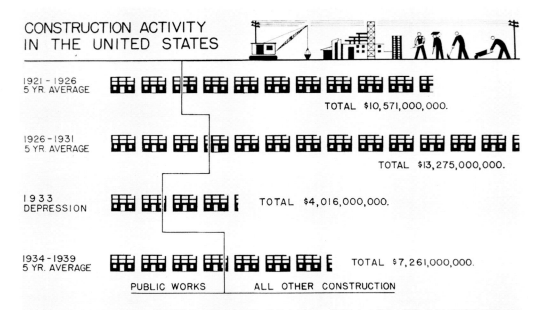

CONSTRUCTION ACTIVITY IN THE UNITED STATES

1921 - 1926
5 YR. AVERAGE
TOTAL $10,571,000,000.

1926 - 1931
5 YR. AVERAGE
TOTAL $13,275,000,000.

1933
DEPRESSION
TOTAL $4,016,000,000.

1934 - 1939
5 YR. AVERAGE
TOTAL $7,261,000,000.

PUBLIC WORKS   ALL OTHER CONSTRUCTION

EACH BUILDING REPRESENTS ONE BILLION DOLLARS OF CONSTRUCTION

Harold Ickes, appointed to head the Public Works Administration by President Roosevelt in 1933. Ickes described himself as having "at least the negative and austere qualities which the handling of so much public money requires. . . ." A veteran of many wars against corruption in Chicago city government, "honest Harold" scrutinized even the minutest details of every loan and grant request, looking for any hint of waste or corruption.

New Deal Plan for Enlarged Supreme Court, C. K. Berryman, February 10, 1937, satirizing Roosevelt's attempt to circumvent the Court's negation of New Deal programs by sending a bill to Congress that would have allowed him to add six justices to the Court and about fifty to the lower courts. In the cartoon, Ickes's publicly recognized integrity is challenged by the President's dubious and unsuccessful court-packing plan.

" . . . Enforced economy sired the virtue of thrift in design and, while effects of monotony and of institutionalism occasionally resulted, for the most part the enormous scope of the housing venture and the realistic restrictions of minimum standards, stimulated housing designs to new approaches in design. The results were not only safe, sanitary and decent shelter, but an architectural straight forwardness and simplicity of treatment which cannot fail to leave a deep impress on all of the architecture of our time."

The Federal Architect, January 1947

"The development of neighborhoods—rather than individual homes—was accepted as a guide not only for the stability it would give to communities, but also because of the reduced municipal expenditures it could bring about. . . . In its 51 projects, the Housing Division was able to remodel existing street patterns and to reduce the necessary street area as much as 30 percent."

America Builds: The Record of the PWA, 1939

The PWA's Williamsburg project in Brooklyn, New York. This city-within-a-city replaced twelve of the most blighted slum blocks in New York City.

Children's playroom, PWA-built Harlem housing project. Mural by Elsie Driggs, done under the Treasury Art Projects.

Houses, Williamsburg project. The development was built to accommodate a total of 1,622 families. Buildings contained craft centers and social rooms, laundries, and nurseries. The project also contained a nursery school. Its buildings covered about 32 percent of a 20.2-acre site.

List of the PWA's federal projects involving buildings, from C. W. Short and R. Stanley-Brown, *Public Buildings: A Survey of Architecture of Projects Constructed by Federal and Other Governmental Bodies between the Years 1933 and 1939*, Washington, D.C., U.S. Government Printing Office, 1939.

Abattoirs
Airfields
Airway equipment
Ammunition manufacturing
Ammunition preserves
Amphitheaters
Animal houses
Animal pens
Animal shelters
Apartment buildings
Army posts
Asylums
Barns
Barracks
Bathhouses
Blacksmith shops
Boathouses
Border stations
Bridges
Building repairs
Bunkhouses
Cabins
Camp grounds
Club buildings
Comfort stations
Customs buildings
Departmental buildings
Dining halls and kitchens
Dispensaries
Dormitories
Drill halls
Electric plants
Experimental stations
Feed sheds
Field quarters
Fire lookouts
Fire stations
Fish hatcheries
Game shelters
Garages
Gatehouses
Gates
Gage stations
General reconditioning
Greenhouses
Gun sheds
Gymnasiums
Hangars
Hay sheds
Headquarters buildings

Inspection stations
Jails
Laboratories
Landing fields
Life stations
Light fog stations
Lighthouses, etc.
Loading docks
Lock houses
Lodges
Machine shops
Memorials
Mess halls
Meter houses
Monuments
National parks
Navy-yard improvements
Nurseries
Observatories
Outdoor gymnasiums
Paint shops
Parachute shops
Piers, etc.
Post construction—Army
Post offices
Reconstruction depots
Refrigeration plants
Rehabilitations
Rest rooms
Restoration of mansions
Restaurants
Riding halls
Rostrums
Sanatoriums
Schools
Screen porches
Sentry houses
Sewer systems
Sheep barns
Silos
Smokehouses
Soil sheds
Stables
Theaters
Tool caches
Towers
Vehicle sheds
Veterans homes
Warehouses
Wash houses

"The new West's new hotspot is a town called 'New Deal,'" from story of construction of the federal government's Fort Peck Dam, *Life*, November 23, 1936. Photo by Margaret Bourke-White. However slight the ultimate influence on the national economy, the effect of the infusion of PWA money on the local economy was sometimes spectacular. The construction of Fort Peck Dam in eastern Montana spawned six disorderly frontier towns with names like New Deal and Square Deal as well as Fort Peck City, built for dam workers—but not their families—by the Corps of Engineers.

The National Estate

Fort Peck Dam, a federal PWA project for the Bureau of Reclamation. Photo by Margaret Bourke-White for the cover of the first issue of *Life* magazine. Note comparative size of two men at bottom of photograph.

"Franklin Roosevelt has a wild west. . . . It is about as wild and about as far west as the Wild West which Franklin's cousin Theodore saw in the Eighties. Its shack towns . . . are as wide open and as rickety as git-up-and-git or Hell's Delight. The only real difference is that Theodore's frontier was the natural result of the Great Trek to the Pacific, whereas Franklin's is the natural result of $110,000,000.

"The $110,000,000 is being spent on a work-relief project in Northeastern Montana. The project is an earthen dam—the world's largest—2,000 miles up the Missouri from St. Louis. The dam is intended to give work to Montana's unemployed and incidentally to promote the carriage of commerce on the Missouri. Whether or not it will promote the carriage of commerce is a question, but as a work maker it is a spectacular success."

Life, *November 23, 1936*

Federal high speed wind tunnel, Langley Field, Virginia.

Examples of Nonfederal Projects Built with PWA Assistance

City Hall, Libby, Montana, before and after PWA.

Coast Highway Bridge, Oregon.

Courthouse, Alameda, California.

Recreational building, Huntington Beach, California.

Relief worker for the WPA
displaying his government
paycheck.

When Roosevelt took of-
fice, nearly a third of the
nation's work force was
on relief. Private charities
and municipal and state
governments, their re-
sources dwindling, could
not begin to meet the
needs of the unemployed.
The federal government
stepped in with a system
of loans to states and mu-
nicipalities and later with
grants-in-aid. But the dole
programs were
inadequate.

Relief administrator Harry
L. Hopkins favored instead
a program that would em-
ploy reliefers on projects
of public benefit. Work for
the unemployed, Hopkins
contended, "preserves a
man's morale. It saves his
skill. It gives him a chance
to do something socially
useful." When angry mobs
marched on city halls protesting the dole and de-
manding jobs, Hopkins got
to try his hand at adminis-
tering a work relief pro-
gram—first the temporary
Civil Works Administra-
tion, then the Works Progress Administration (WPA;
later the Work Projects
Administration), created
by executive order in
1935.

Between 1935 and 1943
eight and a half million
different persons, with
30,000,000 dependents,
performed nearly 19 bil-
lion hours of WPA work
for nearly $9 billion in
wages. At its peak, the
WPA provided relief to a
third of the nation's unemployed—over 3 million.

About 75 percent of WPA
projects were in construction; the remainder were
"service projects"—every-
thing from the running of
adult education classes
and nursery schools to
gardening and canning of
foods for distribution to
the needy.

The majority of projects
were planned, initiated,
and "sponsored" by cities,
counties, and other public
agencies; the proportion
of sponsors' contributions
ranged from 10 percent of
the total cost of all WPA
projects in 1936 to about
30 percent in 1943. About
3 percent of WPA projects
were federally sponsored,
notably the federal arts
projects and several re-
search surveys.

Unlike Public Works Ad-
ministrator Harold Ickes,
Hopkins spent money fast
and furiously. Inevitably, a
certain amount of make-
work resulted. One image
that would remain synony-
mous with the WPA was
"leaf-raking," but as economist Garth Magnum later
observed, "It is difficult to
find fault with leaf raking
if there are leaves to be
raked."

The pejorative image
stuck, however, and the
WPA and its freewheeling
administrator were con-
stantly under attack. Hopkins defended his administrative approach as one of
"experimenting . . . in various parts of the country,
trying out schemes which
are supported by reasona-
ble people and see if they
work. If they do not work,
the world will not come to
an end."

The result was an incredi-
bly rich and varied output:
construction or repair of
650,000 miles of high-
ways, roads, and streets,
including farm-to-market

roads; construction of
nearly 40,000 new public
buildings and the repair or
improvement of more than
85,000 existing buildings;
the construction or im-
provement of thousands of
parks, playgrounds, and
other recreational facilities; the installation or improvement of public utilities service and sanitation
facilities; the extension of
flood and erosion control,
irrigation, and conserva-
tion; the construction or
improvement of thousands
of airports and airways facilities; and preservation
of numerous historic
buildings, including Independence Hall in Philadelphia and Boston's Faneuil
Hall. In Indiana WPA
workers demolished slum
housing and erected, on
leased sites, minimal, portable, prefabricated houses
designed for relief work-
ers' use.

While most WPA facilities
continue to be used and
enjoyed, most Americans
have long since forgotten—
if they ever knew—their
WPA origins.

Photographic "pie," representing the allocation of the WPA dollar. From the WPA archives.

Harry Hopkins, administrator of the WPA. At a luncheon speaker's table Hopkins is flanked on his left by Eleanor Roosevelt and Ellen S. Woodward of the WPA's Women's and Professional Division. Florence Kerr, Woodward's successor, is at Hopkins's right. "For a social worker," historian William Leuchtenburg wrote, Hopkins "was an odd sort. He belonged to no church, had been divorced and analyzed, liked race horses and women, was given to profanity and wisecracking, and had little patience with moralists." He gave off, according to another observer, "a suggestion of quick cigarettes . . . brief sarcasm, fraying suits of clothes, and a wholly understandable preoccupation."

"I am getting sick and tired of these people on the WPA and local relief rolls being called chiselers and cheats. It doesn't do any good to call these people names, because they are just like the rest of us. They don't drink any more than the rest of us, they don't lie any more, they're no lazier than the rest of us—they're pretty much a cross section of the American people. . . ."

Harry Hopkins, 1936, quoted in Depression, Recovery, and War, ed. Alfred Brooks Rollins, Jr., 1966

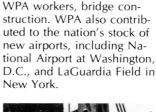
WPA workers, bridge construction. WPA also contributed to the nation's stock of new airports, including National Airport at Washington, D.C., and LaGuardia Field in New York.

WPA workers, North Dakota. "Leaning on shovels" rivaled "leaf raking" as the pejorative image of WPA relief work. Addressing his staff in June 1935, administrator Hopkins said: "What is more important, that the fellow who has been kicked around now for years and given a lot of relief some of it pretty miserable and uncertain, be given a job, or that some great bridge be built and he not get a job? . . . Never forget that the objective of this whole program as laid down by the President . . . is the objective of taking 3,500,000 people off relief and putting them to work, and the secondary objective is to put them to work on the best possible projects we can, but don't ever forget that first objective, and don't let me hear any of you apologizing for it because it is nothing to be ashamed of."

Swimming pool, part of WPA work in building a dozen recreation centers in New York City. Looking back on the WPA era, New York building czar Robert Moses pointed out, "These centers are alive with kids today, and they certainly don't represent boondoggling. . . ." Among WPA's more notable recreational projects were New York's Central Park Zoo, San Francisco's Aquatic Park, and Chicago's waterfront improvement.

WPA worker, toy making.

WPA workers, Philadelphia
Art Museum.

"I was brought up in that school of thought that believed that no one went on the public payroll except for political purposes or because he was incompetent or unless he had a job that he didn't work at. One of the most insidious things is the propaganda that something is wrong about one that works for the people. . . . I am proud of having worked for the government. . . . I have signed my name to about $6,000,000,000 in the last three and a half years. None of it has stuck to the fingers of our administrators. You might think some of it has been wasted. If it has been wasted it was in the interest of the unemployed. You might say we have made mistakes. I haven't a thing to apologize for about our so-called mistakes. If we have made mistakes we made them in the interest of the people that were broke."

Harry Hopkins, 1936, quoted in Depression, Recovery, and War, ed. Alfred Brooks Rollins, Jr., 1966

In addition to its construction programs, the WPA engaged in community services as public works. WPA reliefers were employed to provide society with important services in health, education, and welfare. These workers assisted public health agencies in the operation of clinics; prepared hot lunches for school children from fruit and vegetables canned from food produced on WPA gardening projects; sewed garments for distribution to the needy; repaired and salvaged toys for distribution through toy lending libraries; operated libraries and book mobiles; repaired books; and prepared visual education devices for use in public schools. WPA housekeeping aides visited needy homes. Relief workers also ran WPA nursery schools and adult literacy classes.

Timberline Lodge at Mount Hood, Oregon, built by WPA for the Forest Service in 1936. WPA workers not only built but also designed the lodge. A booklet published at the time described the hope and pride that this lodge infused in the workers. To many the project exemplified a progressive social program, which forged a new community work ethic.

"The crudity of evolving form, symbolic perhaps of the changing social order in which this recreational project has had a part, is evident not only in the exterior of Mt. Hood Timberline Lodge, with its projecting and rudely carved beams, its sturdy basaltic foundation, and its stalwart battens and shakes, but may be found in all the interior details. The only permanency, change, is exemplified in stone and wood. Cruel or beautiful, nature is shown in exquisite expressions of a universal power."

The Builders of Timberline Lodge, *1937*

"Its challenge may be the chiefest of all the values evoked by Timberline Lodge. Like the mountain upon which it is built it is symbolic of many things not seen in the timber and stone which make it. As the winding road leading to it represented progress by laborers, not the least of whose rewards was the daily inspiration of the enlarged and expanding view of mountain tops, so the building itself exemplifies a progressive social program which has revived dormant arts and pointed the way for their perpetuation. It presents concretely the evidence that men still aspire to the dream, often secret but always universal, of becoming greater than themselves through association with others in a common purpose."

The Builders of Timberline Lodge, *1937*

"Those who view the magnificence of this solitary dawn and who salute the sun as a symbol of the renewal of life and the triumph of faith over darkness, have exemplified an age-old ritual. Moreover, in facing the east and its white mountain wedged into the roseate sky, they gaze toward Timberline Lodge, a recreational project which is a concrete manifestation of faith and of the triumph of intelligence over economic distress."

The Builders of Timberline Lodge, *1937*

Cover and illustration from the booklet, *The Builders of Timberline Lodge*, "preparation and publishing conceived by the administrative staff, the text written by the Writers' Project, and the drawings prepared by the Art Project of the Oregon WPA, 1937, dedicated to the Project Workers of the Works Progress Administration who have combined industry with skill to make the work program in Oregon a success."

"Brought together under WPA with intelligent direction, they worked out in combination something bigger than any of them individually. Each, in acquiring a new skill, a new ideal, and a new technique, opened the way for subsequent individual participation in an American renaissance."

The Builders of Timberline Lodge, *1937*

Interior, Timberline Lodge. Railroad ties and telephone poles were recycled in the construction. WPA workers designed and made the fabrics and furniture for the lodge.

CCC workers.

The Depression affected not only the adult population, but also millions of young people. To lighten family burdens, many tried to find employment. But there were no jobs, and boys joined wandering hordes of the unemployed. They could be seen at roadside campfires, on freight trains, on the streets, in flophouses, rescue missions, soup kitchens, and breadlines, begging, stealing, and in jail.

One of Roosevelt's first acts as President was to enlist the vagrant youths into an army that would do battle for one of his pet concerns—conservation. The Civilian Conservation Corps (CCC) put unemployed, single young men between the ages of 18 and 25 to work restoring the nation's forests, reclaiming its land, enriching its park system, and otherwise conserving its natural resources. Another part of CCC work was its development of Recreation Demonstration Areas on submarginal land near cities.

The idea of the CCC was that the youth in the Corps—all from needy families—would earn money both for themselves and their families ($30.00 a month, of which $22.00 was sent home), learn new and employable skills at worthwhile jobs, and become physically fit in the process.

Roosevelt put four departments to work on the project, noting, "I want to personally check the location, scope, etc. of the camps, size, work to be done, etc." The Labor Department was responsible for recruitment; the War Department, for transporting, paying, feeding, clothing, and housing the boys; and the Forest Service, Park Service, and Army Corps of Engineers, for planning projects and supervising the work. An Army reserve officer was in charge of each 200-man camp, though discipline was "by character rather than command."

No militarization was allowed in the camps, though some critics nonetheless liked to compare them with German and Soviet camps. In 1934 the White House reprimanded the Assistant Secretary of War, Harry H. Woodring, for suggesting that the Army should organize the CCC along with war veterans and people on relief into "economic storm troops."

At its peak, the Corps had an enrollment of nearly 506,000 working in 2,635 camps in every state, plus 10,500 in Indian camps located on Indian reservations. Most of the boys stayed from six months to a year.

Roosevelt had envisioned some form of universal youth service since World War I and intended to make the CCC permanent, but World War II enlisted the boys in a different kind of army, bringing the Corps to an abrupt end.

CCC recruiting poster made by the Illinois WPA Art Project, Chicago.

"[CCC boys] thinned four million acres of trees, stocked almost a billion fish, built more than 30,000 wildlife shelters, dug diversion ditches and canals, and restored Revolutionary and Civil War battlefields. They fought spruce sawflies and Mormon crickets in western forests, grasshoppers in the Midwest, gypsy moths in the East. They built a network of lookout towers and roads and trails so that fires could be detected and reached more easily; when fires broke out, regiments of Roosevelt's 'Tree Army' were rushed to the front— forty-nine firefighters lost their lives. Above all, they planted trees—saplings of cedar and hemlock and poplar—in burned-over districts, on eroded hillsides, on bleak mountain slopes ruthlessly stripped of virgin timber. Of all the forest planting, public and private, in the history of the nation, more than half was done by the CCC."

William E. Leuchtenburg, Franklin D. Roosevelt and the New Deal, 1963

President Roosevelt visits the CCC camp at Big Meadows in the Shenandoah Valley, Virginia, August 12, 1933. Beginning second from left are Louis Howe, Harold Ickes, Robert V. Fechner, F. D. R., Henry A. Wallace, and Rexford G. Tugwell.

CCC recruits.

CCC workers, dam construction.

A pool developed by the Civilian Conservation Corps at R. H. Treman State Park in New York provides recreation while preserving the environment. The CCC played a major role in expanding the state park network.

"East Side New York boys found themselves one morning in the high meadows of the Glacier National Park; New Jersey and Connecticut youths waded through late spring snows in the Mount Hood National Forest in Oregon; Texas farm boys saw their first mountains in Wyoming. Here was real adventure."

F. A. Silcox, Chief of the U.S. Forest Service, 1937

Indian CCC workers restoring a totem pole, Tongass National Forest, Alaska.

Although the WPA was originally envisioned as primarily a construction program for the unskilled, administrators managed to adapt both legislation and organization to embrace easel painting, sculpture, archaelogical digs, theater, guidebooks, and research and records programs. Under an administrative device known as Federal Project Number One, the WPA coordinated a national program of work in music, art, writing, theater, and historical records. The cultural programs were concerned with using the skills of unemployed artists and at the same time providing useful services to the community; with the arts *as* public works. Judgments about quality were largely left to posterity.

Holger Cahill, Director of the Federal Art Project (FAP), voiced the concept: " . . . it is not the solitary genius but a sound general movement which maintains art as a vital, functioning part of any cultural scheme. Art is not a matter of rare occasional masterpieces. The emphasis upon masterpieces is a 19th century phenomenon. It is primarily a collector's idea and has little relation to an art movement . . . in a genuine art movement a great reservoir of art is created in many forms both major and minor." Directors under Cahill dictated neither style nor subject; applicants need only be reliefers who were legitimate artists. Originally these artists worked

96 hours a month and were paid according to their classification of skill until Congress later required state administrators to pay each area's prevailing wage. Like most New Deal agencies, the FAP observed local customs on racial segregation.

The arts projects brought American artists and a wide American audience together to produce what *Fortune Magazine* called "a sort of cultural revolution in America." But the programs of Federal One were to be shortlived. In 1938 the newly created House Committee on Un-American Activities made headlines with a series of sensational charges that the WPA cultural projects—including the art, music, and the more radical Federal Writers' and Federal Theatre projects—were "hotbeds for communists." And though a majority of reporters covering the hearings found them unfair, the charges made the front pages; the refutations, the back pages. The damage done to the projects was irreparable, and the conservative coalition in Congress set about weakening and dismantling them. In the case of the FAP, funds were cut; control of projects was turned over to the states; wages were reduced; artists with more than 18 months of FAP employment were fired and remaining artists were required to sign a loyalty oath. As war approached what was left of the FAP undertook projects for defense agencies until the program was terminated in 1943.

Display of publications of the Federal Writers' Project. Guidebooks for each state and territory, the now-famous American Guides, were prepared as well as local guides to cities and regions, schoolbooks that utilized information gathered on local history, and studies of racial groups and folklore. Administrator Henry G. Alsberg credited the guides with bringing about a rediscovery of American culture not only by readers, but also by writers on the project.

Across the country, 158 theatrical companies played to more than 25,000,000 people in conventional and makeshift theaters and in theater caravans as part of the Federal Theatre Project. The Federal Music Project gave American composers and soloists heretofore undreamed-of exposure. WPA orchestras gave performances before an estimated 150,000,000 persons, many of whom had never heard live music before.

The Federal Theatre Project performed the works of native playwrights and experimented with new dramatic forms like the "Living Newspapers" (right), which translated social problems into dramas.

"I only know the best of today's writing must be 'in the present, it is this earth today'. It is the life of one man or one woman today—the average man of today, any man. I only know that to write well today you've got to go out to the people and hear what they're saying, and in so doing believe as Walt Whitman did, that 'not till the sun excludes you do I exclude you'. And this, I believe, is what we on the folklore project are trying to do."

Hyde Partnow, of the Living-Lore Unit of the New York City Federal Writers' Project, c. 1939

Culture as Public Works

Mural by noted abstract expressionist Stuart Davis for New York City municipal radio studio, c. 1939. For many years obscured by a curtain, the mural—which cost taxpayers $245.00—in 1965 was valued at about $100,000. In the confusion of the project's last days, some FAP art was improperly disposed of: a group of canvases by Jackson Pollock, Mark Rothko, Adolph Gottlieb, and Ben Benn ended up in a New York second-hand store, where they sold for around $5.00. Eventually, a good many murals and easel paintings were destroyed by unappreciative recipients—or simply disappeared.

Arshile Gorky painting his mural, *Aviation*, at Newark Airport, New Jersey, 1936. The mural became a center of controversy because, as completed, it contained a star—viewed by critics as a Communist symbol. When the Army began operating Newark Airport in World War II, the mural was painted over. Recent discovery of its location has prompted restoration efforts.

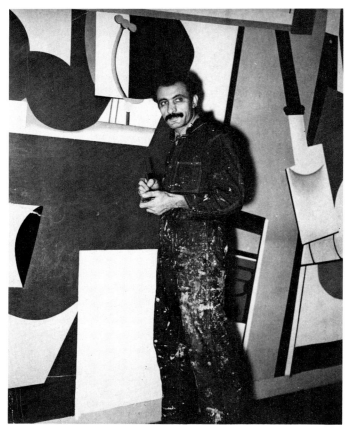

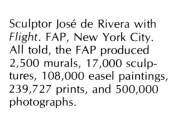

Sculptor José de Rivera with *Flight*. FAP, New York City. All told, the FAP produced 2,500 murals, 17,000 sculptures, 108,000 easel paintings, 239,727 prints, and 500,000 photographs.

"Mural painting does not serve only in a decorative capacity, but an educational one as well. By education, I do not mean in a descriptive sense, portraying, cinema-like, the suffering or progress of humanity, but rather the plastic forms, attitudes, and methods that have become the heritage of the art of painting. Since many workers, schoolchildren, or patients in hospitals (as the case may be) have little or no opportunity to visit museums, mural painting could and would open up new vistas to their neglected knowledge of a far-too-little-popularized art."

Arshile Gorky, "My Murals for the Newark Airport: An Interpretation," in Art for the Millions, *ed. Francis V. O'Connor, 1973*

"WPA/FAP has been the hope of the greatest culture renaissance in recent times. For the present we have steel, stone, and tools. We have the spirit of great men and great cities to move us. We are busy."

Beniamino Benvenuto Bufano, San Francisco FAP artist, "For the Present We Are Busy," in Art for the Millions, *ed. Francis V. O'Connor, 1973*

"The Project was a great purgative. Artists entered it from all levels and they began to see the limitations of the acclaimed American contemporaries. The reason for this is in the fact that working on the Project they were under no real pressures. They could experiment. A lot of what they did was bad but the freedom to be bad acted as a sort of purgative. Finally, gropingly, they found roots by pulling together certain aspects of Expressionism, Surrealism, abstraction—but always in American terms, in terms of their own experience. It was very tentative but out of it I think American art suddenly came of age because it had this big experience. Right after the Project American art developed enormously. It couldn't possibly have done it without the WPA/FAP. The artists still would have been uncertain, still would have had all the provincialisms."

Jacob Kainen, "A Dialogue," in The New Deal Art Projects: An Anthology of Memoirs, *ed. Francis V. O'Connor, 1972*

Holger Cahill (fourth from left), who, before he was named director of FAP, pioneered in the study and exhibition of American folk art. Next to him is Audrey McMahon, director of the New York FAP, which at one point received 45 percent of total FAP funds and was "the source of the best art and the worst disorders," according to historian Richard P. McKinzie. Mrs. McMahon fought a constant battle to keep the Project—and artistic freedom— alive in the face of opposition from the local WPA administrator, Colonel Brehon Somervell, who called FAP artists "those Reds" and told reporters, "As a painter, I'm a good bricklayer."

WPA artist copying the pattern of an eighteenth-century coverlet for the Index of American Design. Over a thousand artists combed the countryside in search of objects illustrating the evolution of native arts and crafts, which were then reproduced for the 22,000-plate Index. WPA workers also collected and studied native folklore, recorded folk songs, and compiled an index of American composers. For the Historic American Buildings Survey, representative types of American buildings were drawn or photographed. Under the newly formed National Archives, a WPA Historical Records Survey also located, arranged, and cataloged historical records in every county in the country.

Public school art class, Federal Art Project.

Department for Lettering, Signs, Project Markers and Miscellaneous in Chicago, run by the Allied Arts Department for the Illinois Federal Art Project. Also in Illinois a Craft Project, cosponsored by Eliel and Eero Saarinen, maintained production facilities in workshops under master craftsmen to stimulate interest in American craft work and to train workers for jobs in private industry. These workshops produced furniture, fabrics, and office, library, and school room equipment for public buildings.

Federal Art Project posters produced for the New York State Department of Health, the New York City Housing Authority, and the Harlem Community Art Centers. Administrator Holger Cahill reserved a considerable part of the FAP's quota for employment of commercial artists, art teachers, and the less skilled on "socially useful" projects such as poster making and photography for public institutions and agencies, art education in public schools and settlement houses, traveling art and crafts workshops, and production of architectural models, relief maps, and dioramas for schools, city museums, and local projects.

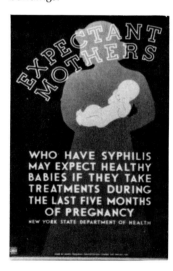

*Blossom Restaurant, The Bow-
ery, Manhattan, October 4,
1935*, photo by Berenice Abbott, Federal Art Project,
Changing New York, 1939.

Art center, Melrose, New Mexico. The Federal Art Project sent experienced New York artists to help communities around the country set up and run art centers, which held exhibits and offered art classes. The WPA provided staff, traveling exhibitions, and some equipment, while a sponsoring group in the community donated the building or paid the rent and utilities and helped plan the program. In 1941 there were 103 centers to which communities had contributed over $850,000 in cash and kind. Visitors to the centers numbered over eight million. Some centers, such as the Walker Art Center in Minneapolis, became permanent fixtures in their communities.

Cartoon, Jack Markow, from *12 Cartoons Defending WPA by Members of the American Artists Congress*, New York, 1939.

Art in Public Buildings

In contrast to the WPA's method of supporting artists, the Treasury Department supported art in the manner of the traditional patron, picking and choosing both artists and subjects to embellish the Department's extensive public building programs. As a dividend, art was viewed as a way to bring the social ideas of the New Deal to large numbers of people in an easily comprehended form.

Treasury official Edward Bruce promoted these ideas in a Public Works of Art Project (PWAP) and talked relief administrator Harry Hopkins into setting aside over $1 million for government employment of artists in federal buildings. In its short lifetime the PWAP—part of a stopgap relief appropriation which expired in June 1934—employed at low daily wages about 3,750 artists who produced over 15,600 works of art for use in public buildings.

After PWAP, Bruce convinced Treasury Secretary Henry Morgenthau, Jr., to create a Section of Painting and Sculpture (later renamed the Section of Fine Arts) to commission art for new public buildings. A small percentage of building costs—usually one percent or less—was reserved for art, so long as actual construction did not exceed estimated costs.

The Section settled on anonymous competitions as the fairest means of obtaining "quality." Artists were invited to participate in a few large national competitions, but most of the contests were local.

The Section chose an "expert" from the area where the building was located, who in turn selected one to three people to form a jury (which always included the architect). Recommended designs were then sent to Washington for evaluation by Section staff, who sometimes disregarded the local jury selections. To encourage artists to enter the competitions, the Section let them know that all the "outstanding" designs submitted that failed to win a competition for a particular building would be commissioned for use elsewhere. So, although the Section held 190 competitions between 1934 and 1943, it actually awarded 1,371 commissions. A subsidiary Section program called the Treasury Relief Art Project (TRAP), supported by grant money from WPA, was used over a five-year period to hire only such "good" relief artists as could be found. *Time* magazine dubbed TRAP "the Ritz" of the relief art projects.

The Section made clear what it considered appropriate style and subject for all its programs: literal representations of "the American scene." And although some artists viewed such standards as repressive, many critics praised the Section for breaking what one called "the stranglehold of the romantic-escape school . . . on officialdom" and for bringing art out of studios and museums and into more than a thousand public buildings—some in towns where people had never seen an original work.

With the advent of World War II, Section funds gradually dried up.

Mural, Harold Weston, Procurement Building, Department of the Treasury, Washington, D.C., portraying the work of the Section.

"Unveiled yesterday, before the approving eyes of Secretary Morgenthau and a host of dignitaries, one mural panel in the lobby of the Federal Warehouse disclosed a Lady Justice with her blindfold askew and another panel, burlesquing the celebrated Indians-scalping-ladies painting in the Postoffice Building, showed an unclad damsel lying prostrate as a frontiersman draws a bead on a redskin. . . . Secretary Morgenthau, in a short informal speech, praised Mr. Weston's work and laughingly accepted his explanation of the unconventional Lady Justice and the postoffice travesty. The latter shows a self-portrait of Mr. Weston, who is depicted as the painter working on the mural."

The Washington Post, June 1, 1938

Opening the Public Works of Art Project, Washington, D.C., 1933. From left to right, Edward Bruce, Eleanor Roosevelt, Lawrence W. Robert, Assistant Secretary of the Treasury, and Forbes Watson, technical director of PWAP.

The Cabinet Room, spring 1939, before the President and Cabinet arrived to view the entries in a competition run by the Section of Fine Arts, Treasury Department, for a mural in the post office at Wausau, Wisconsin. Bruce told his audience that the Section was turning rural post offices into "little cultural centers" that would counter "all the unrest" by bringing beauty into people's lives. "I do not believe that one of these artists who painted these pictures liked either Hitler or Mussolini . . . I have a feeling they all know and like the Twenty-Third Psalm."

In a nationwide competition for a mural for a post office in each of the 48 states, judges reviewed 1,477 designs.

Section of Fine Arts mural, Department of the Interior, inspired by a sixteenth century account of the French landing in Florida. The original appears in the introduction to this book.

"Art critics supported or attacked the [Fine Arts] Section according to their feelings toward the style they described as contemporary realism, since that style characterized so much Section art. Critics of academic bias felt strongly that mural art ought to be closely related to the architectural style of the building and room containing it. Only when subject, design, and colors harmonized with the rest of the building would the mural be a part of the wall, not a mere painting on it. Accept that view, other critics argued, and the government classical architecture of Washington, imitated and bastardized in public buildings across the country, would force American artists to paint in the manner of Raphael, to produce art wholly unrelated to the mood of the times. Few government muralists tried to reconcile the contemporary American scene with what the Section considered the architectural sins of the fathers."

Richard D. McKinzie, The Now Deal for Artists, 1973

Mural by Lloyd Ney in the New London, Ohio, Post Office—the only abstract work the Section approved for a post office. The central triangle represents the Great Seal of the United States. According to historian Richard D. McKinzie, Bruce, who was somewhat bamboozled into accepting Ney's work, rationalized, "It isn't a bad idea to have one experimental picture in the project, as this abstract art stuff is certainly getting a lot of attention these days."

Mine Rescue, study for a mural by Fletcher Martin for the Kellogg, Idaho, Post Office. While liked by miners, the mural was rejected after complaints from town industrialists. An uncontroversial scene from local history was approved in its place. In another protest, Cheyenne Indians camped out on the lawn of the Watongo, Oklahoma, Post Office until artist Edith Mahier altered what they considered objectionable features of her mural. Chief Red Bird claimed Indian ponies in the mural looked like oversized swans and Indian children like cornmeal-bloated pigs.

Full-scale clay model of one of a set of matched eagles, by Heinz Warneke, commissioned by the Section for the Social Security Building. One observer commented that the eagles looked as if they had "washed down pistachio ice cream with Irish whiskey." The $5,000 eagles were later removed and sold as surplus for $25.

"In behalf of many smaller cities, wholly without objects of art, as ours was, may I beseech you and the Treasury to give them some art, more of it, whenever you find it possible to do so. How can a finished citizen be made in an artless town?"

Postmaster Basil V. Jones, Pleasant Hill, Missouri

Mural by Ben Shahn in the U.S. Post Office, Bronx Central Annex, New York.

Sculpture by David Olney for TRAP at the PWA Langston Terrace Housing Project, Washington, D.C.

" . . . From dust and shrinking land, from the thunder of tractors and shrinking ownership, from the desert's slow northward invasion, from the twisting winds that howl up out of Texas, from the floods that bring no richness to the land and steal what little richness is there. From all of these," wrote John Steinbeck, "the people are in flight."

The Farm Security Administration (FSA), successor to Rexford Tugwell's Resettlement Administration, attempted to stem the migratory tide through rehabilitation and farm purchase loans. But for many, FSA help came too late, and they traveled the highways, following the harvests from one state to another, moving from one squalid, makeshift encampment to another. The FSA described them as having the lowest living standards of any group in the United States: "Their only homes are temporary roadside camps, which seldom have any kind of sanitary facilities or even a decent water supply. Their children have little chance for education, adequate medical care, or normal community life. Malnutrition and disease are common among both adults and children." Virtually unnoticed by the federal government, however, was the plight of tenant farmers so movingly documented by James Agee and Walker Evans on a private assignment. (Tenant farmers were officially considered to be employed.)

Largely in the interests of health and sanitation, the FSA began building camps for migrants in 1936. By 1941, there were 49 such camps, which could accommodate more than 10,000 families at any one time—or nearly 200,000 people a year. Nine of these camps were portable, for use in areas with short harvest seasons. The rest of the camps were considered permanent and included small units with subsistence gardens for families able to find year-round work in the area. The FSA used precutting and prefabrication and, in its efforts to cut costs, experimented with houses of rammed earth, stone, steel, adobe, and even cotton duck stretched over plywood.

The FSA projects received high praise. The New York Museum of Modern Art included several FSA communities in its 1944 "Built in USA" exhibit, noting that the FSA's San Francisco office "has shown that 'bureaucratic architecture' can also be distinguished." *Architectural*

Approaching dust storm in the Midwest, 1934. Devastating dust storms and floods exacerbated the plight of migrant workers.

Forum (January 1941) commended "the quality and thoroughly American character" of FSA design. "The freshness and inventiveness displayed in its best work are due, in part, to the fact that there was no architectural precedent for Southern farm buildings to precondition design. . . . Also virtually unique in Government is Farm Security's willingness to experiment, a reflection of the large measure of local autonomy enjoyed by the planners. In five years of trying solutions to minimum house problems there have naturally been mistakes, but the large scale adoption of successful methods has more than paid for them."

One of the most vivid documentation efforts of the Depression era was carried out by FSA in an effort to publicize the plight of the rural poor and gain support for the agency's policies. As part of its Information Division program, filmmaker Pare Lorenz made two historic documentary films—"The Plow That Broke the Plains" and "The River." But what was to leave the most lasting record of the Depression years was the work of the Photographic Section under the direction of Roy E. Stryker.

Among the young photographers who worked for the section were Walker Evans, Arthur Rothstein, Dorothea Lange, Ben Shahn, Carl Mydans, Gordon Parks, Marion Post Wolcott, John Collier, John Vachon, Russell Lee, and Jack Delano. Between 1935 and 1943, with no more than six of them working at any one time, they took more than 272,000 photographs, producing what Edward Steichen described as "the most remarkable human documents that were ever rendered in pictures."

"It is therefore not surprising that they are constant readers of the sky; that it holds not an ounce of 'beauty' to them (though I know of no more magnificent skies than those of Alabama); that it is the lodestone of their deepest pieties; and that they have, also, the deep stormfear which is apparently common to all primitive peoples. Wind is as terrifying to them as cloud and lightning and thunder: and I remember how, sitting with the Woods, in an afternoon when George was away at work, and a storm was building, Mrs. Gudger and her children came hurrying three quarters of a mile beneath the blackening air to shelter among company. Gudger says: 'You never can tell what's in a cloud.'"

James Agee, Let Us Now Praise Famous Men, *1939*

People in Flight
378–379

Of her famous picture of a migrant mother, Dorothea Lange wrote: "I did not ask her name or her history. She told me her age, that she was 32. She said that they had been living on frozen vegetables from the surrounding fields and birds that the children killed. She had just sold the tyres from her car to buy food. There she sat in that lean-to tent with her children huddled around her, and seemed to know that my pictures might help her, and so she helped me. There was a sort of equality about it." The pea crop at Nipomo had frozen and there was no work for anybody. But only hours after, the photographer appeared at the *San Francisco News* office, prints in hand, whereupon relief authorities were contacted. The paper ran the following footnote to the story: "Ragged, ill, emaciated by hunger, 2,500 men, women and children are rescued after weeks of suffering by the chance visit of a Government photographer."

New Mexico. Photo by Dorothea Lange, December 1935.

Oklahoma sharecropper and family stalled in the desert in California. Photo by Dorothea Lange, 1937.

Drought refugees from Abilene, Texas, in California. Photo by Dorothea Lange, August 1936.

" . . . The documentary photographer feels obliged to bring home more than a cold record. Somehow he has to incorporate into that rectangle which he has cut out from the surrounding and therefore formless reality, what the real thing sounded like, what it smelled like—and most important, what it felt like."

Roy E. Stryker, director of the Photographic Section of the Information Division, FSA, "Documentary Photography," The Complete Photographer, April 1942

Drought refugee family from McAlester, Oklahoma, near Tulare, California. Photo by Dorothea Lange, November 1936.

"Lady, you're having a hard time, and a lot of people don't think you're having such a hard time. We want to show them that you're a human being, a nice human being, but you're having troubles."

Russell Lee, FSA photographer, quoted in Roy E. Stryker, in Just Before The War, edited by Thomas H. Garver, exhibition catalog, 1968

"Highway 66 is the main migrant road. . . . Two hundred and fifty thousand people over the road. Fifty thousand old cars—wounded, steaming. Wrecks along the road, abandoned. Well, what happened to them? What happened to the folks in that car? Did they walk? Where are they? Where does the courage come from? Where does the terrible faith come from?"

John Steinbeck, The Grapes of Wrath, 1939

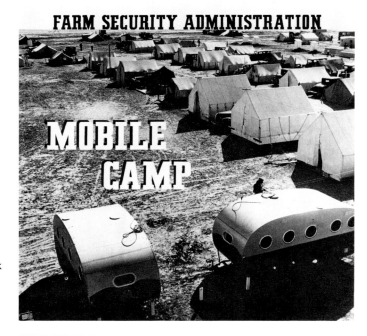

Illustration from an information panel on camps for migratory farm workers, prepared by the FSA in 1941. The trailers contained a first-aid clinic, 24 shower baths, and 18 washtubs. Tents and platforms, usually for 200 families, were moved by truck to give emergency shelter. When work was over, the camp moved to the next site on its route.

"Resting after a hard day's work" in a migrant work camp, Jefferson County, Oregon. Photo by Arthur Rothstein, 1936.

*"We lived in a gov'ment camp
a while, an' then we went
north, an' when we come back
it was full up. That's a nice
place to live, you bet. . . .
Well, it costs, but if you ain't
got the money, they let you
work it out—couple hours a
week, cleanin' up, an' garbage
cans. Stuff like that. An' nights
they's music an' folks talks together an' hot water right in
the pipes. You never seen
nothin' so nice."*

John Steinbeck, The Grapes of
Wrath, 1939

Camp manager talks to new
farm worker arrivals at FSA
migrant camp, Wilder, Idaho.
Photo by Russell Lee, May
1941.

*"Farm Security's organization
consists of a group in Washington and twelve regional offices.
The number of architects in any
one regional office varies with
the amount of work on hand.
To Washington falls the work of
allocating projects within the
budget, and of checking final
plans and cost estimates. All of
the architectural design, engineering and site planning is
handled locally, independently
—and intelligently. Since the
regional offices are in constant
touch with local conditions, the
programs are established in
these offices. In addition, there
is an interesting device known
as a plan pool, whereby all architects in the field can study
the solutions arrived at in other
parts of the country. . . . Today, in face of a national emergency, Farm Security stands
out as the agency most experienced and successful in the
work of building houses quickly
and cheaply. Also, its accomplishment lends credence to the
view that local architecture locally arrived at, whether private or public, achieves results
in speed, quality and cost."*

Architectural Forum, Jan-
uary 1941

Nursery school, FSA community, Woodville, California, 1941. Woodville was designed by a team headed by architect Vernon DeMars. It was one of the most complete of the FSA communities. In addition to metal shelters provided for migrant agricultural workers, there were single and row houses for resident farmers and commun. , service buildings, including a co-op store, social center, and medical clinic.

Migrant camp at Yuba City, California, Burton D. Cairns and Vernon DeMars, architects. Photo by Arthur Rothstein, 1940.

Aerial view, Westley Migratory Camp, California, 1937.

"The bigger the city, the less thought of man," F.D.R. said. In June 1933 Congress appropriated $25 million with which he hoped to realize a long-time dream: settling families in planned rural communities. The government would buy the land, build the houses, acquire livestock and machinery, and put in roads, water, and utilities. Homesteaders would have 30 years to pay the government back.

Under the new Subsistence Homestead Program, 99 communities were built: some were rural industrial communities where low-income families could have small plots for subsistence farming; others were agricultural communities.

As the first such community, Arthurdale, begun in 1933 near the small town of Reedsville, West Virginia, received the most publicity. Coal was no longer mined in Arthurdale and some miners had

not worked for eight years. According to one observer they "shuffled around like ghosts, and a miasmic silence hung over the grimy company houses that clung to the mountainside along the polluted gullies." Of the plight of the miners and their families, Mrs. Roosevelt said: "It is not purely a housing problem. You cannot build houses and tell people to go and live in them. They must be taught how to live. Therefore this is a resettlement problem."

Arthurdale was Mrs. Roosevelt's "baby"—one on which she expended a considerable amount of her own money. She viewed it as a proving ground for those to follow. She wanted it to have the most advanced educational system, a model public health system, a producers' and consumers' cooperative, and a program of handicrafts and music that would preserve the Appalachian folk culture. She interested herself

Agricultural version of the American dream as depicted in four scenes of the evolution of a New York farm, which appeared in O. Turner's *History of the Holland Purchase*, published in 1850. The dream, as well as public policy, was grounded in the belief that success was inextricably connected with the land and its resources. The subsistence homestead program of the 1930s attempted to graft postindustrial reality to the dream by providing community-based jobs for families living on rural farmettes.

in every detail of the planning from selection of homesteaders and the principal of the school, to shopping for refrigerators and inspecting plumbing fixtures.

The success of Arthurdale and other new homestead communities, like the rural homesteading of the nineteenth century, depended on economic independence for residents. But despite Mrs. Roosevelt's ar-

dent efforts to attract industry to the area, at no time during the decade in which it was established was more than a third of Arthurdale's work force employed by private industry. An effort to authorize funds for a factory to manufacture post office equipment was denounced as an assault on private enterprise and defeated by Congress.

The Subsistence Homestead projects drew heated criticism. Costs were

sometimes driven up by hasty planning, high housing standards, and expensive experimentation in construction methods. One Senator condemned the program for providing "simple mountain people" with such "extravagances" as electricity, refrigerators, and indoor privies. Another complained of a relief worker "living in a stone mansion very much handsomer than I have ever lived in in my life." Complaints that the government was subsidizing a life of middle-class affluence were countered by

Communist characterization of the homesteads as a design for permanent poverty. In 1935 the President moved the projects into the Resettlement Administration.

When war came, Congress, under the pretext of cutting back nondefense expenditures, liquidated the program, which had spawned 10,938 homesteads.

View of Arthurdale project, Reedsville, West Virginia. Photo by Walker Evans, June 1935.

Arthurdale, West Virginia, a New Deal version of homesteading. Photo by Walker Evans, 1935.

"Although the leaders of the movement believed they were affording people the opportunity to escape the evils of a vulgar industrial society, the subsistence homesteads which proved most successful were precisely those . . . which quickly took on the character of any suburban subdivision. As soon as the pall of the early depression years lifted, people hurried to get back into the 'real' world of the bustling city streets. Ostensibly experimental and utopian, the subsistence homesteads movement soon seemed rather a quest for an ark of refuge, an indication of the despair of the early thirties."

William E. Leuchtenburg, Franklin D. Roosevelt and the New Deal, *1963*

"There is inherent weakness in cities which become too large for their times and inherent strength in a wider geographical distribution of population."

President Franklin D. Roosevelt

Architect working on designs for a homestead project in Missouri, May 1938. Where prefabrication was used, houses were of standard design with two sizes of sections. Completed sections could be bolted together in various designs, shaped, according to the Washington Post, "like an 'h,' or an 'l,' or 't,' or perhaps some other alphabetical symbol dear to the New Deal."

Schoolchildren building houses, Arthurdale. Photo by E. Johnson, April 1936.

F.D.R. advisor Louis Howe, who shared Mrs. Roosevelt's enthusiasm for Arthurdale, was in such a hurry to get the project underway that he ordered 50 Cape Cod prefabricated houses, fine for a couple on a summer vacation but inadequate for large Appalachian families in the winter. Also, when Howe's prefabs arrived, they didn't fit the foundations planned for them, and had to be redesigned at great expense. *The Saturday Evening Post* (August 4, 1934) wrote that "the camp houses" had been "slowly tortured" into shape and buried in a "meringue of wings, bay windows, fireplaces, porches, terraces, and pergolas." *The Washington Post Magazine* voiced similar complaints.

The Washington Post Magazine

WASHINGTON, D.C., SUNDAY, AUGUST 12, 1934

Flimsy Homesteads Cost Fancy Prices!

BLUNDERS AT ARTHURDALE

Put Burden on Miner and Taxpayer

"It is not unfair to note . . . that in the period of prelude to Arthurdale the planning was carried on with the idea of helping the homesteaders to help themselves on a scale in line with their possibilities and their earlier way of life. When government stepped in with relatively unlimited resources of both planners and funds a new note was struck. Planning was done for, rather than with, prospective homesteaders. Perfection rather than reality became the goal. There is much testimony and ample evidence that as the perfectionist idea grew the zeal of the homesteaders diminished until it became an attitude of grateful resignation."

Millard Milburn Rice, "Footnote on Arthurdale," Harper's Magazine, *March 1940*

Back to the Land

388–389

Community center, Arthurdale. Photo by E. Johnson, June 1934. The basic form of the center was provided by an abandoned Presbyterian church, which was bought, torn down in sections, and rebuilt as the Arthurdale community center. The pillared portico was added, as were the side wings.

Furniture factory, Arthurdale. Photo by Ben Shahn, 1937.

Room of a model house, Arthurdale, 1934. In the haste to attain near-perfection for the model, wild grapevines were reportedly brought in and trained over a trellis beside the house so photographers could record a finished look. Furniture, provided by the government, was made by hand by a local crafts cooperative. Besides the furniture, the first fifty homesteaders were offered a free cow.

"The theory was that we would be able to set up families on subsistence homeeteads at a family cost from $2,000 to $3,000 and here we have already run above $10,000 per family. I am afraid we are going to come in for a lot of justifiable criticism."

Harold Ickes, The Secret Diaries of Harold Ickes, 1933–1936

Cooperative store, Arthurdale, December 1936. Capital for the store was provided by the government.

Kindergarten children with trained nurse, Arthurdale. Photo by E. Johnson, April 1935.

One New Dealer who looked none too fondly on the "back to the land" movement was Rexford Guy Tugwell, a Brains Truster whom F.D.R. in 1935 named to head a new umbrella agency dealing with problems of the rural poor. Tugwell considered the small family farm an anachronism in an age of advancing technology. The job of his new agency, Tugwell explained, was "to assist the families in the worst situations to find new and more economic farms or to locate elsewhere in other occupations with a prospect of

work and income." To Tugwell, "elsewhere" meant near cities, where the jobs were and would most likely continue to be. As for the subsistence homestead projects he inherited, Tugwell had little use for them. Rather than attempting to attract industry to rural areas—an undertaking he viewed as both impractical and impossible—Tugwell proposed that the federal government "go just outside centers of population, pick up cheap land, build a

whole community and entice people into it." Tugwell wanted literally to bring the small town to the city—to show that the advantages of both country and city life could be combined.

Within the Resettlement Administration (RA) Tugwell set up a Suburban Resettlement Division and began studying 100 cities as potential sites for new planned communities for families fleeing the poverty of the marginal farm. From a pared-down list of 25, F.D.R. approved eight.

The number of new towns was further reduced when dollar allocations were cut by more than one half. Ultimately construction was begun on only three towns: Greenbelt, Maryland, near Washington, D.C.; Greendale, Wisconsin, outside Milwaukee; and Greenhills, Ohio, near Cincinnati. A fourth, Greenbrook, New Jersey, was held up by local opposition.

Originally Tugwell envisioned a new town on the order of Le Corbusier's Ville Contemporaine, a model city for three million inhabitants, which was displayed at the Paris

Architects' drafting room at 2020 Massachusetts Avenue, N.W., Washington, D.C., February 1936. The planning ideas of the Suburban Resettlement Division of Tugwell's Resettlement Administration attracted some of the nation's top architects and planners.

Exhibition of 1922. Le Corbusier's city was surrounded by a "green belt" of undeveloped land several miles wide, permanently isolating and protecting it. A group of skyscrapers, spaced apart in a cross shape, contained housing, stores, and office space. Tugwell was talked out of this idea, though the "greenbelt" concept remained.

Tugwell hired a separate planning and architectural team for each of the four new communities to demonstrate different approaches. A Tugwell aide commented that "the young architects felt sure that this Resettlement Administration was going to revolutionize the concept of urban built form." Columnist Marquis Childs observed, "They thought they were planning a new world."

A short 13 months after the project began, the U.S. Court of Appeals in Washington ruled that the federal government did not have the power to engage directly in building housing, such activity having "no connections with the general welfare," and being the exclusive jurisdiction of the states. And while the U.S. Attorney General declared that the decision applied only to the proposed new town of Greenbrook, the court ruled unconstitutional the legislation which provided funds to build the towns. The three towns in progress were pushed to completion with the limited funds remaining; six months later Tugwell resigned and the Resettlement Administration was dismantled after having resettled only 2,267 families in its greenbelt towns.

Although critics called the towns "Communist" and judged them to be expensive, they were visited by more than two million people—including many European planners—during their first year of operation and were praised by those who saw in them the potential for a well-planned urban-suburban pattern for the future. In 1955 the federal government sold the greenbelt towns to private developers. More than a decade would elapse before it became interested once more in the concept of new communities.

Rexford Tugwell, left, with President Roosevelt. Tugwell acquired the image of a Bolshevik, though one associate contended that he was "about as red as a blue hen." Texas Representative Maury Maverick once told him, "Nobody wants to listen to your academic phrases. Nodule my eye! Put your speech in simple language. I never heard of a nodule before, so I don't like it. Besides . . . it sounds like sex perversion."

"There is only one part of the United States government that has caught even a glimmer of what modern design means. And that is the various departments in Washington that are concerned with housing. On a recent tour of inspection at the PWA and the Suburban Resettlement Division, I was surprised at the large number of sensible, straightforward designs, and at the generally hig level of the work."

Lewis Mumford in The New Yorker, *February 29, 1936*

"I really would like to conserve all those things which I grew up to respect and or love and not see them destroyed. I grew up in an American small town and I've never forgotten it. No one was very rich there, but no one was very poor either. I can't make this Park Avenue country club life seem right, along with slums and breadlines, ballyhoo speculation; I can't make this fit into my picture of American institutions."

Rexford Guy Tugwell, *quoted in Albert Lord,* The Wallaces of Iowa, *1947*

"A farm is an area of vicious, ill-tempered soil with not a very good house, inadequate barns, makeshift machinery, happenstance stock, tired, overworked men and women . . . and all the pests and bucolic plagues that nature has evolved . . . a place where ugly, brooding monotony that haunts by day and night, unseats the mind."

Rexford Guy Tugwell, *quoted in* AIP Journal, *1930*

President Roosevelt viewing the plan of Greenbelt, Maryland. "There are fewer streets in Greenbelt than in the ordinary community. Blocks are five or six times as big as the average city square. Resembling small parks, each block has grouped around its borders about 120 dwellings. In the center of each block are recreation and play areas safely separated from the hazards of traffic. . . . Instead of facing only a barren street, the homes look out upon the grass and trees in the center. While each house has its own yard, much of the space is pooled for the common use . . . a network of paths runs through the safe and pleasant surroundings of the interior park." (O. Kline Fulmer on Greenbelt, quoted in *The Federal Architect*, October 1946.)

"The significance of a 'greenbelt' town extends far beyond its own boundaries. Every growing metropolis should, if it is wisely planned, develop a chain of similar suburban communities around its borders. Such communities offer an opportunity for orderly, efficient expansion and their 'greenbelts', linked together, form continuous permanent open space around the city."

The Federal Architect, October 1946

"Yet there could be no question that, in backing Suburban Resettlement, Tugwell understood, perhaps prematurely, a tendency in American life which in another decade and a half would be compelling—the flow of population from the cities to the suburbs. The Greenbelt idea of the thirties found a kind of distorted realization in the suburban developments of the fifties. Ironically for the Resettlement planners, when success at last took place, even in their own projects, it only completed the defeat of the original conception of an autonomous community."

Arthur Schlesinger, Jr., The Age of Roosevelt: The Coming of the New Deal, 1958

". . . These towns never had a chance to prove whether the original high objectives and methods were valid, or could be effectuated. . . . The greenbelt towns might, and should indeed, have constituted the genuine powerful spearhead for a new dimension in American life and urban development: creative prototypes for the current crop of new cities. Instead, they remained vestigial."

Albert Mayer, "Greenbelt Towns Revisited," AIP Journal, 1968

Aerial view, Greenbelt, Maryland.

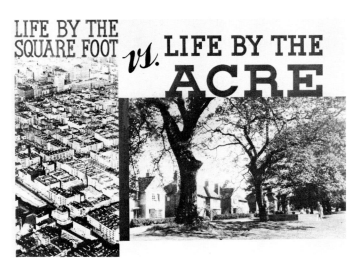

Part of a series of traveling information panels on greenbelt towns prepared by the records section of the Suburban Resettlement Division of the Resettlement Administration.

"Automotive transportation makes it possible for men to live a considerable distance from their work; pure air, rural surroundings, and contact with the ground, are physically and psychically good; life is better in a small town where social cooperation is possible; by eliminating inflated land values, by appropriate planning, by large-scale construction, and by taking advantage of every reasonable means for reducing living costs, working-class families can afford to live in small, special-built suburban towns. The plan of Greendale has been directed toward making these statements true—particularly the last of them."

Elbert Peets, one of the planners for "Greendale," from Werner Hegemann et al., City Planning and Housing, 1937

Street in Greendale, Wisconsin. In all the greenbelt towns low residential density was considered desirable. Originally 3,400 to 5,900 acres were purchased at each site, which was planned for 1,000 units or less.

"The special way of putting together street, house, and lot that distinguishes the Greendale street . . . appears most novel to those whose knowledge of town planning history is least. The type of house it implies is much like the side-garden house of our colonial towns, a house built on the street and along one side of the lot, with a garden between it and the neighbor. Even more it resembles the ancient and universal arrangement of the houses in farm villages, where one does not enter the house directly from the street but through a court around which the buildings are grouped. Not unexpectedly, visitors to Greendale . . . have sometimes found an Old World flavor in its residence streets. They are narrow, for one thing."

Elbert Peets, "Greendale," from Werner Hegemann et al., City Planning and Housing, 1937

Speaking of the flood-ravaged Tennessee Valley, eminent engineer Arthur E. Morgan told Roosevelt: "The wreckage of rugged individualism has been handed to us with a request that we try to do something about it." Lumber, oil, and gas interests had come and gone, leaving devastation and poverty in their wake. In the fall of 1933 there were counties in the southern highlands where more than half of the families were on relief—one where there were more than 87 percent. Morgan, who served as the first chairman of TVA, found "a considerable part" of that population "on the verge of starvation." Of 26 million acres in the Valley—which included portions of seven states—7 million acres were eroded. Annual flood damage was estimated at $1,780,000. Only two out of every 100 farms had electricity.

In April 1933—a little over a month after he assumed office—Roosevelt proposed creation of "a corporation clothed with the power of government but possessed of the flexibility and initiative of a private enterprise." Though branded "a Soviet dream" by critics, legislation creating a Tennessee Valley Authority passed Congress within a month.

The major objectives of the TVA were to improve navigability and provide for flood control, agricultural and industrial development, reforestation, and the proper use of marginal lands. How these objectives were to be achieved was the business of management, which was given authority to buy, build,

Power generators at Pickwick Landing Dam, 1935–1938. Note for scale the man standing on the third generator.

and operate dams, generate and sell electric power, manufacture fertilizer, and engage in a host of other activities. Corporation headquarters were to be in the region, and the Authority was to cooperate with local agencies in meeting its goals. Hiring and firing was to be free from both political patronage and Civil Service regulation.

As Morgan, who was named chairman of the board, envisioned TVA, "the improvement of that total well being, in physical, social, and economic condition, is the total aim." In its first decade of operation—besides replenishing the land and producing power—TVA encouraged cooperatives and rural industries; constructed roads and scenic highways; built Norris, a model "new town" for personnel; provided employees (40,000 in a peak year) with schools, librar-

ies, parks, and recreational and health facilities (shared with adjacent communities). TVA also pioneered in the design of low-cost demountable structures, used for its temporary settlements, which could be trucked to sites and bolted together into a solid house.

TVA distinguished itself architecturally as well as politically and socially. At the opening of an exhibit of TVA work at the Museum of Modern Art in 1941, the director of MOMA said that the architecture of TVA was "the greatest that America had yet produced." TVA board chairman David E. Lilienthal noted: "We had to search for architects who were not in a constant delirium of nostalgia for the past, men who could interpret the functional strength the engineers would build into these structures; and we

had to find engineers willing to collaborate with architects with open and eager minds." An architect who fit that description was Roland Wank, designer of the Cincinnati Union Terminal and member of an architectural firm whose practice was in heavy construction. Wank joined the TVA staff as chief architect, Frederick Gutheim wrote in *Architectural Forum* of September 1970, "not far from the point in historical time when the sculptor Jo Davidson could seriously propose to President Roosevelt that he design the massive downstream faces of TVA dams along the lines of the heroic sculptures of Gutzon Borglum. Wank could have contented himself with such a frankly decorative approach to engineering works. Ample precedents existed then. . . . He chose instead the teamwork approach, and created instead the architecture of engineering."

Senator Norris (in bowtie); Chief Architect of the TVA, Roland Wank (center); David Lilienthal (far right); and TVA engineers tour the lake then rising behind the Norris Dam, 1936. In the 1920s Norris led a protracted fight against private takeover of the government's wartime dams and nitrate plants at Muscle Shoals, Alabama, on the Tennessee River. David Lilienthal wrote of Norris that his "statesmanship and integrity are deeply engraved upon every chapter of TVA's legislative history."

"Many hard lessons have taught us the human waste that results from lack of planning. Here and there a few wise cities and counties have looked ahead and planned. But our Nation has 'just grown.' It is time to expand planning to a wider field, in this instance comprehending in one great project many states directly concerned with the basin of one of our greatest rivers.

"This in a true sense is a return to the spirit and vision of the pioneer. If we are successful here we can march on, step by step, in a like development of other great natural territorial units within our borders."

President Franklin D. Roosevelt, April 10, 1933

Roland Wank, Chief Architect for the TVA. Julian Huxley wrote in his *TVA: Adventure in Planning* (1943): "Small wonder the engineer felt bewildered when the slightly younger edition of the architect came back and said that he was no longer interested in columns and cornices, but that he would like to see how the engineer was making out on the disposition of the structure to its surroundings and of its component parts to each other. The matter was finally resolved, within TVA at least, upon the mutual discovery that both were interested in good, honest, efficient structures, and never mind the mayonnaise."

". . . Because the engineer, like the architect and artist, has a strongly disciplined sense of order, and because the purely functional is generally esthetically satisfying, these dams and their adjuncts are over-whelmingly beautiful. . . . Such objects . . . make up a new grammar of design which cannot be disregarded by the architect."

Architectural Forum, *August 1939*

"Architects were for too long dreamily content with the application of 'tasteful' superficial ornament to the daring construction of the engineers. Sometimes their decoration grew so bold that it swallowed up and denied the structure beneath.

"Modern architecture has brought a new set of values, dependent for their realization upon the complete collaboration of architect and engineer. There is no better example than the work of the Tennessee Valley Authority and this early group at Norris."

Museum of Modern Art, *catalog for the exhibit "Built in U.S.A.," 1944*

Guntersville Dam, drawing by Roland Wank, July 28, 1937.

TVA construction. This photo was used on the cover of *The Valley and Its People: A Portrait of TVA*, prepared in 1944 by TVA. Pride of workmanship is as evident in the quality of reproduction of the book's text and photographs as it is in the massive dam structures.

"*In the Valley . . . architecture has taken hold of an area of 40,000 square miles, inhabited by 2,000,000 people, based on 650 miles of the all-important river.*

"*Really to get hold of the idea, it is necessary to be quite strict in thinking of the whole Valley as the unit that was re-shaped. The dams are merely the climaxes. . . . means were shaped to several sets of ends and the entire area so homogenously treated that there could be no reason for confining the term 'architecture' to the one part where the materials used happened to be concrete and steel instead of soil, trees, water surfaces, or rock. . . . The glimpse that is given is of man working upon the whole of his environment to put it into habitable, workable, agreeable, and friendly shape. As a concept, architecture can today be no less.*"

Douglas Haskell, "Architecture of the TVA," The Nation, *May 17, 1941*

"*We wanted those dams to have the honest beauty of a fine tool, for TVA was a tool to do a job for men in a democracy.*"

David Lilienthal, quoted in R. L. Duffus, The Valley and Its People, *1944*

Powerhouse, Norris Dam, 1933–1936, the first dam built by TVA and the only TVA structure named for a contemporary American—public power advocate Senator George Norris.

Norris Dam, 1933–1936, TVA's highest dam and the highest concrete dam east of the Rocky Mountains. This dam can store more than a million acre-feet of water to control floods hundreds of miles away.

". . . *The Board of the TVA decided at the beginning to build the dams by 'force account'—that is, that the TVA should directly select, hire, train, and supervise the workmen and be responsible for the policies governing wages and conditions of work. The almost universal federal practice is otherwise. Government construction projects are generally 'let out to contract'—that is, a contractor agrees to do the job, to buy the materials, select and pay the employees, and turn over a finished job for a price. With a few exceptions, for work of a special and temporary nature, such as tunnel building or the raising of a bridge, every man who has worked on these Tennessee Valley projects has been employed directly by his government. All were recruited and employed by the TVA.*"

David Lilienthal, TVA: Democracy on the March, *1944*

"The TVA could not close the gates of the dam, pay off the landowners and townspeople, and call it a day. That would not do because Congress had directed that the resources of the region—human energies included—were to be seen as a whole, and the development of a river was only a single part of the total job of regional building."

David Lilienthal, TVA: Democracy on the March, 1944

Tennessee Valley Region, showing the system of dams and reservoirs, which provide a navigable waterway, flood regulation, and hydroelectric power.

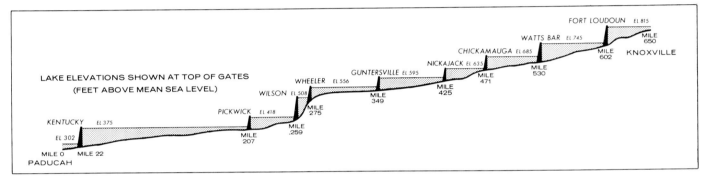

LAKE ELEVATIONS SHOWN AT TOP OF GATES
(FEET ABOVE MEAN SEA LEVEL)

FORT LOUDOUN EL 815
MILE 650
WATTS BAR EL 745
CHICKAMAUGA EL 685
MILE 602
KNOXVILLE
NICKAJACK EL 635
MILE 530
GUNTERSVILLE EL 595
MILE 471
WHEELER EL 556
MILE 425
WILSON EL 508
MILE 349
PICKWICK EL 418
MILE 275
MILE 259
KENTUCKY EL 375
MILE 207
EL 302
MILE 0   MILE 22
PADUCAH

"For when provisions for good food and a decent place for rest and recreation are made—assumed requirements on every TVA construction job—the stage is well set for the more important conditions of an efficient job: union organizations if the men want them, the procedures of collective bargaining, and joint committees to deal with problems of project efficiency. The unit costs of TVA construction have been low compared with private and public undertakings the country over. TVA came within about 3 per cent of keeping within its cost estimates even though many of the major projects were built in wartime when costs were rising rapidly. The jobs have been done with unusual speed. Thus, from the day the Douglas Dam—a major structure on a fractious stream—was authorized by Congress until it was built and producing power took thirteen months, a world's record."

David Lilienthal, TVA: Democracy on the March, 1944

The town of Tupelo, Mississippi, celebrating the signing of a contract with TVA for electric power. Tupelo was the first city to sign.

Fontana Dam, 1942–1945, showing construction at the halfway mark.

Powerhouse, Fontana Dam, 1942–1945, TVA's highest dam and the highest concrete dam east of the Rocky Mountains. The inscription reads: "Built for the people of the United States of America." This legend also appears on the tablets put on TVA dams instead of the conventional hierarchical list of board directors or engineers. The generators in the foreground help produce the electric power that the TVA supplies to a total area of about 80,000 square miles. By 1951 the integrated system of Tennessee Valley dams, including those of the TVA, the Corps of Engineers, and the Aluminum Company of America, produced about 18 billion kilowatt hours of electric energy in a single year. (One kilowatt hour equals about ten hours of human energy.)

Gantry crane at Kentucky Dam, 1938–1944. By regulating the flow of the Tennessee River, this dam can lower the crests on the Ohio and Mississippi Rivers at Cairo, Illinois.

Watts Bar Steam Plant. Even the street lights were TVA-designed.

The Scandal That Failed, by Fitzpatrick, in the St. Louis Post Dispatch, 1938. The cartoon comments on a Congressional investigation of TVA that failed to prove improprieties on the part of the board. During the first five years of its existence TVA withstood 57 court challenges. Its operations were impeded by 26 injunctions of which all but one were later resolved.

Workers' housing, Fontana Dam. Fred Schlemmer, project manager for the dam, observed, "If the men and women in the construction camp are contented and happy, the price of concrete comes down."

"It has been TVA's purpose . . . to weave the housing programs, the library service, and the public health facilities available to construction workers into the fabric of the adjacent community institutions, where they have remained ever since, as locally supported services, long after the workers departed."

David Lilienthal, TVA: Democracy on the March, *1944*

". . . The job of providing adequate housing for the workers at dams built at isolated points was undertaken by the TVA itself. Creative engineers, architects, and builders spent several years developing various types of low-cost housing—demountable houses, for example, houses that could be set up on one building site and then moved to another, always with the widest general use for the region in mind. The influence of these standards of housing, by the contagion of example, upon the private housing development throughout the valley is not difficult to detect even by the casual visitor, and the designs of prefabricated, demountable, and more conventional low-cost housing that have come out of this effort have been made available and are being used by private builders over the country."

David Lilienthal, TVA: Democracy on the March, *1944*

In the boom years of the late 1920s a commission of graduates of the Ecole des Beaux-Arts began planning for a world's fair at Chicago in 1933. Science and industry had made great strides in new applications of electrical power. It was the dawn of the pushbutton age. The theme of the fair was "Progress through Science."

Undaunted by the intervening depression, chief designer Louis Skidmore and his assistant, Nathaniel Owings, pieced together materials and services to stretch scarce dollars for a celebration of a Century of Progress. And nearly 45 million visitors came to be distracted from the harsh realities of the real world. They saw a sleek-looking architecture; their official program guide proclaimed, "Science Finds/Industry Applies/Man Conforms."

By the time of the 1939 World's Fair at New York, the fascination with the look of science had become a fascination with the promise of it for the "World of Tomorrow." Industrial designers like Norman Bel Geddes and Henry Dreyfuss had a heyday conjuring up problem-free utopias (on a Beaux-Arts site plan) where science, technology, and design would guarantee the good life for all. As an answer to economic and political distress, this futuristic vision was in complete contrast to New Deal programs such as subsistence homesteading and greenbelt towns that looked to a simpler past.

Volcano of Light and Water, proposed symbolic structure for Chicago's Century of Progress. Designed by Ralph Walker. Rendering by Hugh Ferriss. The design featured aluminum fins radiating from a floodlit tower with water cascading from the top. Although well received, Walker's proposal was never built for financial reasons.

"In reflecting on its entirety, the thought persists that the Exposition was conceived in the spirit of the roaring, smashing Twenties that came to a crash in October 1929, that the symbol of that time as expressed in the architecture and coloration is the lipstick, the hip flask and the cocktail shaker; that it expresses psychologically a passing era. Every architect should see it. Architecture is on its way, but whither is it going?"

Arthur F. Woltersdorf, *"Carnival Architecture,"* American Architect, *July 1933*

"It would be incongruous to house exhibits showing man's progress in the past century in a Greek temple of the age of Pericles, or a Roman villa of the time of Hadrian. . . . We are trying to show the world not what has happened in the past, because that has already been effectively done, but what is being done in the present, and what may happen in the future."

Members of the Architectural Commission for Century of Progress, Chicago, 1933

"The Chicago Century of Progress was mixed . . . in a hundred-million-dollar bowl but was baked, alas, in a thirty-million-dollar oven. The bakers did their best, but the loaf fell. The Fair had no general plan and at a dozen points no perceptible local plan. The mixture of chic science, architectural bontonism, architectural jazz, big-shot advertising, Coney Island entertainment, and sentimental archaeology caused the physical and emotional collapse of all but the sturdiest visitors. The confusion was complete. . . . Yet I spent a dozen Saturday evenings at the Fair and enjoyed them all. What was irrational by sober daylight became at the day's end a fairyland for optical adventure. . . . The pale-dark towers of tragic Chicago and the leaden lake seemed more unreal than these meaningless but hypnotizing shapes when familiarity had drawn them together."

Elbert Peets, *"The Century of Progress,"* in Werner Hegemann et al., City Planning and Housing, *1937*

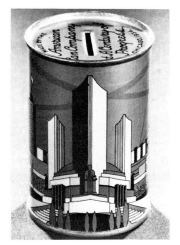

Federal Building, Edward H. Bennett and Arthur Brown Jr., Century of Progress, Chicago, 1933, pictured on a souvenir can bank made by the American Can Company for sale at the fair. The building dome is flanked by three pylons ascribed to the legislative, executive, and judicial branches of government. A pseudo-streamlined Sky Ride dominated the fairgrounds. Down to earth, a bare-skinned Sally Rand created a sensation when she rode a white steed through the opening night ball. The most popular exhibits were the antiquarian villages, especially the Belgian Village and the Black Forest.

"The architectural design of the fair was functional in the extreme. Forced by economics to abandon the nit-picking, fussy mode of the Art Moderne designs proposed by the original Architectural Commission, we gained in simple building masses the lake's gigantic scale. We covered the raw wallboard surfaces with the cold water paint of penurious necessity and produced a masterpiece of contemporary art, topped off by millions of yards of blood red bunting splashed from slanting shafts pressed upon the throngs at the entry gate. We depended upon primitive devices: color, motion and light. . . . There was a certain eerie quality about the uncompromising huge, flat, windowless surfaces, strange in volume and shape, as they blazed in crude, primitive, startling color combinations."

Nathaniel Owings, The Spaces In Between: An Architect's Journey, *1973*

American pavilion, Paris Exposition Coloniale, 1931, an incongruous contrast to the domestic fairs of the 1930s. Designed by Charles K. Bryant. Shortly after the fair, one of the wings of this copy of Mount Vernon was erected as a private residence for an American in Chantilly. During the war the house was occupied by Germans and subsequently destroyed by the French Underground.

"It will be generally admitted that the most extreme modernistic and unique design of the entire exposition is the $300,000 Federal Building, which has the largest floor area and is the highest structure on the grounds. The hue and cry of the moderns, of course, is functional architecture which serves utilitarian requirements, yet here is a triangular tower 175 feet high serving no such purpose, yet very effective. . . . Here is a tower surmounted by a gilded eagle emblematic of the supreme authority of the Government itself. However, the poor old bird has been given the modern touch to the extent that he is well nigh indistinguishable."

William Nichol, "Exposition Discovered at Dallas," The Federal Architect, *October 1936*

The U.S. Government Building, the Texas Centennial Exposition, Dallas, 1936.

"The Federal Building is that rarity in official U.S. exposition architecture, a building actually designed to house exhibits. In addition it represents a creditable and highly interesting attempt to develop a non-traditional design which would at the same time have what is commonly recognized as government character."

Architectural Forum, *June 1939, on the Golden Gate Exposition*

Dedication at the Federal Building, Golden Gate International Exposition, San Francisco, 1939. The building was designed by Timothy L. Pflueger, with murals by the WPA Art Project. *Architectural Forum* of June 1939 judged Government exhibits "superlatively designed": "they establish a new, important precedent by demonstrating that Government can show its activities in a comprehensive, eye-filling and intelligible manner."

Federal Building, New York World's Fair, 1939, designed by Howard L. Cheney. An observer, writing in *Architectural Forum* of September 1939, said that the building's "severe white exterior expresses its official character"—an unwitting testimony to such character's place in the public mind as the epitome of government architecture. Sculptors, muralists, and craftsmen for the building were chosen by competitions.

"The focal exhibits of the 1939 New York World's Fair were designed around a theme promoting an optimistic vision of the future. Their message was that the good will and cooperation of men, combined with the advances of science and technology, could be directed to the building of a cleaner, safer, more efficient and happier tomorrow. That vision was the latest of a series of utopian plans that dated as far back as the ancient Greek philosophers. It was modern in its stress on materialistic solutions to man's problems."

Donald J. Bush, The Streamlined Decade, 1975

Trylon and Perisphere, shown on a U.S. postage stamp issued to commemorate the New York World's Fair, 1939.

" . . . The important effect on architecture of the New York World's Fair is not the creation of a style so much as a dreadful altering of the role of architecture and the architect. For the spectacle on Flushing Meadows witnesses the discovery by big business of the propagandist role of architecture, and the discovery by the architect that this immediate role is lush beyond all expectation. If a style is born it is the Corporation style—a bastard dialect of architectural larceny and advertising."

F. A. Gutheim, "Buildings at the Fair," Magazine of Art, August 1939

Work—The American Way, mural by Philip Guston, Federal Art Project, for the WPA Building, New York World's Fair, 1939.

"The city of tomorrow . . . will be composed of a central town or 'brain center' surrounded by satellite towns containing factories. . . . In the satellite town there will be a public market where the farmers living in the greenbelt will bring their produce. People will not eat concentrated food capsules; they will eat fresh green food direct from the gardens. They won't have artificial flowers because they will get fresh ones from the garden. The family will develop good taste because they will be surrounded by good things—music, trees and other cultural advantages.

"A man will be loyal to his employer because he makes this city possible. . . .

"Automobiles will have glass roofs so that their occupants may look out above, as well as to the sides, front and back. The traffic force in our city will be cut to a minimum. We see no great amount of crime in tomorrow's city because everybody is so happy, thus we will have a police force of only 100 men. Slums develop criminals, but we will have no slums."

Henry Dreyfuss as told to Julian Leggett, Popular Mechanics Magazine, *March 1939*

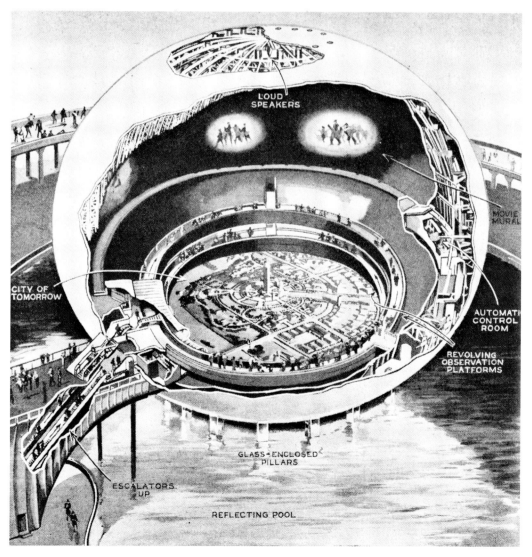

Perisphere with the 200-foot model of Democracity, New York World's Fair, 1939, shown in a drawing and photo published in *Popular Mechanics*, March 1939. Henry Dreyfuss created the fair's theme exhibit with the central feature of Democracity, a futuristic planned community to cover eight million acres with seventy towns and a population of one and a half million. According to *Popular Mechanics*, "There will be only one tall building in the hub. This is a city of low buildings and our only reason for putting a tall building is a dramatic reason—an architectural accent which points up the city. It will house the government for Democracity." *Architectural Forum* (June 1939) reported: "Henry Dreyfus' imaginative conception gives an exciting picture of a way of living that is technically possible today." The fair incidentally commemorated the 150th anniversary of Washington's first inauguration.

remember
PEARL
HARBOR

PURL
HARDER

WPA Federal Art Project poster, New York City Poster Division, 1942.

In 1937, Roosevelt, fearing inflation from deficit spending, cut the budget drastically, and the economy suffered what came to be known as "the Roosevelt recession." In response F.D.R. again stepped up spending on New Deal Programs. But it would be war—and not the New Deal—that ultimately would rescue the nation from its economic woes.

Within six months after war was declared in 1941, Congress had appropriated $100 billion to the defense effort; by mid-1943 war costs were running as high in one month as the New Deal budgets ran in a year. The war would virtually wipe out unemployment.

Unlike other New Deal programs, the Tennessee Valley Authority became an important cog in the war machine—producing munitions and explosives, powering factories and transporting goods, and, finally, providing the enormous energy required to manufacture the atomic bomb.

In the early months of the war, WPA workers were employed on defense construction projects or underwent training for defense industries; still others provided recreational facilities for military and defense workers and their families. They also operated nursery schools and a school lunch program. What was left of the Federal Art Project turned to such services as giving classes on camouflage for military officers and recreational craft instruction for enlisted men. Government artists also decorated military installations and produced posters and visual training aids related to the war effort. As the armed forces and defense industries began absorbing more and more of the unemployed, Roosevelt ordered WPA projects phased out by mid–1943. WPA had served with distinction, he said, and had "earned its honorable discharge." The Civilian Conservation Corps met the same fate.

In World War II, more than any other war, battles were as much struggles between factories as between armies. British Major General J. R. C. Fuller contended that "God now marched with the biggest industries rather than with the biggest battalions." And in the U.S. the legion of new war workers created an acute housing problem. Before Pearl Harbor, 16 federal offices were somehow involved in producing or financing of defense housing—and were engaged in constant competition for materials and funds. After war was declared, the President quickly consolidated all housing efforts into a National Housing Agency (NHA), which absorbed the U.S. Housing Authority into a new Federal Public Housing Authority (FPHA).

About half of the 1.3 million new war housing units were privately financed, mostly under a special Federal Housing Authority mortgage insurance program for privately built war housing; the rest were publicly financed. Overseas, the Corps of Engineers devoted herculean efforts to building logistic facilities in far-flung arenas, including the Burma Road and the Alcan Highway.

Before Pearl Harbor, in 1940, when the U.S. Army held peacetime maneuvers in New York, the troops were "armed" with pieces of stovepipe, beer cans, rainpipes, and broomsticks. The Army's only fully armored unit was busy in southern training centers. No combat planes were available, and trucks sported signs with the word "TANK." In early 1940, before the draft took effect, little more than half a million men were in the armed forces. By the end of the war 15 million men and more than 200,000 women would serve in the armed forces.

Roosevelt called on America to be "the great arsenal of democracy," and within six months of Pearl Harbor "the most enormous room in the history of man"—the Ford plant at once idyllic Willow Run near Detroit—was belching forth a bomber an hour. By late 1943 arsenal America was turning out a plane every six minutes and a ship every five hours.

Employees of a defense plant in Chattanooga, Tennessee, form the victory sign. In the first year and a half of the war, about 3 million workers migrated to war-related jobs, creating an acute housing problem.

"By spring the floodgates were open. Equipped with virtually unlimited financial authorizations, the procurement agencies went to work to place their contracts with the industries of America. . . . [W]e built many new factories, and expanded many others, which we could not use and did not need. . . . In light of the tremendous contracts outstanding . . . however, these plants seemed necessary to some people, and under the system they were given high priorities. In most cases they were also financed by the Government. The result was, however, an overconcentration of contracts in the larger corporations and a failure to fully utilize the 'bits and pieces.'"

U.S. Bureau of the Budget, The United States at War: Development and Administration of the War Program by the Federal Government, 1946

Tail sections of B-17F (Flying Fortress) bombers ready for assembly at the Boeing plant in Seattle, December, 1942. Photo by Andreas Feininger.

David E. Lilienthal, Chairman of the Board of TVA, at a ceremony marking the opening of Douglas Dam, a project rushed to completion to furnish electricity for the war effort.

"The engineer of World War II outdid his compatriot of Bunker Hill because, in only 170 years, his area of operation had become the whole world. . . . During World War II the personnel strength of the Corps of Engineers reached 700,000 officers and enlisted men. . . .

"In some areas of the Pacific there were more engineers than infantrymen or any other arm of service. This preponderance of engineer troops was necessitated by the lack of roads, ports, airfields, and other facilities. Thus it can be understood readily why World War II was termed an 'engineer's' war."

History and Traditions of the Corps of Engineers, *The Engineer School, U.S. Army, Fort Belvoir, Virginia, 1953*

WPA team led by artist Lee Krasner, making window display units to advertise war training courses in New York colleges. According to historian Richard McKinzie, abstract painters on the team, including Jackson Pollock, William Eceron, and Ben Benn, "exercised their art on the borders of the displays."

Dymaxion deployment units, designed by Buckminster Fuller. The light, portable Dymaxion units were used as dormitories for aviators and mechanics assembling U.S. pursuit planes at the head of the Persian Gulf. Although many of Fuller's creations gained wide publicity in the late 1920s and early 1930s, it took the war to put them into production.

Torpedo ordinance plant of the Amertorp Corporation, Chicago, 1942, commissioned jointly by the Navy and the American Can Company. The plant was designed by Albert Kahn Associates, whose firm grew proportionately with growing American involvement in the production of war weapons after 1939. In the three years prior to 1943, the government commissioned the office to design $200 million worth of construction, including the Chrysler Corporation Tank Arsenal in Detroit.

Arsenal of Democracy

One of the lightweight transportable hangars made for the Air Force during World War II.

"The federal government has invested something like $16,000,000,000 in plant and equipment and private enterprise about $9,000,000,000 more. . . . The government's share in the plants is not evenly distributed over industry, but is concentrated in synthetic rubber, light metals (aluminum and magnesium), high-octane gasoline, aviation, shipbuilding, and like wartime essentials. The government plants, moreover, are apt to be huge, in units costing upwards of $10,000,000 or more. Since it is the official policy to sell or lease the plants to private enterprises, this means that only big business can touch them."

C. Hartley Grattan, *"Reconversion,"* **Transatlantic,** December 1945

War birds practicing maneuvers over the 170-foot tower of the administration building, Randolph Field, Texas.

Spectators view the "Nature of the Enemy" exhibit mounted by the U.S. Office of War Information at Rockefeller Plaza in New York City, 1943. Note pile of books (left) and "official" sign superimposed on the word "public."

Cover of catalog from the New York Museum of Modern Art exhibit, "Wartime Housing," 1942.

"Sufficient homes for workers in war industries are an essential element in the whole program of making the weapons of war."

President Franklin D. Roosevelt, letter to the Museum of Modern Art, New York, 1942

"Despite bitter and complicated battles over policy (it looked for a time as if we might start the second front right here at home) a really remarkable production job was done with war housing. It will cause headaches later on: much of the publicly built housing was substandard, due to material shortages; . . . But, all in all, the war housing experience is probably leaving us better equipped than we were before to tackle the post-war problem."

Catherine Bauer, "Toward Postwar Housing in the U.S.," Transatlantic, December 1944

Exhibit section, "Wartime Housing," the New York Museum of Modern Art, 1942. Despite materials shortages and construction speed, federal housing officials managed to produce some architecturally distinguished housing by such modern architects as Eero Saarinen, Louis Kahn and Richard Neutra.

As the nation geared up for war, civilians arrived in the capital in droves to offer their services to the myriad new war agencies springing up daily. Between June 1940 and June 1942 the number of federal employees in the Washington area nearly doubled—and before the war was over totaled about 300,000. This influx, coupled with the burgeoning number of government agencies, changed the face of the city, while the emergency of war radically altered the way government business was conducted.

All considerations of planning and symbolism went out the window in the wartime scramble for office space. The housing crisis in Washington became legend. New structures appeared practically overnight all over town— even on the inviolable Mall. The rapid construction of "temporaries" still could not keep pace with the demand, however, and the agencies that lost out in the competition for space found themselves expanding into hotels, apartments—any place they could finagle. Grumbled one loser in the game, "If the Army and Navy could capture territory as well as they grab office space, we might win the war."

As the war agencies created by Roosevelt mushroomed under the War Powers Act, Congress held no less than a hundred investigations into what one Representative called the "cancerous growth of bureaucracy . . . eating the heart of our American way of life." *Reader's Digest* ran a regular column called "Washington Wonderland" which included such items as the story of a frustrated Japanese spy who reported back to Tokyo that there was no point in bombing any Washington office because there would be two or three offices duplicating its work.

No agency felt the wartime crush in Washington as acutely as the War Department, housed in 17 buildings all over the city. Chief of the Construction Division of the Quartermaster Corps, General Brehon B. Somervell, came up with what was then considered an outlandish plan to relocate the entire

Temporary buildings on the Mall. Wrote *The Federal Architect* of April–June 1942: "Among the trees of the parks and the Mall, the buildings arise. They are not of monumental materials but they look efficient and blend with the landscape nestling among the greenery—the hand of iron in the glove of silk, someone has said." President Roosevelt reportedly believed that the war would not last more than four years and wanted the temporaries designed so they would fall apart in no more than seven years. Most of the World War II temporaries were around until the 1960s.

War Department on a single site on the Virginia side of the Potomac. On a Thursday evening in July 1941, he called to his office Lieutenant Colonel Hugh J. Casey and George E. Bergstrom, president of the American Institute of Architects and also employed in the Engineering Branch, and gave them a weekend assignment. On Monday morning they presented plans for a reinforced concrete structure containing twice the floor space of the Empire State building. Fitted to a site bounded by five roads, the building would have five sides. Thus was born what came to be called the Pentagon and would be the largest office building in the world.

The *Washington Daily News* of July 25, 1941, reported: "Not even a castle in the air Wednesday night, 'Defense City, Va., —Pop. 40,000' was on the congressional conveyor belt and the motor was humming. . . . The House was ready yesterday to rubber-stamp the grandiose proposal . . . but there may be some trouble in the Senate."

Trouble there was. The President of the Commission of Fine Arts protested "introduction of 35 acres of ugly flat roofs into the very foreground of the most majestic view of the National Capital." The National Capital Park and Planning Commission wanted the project scaled down and questioned the advisability of locating so many high-ranking officers in one place during a national emergency. The National Association of Building Owners and Managers feared that the structure would become a white elephant after the war "unless we are to look forward to a permanent military establishment vastly greater than we have hitherto maintained. . . ."

However, the plan was approved after Roosevelt insisted that the site be moved three-fourths of a mile south to satisfy some critics, who included the President's uncle. Four thousand men worked three shifts a day to complete the $83 million structure. A new highway system and 51 road bridges were built to bring personnel to work.

Workers "homeward bound" from a Navy "tempo on the Mall." Cartoon by Gluyas Williams.

Congressman Harold O. Cooley inspects one of Washington's early defenses—a dummy antiaircraft gun and a dummy crewman overlooking the Capitol, 1941. The military strategy of such dummies was to confuse the enemy as to the real strength and position of men and guns.

People and paper proliferated as the crisis of depression changed gears to become the even more pressing crisis of war. The inevitable pressure on space in the capital city was apparent—even before the official U.S. declaration of war.

Aerial view of the Pentagon, 1958. When completed, this bureaucratic fortress was the largest office building in the world.

"Rats which psychologists have tormented in mazes for years must be chattering and squeaking with glee over the frustrations of human beings lost in a new . . . man-made maze . . . the nerve center of the nation's fighting forces."

"Race Between Claustrophobia and Agoraphobia for Those Pent Up in Washington's Pentagon," Newsweek, February 15, 1943

"A building so enormous takes on an entirely new quality of interest and excitement, a quality which depends not on the 'architecture' but on its size and the problems that go with it.

"For miles around the results of building the Pentagon are visible: the reclaimed slums; the broad roads and the new integrated approaches to the capital. Perhaps the greatest lesson of the Pentagon is here: as building approaches the scale technically feasible, the distinction between architecture and city planning vanishes. Despite its short comings, the Pentagon gives a real foretaste of the future."

Architectural Forum, January 1943

"If the boss calls, get his name."

Wartime sign in Pentagon office

"Here in Washington the ebb and flow of currents which moved the Nation have left their mark, some of them as dismal as others are inspiring reminders of what has gone before. Washington always has reflected the spirit of the Nation."

Washington Star, February 20, 1944

One of the proposed plans for the Pentagon, architect unknown, 1941–1942.

"Above all, the building must be capable of very rapid construction . . . platform construction is used at all floor lines so that walls and partitions can be framed while lying on the floor and raised into position. This has caused amazement on the part of many Washingtonians who noticed a whole story had been added to a building while they were at the movies. . . .

"As Government telephones are apt to change with the moon, easy access to the wiring is assured by building a continuous conduit near the ceiling resembling a box type cornice. The face is removed by screws, so wiring can be exposed by just reaching in and grabbing a handful."

The Federal Architect, July 1943

A cutaway view of the citylike Pentagon in *Popular Science*, n.d., reprinted in *Newsweek*, February 15, 1943. The complex contains 4 million square feet of floor space (6 million gross); 16½ miles of corridors; a tunnel 1,000 feet long where the working population enters and leaves at the rate of 3,000 per hour; parking lots for 8,000 cars; cabstands and bus lanes in the basement; a large shopping concourse on the first floor; and a six-acre inner court.

Evacuation Day, March 30, 1942, Bainbridge Island, Washington. Photo by *Seattle Post-Intelligencer.*

Not long after the Japanese attack on Pearl Harbor, a Congressman was reported in the *Congressional Record* of February 19, 1942, to have told his colleagues: "I'm for catching every Japanese in America, Alaska, and Hawaii now and putting them in concentration camps. . . . Damn them! Let's get rid of them now!" Whether out of fear, racism, or political and economic opportunism, many Americans agreed with him, particularly those on the West Coast.

In the face of considerable pressure and mounting violence the President signed Executive Order 9066 on February 19, 1942, which permitted the military to declare the West Coast off limits to persons of Japanese ancestry. The order was subsequently enforced by the criminal penalties of a statute enacted March 21, 1942. By January 1943 there were interned in 10 centers 110,310 people,

some with as little as one-sixteenth Japanese blood. No legal charges were ever filed against internees. Only two months later, the director of the War Relocation Authority called the centers "undesirable institutions" that "should be removed from the American scene as soon as possible." Nonetheless, these secret cities were maintained until the end of the war, when the Supreme Court, reversing earlier decisions, ruled that the camps be closed.

Upon release, many Japanese discovered that their property had been stolen, vandalized, or sold. Often their farms had been confiscated by the federal government through escheat proceedings. Eventually the government settled Japanese claims at less than 10 percent of the total $400 million value of their property as assessed in 1942 by the Federal Reserve Bank of San Francisco.

Thaws at Tule Lake Center turned the streets into seas of mud. Photo by Francis Stewart, WRA (War Relocation Authority), Newell, California, February 2, 1943. Evacuee living quarters were a modification of the Army's "theater of operations" construction. Exterior wall and roofs were covered with black tar paper. Unpartitioned apartment units offered little privacy. Lack of ground cover caused the setting to vary from mud to dust. Physical conditions at Tule Lake were considered superior to those at other centers.

"Herd 'em up, pack 'em off and give them the inside room of the badlands. Let 'em be pinched, hurt, hungry and dead up against it."

Henry McLemore, San Francisco Examiner, January 29, 1942

"Now, therefore, by virtue of the authority vested in me as President of the United States, and Commander-in-Chief of the Army and Navy, I hereby authorize and direct the Secretary of War, and the Military Commanders whom he may from time to time designate, whenever he or any designated Commander deems such action necessary or desireable, to prescribe military areas in such places and of such extent as he or the appropriate Military Commander may determine, from which any or all persons may be excluded, and with respect to which, the right of any person to enter, remain in, or leave shall be subject to whatever restrictions the Secretary of War or the appropriate Military Commander may impose in his discretion. . . ."

Franklin D. Roosevelt, Executive Order 9066, February 19, 1942

"The Japanese race is an enemy race . . ."

General John L. DeWitt, Commander, Western Defense Command and 4th U.S. Army, quoted in Maisie and Richard Conrat, Executive Order 9066, 1972

"It is sobering to recall that though the Japanese relocation . . . was justified to us on the ground that the Japanese were potentially disloyal, the record does not disclose a single case of Japanese disloyalty or sabotage during the whole war. . . ."

Henry Steele Commager, Harper's Monthly Magazine, September 1947

Tanforan Assembly Center. Photo by Dorothea Lange, WRA. The photographer commented, "These barracks were formerly horse stalls. Each family is assigned two small rooms. The interior one has neither door nor window."

Photo by Charles Mace, WRA, Newell, California, September 28, 1943.

"Even though some malefactors might have been present—which was never proven—the liberty of the many cannot be forfeited because of the guilt of the few. Indeed, the Department of Justice successfully handled a similar problem involving persons of Italian and German extraction, dealing with them on an individual basis rather than by mass incarceration. The stubborn fact is, our fellow Japanese American citizens lost their liberty simply and only because of their ancestry."

Tom C. Clark, former Associate Justice of the U.S. Supreme Court and wartime civilian coordinator for the commanding general of the Western Defense Command, "Epilogue," in Maisie and Richard Conrat, **Executive Order 9066,** *1972*

Colorado River Relocation Center. While the internees lived behind barbed wire, 25,000 young Japanese American men served in the armed forces in Europe and the Pacific.

"A hot windstorm brings dust from the surrounding desert." Manzanar Relocation Center, July 3, 1942. Photo by Dorothea Lange, WRA.

"Topaz looked so big, so enormous to us. It made me feel like an ant. Every place we go we cannot escape the dust . . . dust and more dust, dust everywhere. . . . I wonder who found this desert and why they put us in a place like this. . . ."

Young evacuee, quoted in Maisie and Richard Conrat, Executive Order 9066.

"Crowded into cars like cattle, . . . these hapless people were hurried away to hastily constructed and thoroughly inadequate concentration camps, with soldiers with nervous muskets on guard, in the great American desert. We gave the fancy name of 'relocation centers' to these dust bowls, but they were concentration camps nonetheless, although not as bad as Dachau or Buchenwald."

Harold Ickes, Washington Evening Star, September 23, 1946

"After many months of operating relocation centers, the War Relocation Authority is convinced that they are undesirable institutions and should be removed from the American scene as soon as possible."

Dillon Myer, Director of the War Relocation Authority, March 1943

Haste and mud were also traits of a different kind of secret city that grew out of President Roosevelt's establishment on August 13, 1942, of a new division of the Corps of Engineers named "The Manhattan District." With a time limit of three years, the mysterious new division was called on to develop atomic energy as a weapon of war.

The Manhattan Project established three major centers: Hanford (wartime code name of "Site W"), a gigantic plutonium manufacturing complex on the Columbia River in the state of Washington; Los Alamos ("Site Y"), a research facility at an isolated site of a private boys' school in the New Mexico mountains; and the Clinton Engineering Works ("Site X") at what was to become Oak Ridge, Tennessee, which used TVA power to build isotope separation facilities. Work was so compartmentalized among the three isolated communities that workers were unaware of the finished product until the first bomb was dropped on Hiroshima, Japan, on August 5, 1945.

From the field headquarters at Oak Ridge, Colonel K. D. Nichols of the Corps of Engineers directed the construction activities of the Manhattan Project, supervised administrative management, and paid the bills. Oak Ridge itself was typical of the speed, secrecy, and instant planning involved in the atomic-age new towns.

On November 1, 1942, a thousand families (3,000 persons) received notices to vacate their homes and farms in an area of 58,800 acres of Anderson and Roane counties, Tennessee, on the Clinch River. By January heavy machinery was working in the area. On the perimeter, communities not listed in the 1942 Postal Guide were receiving huge shipments of War Department materials.

Stone and White Engineering Corporation of Boston had the contract for design and construction of plants for producing uranium-235. The architectural firm of Skidmore, Owings & Merrill was in charge of planning and

building the town. Roane-Anderson Company, a subsidiary formed by the Turner Construction Company of New York City, acted as landlord and housekeeper of the Atomic City, collecting the rents and the garbage, supplying the maids, repairing the faucets, and replacing the fuses.

By 1944 the Skidmore, Owings & Merrill design office for Oak Ridge had grown to 450. By 1945 the town, originally planned for 3,000 families, variously housed 75,000 persons in 10,000 family dwelling units, 13,000 dormitory spaces, 5,000 trailers, and more than 16,000 hutment and barracks accommodations. Peak employment of construction workers was 47,000 in the spring of 1944 and for all workers was 82,000 in May 1945.

Roane-Anderson organized and operated a system of 800 passenger buses, supervised eating establishments that served a million and a quarter meals a month, ran a chicken ranch and a cattle farm, maintained schools, operated public utilities,

brought in private businesses to serve residents, and operated a railroad that kept 3,000 cars of construction materials coming to plants each month. An official later recalled that Roane-Anderson "was the best whipping boy the Army ever had."

On January 1, 1946, the Manhattan Project was transferred to the civilian Atomic Energy Commission. The AEC then hired SOM to develop a master plan for the permanent city. In 1949 security fences and guard gates came down, and on March 19 a parade signaled the opening of the town of Oak Ridge to the public. Security fences were relocated to protect the restricted plant areas.

"The city is progressing boldly in line with its one firm tradition—change," said *Progressive Architecture* in 1951. "Every month, every day the bivouac atmosphere of the place recedes, giving way to the orderly new city that is foretold in the Master Plan and its already completed components."

One of the typical small farm-homes that dotted the Oak Ridge area before 1942. By 1945 the new city of Oak Ridge had a population of 75,000.

"Louis Skidmore and I found ourselves the center of swarming talent gathered from every field of planning, engineering, architecture and building; strangers to each other, unused to working together, separated from their families, available only through an APO address, unable to explain why they were away or where they were. The miracle was that by creating an atmosphere of amused desperation suggestive of Alice and the Mad Hatter, for three years we were able to maintain a state of controlled hysteria."

Nathaniel Owings, The Spaces In Between: An Architect's Journey, 1973

"Yes, we know it's muddy. . . . You think prices are too high in the grocery store. . . . Coal has not been delivered. . . . It takes six days to get your laundry. . . . The grocer runs out of butter and milk. . . . Your laundry gets lost. . . . The post office is too small. . . . There are not enough bowling alleys. . . . Your house leaks. . . . Everyone is not courteous. . . . It takes too long to get your passes. . . . The water was cold. . . . The beer ran out. . . .

"The telephones are always busy. . . . You can't get all the meat you want. . . . Your house isn't ready. . . . There's confusion in the cafeteria. . . . The dance hall is crowded. . . . There's no soda fountain. . . . The guest house is full. . . . Employees are inexperienced. . . . You don't like the way things are run. . . . You could do better. . . . Someone said someone asked someone who told them someone said they knew something, and you don't like it. . . . Your windows aren't clean in your house. . . . You have seen the movie. . . . Your floors aren't waxed. . . . The butcher didn't wait on you in turn. . . . You want more sugar. . . . The roads are dusty. . . . Your shirts come back without buttons. . . . Things were different 'back home'. . . . You would have planned it differently. . . .

"What you want to know is . . . WHAT'S BEING DONE ABOUT IT?
"Well . . . ."

Capt. P. E. O'Meara of the Manhattan District, first town manager of Oak Ridge, Oak Ridge Journal, September 25, 1943

K-25, the original unit of the U.S. Atomic Energy Commission's huge gaseous diffusion plant at Oak Ridge, where fissionable uranium-235 was separated from a chemical compound of uranium. Construction was begun September 10, 1943. Work went on on Christmas Day to avoid even a one-day delay in the future use of the new weapon. Planning for this plant required 12,000 drawings, 20,000 pages of specifications, and 10,000 pages of operating instructions. Additional units were built after World War II. The U-shaped structure, covering 44 acres, with two other process buildings and about 70 other structures, cost approximately $460,000,000. Technical personnel used bicycles to cover the vast interior space.

"With construction on all sides, the dust created a major problem in hospital operations and the job of keeping operating room instruments sterile was a major difficulty. Between July and October, while the hospital was nearing completion, the hospital staff conducted what was almost a mobile hospital unit, setting up clinics and giving typhoid and smallpox inoculations in the cafeterias. A key figure at the hospital was a psychiatrist, for the mental health of the worker was of prime concern. The long, critical hours, the elaborate security and safety rules, the unreality and the need to produce at top efficiency and speed brought about pressure of great magnitude. . . .

"Even fun had an awkward time. Young girls, immaculately dressed for dances, often removed a mud-caked pair of hip boots at the door, stacked them in racks in the hall with others and then slipped on their dancing shoes. Furthermore, it was considered proper to remove one's shoes before entering a house."

George O. Robinson, Jr., The Oak Ridge Story, *1950*

"Magnets nearly 100 times as large as any previous magnet ever built and containing thousands of tons of steel were installed; they were scores of feet long, so powerful that their pull on the nails in a pair of shoes sometimes made walking difficult and snatched wrenches from workmen's hands if the tools were loosely held. . . .

"Because copper was short and time was more valuable than gold, 14,000 tons of silver having a monetary value of over $500,000,000 was borrowed from the United States Treasury and used for electrical conductors and bus-bars in the electromagnetic plant. . . ."

George O. Robinson, Jr., The Oak Ridge Story, *1950*

Oak Ridge, interior at production area Y-12. East Tennessee high school girls, with no idea of what their jobs were about, were trained to operate the controls of the complex equipment that produced uranium-235. At Y-12 on January 27, 1944, Manhattan District officials witnessed the historic first run of uranium-235 on a mass basis by the electromagnetic method. Twelve million square feet of blueprints were used in preparing designs for this plant.

Cars entering Oak Ridge during the war were inspected as part of a rigorous security system. Agents from the Intelligence and Security Division for the Manhattan District at Oak Ridge went halfway around the world to check possible security leaks. The creator of the Superman comic strip was told to delete mention of atom-smashing cyclotrons. Rumors of what was going on at Oak Ridge included anecdotes about seemingly outlandish waste and projects ranging from a home for returning servicemen to a Roosevelt work boondoggle.

Construction workers' hut-ments (foreground) and trailers (background) in a wartime photo of downtown Oak Ridge.

Early makeshift housing at Oak Ridge.

When demands raced ahead of expectations, hundreds of ready-to-use prefabs were hauled into place along the curved streets of the new hillside neighborhoods. A great deal of the wartime development consisted of semipermanent or temporary units.

Some of the earliest permanent wartime housing at Oak Ridge. During peak construction, a home of this type was being completed every two hours. The layout of nearly 200 miles of streets was determined mainly by land contours, with no blocks or squares.

Part of the shopping center in Jackson Square at Oak Ridge, photo taken 1945. In 1943 a shopping center was high on the list of priorities for the new community, and Jackson Square rose almost as quickly as the Administration Building which oversaw its progress. This early shopping area was a forerunner of the modern-day suburban shopping center.

Oak Ridge, view across Neighborhood 6 to the post-war hillside Neighborhood 9 of garden apartments. Step-down ordering of buildings was used to make the most of views. Within the pattern of white-cement-washed concrete block walls were the bright, porcelain-enamel balustrade panels at the stairs—in red, blue, yellow, and green.

Two buildings erected to house efficiency apartments for Oak Ridge workers and their families, 1945.

Oak Ridge, postwar garden apartments, four-family units.

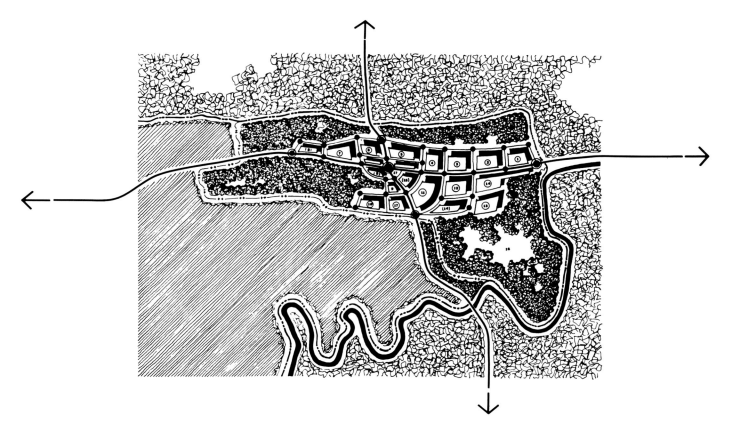

CONCEPTUAL DIAGRAM

New Town
Oak Ridge, Tennessee

LEGEND:
1-13 Thirteen neighborhoods: each having schools, playgrounds, convenience shopping, and churches.
14   Industrial areas.
15   Main shopping center, administrative and cultural center.
16   Riverside Park, camping, picnicking, hiking, riding, golf courses and gun clubs.
17   Athletic fields and recreation.

Conceptual diagram for the postwar new town of Oak Ridge, to serve 50,000 persons and provide a transition from total public ownership to an incorporated municipality with local self-government. The master plan, commissioned from Skidmore, Owings & Merrill by the Atomic Energy Commission, became a major precedent for postwar new town development in America.

**THE MOST
GIGANTIC
BUSINESS
ON EARTH**

8

Interstate highway.
 "Technology has extended the poetic field. . . . It has opened the land of dreams." (Le Corbusier)

Demolition of Henry Ives Cobb's turn-of-the-century federal courthouse in Chicago. In the background is the new federal center, designed by the firm of Mies van der Rohe.

As a result of depression and wartime expansions, the nation accumulated a vast clutter of federal programs, personnel, materiel, records, and structures. In less than 20 years the number of federal civilian employees had risen from half a million to over two million; the number of bureaus and units had grown four-fold to over 1,800; annual expenditures had increased from $3.6 billion to over $42 billion; the national debt per average family had gone from about $500 to about $7,500. By 1949, the Hoover Commission on government reorganization reported, the federal government had become "the most gigantic business on earth."

To order rather than dismantle the physical properties of this leviathan, the Hoover Commission recommended the establishment of a General Services Administration (GSA). Into the new conglomerate agency in 1949 were swept the vestiges of a line of federal building offices dating from the mid-nineteenth century, as well as the government's immense record-keeping, building management, and general procurement functions. The civilian construction role assigned to the GSA was located in its Public Building Service. Agencies with specialized building needs—the Department of Defense, the Veterans Administration, the State Department, the National Park Service—maintained their discrete building operations.

Whatever dwindling status government architects had retained in the depression years had been finally overrun by wartime mobilization. With the birth of GSA their starring role became history, their function largely replaced by private designers. In 1970 the federal client awarded architecture and engineering contracts to 3,400 individuals and firms selected by official boards on the basis of professional credentials and past performance, a selection method that was a powerful force for architectural conservatism. In 1972 government practices for hiring architects and engineers were codified in the Brooks Bill.

The evolution in the management of the design process from designers to administrators and from individuals to teams characterized major building projects, both public and private. Accountability became increasingly diffuse; officials lacked both the detailed knowledge and the opportunity to control actions done in their names. The organization point of view, at its worst, was one that no individual believed in but all upheld. It was an evolution adorned with charts and matrices. In 1974 an administrator of GSA told a gathering of architects and engineers that our society and industry did not want individual artisans, they wanted good members of teams.

Traditional pressures for economy in public works continued, but now in the orderly and organized form of audits by the Congressional investigatory branch, the General Accounting Office. Free of public scandal, federal building projects were nevertheless not free of politics or questionable cost overruns. Although the colorful openness and language of the earlier days of pork barrel were gone, sizable building projects still ran a gauntlet of political approvals; federal office buildings were frequently named for local Congressmen; and military installations clustered in geographic areas represented by legislators on the armed services committees.

Even more decisive for the influence of government on physical design were the massive postwar highway, urban renewal, and mortgage subsidy programs. Money had replaced the popular land subsidies of the nineteenth century as the means of influencing the physical development of the nation. And with federal assistance Americans were on the move again. A major city-to-suburb exodus, underwritten by federal subsidies and regulations, added another chapter to the history of the government's influence on migration. Postwar concern for the destructive power of atomic bombs had lent an early stimulus—and rationale—to this suburbanization, as government campuses sprang up outside the projected perimeter of ground-zero damage. Military emergency was also a useful argument for speeding the construction of a coast-to-coast interstate highway system.

The suburb, which first appeared in the age of the electric streetcar, became, in the age of superhighways and federal mortgages, the line of a new frontier. Urban affairs writer Grady Clay suggested an embellishment of the image: In the zone of warfare on a circular front around large cities, "The weapons are not six-guns and fast cavalry but annexation ordinances, rights of incorporation, housing policy, control over water extension, utility rates, zoning and police."

If there were any protests about the long-range effect of the huge building and highway subsidies on the values and resources of the nation, they were stilled in the historic growth-is-good, bigger-is-better ambience of American progress. The velocity of change and chance, however, overtook tradition and generated its own dynamic on what H. G. Wells once described as "the impartial space, the large liberty" of America. Bulldozers both demolished slums and eliminated landmarks and neighborhoods; highways provided arteries for geographically and upwardly mobile Americans and divided cities; dams provided hydroelectric power and destroyed ecosystems; sewers supported growth and augured strangulation; monolithic office buildings housed the business of government and commerce and created deserts on urban maps. Public spaces became, in planning jargon, "the traffic-flow-support nexus for the vertical whole." Richard Sennett argued in *The Fall of Public Man* that the public space had become a derivative of movement. "The idea of space as derivative from motion," he wrote, "parallels exactly the relations of space to motion produced by the private automobile. . . . In both, as public space becomes a function of motion, it loses any independent experiential meaning of its own." Machines not only consumed urban space; they also consumed ever more sustenance from the natural wealth of the public garden. The Department of the Interior still recognized the wise-use-versus-preservation debate, but on a scale of profitability for use of its resources by private business that suggested not a debate but a conflict of interest.

The most characteristic spatial and social result of federal policies in modern America was segregation—the segregation of activities, of rich from poor, of old from young, of white from black. And in the 1960s social protests swept the country, playing especially dramatically on the symbolic stage of the nation's capital. A quieter revolution was waged on destruction of what was now called "the environment": In

1969 Congress passed the National Environmental Policy Act, which mandated "protection of the environment." Although legislators left the details to time and the courts, citizens had acquired potentially powerful leverage for intervening in decision-making processes and challenging the use of resources. Communities still clamored for "pork barrel projects," but the force of arguments of controlled-growth advocates made many of them more discriminating.

Presidential executive orders directed federal agencies to favor central city locations and to recognize social, economic, and environmental factors in planning, acquiring, and managing prospective federal facilities. Federal legislation protecting water and air and endangered species threw sand in the gear box of traditional practices of federal public works construction and potentially affected the location of human habitation.

By 1974 the federal government was a property holder with worldwide possessions worth $83 billion plus utility systems, roads, dams, bridges, and harbor and port facilities valued at $39.3 billion. It had gone from the construction of less than a dozen buildings annually in the early years of the Republic to a domestic inventory of over 400,000 buildings containing floor space equivalent to 1,250 Empire State Buildings. It leased properties in another 50,000 locations. Overseas it owned or rented additional billions of dollars worth of embassies, war cemeteries, and military installations. On its 200th birthday in 1976 the Corps of Engineers could look back on a record of constructing 4,000 civil works, 25,000 miles of navigable waterways, and 400 man-made lakes. And it had become the country's largest producer of hydroelectric power.

Direct federal public works spending in 1974 was about $5 billion annually; grants, loans, and subsidies accounted for another $10 billion or so of construction. Each year the government was spending some $1 billion on the construction of new federal buildings alone, and $528 million on worldwide rentals. Its holdings included a public domain that was much diminished but still totaled a third of the land of the continental United States. Its holdings also included an unwanted inventory amassed in the course of its subsidized housing ventures: title or mortgage to 250,000 housing units abandoned by their owners or repossessed through mortgage payment defaults—equivalent, by one critic's calculation, to the tenth largest city in the nation.

Federal building types, as well as sheer numbers, proliferated. Visitor centers, research centers, space labs, air traffic control towers, fish hatcheries, wind tunnels, auditoriums, beach houses were as much a part of the federal mix as courthouses, prisons, embassies, and the symbol-laden Capitol and White House. To the postal service were added gigantic, highly automated bulk mail plants and street-side service kiosks. The architectural domain of the military service extended to housing for a new volunteer army and installations under the ice in Greenland and atop the ice in Antarctica, underground missile complexes with living and dining facilities connected by tunnels, military command centers in mountain caverns on giant shock absorbers to withstand near-miss nuclear strikes, and underground cities reportedly complete with sidewalks, street signs, and caches of currency to maintain a post-holocaust civilian government. Some federal projects, like the Kennedy Space Center in Florida, reached such huge proportions that they generated the growth of whole new communities and skewed the development of entire metropolitan areas. Through subsidy programs, federal regulations influenced the design of two-thirds of the nation's health construction, one-fourth of its education building, and virtually all of its housing.

The federal presence, so far as it was expressed symbolically in government buildings used by the general public, represented more and more big business of big government and less and less any tangible local proof of nationality. In 1962 a Presidential committee exhorted the government to adjure any official style. About the same time the line between federal and private style vanished. Only the official seal and perhaps more marble in the lobbies and more hardware on the guards distinguished the big buildings of federal business from the big buildings of private business. Of the two popular business facades—the glass cage and the masonry box—government preferred the masonry box with its sympathetic vestiges of public power: massiveness, whiteness, and columnar pilotis. For all the years and styles and functions that separated the Capitol dome and the President's House from their federal offspring in the capital, whiteness at least united them.

Inside federal buildings modern designers occasionally bowed to a popular concern for the influence of surroundings on behavior by replacing office cubicles with office warrens in an exercise known as "office landscaping." Acting on the report of a task force on federal architecture appointed by the National Endowment for the Arts, Congress in 1976 passed legislation that would allow opening up the ground floors of federal buildings to mixed commercial and cultural uses in order to combat the deadening effects that large office buildings had on urban areas. The act also encouraged acquiring and reusing historic and architecturally interesting buildings for public use. Legislators also took note of changing sentiment about the federal presence by renaming the Senate Committee on Public Works the Committee on Environment and Public Works; its Subcommittee on Buildings and Grounds became the Subcommittee on Regional and Community Development.

Where clarity of building purposes was more evident than in the government's general-purpose buildings, the formal results were more notable. The glamorous glitter of overseas embassies attracted both envy and criticism. Visitor centers in the national parks saw considerable use and acclaim. Federal pavilions at international fairs, freed from the necessity of permanence, often alighted like visitors from some architectural outer space. But for future interpreters of a democratic government's artifacts, the striking forms of nuclear and space age programs, existing outside any recognized grammar of architecture, posed an ultimate paradox of design and meaning.

For well over a century the main expense incurred by a diplomatic officer representing the United States in a foreign country was the cost of renting a residence. The first serious proposal that the federal government should be responsible for providing official residences abroad was made by President Cleveland in his annual message to Congress in 1895. But more than a decade went by before Congress enacted the Lowden Act in 1911, which authorized the acquisition of sites and buildings for the diplomatic and consular establishment of the United States. The primary purpose of the bill was to make it possible for trained personnel, without regard for private means, to serve at the highest diplomatic levels. This was

the beginning of a long-term program to improve the living and working conditions of the Foreign Service, an effort that was allied with the movement to put the Foreign Service on a professional career basis.

From 1926 to 1946 new construction centered on the building of embassy residences in other American republics. In Europe some grand old palaces were purchased or received as gifts. But following World War II the increased foreign responsibilities and the substantial accrued foreign currency assets of the United States stimulated a vastly expanded embassy construction program. From 1946 through 1953 the Foreign Buildings Office (FBO) of

the State Department executed over 200 projects in 72 countries: the results were in the modern corporate idiom. One embassy stylistic tradition spans the cultures in the use of luxurious Barcelona chairs and tables.

In 1953 a directive from ranking officers of the State Department ordered that all buildings henceforth were to be designed in the Georgian and Renaissance neoclassical styles, and 21 projects in the design stage were halted. Pressures for an official style were finessed by the establishment in 1954 of an Architectural Advisory Panel of private architects to advise on the designs and architects for new embassies. The three-person team with changing

membership—originally composed of Ralph Thomas Walker, Henry R. Shepley, and Pietro Belluschi —became a permanent feature of the embassy design process. The State Department and its advisory panel system garnered the most favorable critical attention of federal construction programs. In 1957 the AIA gave the embassy program a citation of honor for "having achieved a new form of expression . . . in which the architecture graciously pays homage due an established style from a government that is a guest." Looking back, Ralph Thomas Walker, as one of the original advisory panel members, demurred, "I did not advocate that they do anything but hire a lot

U.S. Consulate, Yokohama, Japan, built in the 1930s as a replica of the White House. Woodcut by unidentified artist, n.d. Reportedly President Truman believed that all of America's new embassies should be a chain of White Houses.

U.S. Embassy, Ralph Rapson and John van der Menlen, Stockholm, Sweden, 1954.

of youngsters and send them out to see what they could do."

But dissent was also plentiful, especially in Congress. Some members of the Subcommittee on State Department Organization and Foreign Operations found the high-fashion embassies difficult to take. Their criticism took a crucial form in 1960, hamstringing authorizations for the Foreign Buildings Office and requiring committee review of preliminary designs. Despite committee complaints that a small group controlled the program and received all the commissions, in the period from 1954 to 1959, 58 projects were awarded to 55 different architectural offices.

In another vein, some architects and professional critics questioned the appropriateness of America's opulent diplomatic presence. A major sour note came from Eero Saarinen's controversial London embassy, which prompted English architect Peter Smithson to say, "All the U.S. embassies in Europe I have seen—in Oslo, in the Hague, and in London—have been monuments. (As also are those in Athens and in New Delhi, seen in photographs). Now monuments are out of favor in Europe, for obvious reasons, and there is some puzzlement why America —the idea of which we admire without reservation—should have produced these buildings. We are also slightly fearful."

The government's international relations had other architectural results. In 1977, the Corps of Engineers was responsible for supervising $4.5 billion worth of construction for the government of Saudi Arabia. Under the authority of the Foreign Military Sales Act, the Corps managed the design and construction of installations for all of the Saudi armed forces, who reimbursed the Corps for salaries and other expenses. For this work the Corps awarded contracts to American citizens, which supported the traditional Arab opposition to Jewish employees. Although the Corps's Mideastern construction role provoked controversy over

its relationship to American policies, both the General Services Administration and the National Park Service joined the trek of federal contractors to Mideastern markets in 1977.

Also in the Mideast, the American flag flew over an unusual installation. The Sinai Field Mission, permanent base camp for American technicians installed in 1976 to patrol a United Nations buffer zone between Egyptian and Israeli forces, was built of the same prefabricated concrete modules used by the Holiday Inn chain. Unlike the spartan quarters of other Sinai patrol forces, the American facilities offered tennis courts, air conditioning, and carpeting.

Stairway, U.S. Embassy, Stockholm, Sweden.

Interior, U.S. Embassy, Eero Saarinen, Oslo, Norway, 1954, which received an AIA Honor Award in 1955.

U.S. Embassy, Edward Durell Stone, New Delhi, India, 1962. Architect Stone said, "This thing was literally built by hand. There were forges on the site to make the rough hardware. Except for the mechanical equipment, everything has a hand polish. This building was assembled like the Parthenon."

Interior, U.S. Embassy, New Delhi.

"What Ed Stone sought to do was to design a building that would represent this country's democratic vitality and romance, its pleasures as well as its power, its strength, all without ponderous weight. Just completed, his graceful, glittering, eye-luring structure . . . fulfills most of the extravagant hopes aroused by first sketches three years ago, which awoke many people to the possibilities of a new government style. . . .

"Ambassador Ellsworth Bunker has sounded one note of warning, however. He sees a resemblance between his headquarters and a subsequent Stone design for a pharmaceutical plant in the U.S., implying that this use of the New Delhi-type of pierced screen and other devices could debase the governmental character of this architectural currency."

Architectural Forum, January 1959

"[I am] thoroughly convinced that in addition to their salaries our ambassadors and ministers at foreign courts should be provided by the Government with official residences. . . . The usefulness of a nation's diplomatic representative undeniably depends much upon the appropriateness of his surroundings, and a country like ours, while avoiding unnecessary glitter and show, should be certain that it does not suffer in its relations with foreign nations through parsimony and shabbiness in its diplomatic outfit."

President Grover Cleveland, annual message to Congress, December 2, 1895

Showing the Flag

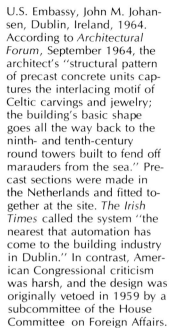

U.S. Embassy, John M. Johansen, Dublin, Ireland, 1964. According to *Architectural Forum*, September 1964, the architect's "structural pattern of precast concrete units captures the interlacing motif of Celtic carvings and jewelry; the building's basic shape goes all the way back to the ninth- and tenth-century round towers built to fend off marauders from the sea." Precast sections were made in the Netherlands and fitted together at the site. *The Irish Times* called the system "the nearest that automation has come to the building industry in Dublin." In contrast, American Congressional criticism was harsh, and the design was originally vetoed in 1959 by a subcommittee of the House Committee on Foreign Affairs.

". . . We have boasted through all our history that this is a country of homes. Shall the nation alone be homeless? Shall America's flag be a tramp in the capitals of the world, protecting not a nation's home but only the temporary abiding place of America's representatives? . . . Now, let this nation do its part. Let us either withdraw from the capitals of the earth, or let us enable our foreign representatives to serve their country abroad on something like equal terms with the rest of the world."

Representative Frank O. Lowden of Illinois, Congressional Record, *March 2, 1910*

"[It] looks as much like a Gaelic tower as the Capitol looks like an aircraft carrier."

Representative Wayne L. Hays on the U.S. Embassy, Dublin, quoted in Architectural Forum, *March 1959*

"It looked to me like a glorified tent or a series of flapjacks with a pat of butter on top. But who am I to criticize? I do not classify myself as a qualified critic of either modern art or modern architecture."

Representative Clement J. Zablocki on the U.S. Embassy, Dublin, quoted in Architectural Forum, *March 1959*

U.S. Embassy, Eero Saarinen, London, England, 1960, the results of a design competition.

The controversial golden eagle with a 35-foot wingspread ready to be hoisted into place atop the new American Embassy building in London's Grosvenor Square, July 30, 1960. For months some Britons had been critical about the bird. According to the Associated Press, one member of Parliament called it a "blatant montrosity."

"The policy shall be to provide requisite and adequate facilities in an architectural style and form which will create good will by intelligent appreciation, recognition, and use of the architecture appropriate to the site."

Design competition program, London embassy, 1955

"What then has gone wrong? The building [the London Embassy] falls between two stools—diplomatic delicacy and American status-seeking.

"Diplomatic immunity from building and planning regulations left the State Department free to build a mile-high skyscraper if it wished. Therefore it became coy and polite; it fell over backward in telling its architect to remember the Georgian scale of Grosvenor Square. There is no Georgian architecture in Grosvenor Square. Hence the false humility—the Georgian proportions and height.

"Then the other 'stool'—the status line—came into action. For all its sham politeness this building had also to be American, new, crisp, and glamorous. Hence the rather aggressive, staccato modeling of the the costume jewelry that overbedecks it all. Every detail contradicts the original and over-polite intentions.

"The rather childish controversy over the xenophobic nature of the 35-foot golden eagle . . . is false. The eagle is consistent with the architecture which in its turn is consistent with the tragedy of Americanism."

R. Furneaux Jordan in The Observer, *quoted in* Architectural Forum, *March 1961*

U.S. Embassy, Harry Weese, Accra, Ghana, 1959.

"[The London Embassy] is built in the mode of our most prosperous and most socially regressive period . . . a period we no longer wish to emulate. . . . And we are puzzled why you should . . . accept such frozen and pompous forms as the true expression of a generous egalitarian society. Surely, the first question for an architect is what is the nature of an embassy? Not what is the style of an embassy."

Peter Smithson, quoted in Architectural Forum, March 1961

"I feel the London Embassy is a complete success in the Grosvenor Square setting. . . .

"A certain amount of bright metal often looks nice on a building. Aluminum in its original color looks too cold with Portland stone. By anodizing it to a straw color, we trim up the building and give it an appropriate official look. Thus the building does create a focal point for the square; it is a symmetrical building and well-defined.

"The straw-colored eagle and the main entrance accentuate the central axis of the building somewhat in the manner of a pediment. We used the eagle as a symbol and as another way to make this building look like an embassy and not just another building. An eagle seems appropriate architecturally and symbolically."

Eero Saarinen, quoted in Architectural Forum, March 1961

"The means chosen to give the building dignity are . . . chiefly a lavish display of gilding in the form of gilded aluminum sheathing to the tips of the exposed beams, the window reveals, and other features of the facades. The result is tawdry, and only emphasizes the more superficial qualities of the design. . . ."

The Times (London), quoted in Architectural Forum, March 1961

"The trouble here appears to be that somewhere inside all this a good architect is fighting to get out. We know Saarinen is a good architect, and the building abounds in details whose consistency and logic bespeak a standard of professional competence that few buildings in Britain can rival. . . . Ultimately, I suspect, the architect deserves our sympathy. In an age when the authority of government depends on personalities, statistics, and communications, any attempt to build 'representational' buildings for prestige will simply produce empty cenotaphs. Saarinen should have been commissioned to design a high-quality office block, and hang the brand image."

Reyner Banham in The New Statesman, quoted in Architectural Forum, March 1961

Casa Thomas Jefferson, Mitchell and Giurgola, Brasilia, Brazil, 1974, designed for the United States Information Agency/Thomas Jefferson Cultural Council.

Showing the Flag

Courtyard, U.S. Embassy, Walter Gropius/TAC, Athens, Greece, 1961. References to ancient temples were made in the podium, quadrilateral plan, enclosed patio, and marble-sheathed columns. According to the designers, "The lavish colors—blue ceramic tile, orange vertical blinds, and bright green planting— parallel the ancient use of paint . . . and respond to the native sparkle of the Greek landscape."

According to Gropius, TAC's intention "was to find the spirit of the Greek approach without imitating any classical means." The Athens newspaper *Ethnos* approved the results as one of the city's most beautiful buildings and observed that "one may become jealous of the people who work in such wonderful surroundings. . . . of the 40 embassies the Americans have built in 40 countries, the embassies in New Delhi and Athens hold first place."

American Embassy, Athens, Greece, April 21, 1975, showing damage done by demonstrators to the chancery. The most curious such use of an embassy as a symbol occurred in Hanoi, North Vietnam, where a Museum of the Revolution featured a complete mockup of the Communist takeover of Saigon, including a helicopter on a string leaving a smoldering model of the American embassy and carrying the American ambassador to safety.

Japanese view ice models of U.S. landmarks, including the Statue of Liberty with oriental features, in Sapporo Park, Japan, April 1976.

Except for the embassy-like pavilion commissioned by the Department of State for the Brussels international fair in 1958, America's more recent overseas pavilions were as light and innovative as their nineteenth-century ancestors had been heavy and modish. In the 1950s the U.S. Information Agency carted about a small geodesic dome to cover exhibits at foreign trade fairs; at Moscow in 1959 a dome plus flower-like plastic umbrellas sheltered America on display. The agency chose a 20-story steel-and-plastic dome for Montreal's Expo 67. Inside, exhibits of "Creative America" dazzled visitors with American movies and Pop Art. The crowning technical achievement for the USIA was its pavilion at Expo 70 in Osaka, Japan, where the U.S. put up the largest air-supported structure ever assembled. Air structures had been first developed in 1946 by the U.S. military, but it was the Osaka pavilion, according to *Engineering News-Record*, that "solved many problems that had held back development of large air-supported fabric structures." Inside were "Images of America"—from Babe Ruth's uniform to a piece of moon rock. Inside and outside, the USIA pavilions all reached for a collaboration of spectacle and technology. Construction of the Osaka pavilion officially got under way

with a centuries-old groundbreaking ceremony presided over by Shinto priests.

At home, the federal buildings at fairs fell to the Department of Commerce, which earned modest kudos for its architecturally stylish pavilions. With one exception: in the land of Robert Moses at the New York World's Fair of 1964, everything was awry. At what was touted as one of the largest single building projects in U.S. history, whimsical pop buildings and mechanistic structures settled uncomfortably on the site plan left over from the 1939 fair, replete with Beaux-Arts axes and radial promenades. And the federal pavilion settled heavily; it was the largest and most expensive of federal

fair structures. One critic called it a "U.S. Government nothing-box, containing several million cu. ft. of nothing." For a decade, proposals for reuse, including a free offer to the city, were made. The building, deteriorating from vandalism and lack of repairs, was demolished in 1976.

For the Bicentennial year, intercity rivalry and domestic tensions defeated attempts to stage a national spectacular. NASA sponsored a Bicentennial exposition of science and technology at Cape Kennedy. In the landscape of the nation's most spectacular technological achievement, paradox, for one thing, was on display. The National Endowment for the Arts filled its exhibit space with a work of art

created by intersecting laser light beams. In another space the Energy Research and Development Administration displayed a 2,600-pound lump of coal, a reminder of the nation's mounting energy crisis. Neither an artful use of technology nor caution about resources could have been imagined by visitors to the 1876 Centennial.

An international exposition with an energy theme was planned for 1982 in Knoxville, Tennessee. The federal government planned to contribute $20 million for a U.S. pavilion.

"A million Muscovites attended the American Exhibition in Sokolniki Park, Moscow, U.S.S.R., last summer to watch fashion shows and square dances under a spectacular reinforced plastics pavilion.

"The building would have been just as exciting if erected on Main St., U.S.A., because it involved daring new concepts in design, engineering, and construction—concepts likely to affect the use of plastics in the building fields for years to come. . . . To students of architecture, to construction engineers, and even to conservationists, the U.S. Pavilion in Moscow offered new ideas for protective construction. In many parts of the world erratic rainfall pattern and peculiar soil conditions make the saving of water a major problem. The lily column makes it possible to collect water automatically."

Albert G. H. Dietz, engineering consultant for the Moscow pavilion, "U.S. Pavilion in Moscow," Modern Plastics, December 1959

U.S. Pavilion, Kabul Trade Fair, Afghanistan, 1956. This pavilion, designed by R. Buckminster Fuller for the U.S. Information Agency, was easy to put up and take down and easy to ship. It was reused about a dozen times over the next few years.

Visitors at model train exhibit, U.S. Pavilion, Kabul Trade Fair, 1956.

Exhibition pavilion, George Nelson, American National Exhibition, Moscow, U.S.S.R., 1959. Sponsoring agency: USIA. Ninety reinforced umbrellas were assembled in clusters. The design was pretested at Mitchell Air Force Base in the United States, using three twin-engine static airplanes to subject the columns to constant hurricane-strength winds. After the exhibit the umbrellas were used by the Russians at a Black Sea resort. American exhibits in Moscow were also housed in one of Buckminster Fuller's geodesic domes.

"World exhibitions during the nineteenth century played a crucial role in letting people experience at firsthand a new machine or process. . . . In the twentieth century efficient means of spreading technical information have developed and now the emphasis is on the individual's relationship to the environment. This is a change in attitude away from concern for the object—its engineering, operation and function, and toward aesthetics—human motivation and involvement, pleasure, interest, excitement."
Billy Kluver, "The Pavilion," in Pavilion Experiments in Art and Technology, ed. Barbara Rose and Billy Kluver, 1972

Multiple-screen film on America for the U.S. exhibition in Moscow, produced by the office of Charles and Ray Eames. A photographic survey of the "Family of Man" was presented in another exhibit. American design prowess was on display in Moscow—in buildings, in displays, and in a photographic exhibit of contemporary American architecture.

Model, U.S. Pavilion, Expo 67, Montreal, Canada, 1967. Architect, R. Buckminster Fuller; exhibit designer, Cambridge Seven Associates. Sponsoring agency: USIA. Sixty-two nations participated in the six-month fair, attended by 50 million visitors. The theme of the fair was "Man and His World."

The largest of Fuller's geodesic spheroids, the pavilion dome was 20 stories high and had a volume equivalent to New York City's Seagram tower. "It will enclose enough space," Fuller said, "for whole communities to live in a benign physical microcosm." The lightweight, space-frame structure supported a transparent skin that allowed the dome to be filled with natural light by day and to glow from internal light by night. Temperature and light inside the bubble were controlled by sunshades that were activated by the sun's rays, changing segments of the skin from transparency to polished chrome.

Interior, U.S. Pavilion, Montreal, housing a multilevel composition of platforms supporting the "Creative America" exhibits. Lunar exploration, Pop Art, and American movies were part of the ebullient mix.

"For close to three years, Masey worked around the clock within that agency [U.S. Information Agency] to make our Montreal pavilion just a little better than it would have been under normal circumstances. . . . Our pavilion at Montreal is a triumph of architecture, interior design, display, dramatization, and all the rest; a demonstration of the ebullient spirit of the young people of our nation and a triumph of sheer courage. . . . this is not only Bucky Fuller's pavilion, not only the pavilion of the Cambridge Seven, nor that of the other contributors. It is the pavilion of one Jack Masey . . . a highly improbable bureaucrat."

Architectural Forum, June 1967

Winning competition entry for the U.S. Pavilion, Osaka, a 15-story air structure later redesigned to reflect, among other things, reductions in budget by Congress. Eleven schemes were submitted by teams of architects and designers, who spent six weeks preparing a jury presentation that was limited to one hour each. A minimum program stipulated little more than site and budget. Presentations were not anonymous, since teams were judged as much for their cooperation potential as their design potential. The unorthodox competition, sponsored by the USIA, was titled an exercise/interview to finesse AIA competition rules. The final design came in under budget, and $1.3 million was returned to the federal government. In 1971 the AIA chose the Osaka pavilion for an Honor Award.

Aerial view, U.S. Pavilion, Expo 70, Osaka, Japan, 1970. Architect, Davis Brody Associates; exhibit designer, Chermayeff, Geismar, de Harak. Sponsoring agency: USIA. Seventy-six nations participated in the first international fair held in Asia, which during six months was attended by over 64 million visitors. Its theme was "Progress and Harmony for Mankind."

The translucent, air-supported cable roof covered a space the size of two football fields, the largest clear-span air-supported roof that had ever been built.

Interior, U.S. pavilion, Osaka. Seven major exhibits were featured: American photography, painting, sports, and space exploration; architecture, folk arts, and new arts. America's outer space feats captured the largest arena in the pavilion and attracted the longest lines at the fair. Especially popular was the moon rock that had been brought back from the Apollo 11 lunar mission. Also featured was a full-scale model of the landing site of the Sea of Tranquility.

"The United States Pavilion was an excellent example of a design that evolves from the requirements set by government. The exhibits were required to show the United States and its products to as many visitors as possible. . . . During those early design discussions for the United States pavilion, every decision seemed to revolve around pedestrian traffic patterns. It was necessary to move the greatest number of people as fast as possible to see as much 'America' as possible."

John Pearce, "An Architect's View," in Pavilion Experiments in Art and Technology, ed. Barbara Rose and Billy Kluver, 1972

"Was Expo 70 really necessary? The Japanese are delighted to have been awarded the first World's Fair ever held in Asia—and Kurokawa has said that this sort of mad celebration is invariably a great popular success, if not always a critical one. As a method of communication it may be less successful, however. After all, there are easier ways of absorbing images and ideas than to wait in line, for hours, to shuffle through a multimedia pavilion.

"Still, Expo 70 has fulfilled its promise in a number of ways. In the areas of technological advance, it has given us the spaceframe roof of Tange's Theme Pavilion and the inflated roof of the U.S. building. In the area of theatrical innovation, it has given us the many-mirrored Canadian Pavilion. And in the area of urban design, it has given us Tange's multilevel grid of people-movers. None of these things would have been investigated in the real world of practical building and city planning. Only in the unreal world of World's Fairs do such things finally get built."

Peter Blake, "Expo 70," Forum, April 1970

"If Montreal's Expo '67 had been the fair for film projections, Expo '70 was shaping up as the fair for mirrors, air structures, and multichannel sound systems."

Calvin Tomkins, "Outside Art," in Pavilion Experiments in Art and Technology, ed. Barbara Rose and Billy Kluver, 1972

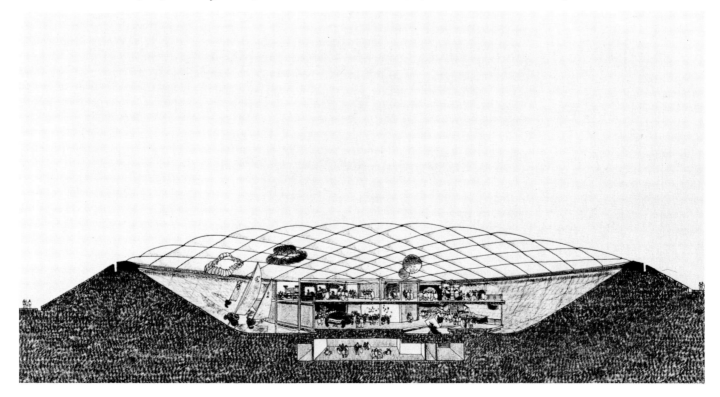

Air structure exhibit building, Atomic Energy Commission, Victor Lundy, 1960, believed to be the first air structure designed in collaboration with an architect. This 22,000-square-foot exhibit building was transported from city to city in South America as part of an Atoms-for-Peace Program. When completely packaged for shipment, the structure was the size of a standard railroad box car. The facility enclosed a theater, an auditorium, and a complete, movable laboratory with technical facilities to show the atom at work in medicine, agriculture, industry, and power. Lundy chose an air structure, in part, to display U.S. technological accomplishment. "I was convinced," he said, "after visits to Brasilia and other South American cities, and out of my own knowledge of the high standards of design in comtemporary South American architecture, that an antiseptic, 'safe,' rehashed solution would be a failure."

"We have standards governing construction by exhibitors, but we do not tell them what they can build . . . Greek and Barbarian, traditionalist and modernist, conservative and iconoclast, right wing and left, they all look alike to us."

Robert Moses on the New York World's Fair, Architectural Forum, January 1964

U.S. pavilion, Expo 74, Spokane, Washington, 1974. Architects; Naramore, Bain, Brady & Johanson of Seattle. One of the constraints imposed by the sponsoring U.S. Department of Commerce was quick demountability, which led, in part, to the tent solution. (A similar tent form had been used by the German government at Montreal.)

In the fairground jumble the most popular images were the tentlike federal pavilion and the surviving clock tower of the Great Northern Railroad Station. While the fair was in progress a campaign was begun to make the pavilion a permanent feature of a city park.

Interior, U.S. Pavilion, Spokane.

"[The landscape design for Expo 74] approaches a reconstruction of the landform and flora that lined the river before the city was founded. It is a classic conception, perfectly fitting the theme of a fair dedicated, as this one is, to the potential harmony of man and his natural environment."

Roger Montgomery, "Expo 74: Nature Festival," Progressive Architecture, *August 1974*

"Before this decade is out" was President John F. Kennedy's prediction, made May 25, 1961, for an American moon landing. And on July 20, 1970, astronaut Neil A. Armstrong stepped onto the moon's surface. By 1975 officials and scientists were sketching the outlines of permanently established space colonies.

America's space adventure also established bases on an ice cap at the South Pole and beneath the frozen surface of the North Pole. Sleek new airport towers and the soaring forms of a new international airport outside Washington symbolized the age of jet travel. Rapid growth and development everywhere demanded energy, and the race was on, too, to develop new energy supplies and to cope with the dwindling of traditional resources. Lawsuits raised questions about the more insidious long-range damage of dams and power plants. The dangers of the spatial feats of dam builders were dramatized by the collapse of Teton Dam, which destroyed both lives and property.

With none of the stops and starts and tentativeness in funds or commitment that characterized urban planning and with none of the burdens of a history of architectural symbolism, technological goals quickly generated thoroughly contemporary design solutions. Spatial landmarks also had an easier time than their urban counterparts. To the background sounds of "Auld Lang Syne" and a recording of the final minutes of countdown, the first moon explorers celebrated the fifth anniversary of their flight by dedicating Launch Complex 39 at the Kennedy Space Center as a national historic landmark. And instead of demolition, the "Pregnant Guppy," the first airship built for NASA to transport oversized space components, was destined for preservation in the Air Force's air museum in Dayton, Ohio.

Ventilators above the nuclear power plant of Camp Century, a village under ice constructed 800 miles from the North Pole in 1960 by the U.S. Army Corps of Engineers to study construction and survival in the polar regions. Operated by the Army's Polar Research and Development Center under agreement with Denmark, the camp supported some 100 research projects in its first two years, including studies of improved weather forecasting, glacial geology, food preservation, radio communication, development of fabrics for cold climates, and special medical problems.

Diagram of Camp Century showing underground complex of barracks and laboratory buildings winding through four levels of ice tunnels. Standard Army prefabricated plywood buildings, installed underground, allowed the camp to accommodate up to 250 persons. Water for citizens of Camp Century was furnished from "flash-thawed" snow and ice taken from a glacial depth that represented 400 years of history. "What we need," said one civil engineering resident, "is women, a few trees, and perhaps a bluebird or two."

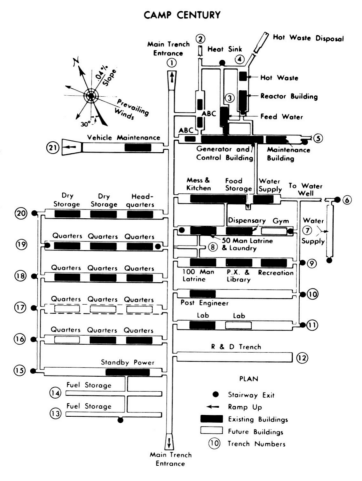

CAMP CENTURY

"What we learn here can be as important—really—or even more important than what we can learn in outer space. . . . This is the one place in the whole world where environment comes first. . . . The station we dedicate today is another announcement to the world that we propose to move onward in the area of polar science."

Representative J. J. Pickle, dedication remarks, Amundsen-Scott South Pole Station, January 8, 1975

U.S. Amundsen-Scott South Pole Station. The dome shelters three two-story buildings that contain a communications center, a store, a library and recreation room, science labs, single-room quarters, a photographic darkroom and laboratory, a meeting hall, and a vault for earth tide measurements. Under the adjacent steel arches are a dispensary, biomedical facilities, vehicle repair and maintenance shops, storage space, and a small gymnasium.

U.S. Amundsen-Scott South Pole Station, 1974. Delivery of materials for construction required 438 flights. Navy Seabees worked 10 hours a day, 7 days a week, often taking advantage of 24-hour sunlight in multiple shifts. Construction season at the Pole covered some 75 days with an average temperature of −32°C. Structures were designed to withstand temperature extremes to −80°C, high winds, drifting snow, and a constantly moving ice sheet. Mementos presented to the station manager during dedication ceremonies included a photograph of Norwegian explorer Roald Amundsen and his party at the Pole in 1911 and replicas of the boots worn by Amundsen when he became the first to reach the Pole.

Vehicle Assembly Building, Urbahn-Roberts-Sealye-Moran, Kennedy Space Center, Florida, 1962, by far the largest building in the world—covering eight acres and enclosing 130 million cubic feet of space—and reportedly so large that sometimes rain falls from cloudlike vapor accumulations formed inside the vast space. By one estimate, four Seagram Buildings could be parked inside the VAB as well as a half-dozen Pepsi-Cola Buildings. The huge mobile plug-in units of the Space Center contribute a fairy-tale quality: 40-story-high structures on wheels; moving platforms the size of half a city block; entire floors within the VAB that slide in and out like trays; prefabricated labs and workshops that are plugged in and removed when not needed.

"[The] juxtaposition of so-called visionary architecture and the accomplishment of the engineers of the space program demonstrates a serious gap between even the farthest-out fantasies of architects and the reality accepted daily in advanced, nonbuilding technology. . . . Yet, in visionary architecture such concepts as prefabbed apartments hoisted into position on a skeletal frame, to be plugged into prepared utilities, are still considered impractical by most designers and builders. . . . The proud achievements at Cape Kennedy are proof of our ability to tackle the most staggering problems; and, by implication, they are an indictment of those who would not expend the same kind of effort on our urban ills. It is unfortunate that the U.S. has only twice, in recent history, committed itself to such efforts—and that, in both instances, one motivation was fear. The other program, of course, gave us the H-bomb."

Peter Blake, "Cape Kennedy," Architectural Forum, January/February 1967

Transonic wind tunnel, NASA
Langley Research Center,
Langley Station, Hampton,
Virginia, 1961. Note size of
man.

Dulles International Airport, Eero Saarinen, Washington, D.C. To solve some of the problems of large airports—getting to the airport, checking in, claiming baggage—Saarinen used a device of nineteenth-century train stations—space and closeness to departure points—plus a limited-access highway and mobile lounges that carry passengers from the terminal to airplanes. The terminal is generally acknowledged to be one of America's great twentieth-century buildings.

"The airport sets an implied standard of quality. Everybody out here is proud of Dulles and that's not a common attitude around airports."

Joseph Trocino, Loudoun County planner, The Washington Post, March 7, 1977

". . . Eero Saarinen did on that job [Dulles airport] something he never had to do on other jobs and something that other architects have not recognized needs to be done. He generated a tremendous amount of enthusiasm for the design itself. He convinced the Federal Aviation Authority that this was their great opportunity to raise the level of airport design all over the country. He was able to overcome the forces of indifference and inertia by personal appearance and by the most effective kind of selling; he was able to overcome the different processes of review by unremitting labor on his own part and by what I can only describe as a remarkable example of architectural leadership. . . . these are not activities that architects in private practice are called upon to do in most cases, but they are the most rewarding kinds of activity if our objective is the highest standard of design in Federal building."

Frederick Gutheim, AIA Journal, June 1963

High-activity airport traffic
control tower, I. M. Pei and
Partners, 1964. The prototype
tower was designed for installation in one of 13 look-alike
variations at 60 U.S. airports.
Congress had decided in 1961
that all future airport towers
should be designed by the
Federal Aviation Administration instead of by localities.
The Pei office was recom-
mended for the job of designing the prototype tower by a
committee of private citizens
established by FAA Administrator Najeeb Hallaby to advise on the design of FAA facilities. The substantial
increase of construction costs
over budget of a related design
for low-activity airports
caused an investigation by the
General Accounting Office in
1965. The GAO attributed the
additional costs to "aesthetic
factors inherent in the non-
conventional design of the
new towers." Hallaby's successor as FAA Administrator
agreed to use lower-cost design in the future on both
low-activity and high-activity
towers.

Three 437-foot-high cooling towers at TVA's Paradise Steam Plant in Kentucky, which has a generating capacity of 2,558,200 kilowatts —larger than any fuel-powered station now in operation anywhere in the world. TVA's major use of nuclear power has aroused the "valley people" to protest and litigation.

"Dolos" installation by the Corps of Engineers to protect a jetty from wave damage, 1972. South Africans invented the 20-ton concrete "dolos," which can be left untied without rolling and provide a sturdy guard to the breakwaters. The Corps modified that design for a dolos weighing 42 tons. Over 4,700 dolos were cast and placed in two layers up to 200 feet away from shore in their first use in the United States.

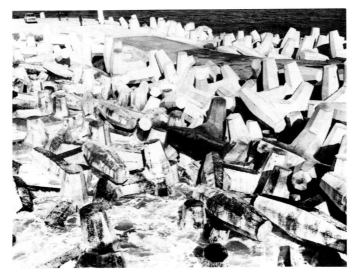

Grand Coulee Third Power Plant, Marcel Breuer and Hamilton Smith/Thomas Hayes, Associate, Bureau of Reclamation, Columbia Basin Project, Grand Coulee, Washington, 1968. Structural folds create the stiffness needed to support machinery within the 1,100-foot-long power plant.

"Architects and engineers, because of their different approaches to projects, are frequently at odds with each other. Grand Coulee Dam's Third Powerplant happily reverses this situation. [Bureau of Reclamation] specified in classic architectural terms that the design should provide 'continuity, visual interaction and structural integration.' The engineers also mentioned that the building had to house the world's largest hydroelectric turbine-generators. . . . [The architects] have given BuRec and those Americans who are lucky enough to visit Grand Coulee Dam a marvelous example of architecture and engineering at its best."

Engineering News-Record, *August 8, 1974*

"When completed the complex [Grand Coulee] will be the world's largest single power facility, as well as one of the most massive structures erected since antiquity. (Indeed, its forms as well as its dimensions seem vaguely Egyptian.) . . . The fact that the Federal Bureau of Reclamation decided to turn to an architect of Breuer's stature, rather than to consider such construction as just an engineering project, is heartening, and the results promise to well repay that decision."

Architecture Plus, *May–June 1974*

SKYLAB ORBITAL WORKSHOP

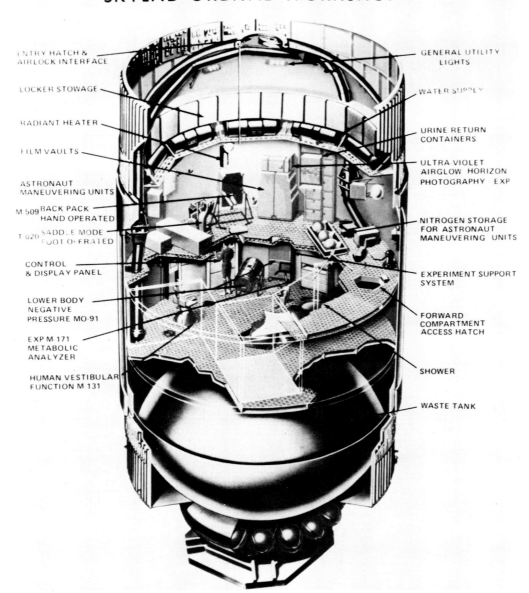

ENTRY HATCH &
AIRLOCK INTERFACE

LOCKER STOWAGE

RADIANT HEATER

FILM VAULTS

ASTRONAUT
MANEUVERING UNITS

M 509 BACK PACK
HAND OPERATED

T 020 SADDLE MODE
FOOT OPERATED

CONTROL
& DISPLAY PANEL

LOWER BODY
NEGATIVE
PRESSURE MO-91

EXP M-171
METABOLIC
ANALYZER

HUMAN VESTIBULAR
FUNCTION M-131

GENERAL UTILITY
LIGHTS

WATER SUPPLY

URINE RETURN
CONTAINERS

ULTRA-VIOLET
AIRGLOW HORIZON
PHOTOGRAPHY EXP

NITROGEN STORAGE
FOR ASTRONAUT
MANEUVERING UNITS

EXPERIMENT SUPPORT
SYSTEM

FORWARD
COMPARTMENT
ACCESS HATCH

SHOWER

WASTE TANK

Artist's conception, cutaway
view of the Skylab 1 Orbital
Workshop, one of the five
major components of the Skylab space station cluster,
which was launched by a Sat-
urn V on May 14, 1973. The
space station consists of a
100-ton laboratory complex in
which highly versatile medical, scientific, and technological experiments can be performed in earth orbit. Three-
man crews visit the station
three times over an eight-
month period. The Navy has
developed a counterpart,
called ''Sealab,'' for underwa-
ter exploration.

*''. . . We will be seeing more or
less permanent human habitats
in outer space by the late '80s,
maybe even the mid '80s. This
will challenge the whole society, and especially architects.
. . . By the time we get to the
point of building and testing in
orbit, there will be a new freedom to deal with an architecture of volumes.''*

Russell Schweickart, former astronaut, AIA Journal, May
1977

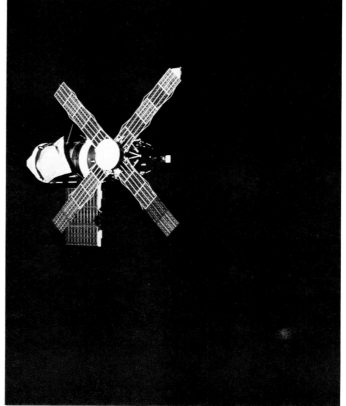

Artist's conception of a suggestion by Gerald K. O'Neill of Princeton University for a twenty-first-century space colony, part of a NASA-sponsored study of space colonization. The design represents the largest of four types of space habitations suggested and could accommodate a population of 200,000 to several million, depending on how the interior is planned. The cylindrical portion is the living area, and the interior could be fashioned to resemble any landscape of the American dream—the plains of South Dakota, San Francisco Bay, or the tidy village squares of New England. Each cylinder would rotate around its axis once every 114 seconds to create earthlike gravity. Solar energy would be the source of power and lunar or asteroid raw materials would be used for construction. The cylinder is capped by a manufacturing and power station and ringed by tea-cup-shaped containers that are agricultural stations.

Skylab space station, overhead view taken from the Command Service Module during final "fly-around" inspection.

Space colony agricultural area, artist's conception, designed by a NASA-sponsored study in 1975. The area is shown situated between two parks. On the top four levels of the farm, soybeans, wheat, sorghum, and some other crops would be grown. Water would be supplied directly from the river and indirectly through the fish tanks that line the sides. Altogether, these tanks could hold about 260,000 fish. The half-mile-long farm would also be inhabited by rabbits and 2,800 cattle. Since moisture, sunlight, and heat conditions are controlled, the farm could yield far more than a farm of comparable size on Earth.

Proposal for an experimental
air-supported megastructure to
house federal offices, Megastructure Environments Group
for the GSA, 1973.

Model, Federal Building,
Smith Hinchman & Grylls,
Saginaw, Michigan, 1976,
completed as a GSA environmental demonstration project.
The solar collector was designed to produce in excess of
70 percent of summer air
conditioning and 50 percent
of winter heating. Half the
roof area is covered with
lawn, shrubs, trees, and seat-
ing, which provide additional
insulation. The other half of
the roof is a parking lot,
which becomes a community
playground after business
hours.

Federal Aviation Administration building with an air-age look, Daniel Mann Johnson & Mendenhall, Hawthorne, California.

Central Laboratory and Office Building, U.S. Atomic Energy Commission, Batavia Area Office, Batavia, Illinois.

With the detonation of the atomic bomb at Hiroshima, national defense took on new meanings, new forms, and new budgets. The progeny of nineteenth-century weapons and forts now appeared as ABM, MSR, IBM, ICBM, Sentinel, Safeguard, Sprint, and Spartan. Borders were BMEWS and DEWline. Patrols and scouting parties were supersonic aircraft and nuclear submarines. Scenarios replaced battle plans. And the enemy, as often as not, wore gray flannel suits. When the superpowers sat at bargaining tables, calculations included their split-second kill and over-kill capacities, the nuclear potential of smaller powers, and the political dangers back home. Defense in such a world was, at best, speculative deterrence. Deterring the enemy abroad might be simpler than deterring the critics at home. When the Secretary of Defense acknowledged in 1967 that he supported the decision to authorize an ABM on "marginal grounds," he provided opponents with another brand of weaponry. Sentinel, went the humor of the mid-1960s, was largely a defense against American Republicans, not Chinese Communists.

Wherever political and military and moral reality lay, architecture-engineering firms competed eagerly for part of the fast-breaking action. The Safeguard antiballistic missile facilities in North Dakota became in half a decade symbolic of record-breaking structures built in record time with record budgets. Begun in 1970, crash schedules for construction left a record by 1973, according to a GAO investigation, of change orders that could add 87 percent to the original contract price. By 1976, the system was abandoned, victim of détente and Congressional disfavor. Recalling the pyramid of Cheops and the ruins of Stonehenge, the huge, abandoned structures of the ABM program joined the twentieth-century archaeology of the concrete bunkers that once protected the perimeter of "fortress Europe." For architects the concrete coffins might ironically recall Le Corbusier's claim that architecture is "the masterly, correct, and magnificent play of masses brought together in light."

Radar site with a 30-foot antenna and a radome, Cam Main, Canada, distant early warning (DEW) line, U.S. Air Force. Radomes emerged from the military development of Buckminster Fuller's geodesic domes in the 1950s.

Interior view of the SATCOM radome, Shemya Air Force Base, Alaska, October 1968. The antenna acts as a mobile ground terminal link, which transmits and receives through defense communications satellites.

Radar surveillance antennae, U.S. Air Force ballistic missile early warning system (BMEWS) station at Clear, Alaska.

"Located forty-seven miles west of Washington, D.C., in rural Virginia, Mount Weather and almost 100 other 'Federal Relocation Centers' are officially described as the backbone of America's 'Continuity of Government' program. The system was designed in the early 1950s as a civil defense program for the Executive branch of the Federal Government, . . . a massive underground fallout shelter system that could protect the essential leaders of government during times of crisis. Under the code name 'Operation High Point,' the Army Corps of Engineers combed the countryside around Washington in search of a suitable site. . . .

"The cumbersome excavation work took years to complete. But when it was finished, say sources who formerly served as supervisory personnel at Mount Weather, the shelter more closely resembled a city than an emergency installation. Mount Weather was equipped with such amenities as private apartments and dormitories, streets and sidewalks, cafeterias and hospitals, a water purification system, power plant, and general office buildings. The site includes a small lake fed by fresh water from underground springs. It even has its own mass transit system—small electric cars that run on rechargeable batteries and make regular shuttle runs throughout the city."

Richard P. Pollock, "The Mysterious Mountain," **The Progressive,** *March 1976*

Movie version of The Pentagon "war room," from "Dr. Strangelove," 1964. Pictures of the real version, published in 1976, were remarkably similar.

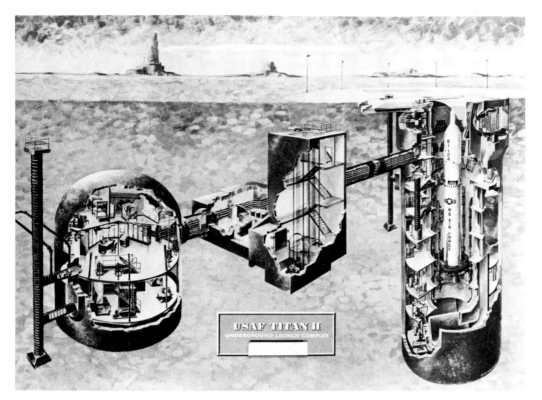

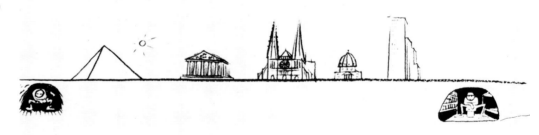

Artist's concept of an underground view of a Titan II site, part of the nation's deployment of intercontinental ballistic missiles. Each 160-foot-deep missile silo (on the right) is flanked by a 40-foot-deep silo for launching equipment and a 20-foot-deep silo containing fuel storage tanks. The silos are connected by 10-foot-diameter steel tunnels.

History of Man, Robert Osborn, 1950s, commented on the bomb shelter scenario for "Thinking the unthinkable." Beginning in 1956 the Office of Civil and Defense Mobilization (OCDM) and the Department of Defense worked with the Atomic Energy Commission, the National Bureau of Standards, and the National Academy of Science to test and develop standards for shelter design. These were incorporated in a booklet issued in 1960 by OCDM: *Fallout Shelter Surveys: Guide for Architects and Engineers.*

"There are few ground rules, and the changes in missile development itself, as well as policy shifts affecting their deployment and housing, make it unlikely that there will ever be very many firm rules. But architect-engineer firms and contractors that have so far played major roles in missile and space-development work have shown their enthusiasm in the vigor with which they attempt to garner new contracts for such work."

David B. Carlson, "Buildings for the Space Age," **Architectural Forum,** *September 1960*

Abandoned $5.7 billion missile tracking station, at the U.S. Army's Safeguard anti-ballistic missile defense system tactical facilities near Grand Forks, North Dakota, December 1975, built in 1970. After a 1972 Soviet-U.S. arms limitation treaty, construction was called off at another ABM site in Great Falls, Montana and plans for a site near Washington, D.C., were canceled. The remote plains of North Dakota still harbor ICBM missiles which the Air Force began installing in 1965. A local resident reportedly claimed, "If Cavalier County [North Dakota] were to secede from the union, it would be the world's third greatest nuclear power."

"Passion can create drama out of inert stone."

Le Corbusier, Vers une architecture, *1923*

". . . The stark engineering composition of severely abstract forms, grimly silhouetted against open sky and flat land, upstages architecture totally. It is without doubt one of the most peculiarly impressive built groups of our time. Architects trying consciously for impact and meaning might just as well call it quits in the face of this kind of brute force. . . . In the case of the ABM structures, we are assaulted; our senses are shattered. The architectural power, the imagery and symbolism, are overwhelming. . . . Next to the reality that produces an ABM the monuments of architects often seem like arbitrary toys."

Ada Louise Huxtable, "A Bizarre Monument to Non-Architecture," The New York Times, *December 14, 1975*

Air Force Titan intercontinental ballistic missile site 1A at Lowry Air Force Base, Denver, Colorado, February 1960. The complex consists of three launching sites, two steel-concrete domes housing the control center, an electric power generator, and elevated radomes used as part of Titan's guidance system.

Federal Reserve Board complex, Culpeper, Virginia, built to withstand both blast and radiation from a nuclear attack. Lead shields can be raised over windows in case of attack. Design of the installation is predicated on the belief that there would be survivors to use the bank and its cash reserves. The guard tower resembles the bastions of nineteenth-century forts.

U.S. Air Force Academy, showing something of the ruggedness and vastness of the 17,500-acre site in the foothills of the Rocky Mountains. In 1955 Congressional criticism of the architectural design threatened to stop funding on the project. A leading Congressional critic believed the steel and glass design a monstrosity because it lacked brickwork. Another promoted the use of his home-state limestone. Sympathetic with these positions were the Allied Masonry Council and its component Bricklayers, Masons & Plasterers International Union.

The nation's postwar increase in international defense responsibilities coincided with the arrival of the air age. To train officers for the youngest branch of the military, a new brass factory was planned for a site in the Rocky Mountains of Colorado. Perhaps no architectural debate over government building in the 1950s equaled the discussion about the design for the new U.S. Air Force Academy.

Architect selection and design review were assigned to a panel of private architects: Welton Becket, Pietro Belluschi, and Eero Saarinen. Interprofessional conflict marred the design competition. The firm of Skidmore, Owings & Merrill emerged the victor. When the model was unveiled in 1955, another controversy ensued over the austere metal-and-glass design. The focal point of the campus, the chapel, was the lightning rod for both praise and blame. Architect Frank Lloyd Wright, earlier a competitor in the design competition, was embroiled in Congressional hearings as a critic of the choice of architects. Congress threatened to cut off vital building funds. True to these beginnings, controversy flared again a decade later, when the original architects lost out on the chance for designing extensions to the Academy.

The "look" of military bases was changing. They were total communities, providing ever more civilian signs of permanence—theaters, shopping centers, recreation. Quality was needed to attract and keep recruits. Family housing had to appeal to the spouse who could discourage enlistment or reenlistment. Experiments with prefabricated family housing to stretch housing dollars were disappointing. By 1973 the Air Force found that its systems building program was not as economic as expected—a conclusion also reached in the much-heralded Breakthrough Program of the Department of Housing and Urban Development.

Through the 1960s the budgets for military housing grew, but the most

U.S. Air Force Academy chapel, Walter Netch/Skidmore, Owings & Merrill, Colorado Springs, Colorado. The enclosing space frame of the chapel, the focal point of the new campus, was made by assembling 100 tetrahedrons of steel pipe clad on the outside with aluminum sheets. The spaces were filled with strips of stained glass in a progression of 24 colors. The new academy was authorized by Congress in 1954; the first class graduated in 1959. In addition to the cadet facilities the complex includes housing for support personnel, a high school and two elementary schools, a shopping center, hospital, golf course, and an airplane landing strip.

momentous change followed the end of the war in Vietnam. In January 1973 Congress ended the draft, requiring the military to rely exclusively on recruits. The Modern Volunteer Army was official. Preparations and adjustments for the new era would have astounded G.I. Joe and his predecessors. To attract recruits the military gave formerly undreamed-of attention to the privacy and amenities of living quarters. Through a design competition, the

Army Corps of Engineers selected architectural firms to give expression to the concept of the soldier as an individual. The architectural results were exemplary; living quarters for single personnel emphasized homelike arrangements and detailing. But a postoccupancy evaluation of one project carried out in 1976 revealed that in some ways the Army was still the Army. Army policy required assigning a room to each bachelor enlistee but did not require sleeping in it.

In a practice called "ghosting," many enlisted personnel rented off post rather than live in the new free quarters. Enlistees cited the reasons as restrictive regulations on visitors and social activities.

As the ranks of soldiers grew so did the ranks of veterans, and the Veterans Administration grew to one of the largest of federal construction agencies. Hospitals for veterans abandoned the Veterans

Administration's traditional colonial and regional styling for a favored white "brut" style. Earthquake damage and loss of life at a VA center in San Fernando, California, caused the VA to develop seismological evaluations and standards, which served to highlight the choice of one new site at the intersection of three geological faults—a choice humorously tagged as a candidate for the "fickle finger of fate award."

Interior, chapel, U.S. Air
Force Academy.

"Glass and metal, of course,
are alien to American monumental design—even European.
This is so obvious it needs no
further comment."

Representative John E. Fogarty,
1955

"We regret that the Air Force
and its architects have seen fit
to listen to the loud criticism
evoked by preliminary plans
and building models for the
new Academy—criticism that
had little validity outside the
curious doctrine which holds
that election to Congress automatically transforms the electee
into an infallible authority on
every art, technology and
method of doing business. . . .
We wish [the] architects had
stood by their guns. We lament
the circumstances that make
them susceptible to Congressmen who are architects by
suffrage."

San Francisco Chronicle,
1955

"Any structure or work of art
will find itself the target of criticism, sometimes voiced without
knowledge of the problems involved. . . . The AIA is firmly
convinced that the commissioned architects should continue [developing] their plans
and the Air Force should proceed with confidence knowing
that the final result will be in
the best interest of the American people."

American Institute of Architects, 1955

"Just as West Point, with its
medieval fortress-like appearance symbolizes the traditions of
land warfare, so does the sharp-
lined and soaring Air Force
Academy represent the newest
and swiftest military science.
But the emphasis of its training
system will not be on technology alone, for the Air Force has
announced that an almost equal
balance will be maintained between studies in the physical
and natural sciences and in the
humanities. Perhaps it is no
accident, then, that the domi-
nating structure of the academy
will be a modern chapel, sym-
bolizing, as the other buildings
do, man's quest for scientific
advances within the framework
of ancient traditions and immutable values."

New York Herald Tribune,
May 16, 1955

Accommodating Defenders

480–481

"In this age of enforced decentralization, of congested cities, snarled traffic, creeping slums, here we have a vivid contrast—17,500 acres of untouched nature couched in quiet dignity and grandeur against the ever changing faces of the Rockies. The Academy site represents a virtual island of unspoiled country, situated at the hub of the network of roadways, railways, and airways. . . .

"We believe that the architectural concepts of the Academy buildings should represent this national character of the Academy, that they should represent in steel and glass, marble and stone the simple, direct, modern way of life—that they should be as modern, as timeless, and as style-less in their architectural concept, as efficient and as flexible in their basic layout as the most modern projected aircraft. . . .

"Through the ages, man has gone to the heights for contemplation and inspiration. We believe that this Academy, tucked in among the mountains, proudly standing on our modern Acropolis, will create a vibrant cultural and spiritual sense of forward-looking accomplishment in these young men."

Nathaniel Owings, introductory comments to a presentation of the architectural concepts of the U.S. Air Force Academy, May 1955

"Now the halls of Congress resounded to the complaints of Representative Fogarty and others; and of their special witness, Frank Lloyd Wright, who denounced the advisory commission of Saarinen, Belluschi and Becket as a team of a small boy, a schoolteacher and a man who had done a great deal of harm to American architecture. Congressman Hardy of Virginia thought the Academy looked like a cigarette factory. Senator Flanders was not alone in calling the chapel sacrilegious. President Eisenhower, whose sophistication and taste in architecture were not great, is said to have 'flushed with anger' when he learned that the proposed design of the chapel was seriously advanced."

John Burchard and Albert Bush-Brown, The Architecture of America, 1961

"This tabernacle of aluminum and glass, raised up in the name of the American people with such pride before Colorado's awesome Rampart Range, is in truth our first militant monument to Mass Cult. . . . Can it be the last major structure of its kind? Except to the 'God is my copilot' school of theology, the notion of divine intervention in very worldly affairs—for example, thermonuclear warfare—no longer carries much weight. For this reason alone the choice of the chapel as the dominant focal structure of the Academy, even if it was not the architects' choice, is open to serious question."

Allan Temko, Architectural Forum, December 1962

"The new chapel at the Air Force Academy creates a compelling focal point for the entire complex in its mountain setting, reminiscent of the dominance of the cathedral over a medieval town. . . . By means of a different kind of architecture, and at a different time, this chapel appears likely to become a national shrine, as did the chapel at West Point. . . . The cohesiveness of the [Air Force] chapel has brought into being a unifying symbol for its several creeds that is particularly appropriate for our democracy in a world of conflict."

Architectural Record, December 1962

"In wrestling with . . . factors in planning the expansion, designers were restricted by . . . complications peculiar to the academy job. Air Force officials, who concede that the cadets' schedule crams 26 hours into a 24-hour day, demanded a design that conserves the cadets' productive time. Time-motion studies provided criteria not only for location and design of the buildings, but for functional details as well. The dining room doors, for example, were located on the basis of studies that showed a way to eliminate a right-angle turn for cadets marching in formation. The door width enables cadets to march nine abreast into the hall without breaking ranks."

Engineering News-Record, August 18, 1966

"I don't want to generalize about my Air Force Academy classmates . . . but I have to agree that the academies do indeed mold one-dimensional thinkers—or, as a classmate of mine put it, 'thinking in a strait jacket.'"

Letter to Newsweek, July 2, 1973

Michelson-Chauvenet Hall, John Carl Warnecke and Associates, U.S. Naval Academy, Annapolis, Maryland. According to the designers, "The structure was designed to be military in character, to respect the architecture of its historic surroundings, and yet to be modern in its expression. The facade of the building has military orderliness, and the boldness of the heavy granite structure is reminiscent of its neighbors." A master plan prepared in the 1960s for campus development included rehabilitation of existing buildings.

Midshipmen Activities Facility, Ellerbe Architects-Engineers, U.S. Naval Academy, Annapolis, Maryland, adaptive use of an armory dating from Ernest Flagg's redesign of the campus early in the century.

Chapel and religious education building, James A. McDonald, U.S. Naval Training Center, Orlando, Florida.

Theater, Barrett Doffin & Figg, Whiting Field Naval Air Station, Milton, Florida.

Sample living room that serves each module of four three-person bedroom areas, Modern Volunteer Army living quarters, Lyles, Bissett, Carlisle & Wolff, Columbia, South Carolina. Requirements for design to support the MVA included increased privacy and security, decentralized bathrooms, and less active social spaces.

Accommodating Defenders

Modern Volunteer Army Bachelor Enlisted Housing, Lyles, Bissett, Carlisle & Wolff, Columbia, South Carolina. Work and living spaces are separated, a marked departure from traditional barracks design. Each level houses 12 persons in four furnished bedroom suite areas, which each open onto a central living room. Larger combinations of units form clusters around courtyards, which can be multiplied in townhouse fashion according to military unit size.

Bachelor Enlisted Housing, Delanie, Macy & Henderson, U.S. Naval Air Station, San Diego, California, 1970.

Family housing, George Mat-
sumoto and Associates, Presidio of San Franscisco, California, 1972. Suburban
expectations of military family
housing are acknowledged in
site planning and in subdivision names like Custer Terrace and Argonne Hills.

Navy/Marine Corps Reserve
Training Center, Campbell
Yost Grube, Portland, Oregon,
1976. A 1976 Defense De-
partment design awards jury
commented on the building's
"nautical character."

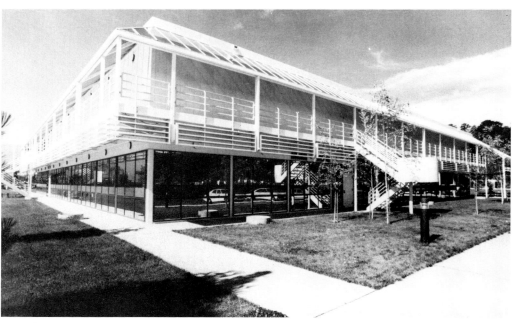

In the early days of the Republic the prison was considered a worthy challenge for gentleman architects who gave thought and sketches to the problem of housing offenders. But it took the national government a century to develop its own system of prisons.

In its first century, the federal government condemned violators of its laws to do penance in state prisons. Abuse of the state system of selling prisoner labor to private citizens led Congress to prohibit the practice, and by 1910 federal penitentiaries were established at Fort Leavenworth, Kansas; Atlanta, Georgia; and McNeil Island, Washington. A Superintendent of Prisons in the Justice Department had control over these institutions. Prison offices were patronage appointments, and appropriations varied widely and arbitrarily.

In 1929, Congress responded to reformers' complaints by naming a committee to study the conditions of prisons and recommend remedial legislation. The extensive report documented the archaic and sometimes brutal conditions of federal prisons and of prisoner treatment. New legislation raised the standards of prison construction and administration and created the U.S. Bureau of Prisons to develop an integrated system of classified institutions.

The current view that society is responsible for rehabilitating prisoners has led to major changes in the design and appearance of new prisons. Campus layouts, urban locations, and personalized interiors are among the contemporary innovations.

Newgate, Connecticut's eighteenth-century prison, commonly called "Hell." During the Revolution, Loyalists, often chained, worked a nearby copper mine.

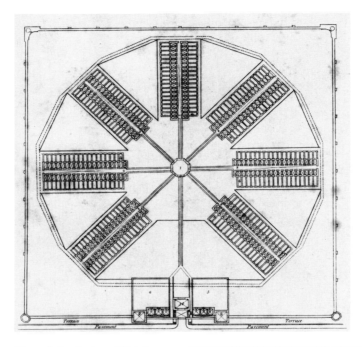

Plan of the Eastern [State] Penitentiary, John Haviland, Philadelphia, 1829, showing the Pennsylvania-type plan of short, radial wings of cell blocks. Most of the nineteenth-century prisons followed either the Pennsylvania system of continuous, solitary confinement or the Auburn, New York, approach of confining prisoners to individual cells at night but bringing them together for daytime labor. Both systems demanded total silence of their involuntary denizens.

The entire staff of the McNeil Island (Washington) Penitentiary, c. 1890. Originally built by the Supervising Architect's Office as a jail for the Washington Territory, it was designated a federal penitentiary in 1907. In 1891 there were only 1,600 inmates in federal prisons; the total nearly doubled during the Depression of 1893.

Federal Penitentiary, Alcatraz Island, California. Originally the haunt of pelicans (the name Alcatraz derives from the Spanish word for pelican), the island was reserved for unnamed ''public purposes'' by President Fillmore in 1850. It was the site of the first U.S. lighthouse on the West Coast (1853–1858) and was used by the military until 1934, when it was designated a civil penitentiary. It served that purpose for less than thirty years and is now under control of the National Park Service.

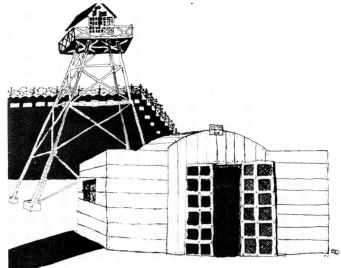

Guard's tower, Alcatraz, drawing by Andrew Delano, 1969. Until it was closed in 1963, ''the Rock'' was the ultimate symbol of impregnability and maximum-security discipline.

Federal Penitentiary, Atlanta, Georgia, built c. 1910, showing the long hall with flanking cell houses, which was typical of the so-called Auburn or Sing Sing system of confinement.

The yard at the federal penitentiary, Atlanta, Georgia, c. 1910.

Federal Penitentiary, Eames and Young, Leavenworth, Kansas, 1907. From 1895 to 1906, the Department of Justice used the former Military Barracks at Fort Leavenworth. The new prison combined the Auburn–Sing Sing style of long flanking cell rows with Pennsylvania-type radial wings.

Chapel, Moritz Kundig, Federal Penitentiary, McNeil Island, Washington, 1962. The design was selected through a statewide design competition.

Federal Correctional Center, Harry Weese, Chicago, 1976. Construction was temporarily delayed by local protests against locating a prison in the heart of downtown.

Interior, Federal Correctional Center, Chicago. Inmates of another new federal jail, the Metropolitan Correctional Center in lower Manhattan, filed suit in federal court to protest "double-celling," the practice of putting two inmates in cells designed for only one. Judge Marvin E. Frankel of the the Federal District Court in Manhattan ruled against this practice in early 1977. Frankel also ordered prison officals to do away with bans on written material from anyone on the outside. By 1976 Justice Department figures for the federal system of prisons showed a record population of 26,700 for a system built to hold 21,322 prisoners.

Dedication ceremonies, Robert F. Kennedy Youth Correctional Center, for the Bureau of Prisons, Morgantown, West Virginia, December 9, 1968, one of the Bureau of Prisons' campuslike facilities.

Federal Youth Center, Pleasanton, California, 1974.

National Park Service rangers,
Yellowstone National Park,
Wyoming, summer 1936.
Third from left is future Presi-
dent Gerald R. Ford.

Pearl Harbor marked the end of the great spurt of federal conservation and recreation work of the Depression years, and the National Park Service entered a period of decline. Parks had not been so neglected since the U.S. cavalry was used to protect the first Western parks from itinerant vandals. With the end of the Korean war the demand for outdoor recreation facilities increased, but the appropriations, which had dropped from $21 million in 1940 to $5 million during the war, rose only slowly. By 1954 the parks were hosting 54 million

visits a year with facilities and staff designed for the 17 million visitors of 1940.

In 1956 Conrad Wirth, then-Director of the National Park Service, inaugurated Mission 66, a ten-year program to bring every park up to standard by the time of the Park Service's fiftieth anniversary. Today the NPS operates 286 parks covering 30 million acres with a visitation level of 250 million, and the quality of its visitor centers has received a great deal of praise. In 1970 NPS won the special AIA Citation of an Organization.

Design and planning activities of the NPS are centralized in the Denver Service Center. In contrast to the prevalent practice of civilian federal agencies, staff architects design many of the agency's smaller facilities. Exhibit, film, and publication work are carried out by the Interpretive Design Headquarters in Harpers Ferry, West Virginia. The NPS is known worldwide for its development of interpretive exhibits.

In the 1970s the Park Service expanded its role as host by revising its planning procedures to invite the public into a broader review. In 1973

public outcry over aggressive commercial proposals for Yosemite National Park by a private concessionaire had caused NPS to junk over half a million dollars of conventional master planning efforts. To start all over again, the NPS conducted 34 public workshops in California and 14 in seven cities throughout the country. Results were used to design the *Yosemite Planning Workbook*. Hundreds of questions posing alternative futures for the park were answered by 20,700 citizens who requested the workbooks. The major choices were made part of

Coquina Beach Facilities, Donald F. Benson, NPS architect, Cape Hatteras National Seashore, North Carolina, 1956. Severe beach erosion required the replacement of this structure in 1975.

Coquina Beach Facilities, Richard J. Kusek, NPS architect, Cape Hatteras National Seashore, North Carolina, 1975.

the required Environmental Impact Statement for the park. And the Yosemite approach became park policy to be extended in variations to other parks.

Conventional wisdom has it that politicians, especially presidents, don't veto public parks. But budget examiners can be another story, and the Park Service personnel numbers fall behind program dollars. The 1976 ratio of one permanent NPS employee for every 44,000 park visitors reflected the manpower ceiling of the Office of Management and Budget. Legions of contract and part-time workers bridge the gap to meet new public assignments.

Other agencies do the same, accounting for the appearance that government doesn't grow. But in the case of NPS, contractors and part-timers don't receive the traditional service training that is the hallmark of NPS responsibilities.

At home in the Department of the Interior, the Park Service has always had to straddle the wise-use-versus-preservationist attitude toward natural resources. The nation's growth needs increase the pressures for development of all public lands, including those administered by the NPS. Behind the image

of stewardship and the well-designed visitor center can be the unnecessary road and strip mine. Ironically one of the government's most public-service-oriented agencies exists within a department that *Fortune* magazine identified as running a profitable business on the scale of General Motors.

The newest challenge to the NPS is the demand to meet burgeoning urban recreational needs. With the exception of its popular historic parks, Park Service ventures onto urban turf, althrough met with public enthusiasm, have run into huge planning problems. The giant Gateway parks planned to

serve the cities of New York and San Francisco cross many government jurisdictions and include both open space and urban areas. The wilderness-trained ranger striding out of a Wall Street headquarters office is faced with new and troublesome challenges to his hospitable equanimity.

Outside the Park Service, federal agencies, among them the TVA, the Bureau of Reclamation, and the National Forest Service, built visitor centers as educational adjuncts to the management of natural resources.

Visitor center, Anshen and Allen, Dinosaur National Monument, Utah, 1958. In 1967 researchers from the University of Massachusetts surveyed over 3,000 visitors across the country as well as 150 selected NPS staff to evaluate twelve NPS visitor centers, ranging from traditional to modern stone-and-glass styles. They reported, "There is . . . an impressive response to the Dinosaur Visitor Center as the single most attractive building depicted . . . [and] preference for the coarser 'natural' materials as represented by the stonework in both the Dinosaur and Glacier buildings."

"When Grand Teton Park was established in 1946, rangers couldn't walk the streets of Jackson without getting abuse. Now, ranchers in the area, who so bitterly opposed the park, are looking for tax relief and want the Park Service to expand park boundaries, taking some of their land and giving them grazing rights."
William Everhart, Assistant to the Director, National Park Service, quoted in **Design** and **Environment,** *Fall 1976*

Observation and fire tower, Benjamin Biderman, NPS architect, Shark Valley, Everglades National Park, Florida, 1964.

"Visitors' perceptions of a visitor center are . . . probably influenced by the social experience which they encounter. . . . A case in point is the charismatic personality of Mr. Warren Perry, ranger at the Cape Cod-Province Lands Center which has one of the more meagre exhibits. When he discusses these exhibits, however, he puts them into a local context and relates them to his personal experiences, [and] they take on added meaning and interest for visitors. There are times when Mr. Perry appears as the Pied Piper of Province Lands with a totally engrossed group of followers. Persons such as he undoubtedly influence visitors' perceptions of buildings and exhibits."

Ervin H. Zube, Joseph H. Crystal, and James F. Palmer (Institute for Man and Environment, University of Massachusetts), **Visitor Center Design Evaluation,** *a study prepared for the Denver Service Center, National Park Service, U.S. Department of the Interior, April 1976*

". . . The Service will employ quality design of a high esthetic and functional caliber. Facilities will be integrated into the park landscape so as to cause the least adverse effect upon it."

Management Policies, *manual of the National Park Service*

"Good designers are not imitating old time styles, and while those who cry for a return to log cabin architecture are entitled to their opinion, the Park Service holds to the philosophy that everything built in the parks should aspire to the highest level of design excellence. Some of the finest architects in the U.S. have done buildings for parks that have received national recognition."

William Everhart, Assistant to the Director, National Park Service, The National Park Service, *1972*

Visitor center, Walter Roth, NPS architect, Fort Pulaski National Monument, Georgia, 1964.

Tlingit house front installed over the entrance of the visitor center, John Morse and Associates, Sitka National Monument, Alaska, 1965.

Visitor center, Mitchell, Cunningham & Giurgola Associates, Kill Devil Hills, Wright Brothers National Memorial, North Carolina, 1960.

Interior, Visitor center, Wright Brothers National Memorial.

Interpretive Design Center, Ulrich Franzen, National Park Service, Harpers Ferry, West Virginia, 1971. All the educational design services of the NPS are centralized and directed from this center, overlooking the Shenandoah River. *Architectural Forum*, July/August 1971, described the new look: "There was a time when the National Park Service . . . seemed a rather fuddy-duddy organization: well-intentioned but dull. . . . This building . . . is a symbol of . . . change."

Restorer at work, Interpretive Design Center, Harpers Ferry, West Virginia.

NPS employee demonstrating sand-cast molding at Hopewell Village, Pennsylvania, one of several historic sites maintained and operated by the National Park Service.

Steel frame outlining Benjamin Franklin's home, Franklin Court, Venturi and Rauch, Independence National Historical Park, Philadelphia, Pennsylvania, 1976. The frame was based on archaeological evidence of outlines of the original house and available floor plans. Lacking enough evidence for a complete restoration, the architects decided on an outline "sign," resembling a three-dimensional drawing. Incised in the floor slates are quotations from Franklin's diaries and letters about how he wanted the house to look. Parts of original foundation walls are visible under concrete hoods. Also included in Franklin Court are five historic houses restored and adapted for museum and office use and an underground museum.

Passageway in the underground exhibit area of the Benjamin Franklin Museum, located under Franklin Court. Mirrors on corridor walls multiply the impressions of activity after visitors have left the sedate eighteenth-century-style reception room. In another exhibit space, closed-circuit telephones simulate conversations about Benjamin Franklin with other historic figures, for example, John Adams and Herman Melville in America, Thomas Carlyle and David Hume in Europe.

"Over 17 Billion Served,"
R. O. Blechman, cover of *Architecture Plus*, March–April
1974, portraying the possibility of a fast-food operation in
the crown of the Statue of
Liberty. The Statue of Liberty,
administered by the NPS, is
part of the huge, complex federal Gateway system planned
to serve the New York City
area.

Queen Elizabeth and Prince
Philip of England on their Bicentennial visit to the United
States in front of Federal Hall,
New York City. The statue
marks the site of George
Washington's inauguration.
Federal Hall, originally built
as a U.S. customhouse, now
houses the headquarters and
visitor center of the National
Park Service for the New York
area.

*"We didn't know what 'parks
to the people' meant. I was
promised everything from the
White House in the way of
manpower and money. It was
acknowledged that if this
administration made some very
strong moves where people
were, there would be strong political rewards. . . . We spent
money there like it was going
out of style. We had the money
and we had the manpower to do
the job. Gateway East got a
massive infusion of talent,
money and police protection.
But by our boundless success in
New York, we're faced with a
crisis. We've got a lit firecracker
in our hand. Any big city
mayor faced with a tight budget
is going to demand that we
come in there and give him a
park. He's a damn fool unless
he does. 'Quick, Uncle,' he will
say, 'come in.' Like in Ohio:
we're owed a national park—
quote, unquote. Come in, National Park Service, and do
your thing. But where is it
going to end?"*

Nathaniel P. Reed, Interior Department official, quoted in The
New York Times, *December
1, 1974*

*"Put yourself in my position as
a politician. I've voted for national parks year after year. Yet
Ohio is the sixth most populous
state and doesn't have a single
national park. . . . I'm not
suggesting that every urban
area have a federal recreation
area such as the proposed Cu-
yahoga Valley park. Not every
urban area has such a unique
and well-preserved large open
space available. And the federal
government cannot afford to
make itself the sole custodian of
all our natural and historic resources or to become the manager of small neighborhood
parks and playgrounds. But the
federal government cannot afford to ignore the recreation
needs of people who live around
our major urban centers, where
the need is greatest."*

Representative John F. Seiber-
ling (D-Ohio), member of the
National Parks Subcommittee,
quoted in The New York
Times, *December 1, 1974*

The nineteenth-century view that public buildings symbolized the government presence readily lent itself to the use of commemorative and historic art to adorn these buildings. But the federal government's most active engagement with art for public spaces was part of meeting the economic needs of the 1930s. Then conversion to a wartime economy abruptly ended federal spending for the arts.

Almost twenty years elapsed before the General Services Administration began incorporating the fine arts in selected new construction. For the adornment of federal buildings, the sculpted and painted rhetoric of heroes and history was supplanted by samplings of contemporary art created under a program called "Fine Art in Federal Buildings," which allowed a percentage of construction costs for ornamentation.

The GSA fine arts policy waxed and waned with the ups and downs of construction costs and appropriations. Following the doldrum effects of a 1966 freeze on new spending for works of art, the GSA program was reactivated in 1972. Under the new program, selection of artists was made through a cooperative procedure between GSA and the National Endowment for the Arts.

Commissioned art works, at their best, rehabilitated some government buildings from architectural anonymity. At their worst they seemed to reinforce the public perception of the impersonality of government. In either case, controversy could be attendant; in many cases, community celebrations that once marked the openings of federal buildings were organized for the dedications of works of art.

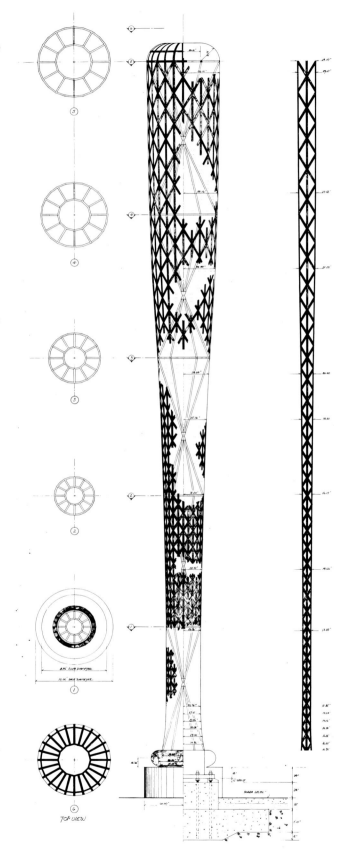

Drawing for *Batcolumn*, sculpture by Claes Oldenburg, Social Security Administration Building, Chicago, immortalizing the city's most popular sport. The column, completed in 1977, is as high as the building and is reflected in its mirror-glass facade.

Claes Oldenburg's *Batcolumn* under construction.

Sculptor Claes Oldenburg. In the background the *Batcolumn* is hoisted into place by a crane.

Bicentennial Dawn, sculpture
by Louise Nevelson, lobby of
the Courthouse and Federal
Office Building, Philadelphia,
1976.

*"There is no need for govern-
ment building, whether federal,
state, or municipal, to build on
the theory of scarcity. To use
the nation's talent and maintain its culture creates a fiscal
asset as great or greater than
the building itself."*

*David Smith, "Modern Sculp-
ture and Society," "Sculpture
and Architecture,"* Arts, *May
1957*

Sculpture by George Segal,
Federal Office Building, Buffalo, New York, 1976.

Maquette for sculpture by George Sugarman, Baltimore Federal Courthouse and Office Building, completed 1976. The proposed sculpture provoked an outcry from judges resident in the building and their supporters among the Marshals' Service, the Baltimore Police Department, the FBI, and Secret Service, who believed the piece might serve as a hiding place for dissidents and explosives. Supporters rallied; the sculpture was saved. In order to temper future controversy the GSA announced that it would seek community involvement at an earlier stage on large commissions and expand the representation on selection panels.

"The artwork could be utilized as a platform for speaking or hurling objects by dissident groups demonstrating in front of the building . . . its proposed location would obstruct natural surveillance by passing patrol vehicles . . . its contours would provide an attractive hazard for youngsters naturally drawn to it; and most importantly . . . the structure could well be used to secrete bombs or other explosive objects."

Chief Judge, United States District Court in Baltimore, letter to GSA, quoted in The Washington Post, *August 13, 1976*

"The world is chock-a-block with dangerous things. But the real hazard in this instance would be to let judges of law become the final arbiters of art."

Editorial, The Washington Post, *August 13, 1976*

"[The sculpture] is something in which the public can stroll and sit, something they can feel comfortable with."

George Sugarman, The Washington Post, *August 13, 1976, on his proposed sculpture for the Baltimore Federal Courthouse and Office Building*

"The ribbon forms that resolve into satellite benches suggest the continuity of the law."

Director of the Neuberger Museum, The Washington Post, *August 13, 1976*

"[People will] walk up to, into and around it, sit, take the sun or rest, collect their thoughts, even eat lunch . . . without worrying that it is Art."

Editor, Art in America, *quoted in* The Washington Post, *August 13, 1976*

"We have decided to go ahead and place the piece as planned. Censorship cannot exist if a program such as this is to survive."

Commissioner, Public Buildings Service, GSA, *October 12, 1976*

Dedication of *Flamingo*, Alexander Calder, plaza of the
Federal Building, Chicago,
1974.

Sculpture by Isamu Noguchi,
Federal Office Building, Seattle, 1975.

*"Back in the Beaux Arts days,
architects and artists had a
working theory of how to operate together, and the decorative
programs were an intrinsic part
of the process of design. These
kinds of precedents were followed, less effectively, in many
of the larger federal projects
during the Depression. Contemporary architects and builders, for a variety of reasons,
have lost the knack."*

Benjamin Forgey, Art News,
April 1977

*"One is tempted to suggest the
alternative of a nicely-placed
large oak tree . . . at a fraction
of the cost, in addition to providing a source of oxygen,
shade, variations through sea-
sonal change and with no need
to be cleaned or re-painted."*

Howard Conant, Leonardo,
vol. 9, 1976

*". . . What we need right now
from 'public art' is an art for
the public, not an art that is
just for public spaces. And,
public spaces being what they
are these days, this means an
art that will take them on and
fight them to a draw."*

Peter Schjeldahl, The New
York Times, January 5, 1977

*"Over the past four years, the
proliferation of public art in
this country has been Medician
in quality and Pharaonic in
scope. . . . The surprise is that
the largest sole patron now is
neither prince nor pharaoh nor
pope, but the people of the
United States, known collectively as Uncle Sam. . . . Art
critics have been uniformly enthusiastic both over individual
works and the program as a
whole."*

Jo Ann Lewis, Art News,
April 1977

*"Patron: commonly a wretch
who supports with insolence,
and is paid with flattery."*

Samuel Johnson, Dictionary,
1755

Model for proposed "Pyramidal Memorial to Man to Be Visible from Mars," Isamu Noguchi, 1947. Proposed size of nose: one mile. Escalation to gigantic scale is taken to its ultimate conclusion.

Lewis Mumford once wrote, "The notion of a modern monument is veritably a contradiction in terms: if it is a monument it is not modern, and if it is modern, it cannot be a monument." And yet Mumford agreed to serve on the Advisory Committee to the Franklin Delano Roosevelt Memorial Competition and helped write the competition program. In 1960 further testimony to the expectation of being able to resolve the dilemma was offered in 574 entries from American architects.

In 1962 the Roosevelt Memorial Commission approved the winning design by Pedersen and Tilney; a month later the federal Commission of Fine Arts (CFA) vetoed it as "lacking in repose, an essential element in memorial art." Over the next decade the history of the Roosevelt Memorial was replete with dilemmas: the winning proposal was redesigned, approved, and scrapped; a new design by Marcel Breuer, chosen by the Memorial Commission in a limited competition, was rejected, redesigned, rejected, and scrapped; a design by Lawrence Halprin, sponsored by the National Park Service, was redesigned and finally approved by the Commission of Fine Arts in 1977. Meantime a small commemorative slab, installed next to the National Archives, reflected, according to Supreme Court Justice Felix Frankfurter, Roosevelt's own wishes.

Other memorials struggled for notice in a modern context of skyscraper and superhighway forms—by contrasting them with landscape solutions or by challenging them in scale. The latter approach characterized the memorials to former presidents in a system of privately built but federally operated and maintained Presidential libraries. The first of the system, the Franklin D. Roosevelt Library, established by Congress in 1939, was designed by Roosevelt himself in the small-scale Dutch style that he favored. The distance in size to the presidential libraries built since World War II seemed greater than the entire span of American history and was, wrote one critic, "homage and money wasted." In Texas, large scale caused little comment; in Cambridge, Massachusetts, it caused an uproar and subsequent relocation and redesign.

A new Jefferson memorial, the Gateway Arch in St. Louis, recalled the triumph of Robert Mills's famous monument to Washington in the nation's capital. It was a traditional form; it was an engineering innovation; and it provided a visual landmark that could organize a city view from many distant points. It was a modern approach to critic Ogden Tanner's query in 1961 about the Franklin Roosevelt Memorial: "Is modern architecture, reflecting all the dynamic divergences and confusions of its era, capable of monuments?"

Winning design competition proposal for the Franklin Delano Roosevelt Memorial, Pedersen and Tilney, 1960. F.D.R.'s words appeared on eight concrete steles finished in white marble aggregate. The slabs were turned back to form plazas on four levels. Critics dubbed the forms "bookends" and "instant Stonehenge," but eventually the design received substantial critical acclaim. In 1962 the federal Commission of Fine Arts rejected it. A revised design was approved by the Commission of Fine Arts in 1964, but the memorial commission chose to solicit an entirely new design.

"What you see is no static form to be merely looked at. It is a dynamic composition variously experienced and always relative. It is a monument for and by modern, post-Einstein men."

Wolf Von Eckardt, quoted in Ogden Tanner, "The FDR Competition," Architectural Forum, February 1961

". . . We have come to a point in architecture and its sister arts in the United States when we can look on monumentality as a matter of scale and of hierarchy within the range of building types and purposes. We still, properly, demand a consistency with the aims of a democratic society. And we still must prove an ability to produce, within the media of modern architecture, a significant and emotionally convincing result. We feel now that we may approach even the problem of a memorial to a 'person, event, etc.' . . . the question remains, can we? . . . Monumentality is fundamentally a problem in expression, not in function, technology, or economics."

Thomas Creighton, The Architecture of Monuments—The Franklin Delano Roosevelt Memorial Competition, 1962

". . . the memorial we have designed . . . is democratic in its accessibility from all sides, its openness, and the human scale of its spaces. . . ."

Pedersen and Tilney, F.D.R. Memorial Competition statement

"Here is a design [Pedersen and Tilney] conceived in terms of our own day, a design that could not have been built under an earlier technology, a design so freed from the limitation of one-point perspective that it cannot successfully be represented on a single plane. Here is a design which recognizes the meaning of extension in space, one which depends not on absolutes but on relatives, one which is truly built on a flow of space experiences. . . .

"Here is a great statement of the vitality of American culture, a statement to the world, a statement which is worthy of the very great man we seek to honor."

Edmund Bacon, Professional Advisor for the F.D.R. Memorial Competition, "A Design of and for a Winner," AIA Journal, March 1962

The Dilemma of Memorials

508–509

"... It seems difficult to fathom why these towering steles ... have anything to do with Roosevelt despite their function as background for his engraved words. One scarcely needs eight concrete slabs 172 feet high to accomplish this end, for FDR's words have adequate grandeur without undue aggrandizement."

Katherine Kuh, "Must Monuments be Monumental?" Saturday Review, September 2, 1961

"Is it possible in these days to memorialize anybody in a significant way through artifacts? If it is possible, is a monumental artifact possible? Do we know how to make one? Do artists have their hearts in the job when they try?"

John Burchard, Architectural Record, March 1961

"In the opinion of the jury the Competition was an unqualified success. ... The Competition proved to be a mirror of our present-day culture; and served to discover new talent and to encourage new talent and to encourage architects to discover enduring monumental qualities in an age engrossed in more commercial pursuits. ...

Jury report, F.D.R. Memorial Competition, 1961

"To be on the winning end of a great national competition is a unique professional experience and one which produces a variety of emotions. ... The comments from the profession ... have generally been competent, understanding and, for the future development of the Memorial, helpful. ... Comments from almost all other sources were a great disappointment. The failure to view the Memorial as a work of art and to so judge it is to my mind a fearsome commentary on the attitude of the public toward architecture as an art and should be of concern to every member of the profession."

William F. Pedersen, winner of the F.D.R. Memorial Competition, "Problems of a Winner," AIA Journal, March 1962

Entry, F.D.R. Memorial Competition, Leo N. Fagnani, 1960, one of several entries that featured globes.

Finalist entry, F.D.R. Memorial Competition, Tasso Katselas, 1960, a pavilion of cantilevered concrete beams over a central statue. Art critic Thomas Creighton classified the 574 competition entries as falling into essentially five basic thematic solutions: inspirational shaft concepts producing space but unenclosed space, usually without buildings; landscape concepts, usually without buildings; pavilions, primarily open; building structures, mainly enclosing usable space; and sculpture or sculptural forms. Among the six finalists were two shaft solutions, two landscape solutions, and two pavilions.

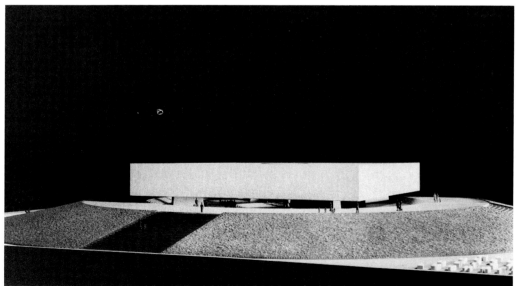

"*. . . I feel that something quite extraordinary could develop if the Fine Arts Commission saw fit to give the American Indian artists . . . an opportunity to create a memorial that would breathe and make men feel as well as see. . . . I am not suggesting that artists replace architects, but merely that the Indian's concepts might be the dream and the drive behind an architect's design. For this Memorial, I think, the architect should be called upon to execute another's inspiration. Let the architect do the foundations and walls; let the Indian deal in fancy and in wings.*"

Harrold S. Bloomgarden, Assistant to the Secretary of the Interior, letter to the Commission of Fine Arts, February 2, 1967

"*To conclude: the Memorial attempts to reflect the spirit of Franklin Delano Roosevelt by an integration of natural elements, basic materials, modern technology and unsophisticated human pleasures.*"

Marcel Breuer and Herbert Beckhard, statement on their F.D.R. Memorial design, December 20, 1966

"*I urge that we get away from bigness as a manner of memorializing great men. A man's place in history is never determined by the size of his monument. . . .*"

William Walton, chairman of the Commission of Fine Arts, letter to Representative Eugene J. Keogh, chairman of the Franklin Delano Roosevelt Memorial Commission, December 22, 1969

Proposal for the Franklin Delano Roosevelt Memorial, Marcel Breuer and Herbert Beckhard, 1966. Each of the 73-foot high slabs of rough granite was to be flanked by water. Plans included a central 32-foot-high square of black polished granite with a profile of the late president cut into one side. Visitors would hear recordings of Roosevelt's speeches and "fireside chats." One critic called the design "a transistorized F.D.R." The hearing record of the Commission of Fine Arts includes the criticism, "He has scattered granite to the winds and sown a crop of grossness." Although approved by the Memorial Commission, the design was rejected by the Commission of Fine Arts and the Roosevelt family. Nineteen leading architects signed a telegram supporting the design. The CFA rejected a redesign, and Congressional members of the Memorial Commission failed in an attempt to pass legislation specifically ordering erection of the twice-rejected Breuer design without CFA approval.

The Dilemma of Memorials

Harry S Truman Library, Voscamp & Gentry, Independence, Missouri, 1957.

"You can tell a lot about a country by the kind of building it has. . . . I don't understand fellows like Lloyd Wright. I don't understand what gets into people like that. He started this whole business of chicken-coop and hen-house architecture, and I don't know why in the world he did it. I think that the building people do show what they are thinking for that period, and that's why I hope that one of these days we'll get back to some real architecture."

Harry S Truman, quoted in Merle Miller, Plain Speaking: An Oral Biography of Harry S Truman, *1974*

"With LBJ weighing in at 500 million pounds, will RMN be far behind?"

Architectural Forum, *November 1971*

Dwight D. Eisenhower Library, John Brink, Abilene, Kansas, 1962.

"Obviously, presidential monuments do not always reflect the presidential personality, though some quite clearly do: LBJ could hardly have been better portrayed if his architect, Gordon Bunshaft, had been a still photographer. . . ."

Architectural Forum, *November 1971*

Lyndon B. Johnson Library, Skidmore, Owings & Merrill, Austin, Texas, 1971.

First proposal, John Fitzgerald Kennedy Library, I. M. Pei and Partners, Cambridge, Massachusetts.

". . . [Cambridge] simply will not put up with a tourist mecca just because it happens to enshrine the personality, philosophy, paper, and paraphernalia of a former president. . . . Cambridge . . . taught the country yet another valuable lesson. The days are over when a building, even a masterpiece of a building, that is meant for the public interest, is gladly embraced without any questions being asked. . . ."

William Marlin, The Christian Science Monitor, *September 10, 1976*

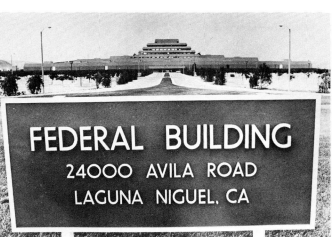

An interim "presidential library," ten miles from San Clemente, California. To store the records of President Richard M. Nixon, the federal government traded $27 million worth of Air Force property for this building, which is one-fourth the size of the Pentagon.

"In an insidious way, the associated memorabilia left behind by Presidents have taken on an inflated life of their own that has come to dominate the repository for Presidential papers, both as an architectural element and a public feature. This has brought a change in emphasis from library to museum, and a change in function from research facility to tourist attraction.

"From simple beginnings, as at Hyde Park, the concept has become an exercise in Presidential oneupmanship, with the Johnson Library, a construction to rival the pyramids, as harbinger of the future. Only inflation and questions of environmental impact have succeeded in slowing down the trend. . . . The latest Kennedy design was a model of taste and restraint; but the Government should not be saddled with an unending series of competitive monuments."

Editorial, The Washington Post, *February 18, 1975*

John F. Kennedy Gravesite, John Carl Warnecke and Associates, Arlington Memorial Cemetery, Washington, D.C. Central symbol of the grave is a flame lighted as part of the burial service by Mrs. Kennedy. The grave is sited on the axis which extends from the Capitol to the Lincoln Memorial across the Potomac to the Custis Lee Mansion.

"The earth resembles some large tablets on which everyone wants to write his name. When these tablets are filled up, it is necessary to erase thoroughly the names which have been written there, in order to place new ones there. What if the monuments of the ancients were to subsist? The moderns would have no room for their own."

Bernard de Fontenelle, Dialogues des Morts, 1693

". . . President and Mrs. Ford joined Lady Bird Johnson yesterday to dedicate the capital's first memorial to Lyndon Johnson—a grove of trees harboring a 19-foot-high granite rock that came, like the late President himself, roughly hewn from the hill country of Texas. . . . When completed the LBJ Memorial Grove will feature about 500 white pine trees, along with rhododendrons, azaleas and other shrubs. . . . [Laurance S.] Rockefeller, like other speakers, stressed that the grove was a memorial to be used by strollers and bikers, and was not another marble edifice to History."

The Washington Post, September 28, 1974

Gateway Arch, Jefferson National Expansion Memorial, Eero Saarinen, St. Louis, Missouri, 1965, the result of a design competition. The arch, a symbolic form rooted in the Roman architecture admired by Jefferson, set a contemporary precedent for the use of new structural techniques. The ¼-inch stainless steel outer skin with a backup sheet of carbon steel acted as a load-carrying membrane, a radically different engineering approach to tall structures. The 630-foot-high arch is visible from a great distance throughout the city. *Architectural Forum*, November 1963, observed that "while its height . . . shatters no records, this plus its enormous span (also 630 feet) and structural method makes the arch a most daring piece of construction."

Gateway Arch is "topped out" as the final section is inserted on October 28, 1965.

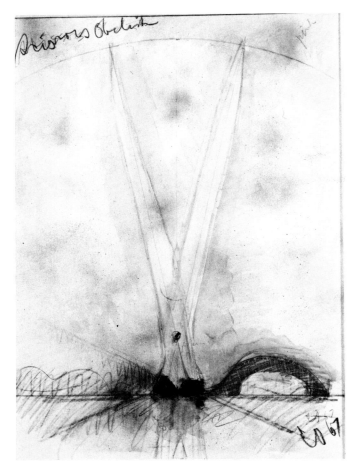

"Proposed Colossal Monument to Replace the Washington Obelisk," Claes Oldenburg, 1967.

The United States' obsession with division ('united we stand . . . ,' etc.) all suggested a scissors. A strange intolerance of division, separation, in the U.S.A. is expressed by the cruelty of the scissors in obtaining union: as the scissors close—unifying—they separate the material they close about.

"Like the scissors, the U.S.A. is screwed together—two violent parts destined in their arc to meet as one. The scissors have played as important a part in the U.S.A. history as the neoclassic inheritance from the French architects around the revolution (the last brilliant symbolist architects). Betsy Ross cut her flag from a dress, didn't she? The capacity to separate material is as great an invention as fire and the mirror.

"The scissors are an obvious morphological equivalent to the obelisk, *with interesting differences—metal for stone, humble and modern for ancient, movement for monumentality.*

"The handles of the monument are underground, balanced in great troughs which may be looked into. The blades part in the course of a day. At the evening, the colossal red handles rise above the ground; they sink out of sight sgain when the sun sets. The closing continues slowly all night until dawn when the colossal blades are joined, forming a structure like the obelisk, catching the sun's light at the tips."

Claes Oldenburg, quoted in Barbara Haskell, Claes Oldenburg: Object into Monument, *1971*

Proposed monument, Philip Johnson, Ellis Island National Park, New York City, 1966. Mounted on the ramps that encircled the monument would be the photographic reproduction of the names of all the immigrants that passed through the Ellis Island control point.

USS *Arizona* Memorial, Johnson & Perloms & Preis, Pearl Harbor, Oahu, Hawaii, 1962. The concrete rectangle, both museum and monument, was built over a steel cage and decorated with abstract patterns formed by inlaid cast stone, marble, and glass. It replaced the makeshift use of the original wreck for flag-flying ceremonies when the rusty *Arizona* became unsafe.

"The form, wherein the structure sags in the center but stands strong and vigorous at the ends, expresses initial defeat and ultimate victory.

"Wide openings in walls and roof permit a flooding by sun- light and a close view of the sunken battleship eight feet below, both fore and aft. At low tide, as the sun shines upon the hull, the barnacles which encrust it shimmer like gold jewels . . . a beautiful sarcophagus.

"The overall effect is one of serenity. Overtones of sadness have been omitted to permit the individual to contemplate his own personal responses . . . his innermost feelings."

Alfred Preis, architect for the USS Arizona *Memorial*

Architectural image making has nowhere been so concentrated as in the capital city. And nowhere were the political restraints so close to the planning and design processes. Each building stands as a monument to something—an agency, an architect, a legislator, economy or cost overruns, conflict, power. Most Americans judge the results as postcard images, television backgrounds, or glossy magazine illustrations. To the architect, wrote James Marston Fitch, "a picture is worth a thousand words, and since the introduction of photography ten thousand." But as aerial views and pedestrian experience reveal, many of Washington's monumental buildings are, as of the mid-1970s, surrounded by jarring neighbors, leftover spaces, and tangles of concrete streets and highways. Some of the lesser mistakes are softened by green leaves.

Contrasting with the impression of a green and white city of parks and monuments is the other, grittier Washington, which, like many American cities, has suffered from flights to the suburbs, overexpectations of urban renewal, from poor housing, inadequate public facilities, racial tension—plus a schizophrenic structure for decision making. Local government composes and Congress disposes, for, in spite of the trappings of elected government, the capital is a company town. The federal company is the major

metropolitan employer. Further, it owns half the land in the city, which it fills with its headquarters facilities. In the early 1960s *Architectural Forum* observed that the assemblage resembled "a cemetery of neo-classic plaster casts, stacking ennui alongside tedium."

In the 1960s city planning for the year 2000 was followed shortly by planning for the year 1985, in both cases accommodating the trend of dispersal outward from the "civil service anthill." President Kennedy inaugurated a new attempt to aggrandize Pennsylvania Avenue, which in its first view pictured completion of the Federal Triangle and, near the White House, a grand 800-by-900-foot plaza—a space uncomfortably reminiscent of organized political rallies rather than careless American parades. Some solid nineteenth-century buildings that stood in the way of or near ceremonial visions were marked for demolition.

But the very complexities and contradictions of the exercise of power in a democracy—whether for putting together parades or city plans—resulted in a lot of in-the-meanwhile forces messing up the designers' renderings. In the meanwhile a large hunk of inaccessible concrete for the FBI headquarters claimed a piece of Avenue real estate. And in the meanwhile preservationist and anti–big building sentiments were rising across the country.

Drawing depicting the architectural mishmash of Washington, John Corkill, Jr.

Successive plans for the Avenue reflected these changes. By 1976 the plan approved by Congress bore faint resemblance to the sweeping imperial right of way of 1964. Once obsolete buildings would be adapted to new uses; some housing would be mixed with commercial development. Some people were emboldened to suggest ways of making the FBI building more accessible to imagined lively pedestrians in an imagined revitalized downtown setting on an imagined enhanced street.

On Capitol Hill the extension of the east front and the proposed extension of the west front of the Capitol building provoked protest from the architecture and planning professions. In the 1970s legislators finally responded to years of criticism of the architectural expansions of their own domain by at least trying a master planning process and, in one case, opening a usually closed hearing on a new legislative office building. There even appeared an exception to the headquarters look of impenetrable masonry. On Lafayette Square new red brick government buildings took a second-row site to nineteen-century townhouses restored for modern office use. Nearby, Mullett's once-maligned State, War, and Navy Building was saved, cleaned up, and used to provide office space for an expanding White House staff.

Aerial view of modern Washington. By the 1960s the Federal Triangle (right) had become an architectural and planning battleground. Cars still filled the unlandscaped Grand Plaza (foreground). Proposed extensions to the Triangle became embroiled in partisan politics; the architect of one party was replaced by the architect of another party and nothing at all resulted. The old Post Office (right, center) held its grounds through the efforts of the 1960s to demolish it to make way for completion of earlier Triangle planning. By the 1970s popular preservation

sentiment marked it for refurbishment and reuse. Alongside the Triangle, Pennsylvania Avenue (from lower left to upper right) stimulated a succession of redevelopment plans for the ceremonial avenue, but lack of funds delayed fulfillment. Congress voted Avenue funds in 1976 for development remarkedly different from the intentions of the early 1960s.

"One of these days this will be a very great city if nothing happens to it. Even now it is a beautiful one, and its situation is superb."

Henry Adams, 1877

"Conceived in grandeur, Washington is being executed in poverty of means and spirit."

Architectural Forum, *January 1963*

Proposed new square as terminus of Pennsylvania Avenue in front of the White House, from *Report of the President's Council on Pennsylvania Avenue*, 1964. A new gate (far side of square in above picture) would lead to the White House grounds. The gate, said the planners, "would be large enough to be seen from far down the Avenue, would be designed by a master, would be strong enough to command respect, and would be enhanced by being sturdily flanked."

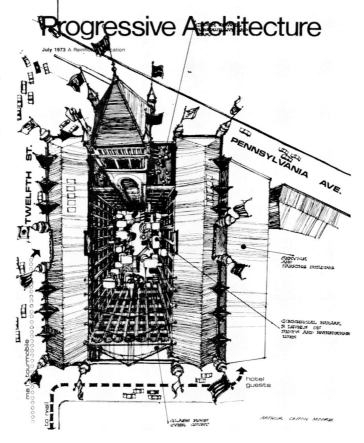

A commercial proposal, designed by Arthur Cotton Moore, for saving the embattled nineteenth-century Post Office, which continued to cling to one corner of the Federal Triangle. Cover, *Progressive Architecture*, July 1973. In 1977 architect Moore won a public design competition for remodeling the building for government offices and ground floor commercial use.

"This is the capital of a leading country of the Free World, and it will be to our disgrace if we have any situation develop in the city of Washington—this rather beautiful city, in some ways—which is not a credit to all of our people. . . ."

President John F. Kennedy, December 12, 1962

The New Executive Office Building (Federal Office Building No. 7), John Carl Warnecke and Associates, 1970. This and a similar Court of Claims building flank Lafayette Square, the Presidential park, behind the rows of nineteenth-century houses that were restored for contemporary office use. During the Kennedy administration the White House intervened to stop plans to demolish the houses and replace them with large, monolithic government office buildings. Adjacent to the southwest corner of the square, Mullett's old State, War, and Navy Building was also saved and restored.

"The primary battleground of ideas about Washington's development is in the middle area of the power structure, inhabited by myriad agencies, boards, committees, and commissions. . . . The process of Washington's development can best be described as the bringing of chaos out of chaos."

Donald Canty, "How Washington is Run: An Ungovernment without Top or Bottom," Architectural Forum, January 1963

"Washington is a city of ragged edges, gaping holes, freestanding buildings which should be walls defining exterior spaces. The notion that important buildings should stand in a park is unrealistic and an offense to L'Enfant's concept. . . . Although Washington is based on classical and Renaissance concepts for the buildings themselves, these concepts have been ignored in creating the spaces between *the actual buildings."*

Paul Rudolph, Architectural Forum, *January 1963*

"Tragic as is the loss of many fine old buildings, this basically traditional city is still textured, warm and colorful . . . a city ever more unique and beautiful among the capital cities of the world."

Charles Blessing, AIA Journal, *July 1976*

Hirshhorn Museum of the Smithsonian Institution, Gordon Bunshaft for Skidmore, Owings & Merrill, 1974.

National Air and Space Museum of the Smithsonian Institution, Gyo Obata for Hellmuth, Obata & Kassabaum, 1976. The building is faced with Tennessee marble and stretches for three blocks along the Mall.

Interior, National Air and Space Museum.

Interior, Renwick Gallery of the Smithsonian Institution, interior restoration by Hugh Newell Jacobsen. Originally the building housed the Corcoran Gallery of Art and later the U.S. Court of Claims.

Interior, Patent Office building, remodeled for the Smithsonian's National Collection of Fine Arts and National Portrait Gallery by Faulkner, Stenhouse, Fryer & Faulkner.

Cartoon by Saul Steinberg from *Steinberg at the Smithsonian—The Metamorphoses of an Emblem*, exhibit catalog for the National Collection of Fine Arts, Smithsonian Institution Press, Washington, 1973. While Steinberg was Artist in Residence at the Smithsonian he recorded his encounter with the official stationery of the institution.

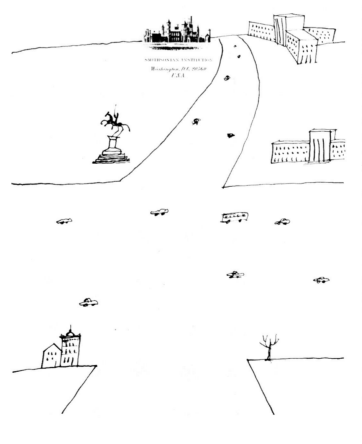

"Imperial grandiosity as an ideal—that is the great danger to Washington. Spacious monumentality may produce great beauty, but let there be a hair's breadth of deviation from good taste, and nothing remains but pompous banality. Too great an emphasis on the national scale, the impersonally monumental, is more likely to produce dullness than grandeur. Lining the Mall, Capitol Square, and Lafayette Square with monumental buildings of granite and marble may be financial and administrative daring—it may also be artistic timidity. . . . Until we overcome this small sector of our deadly national idealism and realize that art is something more than liberal expenditure and good intention, students of civic art will continue to study plans of the capital of the United States—and to make pilgrimages seeking the living touch of beautiful cities, to Paris and Rome—to Bath, Richelieu, Nancy, Ludwigslust, and Pompeii."

Elbert Peets, "The Plan of Washington," in Civic Art, the American Vitruvius, *by Werner Hegemann and Elbert Peets, 1922*

Kennedy Center for the Performing Arts, Edward Durell
Stone & Associates, 1971. The
design for this cultural headquarters on the Potomac, chosen by the late President's
family, acquired a collection
of critical sobriquets—"Soviet
Kleenex box" and "the box
the Guggenheim came in"
were on the list. Its massive
scale and auto access made it
a product more of the age of
freeways than of the pedestrian intentions of L'Enfant.
Eventually criticism waned;
praise for the variety and
quality of events staged in the
Center's four theaters waxed.
And architectural design became a Congressional head-
ache—in 1976 the House
voted $3.3 million to repair
the leaking roof.

Department of Housing and
Urban Development, head-
quarters building, Marcel
Breuer, 1968, the first use of a
modular precast concrete
building by the federal government and acclaimed for
being completed for $6 mil-
lion under estimate and $3
million under appropriations.
The new building consoli-
dated 4,300 employees who
had previously been housed
in 20 separate buildings. In
the interest of the administra-
tively popular idea of efficiency through consolidation,
employees lost access to
downtown parks and gained
the huge masonry spaces of
L'Enfant Plaza. The street level
experience of the building is
far from that conveyed by this
architectural photograph. A
bleak entrance court of stone
pavement and concrete barriers leads to bleak lobbies
decorated mostly by guards
who limit access to the building. The rooftop lunch area,
with a superb view of the city,
has backless benches and no
wind barriers.

U.S. Tax Court, Victor A. Lundy/Lyles, Bissett, Carlisle & Wolff, 1976. The foreground grid is part of construction to cover over a busy highway that runs directly in front of the building. The building won critical acclaim as a "suitable" and "classical" contemporary building and as "one of the best public structures to be built in this country in the past decade." But its siting was considered deplorable— "the right building in the wrong place in the right city." Critic Wolf Von Eckardt wrote of the misfit: "It is cruel arrogance, because artistic talent has here been sacrificed to the incompetence of Washington's planning bureaucracy."

"In its eighth year, there is already about the [HUD] building the beginning of traces of reduced investment, a clue that HUD employees are schooled to recognize elsewhere as the sign of deteriorating neighborhoods and structures. . . . Symbolically, the HUD building does say a great deal about the department and government of which it was a part when it was designed. Perhaps anonymity or ambiguity is what it says best. . . . In a city which has attracted little architecture of note in the past 50 years, it is in appearance and utility superior to most. This is faint praise."

Lawrence O. Houstoun, "Evaluation: Housing the Department of Urban Development," AIA Journal, April 1977

"In sum, what is required is an extremely large, but low building, to accord with a zoned, low skyline, in a non-style tortured to conform to something viewed as a 'classical' tradition. . . . The problem might be called how to slipcover a building, according to the Washington cut. . . . Architects who do well in other places flunk out in Washington with predictable regularity."

Ada Louise Huxtable, "How to Slipcover a Building, Washington Style," The New York Times, June 23, 1974

"It takes time to build on Washington's bureaucratic quagmire. . . . That's why our latest public buildings seem to be ludicrously anachronistic expressions of Late Kennedy, High Johnson and Early Nixon—expressions of the Arrogance of Power. Now that Vietnam, Watergate and dawning One Earth awareness may have made us more humble, the powerful arrogance of these buildings is hard to take."

Wolf Von Eckardt, The Washington Post, October 26, 1974

"Nowhere is much flatter than Washington. The ground is flat. The style is flat. The architecture is deliberately flat. From up there in the Arlington cemetery the whole city seems to lie in a single plane, without depth or perspective, its layered strips of blue, green and white broken only by the obelisk of the Washington Monument and the Capitol dome, as the massed ranks of Arlington are interrupted only by the graves of specially important corpses. It looks like a city of slabs, reverently disposed."

Jan Morris, "The Elements of Washington, D.C.," Rolling Stone Magazine, reprinted in The Washington Post, November 24, 1974

J. Edgar Hoover Building, headquarters for the Federal Bureau of Investigation, C. F. Murphy Associates, 1975. As of 1977 the new FBI building held the record, at $126 million, of being the most expensive federal building. Washingtonians, however, objected to the building chiefly as an urban misfit—an inaccessible, high-security behemoth with a solid ground-floor wall lining Pennsylvania Avenue and extravagantly out of character with hopes for pedestrian-oriented development of the Avenue.

Metro subway station, Harry Weese, architect. The new transportation system, which began limited operation in 1977, promised to give employees of some isolated federal enclaves access to urban variety and to stimulate some of that variety around the enclaves themselves.

"Weaned on the milk of the
thirties, and fed thereafter on a
balanced diet of efficiency studies, cost analysis and manufac-
turers' catalogues, it is a Federal architecture still to be
named. It is more closely related to the new faceless commercial buildings of the city today than to the Federal
buildings of the past, and with
good reason, for it is designed
for the same purpose: to enclose
as many Federal employees as
possible for approximately the
same cost per square foot."

Francis D. Lethbridge, "The
Federal City as a Client," AIA
Journal, May 1965

". . . Perfection of planning is
a symptom of decay. During a
period of exciting discovery or
progress, there is no time to
plan the perfect headquarters.
The time for that comes later,
when all the important work
has been done. . . ."

C. Northcote Parkinson, 1957

The James Forrestal Building
(Federal Office Building No.
5), Curtis and Davis, Fordyce
& Hamby Associates, Frank
Grad & Sons, 1969, a com-
plex of three buildings bridging one end of L'Enfant Plaza.
The site served as headquarters for the Corps of Engineers
until 1977, when the Corps
was to be replaced by the Department of Energy. Six different schemes for FOB No. 5
accompanied changes in the
membership of the Commis-
sion of Fine Arts. Originally a
three-building design was to
have a steel and glass facade.
An intervening scheme presented one building block. In
final form, the three-building
approach was restored—but
with a white masonry facade
to satisfy the CFA's demand
that it relate "to the character
of major structures in the vicinity"—which included, in
fact, the Department of Agriculture, faced in buff and
limestone, the Smithsonian in
red sandstone, FOB No. 10 in
bluish-white marble, and the
pinkish concrete pavement of
the future L'Enfant Plaza.

Rayburn House Office Building, Harbeson, Hough, Livingston and Larson, 1965. Until construction of the FBI building, this Roman-style legislative office building held the record as the government's most expensive, most criticized modern-era building. Only 15 percent of its space accommodated offices and hearing rooms. Closed hearings, accusations of pork barrel contracts, building dysfunctions, and escalating costs were all part of its early history.

"The worst thing about the Rayburn Building is the very thing it symbolizes best: the power system that created it."

Harold B. Meyers, Fortune, *March 1965*

"The Rayburn building . . . is such an eloquent expression of the sterile grandiosity which has beset Washington since the modest days of the Eisenhower pastorale. One sees efforts everywhere to emulate its arrogance.

"The Kennedy Center nearly succeeds for barefaced oppression of the individual spirit. Poor Lincoln, down the road a piece in his serene little Greek temple, would be crumpled like a candy wrapper if the Kennedy Center could flex an elbow. The Pentagon of the warlike forties is matched by a monstrous new Copagon, home for the F.B.I., astride Pennsylvania Avenue. The vast labyrinths bordering the Mall would make a minotaur beg for mercy.

"My misgivings are not about the wretched architects, who must give Washington what it pays for, but about their masters who have chosen to abandon the human scale for the Stalinesque. Man is out of place in these ponderosities. They are designed to make man feel negligible, to intimidate him, to overwhelm him with evidence that he is a cipher, a trivial nuisance in the great institutional scheme of things.

"Those most likely to be affected are men who work in such arrogant surroundings. And so, it is not surprising that of late we have seen a curious tendency for Government people to differentiate between duty to Government and duty to country in a most ominous way.

"It is as if the United States Government were a separate power to which Washington owes prime loyalty, and the people at large an obstreperous ally, a less truculent France perhaps, to be guardedly eyed and kept in line."

Russell Baker, "Moods of Washington," New York Times Magazine, *March 24, 1974*

Rayburn House Office Building, details.

Public places are magnets
for both protest and celebration. And Washington,
especially in the 1960s,
witnessed a seemingly un-
ending succession of dra-
mas, heightened in their
emotional and political
impact by the settings of
historic buildings and
monuments. The mutual
reinforcement of event
and place had a special
power to send a message
in the age of television.

March on Washington led by
Martin Luther King to demonstrate racial cooperation in
support of civil rights, August
1963.

Servicemen lift the casket of
President Kennedy off the
caisson at the Capitol steps,
November 1963.

Resurrection City, which
housed a poverty protest in
1968. The tent city on the
Mall went up after Martin Luther King's death and was still
up when Robert Kennedy was
assassinated on June 6, 1968.

Antiwar marchers at the Pentagon, November 1967. Military police cordon off the entrance and line the rooftop.

The flag at half mast and soldiers in battle dress at the Capitol following Martin Luther King's assassination, April 1968.

Smoke over the nation's capital from fires burning in the northwest section of the city during rioting that followed Martin Luther King's assassination, April 1968. The Washington Monument and the Jefferson Memorial are in the background. The White House is obscured by the smoke at upper right.

Massive rally of demonstrators protesting the war in Vietnam on the grounds of the Washington Monument, November 15, 1969, the largest such demonstration ever in the nation.

"It was a campus crowd. It was chilled. It was huge. It was obviously proud of its size, tolerant about its diversity and almost smug about its self-control. It was parading a sense of right, and the most important thing for most of the marchers was simply to have been there. . . . The mean or just plain rowdy here this weekend have been flotsam on a sea of serene people who frown upon all violence, in Vietnam or Washington."

Max Frankel, The New York Times, *November 16, 1969*

Tear gas being used against a splinter group from the main antiwar march in front of the Department of Justice during the Vietnam Moratorium, November 15, 1969. Before dispersal, protesters pelted the building with rocks and bottles and twice ran a Vietcong flag up the main flagpole.

Antiwar demonstration in front of the White House, May 1970.

Demonstrators keeping vigil at the Lincoln Memorial in protest against hunger in the world, September 1974.

The Reverend Dr. Billy Graham at the Lincoln Memorial during Honor America Day, June 30, 1974.

"Washington's first line of defense is its ability to inspire awe. The domed, colonnaded and scrolled buildings, the marble boulevards, the parks and fountains humble a person and make him feel small and narrowly limited in life and power against the margin of the temples of government, against the pomp of imperial Disneyland. . . .

"The city is bereft of a sense of fitness of things, of a knowledge of what is meet and becoming conduct. It has confused pomposity with dignity and cannot remember that once these buildings, smaller and less opulent, were guarded not by soldiers, but by citizens' affections and reverence."

Nicholas von Hoffman, "A Welcome to Fat City," The Washington Post, *November 14, 1969*

"Washington is a city made for fists to be shaken at. Shaken at, not bloodied on. Federal buildings are especially constructed to be impervious to blood. You can rush headlong into a marble balustrade smearing brains and blood and bile three yards wide. But as the lady does on television, with a smile and a few whisks of a damp cloth, the wonderful material will come up as clean and white and sparkling as before. . . . The buildings were made to last forever and to forever remain shining and white, the summer sun glaring off their walls, stunning the passerby."

Matthew P. Dumont, "Down the Bureaucracy!" Trans-Action, *October 1970*

"The immense power that the reporters were up against is reflected in the film's ["All the President's Men"] unusual visual style. There are shots of great stone buildings that are enormous, and that dwarf the characters in the film. And you just feel the enormity of the power they represent, the enormity of impersonal government, and our fantasy of it as well. And against that, there are these little cards, these little scribbles that piece together, [that] will cut right through those walls and force certain areas of that power to crumble."

Alan J. Pakula, "The Making of the President's Men," *WMAL-TV, July 6, 1976*

Dustin Hoffman and Robert Redford during the filming of "All the President's Men" at the Library of Congress. The movie, released in 1976, was based on the investigations by reporters of *The Washington Post* into the break-in at the Democratic National Committee offices in the Watergate apartments, which eventually led to the resignation of President Richard Nixon.

"The Centennial," reassembled exhibit of the nation's first birthday celebration as part of the nation's Bicentennial, installed in the Smithsonian's nineteenth-century Arts and Industries Building. Interior restoration by Hugh Newell Jacobsen.

Parade watchers perch on a statue in front of the Federal Trade Commission Building, July 4, 1976.

Fireworks open the Bicentennial exhibit of the National Gallery of Art, "The Eye of Jefferson," 1976. In front of the Capitol dome is a model of Monticello.

Government and the Distant Glance

538–539

Government Bureau, painting by George Tooker, 1956.

Once upon a time a new federal building was the prominent landmark in town, a symbol of membership in the nation, and a cause for community celebration. Its progress was also frequently associated with delays, escalating costs, political and architectural politics, and critical furor. Although less visible in the modern administrative state, these associations endured. But in the comtemporary setting it was difficult for a building to dwarf its neighbors. The federal building encapsulated the general business of government; a general form followed the general function. And it posed, like the private office building, a lot of unresolved problems about what made a good place to work and what role the building should play in an active urban milieu.

Still grafted onto the federal building were bits and pieces that had in the past signaled the governmental presence—massiveness, official emblems, towering spaces, setbacks, and, more often than not, a neoclassically white exterior. These symbolic elements were long separated from their original sources and, wedded to the technology and ideology of modern architecture, were forbidding. No longer did the public building delay the passage or arrest the glance of the passerby. Detail and spaces that might engage visual and active participation had disappeared. So, apparently, had the intention of engagement; lobbies, hallways, offices were fungible. Attempts at change dealt with the details of quality, not with policies for quality.

If public buildings gave form to public values, the forms spoke of a lack of connection between government and the governed. Both parties to the social contract viewed each other from a distance. In the space between, architects, designers, artists, administrators, and building managers had to cope with this dilemma of the public realm.

"Antiquity's sensitivity to the inner life of the architectural detail, its plastic beauty and expressiveness, gives way. . . . The eye is no longer fixed upon the separate building parts. . . . The point of the matter is that the clearly defined form and function of each separate building element is no longer felt. . . . The eye glides over the architectural forms, follows the great movements of the masses, the grandiose rise of vaults and the endless flights of monotonously divided walls. Characteristically abstract, peculiarly far-seeing and therefore summary, the glance skips over detail and articulation in order to rest with mass and dimension."

H. P. L'Orange, Art Forms and Civic Life in the Late Roman Empire, 1965

"There is a rough parallel between the crisis of Roman society after the death of Augustus and present-day life; it concerns the balance between public and private life. . . .
"Intimate vision is induced in proportion as the public domain is abandoned as empty. On the most physical level, the environment prompts people to think of the public domain as meaningless."

Richard Sennett, The Fall of Public Man, 1977

"The one sure way to kill cities is to turn their ground floors into great, spacious expanses of nothing."

Peter Blake, "The Folly of Modern Architecture," Atlantic Monthly, September 1974

"The very term 'public building' has become a contradiction: no one in his right mind now goes into a public building except on business."

J. B. Jackson, lecture, University of Massachusetts, 1966

"The vague institutionalism of contemporary public architecture is a hesitant style, lost in the land between what was and what is to be."

Frederick Gutheim, Potomac, 1949

". . . Our government, in its public buildings, has the responsibility to embody the finest contemporary consensus on a subject such as architectural form. It is not the function of government to experiment, to lead the way. The function of government is to give expression to the thought and values of the American democracy as . . . reflected in the work of the American architects of our time."

Daniel P. Moynihan, AIA Journal, June 1962

"I like boring things."
Andy Warhol

"One of the problems with civic buildings is that you need a universal style which doesn't offend anybody . . . but with a certain character. So my proposal is that civic buildings should be made out of compositions utilizing the letters of the function."

Claes Oldenburg, conference entitled "Art in Public Places," Seattle, Washington, February 20, 1971

"In most situations, design could certainly be improved by a better knowledge of man's nature and of the effects that the environments exert on his physical and mental being. But design involves also matters of values, because free will can operate only where there is first some form of conviction."

René Dubos, So Human An Animal, 1968

"The average citizen, as he looks at his city, is often troubled to know 'who did it.' Large slices of his city seem to be the work of distant, impersonal, and untouchable entities."

Grady Clay, "The Competitors," unpublished monograph, 1961

"We still act as though we had infinite space to overrun. . . . The guts of the problem is thus that most of our building just happens and it happens very badly. We let it happen very badly not so much because we are powerless . . . but because we have only very vague and indifferent notions about what, in terms of modern life and our uncertain esthetics, we expect great architecture that adds up to great cities to be."

Wolf Von Eckardt, "The Age of Anti-Architecture," Arizona Architect, February 1965

"The immense new Federal building just being completed . . . stands aloof from the city's skyline and out of scale with it, unrelated to anything in the topography, no part even of the grandiose civic center nearby. Slick details, giant fountains, and all, it draws back from the street and just stands there. It is one of the West's largest filing cabinets, and it is unfair, of course, to expect from it any attributes of the public realm. Indeed, if San Francisco, one gathers, had not grudgingly stepped aside for it, some distant bureaucrats would spitefully have removed it to Oakland. So much for the Federal Heart of the city."

Charles Moore, "You Have to Pay for the Public Life," Perspecta 9/10, The Yale Architectural Journal, 1965

". . . Twentieth-century America has seen a steady, persistent
decline in the visual and emotional power of its public buildings, and this has been accompanied by a not less persistent
decline in the authority of the
public order."

Daniel Moynihan, introduction, Ada Louise Huxtable,
Will They Ever Finish Bruckner Boulevard?, 1971

"While the Federal Plaza may
please the esthetic sense of some
officials looking down from
their 10th-floor offices, the
lowly taxpayer-pedestrian is beset with impossible circulation
patterns, no place to stop and
sit, total absence of shelter and
a feeling of emptiness that borders on panic. . . . It would be
difficult to find a more symbolic
expression of the attitude of the
federal bureaucracy towards local government. Indeed, if the
goal of the plaza was to impress
the on-foot citizen with the image of federal power, it is a
huge success."

Howard Glazer, Willamette
Week, Portland, Oregon, 1977

"Although a pleasant work environment is a partial stimula-
tion, it is generally not thought
of as being a motivator by most
management experts. 'Office
landscaping' deals with
achievement, the prime motivator, in realizing improvement in
attitudes and operations. The
freedom of communication,
unencumbered by solid walls
and closed doors, contributes
greatly to fostering a goal ori-
ented organization."

"The Planning Forces," Public
Building Service, GSA, 1972

"This destruction of walls, office planners are quick to say,
increases office efficiency, because when people are all day
long visually exposed to one
another, they are less likely to
gossip and chat, more likely to
keep to themselves. When
everyone has each other under
surveillance, sociability de-
creases, silence being the only
form of protection. The open-
floor office plan brings the paradox of visibility and isolation
to its height, a paradox which
can also be stated in reverse.
People are more sociable, the
more they have some tangible
barriers between them, just as
they need specific places in public whose sole purpose is to
bring them together. . . . Human beings need to have some
distance from intimate observation by others in order to feel
sociable. Increase intimate contact and you decrease sociability. Here is the logic of one
form of bureaucratic efficiency."

Richard Sennett, The Fall of
Public Man, 1977

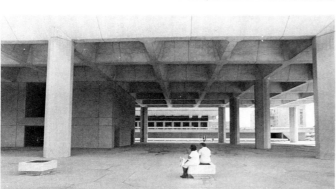

"For beware: the ultimate promise of modern architecture is collective sightlessness for the species. Blindness is the fruit of your design."

Norman Mailer, Architectural Forum, *April 1964*

"What a very little fact sometimes reveals the national character."

Andrew Jackson Downing, 1847

"Little reflection will show that the one and only building which can be constructed from measurements and financial estimate alone, independently of living use, is a coffin."

Patrick Geddes, 1904

"Unlike a genuine Imperial Style, the Sub-Imperial Style is what you get when power is exercised not by individuals, but by organizations. . . ."

Ada Louise Huxtable, Architectural Forum, *April 1972*

"The policy shall be to provide requisite and adequate facilities in an architectural style and form which is distinguished and which will reflect the dignity, enterprise, vigor, and stability of the American National Government. . . . Major emphasis should be placed on the choice of designs that embody the finest contemporary American architectural thought. . . . The development of an official style must be avoided. Design must flow from the architectural profession to the Government, and not vice versa."

"Guiding Principles for Federal Architecture," *Report to the President by the Ad Hoc Committee on Federal Office Space, June 1962*

"These ever-jarring principles of magnificence and economy— laying out millions for dignity and denying the thousands necessary to ensure care, intelligence, and taste, in their conservation and exposition— produce a certain compound pretension and meanness of effect, highly to be deprecated in great public works."

Horatio Greenough, "Aesthetics at Washington," The Travels, Observations, and Experience of a Yankee Stonecutter, *1852*

"Each time we as a people build through our government, we are saying something about ourselves, something about the relationship of government to citizens. Therefore, it is entirely proper that we ask that federal architecture, particularly those strategic buildings used by the general public, reflect the greatness we strive for as a nation—a greatness based not so much on size and splendor as on humaneness, openness and regard for individual dignity. But the message that most federal architecture is giving about us is a distinctly distorted and unflattering one."

"Federal Architecture: A Framework for Debate," Report of the Task Force on Federal Architecture, National Endowment for the Arts, May 1974

"I have long seen the outward environment created by man as a reflection of inner moods and dispositions—a lesson, in Plato's image—written in large letters that all may read."

August Heckscher, "On the Building Art," The Christian Science Monitor, November 5, 1976

"Architecture is the physical form of social institutions. . . . Architecture cannot say anything meaningful about an institution if the institution is not sure what to say about itself. . . . The only way we and the institutions we share can make an architectural environment that says something worth listening to is to clarify for ourselves the things we believe in and then to ask our architects to translate these things into building."

James Ackerman, "Listening to Architecture," Harvard Educational Review, vol. 39, no. 4, 1969

"Those who create our environment today must be aware that their choices are not just aesthetic—they are also political. They imply views about the nature of man, the relation of the individual to society, the nature of the 'good society.' Normally, when we talk about the expression of social and political values, we think of the word, either spoken or written. But things also speak to us. They embody ways in which we think about the world, standing as objective symbols for subjective states of mind."

John William Ward, "The Politics of Design," Who Designs America?, 1965

Of Such Dimensions As May Be Required

In the early years of the Republic, Congressional authorizations for federal buildings directed that construction be "of such dimensions as may be required." As the nation developed and expanded, Congress proposed more detailed specifications. The results interested individual localities and beneficiaries, but general public interest waned.

As the perception of the federal presence has diminished its pervasive influence on the physical surroundings has grown. Today cultural historians, if they consider federal projects at all, find them unimportant. Critics of the building arts consign federal architecture to a second-class status and are virtually unconcerned with those federal policies that affect the use and appearance of American space. Likewise, public concern has been missing. The increasing preference for private over public life has been accompanied by an increase in the physical neglect of the public domain. When the question is asked, "What is the good life?" the assumption is a reference to the pleasurable, personal life. But in Western civilization "the good life" historically meant the life of politics, that which occurred in the public realm for the public benefit.

By the mid-1970s, however, there are signs that concern for the physical quality of public life is reviving. Historic preservation efforts, if not sidetracked into illiberal historicism; energy constraints, if not unfairly distributed; the mixed use of public access spaces, if not thoughtlessly designed; and new technology, if not mindlessly embraced, may all improve the overall physical context of our existence.

The underlying assumption of this volume is that, although we cannot vote for "good" public design, we can marshal a consensus of values, which will increase the chance of its flourishing. And that the scope and volume of federal building and leasing, the vast reach of federal dollars that support a large proportion of state and local as well as private construction, impose a responsibility on us to require that our best values and judgments define the future dimensions of the federal presence.

Astronaut and lunar roving
vehicle, Hadley Rille, the
moon, July 31, 1971.
"Man must explore. And
this is exploration at its greatest." (Astronaut David R.
Scott, Apollo 15 mission)

An early morning birthday
party at the Lincoln Memorial,
1975.

"If the tendencies of our
government are like those of
ancient Rome, we need not
hope for our art unless they
are checked; but there is a
Greek spirit among us, which
yet may save us." (Peter
Wight, *American Architect
and Building News,* March 1,
1876)

BIBLIOGRAPHY

Introduction

The Federal Presence began not as a book but as research to orient a new staff to the concerns of the Task Force on Federal Architecture of the National Endowment for the Arts. No tidy treatment of our subject and no quick collection of references were available. Works on American history neglect the building arts, and works on architectural history overlook the role of government.

Historian Frederick Gutheim prepared a paper for the Federal Architecture Project, which provided an instructive first outline of the history of federal architecture. Diverse books, articles, and interviews furnished clues that directed research into scattered and little-used archives and government records. Finally, a point of view—American history seen through federal building activities—became a compelling motivation that transformed photocopied gleanings first to a scrapbook collection and then a book.

This bibliography is a map of the paths we followed to collect data, events, images, ideas. It is arranged by groupings of general references, references on the city of Washington, and individual chapter sources.

Of the architectural historians consulted, the most useful authors were John Burchard and Albert Bush-Brown, Talbot Hamlin, Hugh Morrison, James Marston Fitch, John Kouwenhoven, and Frederick Gutheim. For the history of planning, we made frequent reference to the work of John Reps and Norman Newton. Francis O'Connor and Richard McKinzie, in both their work and their suggestions, were helpful in assessing the federal art programs of the 1930s. Of the many general histories of the New Deal period that of William Leuchtenberg proved most valuable. Praeger Publishers' series of books on government departments and agencies provided the framework for an understanding of administrative history.

Two major government publications used were the 1901 history of public buildings issued by the Treasury Department and the 1939 history of public buildings under the Public Works Administration by C. W. Short and R. Stanley Brown. In the case of government records, the most frequently used source was the records of the Supervising Architect's office and its progeny, which are located in the National Archives as Record Group 121.

Periodicals found to attend most often to federal architecture were the *American Architect and Building News* for the latter half of the nineteenth century; *Architectural Record, American Architect*, the *Magazine of Art, AIA Journal*, and *Architectural Forum* for the twentieth century. The latter two were particularly useful for recent decades. *The Federal Architect* magazine was a rich reference for the period of its publication, 1930 to 1947. *The Journal of the Society of Architectural Historians*, especially articles by Lawrence Wodehouse, and the Historical Building Studies of the General Services Administration furnished important historical analyses of individual buildings.

Newspaper articles are not included in the bibliography. Quotations in the book, cited by name and date of publication, indicate most newspaper resources. In addition, for the contemporary period, the reader is referred to the regular critical columns of Ada Louise Huxtable in *The New York Times*, Wolf Von Eckardt in *The Washington Post*, and William Marlin in *The Christian Science Monitor*.

Guidance to the sources on the federal role in the development of American space came primarily from John Brinckerhoff Jackson's scholarship in the history of American landscape, William Goetzmann's work on federal exploration of the American West, and Benjamin Horace Hibbard's history of public land policies. For a coherent view of the federal government's relations to cities, two important authors were Mark Gelfand and Daniel Elazar.

Throughout the work on the book we most often kept company with the insights of Henry Adams, Henry James, Elbert Peets, Joseph Hudnut, Edwin Bateman Morris, and, for an overall understanding of American history, Daniel Boorstin and Richard Hofstadter.

Two books seemingly far afield from the federal presence deserve special attention. *Art Forms and Civic Life in the Late Roman Empire*, by H. P. L'Orange, examines the relationship between the organization of political power and the organization of government architecture in a way that is provocative for any place or period in history. And for a study of the balance between public and private life that underlies the crucial values of a society, any list of readings should be headed by Hannah Arendt's *The Human Condition*.

General Sources

Adams, Henry. *The Education of Henry Adams: An Autobiography, 1850–1854.* Boston: Houghton Mifflin Company, 1918 (privately published, 1906).

————. *History of the United States of America during the Administrations of Jefferson and Madison.* Abridged and edited by Ernest Samuels (selections from nine-volume 1921 edition). Chicago: University of Chicago Press, 1967.

Alsberg, Henry G., editor. *The American Guide: A Source Book and Complete Travel Guide for the United States.* New York: Hastings House, 1949.

Amon Carter Museum of Western Art. *The Image of America in Caricature and Cartoon.* Fort Worth: Amon Carter Museum of Western Art, 1975.

Andrews, Wayne. *Architecture, Ambition, and Americans: A History of American Architecture.* New York: The Free Press, 1964.

Armstrong, Ellis L. *History of Public Works in the United States, 1776–1976.* Chicago: American Public Works Association, 1976.

Bailyn, Bernard. *The Origins of American Politics.* New York: Alfred A. Knopf, Vintage Books, 1967.

Banham, Reyner. *The Architecture of the Well-Tempered Environment.* London: The Architectural Press, 1969 (also Chicago: The University of Chicago Press, 1969).

Benevolo, Leonardo. *History of Modern Architecture*, vols. 1 and 2. Cambridge, Mass.: The MIT Press, 1971.

Boorstin, Daniel J., editor. *American Civilization: A Portrait from the Twentieth Century.* New York: McGraw Hill Book Company, 1972.

———. *The Americans: The Colonial Experience; The Americans: The National Experience; The Americans: The Democratic Experience*. New York: Alfred A. Knopf, Vintage Books, 1958, 1965, 1974.

Borklund, C. W. *The Department of Defense*. Washington, D.C.: Praeger Library of U.S. Government Departments and Agencies, 1968.

Bryce, James. *The American Commonwealth*, vols. 1 and 2. New York: The Macmillan Company, 1914 (first printing, 1893).

Burchard, John, and Bush-Brown, Albert. *The Architecture of America*, vols. 1 and 2. Boston: Atlantic Monthly Press, 1961.

Carstensen, Vernon, editor. *The Public Lands: Studies in the History of the Public Domain*. Madison, Wis.: The University of Wisconsin Press, 1968.

Clawson, Marion. *America's Land and Its Uses*. Baltimore: The Johns Hopkins University Press, 1972.

———. *The Bureau of Land Management*. Washington, D.C.: Praeger Library of U.S. Government Departments and Agencies, 1971.

Collins, Peter. *Architectural Judgment*. Montreal: McGill–Queen's University Press, 1971.

Condit, Carl. *American Building Art*. Chicago: University of Chicago Press, 1968.

Cooke, Alistair. *Alistair Cooke's America*. New York: Alfred A. Knopf, 1973.

Cullinan, Gerald. *The Post Office Department*. Washington, D.C.: Praeger Library of U.S. Government Departments and Agencies, 1968.

Davidson, Marshall B. *The American Heritage History of the Writers' America*. New York: McGraw-Hill Book Company, American Heritage Publishing Company, 1973.

———. *The American Heritage History of the Artists' America*. New York: McGraw-Hill Book Company, American Heritage Publishing Company, 1973.

Davis, Colonel Franklin M., Jr., and Jones, Colonel Thomas T. *The U.S. Army Engineers: Fighting Elite*. New York: Franklin Watts, Inc., 1967.

Davis, Grant Miller. *The Department of Transportation*. Lexington, Mass.: D. C. Heath, Lexington Books, 1970.

Elazar, Daniel J. "The Shaping of Intergovernmental Relations in the Twentieth Century," *Annals of The American Academy of Political and Social Science*, no. 359 (May 1965).

———. "Urban Problems and The Federal Government: A Historical Inquiry," *Political Science Quarterly*, vol. 82, no. 4 (1967).

Emerson, Ralph Waldo. *The Selected Writings of Ralph Waldo Emerson*, edited by Brooks Atkinson. New York: The Modern Library, Random House, 1940.

Everhart, William C. *The National Park Service*. Washington, D.C.: Praeger Library of U.S. Government Departments and Agencies, 1972.

Fabos, Julius, Gordon, T., and Weinmayr, V. M. *Frederick Law Olmsted, Sr.: Founder of American Landscape Architecture*. Amherst, Mass.: University of Massachusetts Press, 1968.

Fitch, James Marston. *American Building: The Environmental Forces That Shape It*. Cambridge, Mass.: The Riverside Press, 1972.

———. *American Building: The Historical Forces That Shaped It*. Boston: Houghton Mifflin Company, 1966.

Fogelson, Robert M. *The Fragmented Metropolis: Los Angeles, 1850–1930*. Cambridge, Mass.: Harvard University Press, 1967.

Garrett, W. D., et al. *The Arts in America: The Nineteenth Century*. New York: Charles Scribner's Sons, 1969.

Gifford, Dan, editor. *The Literature of Architecture*. New York: E. P. Dutton and Company, 1968.

Glaab, Charles N. (with A. Theodore Brown). *A History of Urban America*. New York: The Macmillan Company, 1967.

Goldstone, Harmon H., and Dalrymple, Martha. *A Guide to New York City Landmarks and Historic Districts*. New York: Simon and Schuster, 1974.

Gowans, Alan. *Images of American Living: Four Centuries of Architecture and Furniture as Cultural Expression*. Philadelphia: J. B. Lippincott Co., 1964.

Green, Constance McLaughlin. *The Rise of Urban America*. New York: Harper & Row, Harper Colophon Books, 1967.

Greenough, Horatio. "American Architecture," *The United States Magazine and Democratic Review*, August 1843.

Greiff, Constance M., editor. *Lost America: From the Mississippi to the Pacific*. Princeton, N.J.: Princeton University Press, 1972.

Gutheim, Frederick. "The History of Federal Architecture." Unpublished paper for the Federal Architecture Project. Washington, D.C., 1973.

Gutman, Robert, editor. *People and Buildings*. New York: Basic Books, Inc., 1962.

Haefele, Edwin T. *Representative Government and Environmental Management*. Baltimore: The Johns Hopkins University Press, 1974.

Hamlin, Talbot. *Architecture Through the Ages*. New York: G. P. Putnam's Sons, 1953.

Heckscher, August. *The Public Happiness*. New York: Atheneum, 1962.

Hibbard, Benjamin Horace. *A History of the Public Land Policies*. Madison and Milwaukee, Wis.: The University of Wisconsin Press, 1965.

Hill, Forest G. *Roads, Railroads and Waterways: The Army Engineers and Early Transportation*. Norman, Okla.: The University of Oklahoma Press, 1957.

Hindley, Geoffrey. *A History of Roads*. Secaucus, N.J.: The Citadel Press, 1972.

Hitchcock, Henry-Russell. *Architecture: Nineteenth and Twentieth Centuries*. Baltimore: Penguin Books, Inc., 1958.

Hofstadter, Richard. *The American Republic*, vols. 1 and 2. Englewood Cliffs, N.J.: Prentice-Hall, Inc., 1970.

Honour, Hugh. *The New Golden Land: European Images of America from the Discoveries to the Present Time*. New York: Random House, Pantheon Books, 1975.

Huth, Hans. *Nature and the American: Three Centuries of Changing Attitudes*. Berkeley: The University of California Press, 1957.

Jackson, John Brinckerhoff. *American Space: The Centennial Years, 1865–1876*. New York: W. W. Norton & Company, Inc., 1972.

———. *Landscapes: Selected Writings of J. B. Jackson*, edited by Ervin H. Zube. Amherst, Mass.: The University of Massachusetts Press, 1970.

Jensen, Oliver, et al. *American Album*. New York: American Heritage Publishing Company, 1968.

Johnson, Allen, and Malone, Dumas, editors. *Dictionary of American Biography*. New York: Charles Scribner's Sons, 1928–1944.

Johnson, Thomas H. *The Oxford Companion to American History*. New York: Oxford University Press, 1966.

Jones, Howard Mumford. *O Strange New World: American Culture: The Formative Years*. New York: The Viking Press, 1955.

Kammen, Michael. *People of Paradox: An Inquiry Concerning the Origins of American Civilization*. New York: Alfred A Knopf, 1972.

Kirkland, Edward. *Men, Cities, Transportation: A Study in New England History, 1820–1900*, vols. 1 and 2. New York: Russell and Company, 1968 (reprint of 1948 edition).

Kouwenhoven, John A. *Made in America*. New York: Doubleday, Inc., 1949.

———. *The Columbia Historical Portrait of New York*. New York: Harper & Row, 1972.

Lamphere, George N. *The United States Government: Its Organization and Practical Workings*. New York: J. B. Lippincott & Company, 1880.

Lawrence, D. H. *Studies in Classical American Literature*. New York: The Viking Press, 1961 (reprint of 1923 Thomas Seltzer, Inc., edition).

Lewis, R. W. B. *The American Adam: Innocence, Tragedy and Tradition in the Nineteenth Century*. Chicago: The University of Chicago Press, 1955.

Lowenthal, David. "The American Scene," *Geographical Review*, vol. 58, no. 1 (1968).

McCoubrey, John W. *American Tradition in Painting*. New York: George Braziller, Inc., 1963.

McHenry, Robert, editor. *A Documentary History of Conservation in the United States*. New York: Praeger Publishers, 1972.

McShine, Kynaston, editor. *The Natural Paradise: Painting in America, 1800–1950*. New York: The Museum of Modern Art, 1976.

Marx, Leo. *The Machine in the Garden: Technology and the Pastoral Ideal in America.* New York: Oxford University Press, 1964.

Mayer, Harold, and Wade, Richard. *Chicago; Growth of a Metropolis.* Chicago: The University of Chicago Press, 1969.

Metropolitan Museum of Art. *The Shaping of Art and Architecture in Nineteenth-Century America* (eleven papers from symposium held in May 1970). New York: Metropolitan Museum of Art, 1972.

Miller, Charles A. "American Attitudes toward the Land," *Design and Environment,* fall 1975.

Miller, Perry. *Errand into the Wilderness.* Cambridge, Mass.: Harvard University Press, The Belknap Press, 1956.

Mumford, Lewis. *The Golden Day: A Study in American Experience and Culture.* New York: Boni and Liveright, 1926.

————. *Sticks and Stones: A Study of American Architecture and Civilization.* New York: Dover Publications, Inc., 1955 (reprint of 1924 Boni and Liveright edition).

————, editor. *Roots of Contemporary American Architecture.* New York: Reinhold Publishing Company, 1952.

Museum of Fine Arts, Boston. *Frontier America: The Far West* (exhibit catalogue). Boston: Museum of Fine Arts, 1976.

Nash, Broderick. *Wilderness and the American Mind.* New Haven: Yale University Press, 1967.

National Collection of Fine Arts. *National Parks and the American Landscape.* Washington, D.C.: The Smithsonian Institution Press, 1972.

National Endowment for the Arts, Task Force on Federal Architecture. "Federal Architecture: A Framework for Debate." Washington, D.C., May 1974.

Newton, Norman. *Design on the Land: The Development of Landscape Architecture.* Cambridge, Mass.: Harvard University Press, The Belknap Press, 1971.

Novak, Barbara. *American Painting of the Nineteenth Century.* New York: Praeger Publishers, 1969.

Ottoson, Howard W., editor. *Land Use Policy and Problems in the United States.* Lincoln, Neb.: The University of Nebraska Press, 1963.

Pachter, Marc, and Wein, Frances, editors. *Abroad in America: Visitors to the New Nation, 1776–1914.* Washington, D.C.: The Smithsonian Institution Press, 1976.

Peck, Robert A. "Bureaucratic Architecture and the Architectural Bureaucracy: The U.S. Commission of Fine Arts and Federal Government Architecture in the District of Columbia." Unpublished paper, 1971.

Peets, Elbert. *See* Spreiregen, Paul D.

Pevsner, Nikolaus. *A History of Building Types.* Princeton, N.J.: Princeton University Press, 1976.

Potter, David. *People of Plenty.* Chicago: The University of Chicago Press, 1954.

Price, Edward T. "The Central Courthouse Square in the American County Seat," *Geographical Review,* vol. 58, no. 1 (1968).

Puter, S. A. D. *Looters of the Public Domain.* Portland, Ore.: The Portland Printing House, 1908.

Redford, Emmett S. *Democracy in the Administrative State.* New York: Oxford University Press, 1969.

Reps, John W. *The Making of Urban America: A History of City Planning in the United States.* Princeton, N.J.: Princeton University Press, 1965.

Roper, Daniel C. *The United States Post Office: Its Past Record, Present Condition, and Potential Relation to the New World Era.* New York: Funk & Wagnalls, 1917.

Saylor, Henry H. *The AIA's First Hundred Years.* Washington, D.C.: American Association of Architects, 1957.

Scheele, Carl H. *Neither Snow nor Rain . . . The Story of the United States Mails.* Washington, D.C.: Smithsonian Institution Press, 1970.

Schuyler, Montgomery. *American Architecture and Other Writings,* vols. 1 and 2, edited by William H. Jordy and Ralph Coe. Cambridge, Mass.: Harvard University Press, The Belknap Press, 1961.

Scully, Vincent. *American Architecture and Urbanism.* New York: Praeger Publishers, 1969.

Sky, Alison, and Stone, Michelle. *Unbuilt America.* New York: McGraw-Hill Book Company, 1976.

Smith, Henry Nash. *Virgin Land: The American West as Symbol and Myth.* Cambridge, Mass.: Harvard University Press, 1950.

Spreiregen, Paul D., editor. *On the Art of Designing Cities: Selected Essays of Elbert Peets.* Cambridge, Mass.: The MIT Press, 1968.

Taylor, George. "American Urban Growth Preceding the Railway Age," *Journal of Economic History,* 1967.

Taylor, Joshua. *America as Art.* Washington, D.C.: National Collection of Fine Arts, The Smithsonian Institution Press, 1976.

Taft, Robert. *Photography and the American Scene: A Social History, 1839–1889.* New York: Dover Publications, 1964 (reprint of 1938 Macmillan Company edition).

Turner, Frederick Jackson. *The Frontier in American History.* New York: Henry Holt and Company, Inc., 1920. (Includes "The Significance of the Frontier in American History," 1893.)

U.S., Army, Corps of Engineers. *History and Traditions of the Corps of Engineers.* Fort Belvoir: The Corps of Engineers, 1953.

U.S. Army, Corps of Engineers. *The Genesis of the Corps of Engineers.* Fort Belvoir: The Corps of Engineers Museum, 1966.

U.S., Civil Service Commission, Manpower Statistics Division. "Paid Civilian Employment of the Federal Government, Washington, D.C., Metropolitan Area, 1816–1972" and "Paid Civilian Employment of the Federal Government by Branch and Selected Agencies, All Areas, 1816–1972."

U.S., Department of Commerce. *Statistical Abstracts of the United States.* Washington, D.C.: U.S. Government Printing Office, 1971.

U.S., Department of the Interior, Office of Archeology and Historic Preservation. *National Register of Historic Places.* Washington, D.C.: U.S. Government Printing Office, 1972.

U.S., Department of the Treasury. *Annual Report of the Secretary of the Treasury on the State of the Finances.* 1852, 1853, 1854, and 1865. Also 1939–1940.

U.S., Department of the Treasury. *A History of Public Buildings under the Control of The Treasury Department.* Washington, D.C.: U.S. Government Printing Office, 1901.

U.S., Department of the Treasury, Supervising Architect's Office. *Annual Report of the Supervising Architect of the Treasury.* Washington, D.C., 1866–1939.

U.S., General Services Administration, The National Archives and Records Service. *Preliminary Inventory of the Records of the Public Buildings Service (Record Group 121),* compiled by W. Lane Van Neste and Virgil E. Baugh. Washington, D.C., 1958.

Wade, Richard. *The Urban Frontier: Pioneer Life in Early Pittsburgh, Cincinnati, Lexington, Louisville, and St. Louis.* Cambridge, Mass.: Harvard University Press, 1959.

Warner, Sam Bass. *The Urban Wilderness: A History of the American City.* New York: Harper & Row, 1972.

Webb, Walter Prescott. *The Great Plains.* New York: Ginn and Company, 1931.

Weber, Gustavus A. *The Bureau of Standards: Its History, Activities and Organization.* Baltimore: The Johns Hopkins University Press, 1925.

Weisberger, Bernard A. *The American Heritage History of the American People.* New York: American Heritage Publishing Company, 1971.

Wells, H. G. *The Future in America: A Search After Realities.* New York: Harper & Brothers Publishers, 1906.

Whiffen, Marcus. *American Architecture Since 1780: A Guide to the Styles.* Cambridge, Mass.: The MIT Press, 1969.

Willis, Nathaniel P. *American Scenery.* London: G. Virtue, 1841.

Wilson, William H. "A Great Impact, A Gingerly Investigation: Historians and the Federal Effect on Urban Development," in *National Archives and Urban Research,* edited by Jerome Finster. Athens, Ohio: Ohio University Press, 1974.

Yard, Robert Sterling. *Our Federal Lands: A Romance of American Development.* New York: Charles Scribner's Sons, 1928.

Zimmerman, Lawrence. "World of Fairs: 1851–1976," *Progressive Architecture,* August 1974.

The City of Washington

AIA Journal, January 1963. "Washington in Transition" (special issue).

AIA Journal, June 1965. "1965 Official Convention Guide."

Aikman, Lonnelle. "Under the Dome of Freedom," *National Geographic,* January 1964.

American Institute of Architects. *A Guide to the Architecture of Washington, D.C.* New York: Praeger Publishers, 1965.

Architectural Forum. January, 1963. "Washington, D.C." (special issue).

Atwood, Albert W., editor. *Growing with Washington.* Washington, D.C.: Washington Gas Light Company, 1948.

Brown, Glenn. *Memories, 1860–1930: A Winning Crusade to Revive George Washington's Vision of a Capital City.* Washington, D.C.: W. F. Roberts, 1931.

————. *History of the U.S. Capitol,* vols. 1 and 2. New York: Da Capo Press, 1970 (reprint).

Brown, Letitia, and Lewis, Elsie M. *Washington in the New Era, 1860–1970.* Washington, D.C.: Smithsonian Institution Press, 1972.

Cable, Mary. *The Avenue of the Presidents.* Boston: Houghton Mifflin Company, 1969.

Cox, Warren J., et al., editors. *A Guide to the Architecture of Washington, D.C.* New York: McGraw Hill Book Company, 1965.

Cox, William V. *The Centennial Celebration of the Establishment of the Seat of Government in the District of Columbia.* Washington, D.C.: U.S. Government Printing Office, 1901 (56th Congress, House Document no. 552).

District of Columbia, Public Buildings Commission. *Public Building in the District of Columbia.* Washington, D.C.: U.S. Government Printing Office, 1910.

Duryee, Sacket L. *The Corps of Engineers in the Nation's Capital, 1852–1952.* Washington, D.C.: The Washington Engineers District, 1952.

Ewing, Charles. *Yesterday's Washington, D.C.* Miami: E. A. Seaman Publishing, Inc., 1976.

Fairman, Charles E. *Art and Artists of the Capitol of the United States of America.* Washington, D.C.: U.S. Government Printing Office, 1927 (69th Congress, 1st session, Senate Document no. 95).

Fisher, Perry G. *Materials for the Study of Washington* (George Washington University Washington Series, no. 1). Washington, D.C.: George Washington University, 1974.

Goode, James M. *The Outdoor Sculpture of Washington, D.C.* Washington, D.C.: The Smithsonian Institution Press, 1974.

Green, Constance McLaughlin. *Washington: Village and Capital, 1800–1878.* Princeton, N.J.: Princeton University Press, 1962.

Greenough, Horatio. "Aesthetics at Washington," *The Travels, Observations, and Experience of a Yankee Stonecutter.* Washington, D.C.: J. T. Towers, 1852.

Gutheim, Frederick. *Potomac.* New York: Grosset and Dunlap Publishers, 1968 (originally published, 1949).

————. *Worthy of the Nation: The History of Planning for the National Capital.* National Capital Planning Commission Historical Studies. Washington, D.C.: The Smithsonian Institution Press, 1977.

Haas, P. *Public Buildings and Architectural Ornaments of the Capital of the United States at Washington, D.C.* Washington, D.C.: Published and lithographed by P. Haas, 1839.

Hazelton, George C., Jr. *The National Capitol: Its Architecture, Art, and History.* New York: J. F. Taylor and Company, 1914.

Josephy, Alvin M., Jr. *History of the Congress of the United States.* New York: American Heritage Publishing Company, Inc., 1975.

Kimmel, Stanley. *Mr. Lincoln's Washington.* New York: Bramhall House, 1957.

Kohler, Sue A. *The Commission of Fine Arts: A Brief History, 1910–1976.* Washington, D.C.: U.S. Government Printing Office, 1976.

Leeming, Joseph. *The White House in Picture and Story.* New York: George W. Stewart Publishers, Inc., 1973.

Maddex, Diane. *Historic Buildings of Washington, D.C.* Pittsburgh: Ober Park Associates, Inc., 1973.

Moore, Joseph West. *Picturesque Washington: Pen and Pencil Sketches.* New York: Hurst and Company, 1883.

Myer, Donald Beekman. *Bridges and the City of Washington.* Washington, D.C.: U.S. Government Printing Office for the U.S. Commission of Fine Arts, 1974.

Noreen, Sara Pressey. *Public Street Illumination in Washington, D.C.: An Illustrated History.* Washington, D.C.: George Washington University, 1975.

Pennsylvania Avenue Development Corporation. *The Pennsylvania Avenue Plan.* Washington, D.C.: Pennsylvania Avenue Development Corporation report, 1974.

Reps, John W. *Monumental Washington: The Planning and Development of the Capital Center.* Princeton, N.J.: Princeton University Press, 1967.

Rosenberger, Francis Coleman, editor. *Records of the Columbia Historical Society of Washington, D.C., 1971–1972.* Washington, D.C.: The Columbia Historical Society, 1973.

Schwartz, Nancy B. *Historic American Buildings Survey; District of Columbia Catalog.* Charlottesville, Va.: University Press of Virginia for the Columbia Historical Society, 1974.

Slauson, Allan B., editor. *A History of the City of Washington: Its Men and Institutions.* Washington, D.C.: The Washington Post, 1903.

Smith, Howard K. *Washington, D.C.: The Story of Our Nation's Capital.* New York: Random House, Inc., 1967.

Truett, Randall Bond, editor (originally prepared by the Federal Writers' Project). *Washington, D.C.: A Guide to the Nation's Capital.* New York: Hastings House, 1968 (reprint of 1942 edition).

U.S., Commission of Fine Arts. *Washington Architecture, 1781–1861: Problems in Development,* prepared by Daniel D. Reiff. Washington, D.C.: U.S. Government Printing Office, 1971.

U.S., Congress, Architect of the Capitol under the Direction of the Joint Committee on the Library. *Art in the United States Capitol.* 91st Congress, 2d session, House Document no. 91–368. Washington, D.C.: U.S. Government Printing Office, 1976.

U.S., Congress, Senate. *A Manual on the Origin and Development of Washington,* prepared by Hans Paul Caemmerer. 75th Congress, 3rd session, 1939, no. 178. Washington, D.C.: U.S. Government Printing Office, 1939.

U.S., National Archives, Trust Fund Board. *Washington: The Design of the Federal City.* Publication no. 73–1. Washington, D.C.: The National Archives, 1972.

U.S., President's Council on Pennsylvania Avenue. *Pennsylvania Avenue: Report of the President's Council on Pennsylvania Avenue.* Washington, D.C.: U.S. Government Printing Office, 1964.

U.S. Capitol Planning Group. *Survey toward a Master Plan for the United States Capitol.* U.S. Capitol Planning Group Report, Phase One. August 19, 1976.

The Washington Post. Washington, D.C. Washington, D.C.: The Henry E. Wilkens Printing Company, 1903

White House Historical Association (with the National Geographic Society). *The White House: An Historic Guide.* Washington, D.C.: White House Historical Association, 1969.

Young, James Sterling. *The Washington Community, 1800–1828.* New York: Harcourt, Brace and World, 1966.

Prologue

Bridenbaugh, Carl. *Cities in the Wilderness: The First Century of Urban Life in America, 1625–1742.* New York: Oxford University Press, 1971.

Burnett, Edmund Cody. *The Continental Congress.* Westport, Conn.: Greenwood Press, 1941.

Fitzpatrick, Paul J. "Royal Governors' Residences in the Original Thirteen Colonies." *Social Science,* April 1971.

Forman, Henry C. *The Architecture of the Old South, 1585–1859.* New York: Russell & Russell, 1948.

Garvan, Anthony N. B. *Architecture and Town Planning in Connecticut.* New Haven: Yale University Press, 1951.

Harriot, Thomas. *A Briefe and True Report of the New Found Land of Virginia, 1590.* New York: Dover Publications, Inc., 1972.

Hofstadter, Richard, and Ver Steeg, Clarence L. *Great Issues in American History: From Settlement to Revolution, 1584–1776.* New York: Random House, 1968.

Howells, John Mead. *Lost Examples of Colonial Architecture in America.* New York: Dover Publications, Inc., 1963.

Johnson, Adrian. *America Explored.* New York: The Viking Press, 1974.

Lancaster, Bruce. *The American Heritage History of the American Revolution.* New York: American Heritage Publishing Company, Inc., 1971.

Lehner, Ernst, and Lehner, Joanna. *How They Saw the New World.* New York: Tudor Publishing Company, 1966.

Lorant, Stefan, editor. *The New World: The First Pictures of America.* New York: Duell, Sloan and Pearce, 1946.

McCoubrey, John W., et al. *The Arts in America: The Colonial Period.* New York: Schocken Books, 1975.

Millar, John Fitzhugh. *The Architects of the American Colonies.* Barre, Mass.: Barre Publishers, 1968.

Morris, Richard B. *The Making of a Nation, 1775–1789.* New York: Time-Life Books, 1963.

Newcomb, Rexford. *Spanish Colonial Architecture in the United States.* New York: J. J. Augustin, 1937.

Radoff, Morris L. "Buildings of the State of Maryland at Annapolis" (publication no. 9, Hall of Records Commission). Annapolis: State of Maryland, 1954.

Sauer, Carl O. "The Settlement of the Humid East," *Yearbook of Agriculture, 1941.* Washington, D.C.: U.S. Department of Agriculture, U.S. Government Printing Office, 1941.

Smith, John. *Captain John Smith's History of Virginia: A Selection.* Indianapolis and New York: Bobbs-Merrill Company, Inc., 1970.

Trewartha, Glenn T. "Types of Rural Settlement in Colonial America," *Geographical Review,* vol. 36, no. 4 (1946).

U.S., Library of Congress. *To Set A Country Free.* Washington, D.C.: Library of Congress, 1975.

Walsh, Richard, editor. *The Mind and Spirit of Early America: Sources in American History, 1607–1789.* New York: Appleton-Century-Crofts, Educational Division, Meredith Corporation, 1969.

Wertenbaker, T. J. *The Puritan Oligarchy.* New York: Charles Scribner's Sons, 1947.

Whiffen, Marcus. *The Public Buildings of Williamsburg.* Williamsburg: Colonial Williamsburg Press, 1958.

Chapter 1

Adams, William Howard, editor. *The Eye of Thomas Jefferson.* Washington, D.C.: National Gallery of Art, 1976.

American Philosophical Society. *Historic Philadelphia from the Founding until the Early Nineteenth Century,* vol. 43, part 1. Philadelphia: American Philosophical Society, 1953.

Andrist, Ralph K., "Alas, Poor George, Where Is Your Head?" *Smithsonian Magazine,* September 1974.

Bulfinch, Ellen Susan. *The Life and Letters of Charles Bulfinch, Architect.* Boston: Houghton Mifflin Company, 1896.

Butler, Jeanne F. "Capitol Studies, Competition 1792: Designing a Nation's Capitol" (exhibit catalog). Washington, D.C.: AIA Foundation, 1976.

Caemmerer, Hans Paul. *Life of Pierre Charles l'Enfant: Planner of the City Beautiful.* Washington, D.C.: National Republic Publishing Company, 1950.

Carter, Edward C., II, "Benjamin Henry Latrobe and Public Works: Professionalism, Private Interest, and Public Policy in the Age of Jefferson." *Essays in Public Works History,* no. 3. Washington, D.C.: Public Works Historical Society, December 1976.

de Crevecoeur, Hector St. John. *Letters from an American Farmer.* Magnolia, Massachusetts: Peter Smith Reprint of 1782 edition.

The Federal Architect, October 1943. "The Laying of the Cornerstone of the Capitol."

Fortenbaugh, Robert. *Nine Capitals of the U.S.* York, Penna.: Maple Press Company, 1973 (reprint of 1948 edition).

Furneaux, Rupert. *Pictorial History of the American Revolution.* Chicago: J. G. Ferguson Publishing Company, 1973.

Guinness, Desmond, and Sadler, Julius T., Jr. *Mr. Jefferson, Architect.* New York: The Viking Press, 1973.

Hamlin, Talbot. *Benjamin Henry Latrobe.* New York: Oxford University Press, 1955.

Isaacson, Philip M. *The American Eagle.* Boston: The New York Graphic Society, 1975.

Kimball, Fiske. *American Architecture.* New York: AMS Press, 1970 (reprint of 1928 edition).

Kirker, Harold. *The Architecture of Charles Bulfinch.* Cambridge: Harvard University Press, 1969.

Kite, Elizabeth S. *L'Enfant and Washington: 1791–1792.* Baltimore: The Johns Hopkins University Press, 1929.

Lipset, Seymour Martin. *The First New Nation.* New York: Basic Books, 1963.

Maverick, Maury, "The Great Seal of the United States." Article in records of U.S. Treasury Department library, n.d.

Miller, Lillian B. *In the Minds and Hearts of the People: Prologue to the American Revolution, 1760–1774.* Greenwich, Conn.: The New York Graphic Society, 1974.

Morrison, Hugh. *Early American Architecture: From the First Colonial Settlements to the National Period.* New York: Oxford University Press, 1952.

Peterson, Charles E. *The Carpenter's Company 1786 Rule Book.* Philadelphia: Bell Publishing Company, 1971.

———. *Building Early America: Contributions toward the History of a Great Industry.* Radnor, Pennsylvania: The Chilton Book Company, 1976.

Pierson, William H., Jr. *American Buildings and Their Architects: The Colonial and Neo-Classical Styles.* New York: Doubleday and Company, 1970.

Bibliography

Seemes, John E. *John H. Latrobe and His Times, 1803–1891.* Baltimore: Norman Remington, 1917.

Stanislawski, Dan. "The Origin and Spread of the Grid-Pattern Town," *Geographical Review,* vol. 36, no. 4 (1946).

Thrower, Norman J. *Original Survey and Land Subdivision: A Comparative Study of the Form and Effect of Contrasting Cadastral Surveys.* Chicago: Association of American Geographers, Rand McNally & Company, 1966.

U.S., Department of the Interior, National Park Service. "Thomas Jefferson and the National Capital" (pamphlet). Washington, D.C.: U.S. Government Printing Office, 1946.

U.S., Department of State. "The Great Seal of the United States" (pamphlet). Washington, D.C.: U.S. Government Printing Office, 1976.

U.S., Department of the Treasury. "A History of the Seal of the United States" (pamphlet). Washington, D.C.: U.S. Government Printing Office, 1909.

Wheeler, Richard. *Voices of 1776.* Greenwich, Conn.: Fawcett Publications, Inc., 1972.

Zorn, Walter Lewis. *The Capitols of the United States of America.* Monroe, Mich.: published by the author, 1955.

Chapter 2

Adamson, Hans. *Keepers of the Lights.* New York: Greenberg Publishers, 1955.

Architectural Record, January 1893. "Architectural Aberration."

Architectural Record, May 1908. "The Baltimore Customs House."

Arvin, Newton. *Herman Melville.* Westport, Conn.: Greenwood Press, 1973 (reprint of 1950 edition).

Christwick, Mary Louise; Swanson, Betsy; Toledano, Roulhac; and Hulden, Pat. *New Orleans Architecture, Volume 2: The Modern Sector.* Gretna, La.: Pelican Publishing Company, 1972.

Coit, Margaret L. *John C. Calhoun: American Portrait.* Boston: Houghton Mifflin Company, 1950.

Cooper, James Fenimore. *Home as Found.* Washington, D.C.: American Institute of Architects, 1828 (reprint: New York: G. P. Putnam's Sons, 1961).

Cunliffe, Marcus. *The Nation Takes Shape: 1789–1837.* Chicago: The University of Chicago Press, 1959.

Davis, Jane B. "A. J. Davis's Projects for a Patent Office Building, 1832–1834," *Journal of the Society of Architectural Historians,* October 1965.

Dickens, Charles. *American Notes.* Magnolia, Mass.: Peter Smith reprint of 1842 edition.

Dunlap, William. *History of the Rise and Progress of The Arts of Design in the United States,* vols. 1 and 2. New York: Dover Publications, Inc., 1969 (reprint of 1834 George P. Scott and Company edition).

Furman, Bess. *A Profile of the U.S. Public Health Service, 1798–1948.* Washington, D.C.: U.S. Government Printing Office, 1973.

Galbraith, John Kenneth. *Money: Whence It Came, Where It Went.* Boston: Houghton Mifflin Company, 1975.

Gallagher, H. M. Pierce. *Robert Mills, Architect of the Washington Monument, 1781–1855.* New York: Columbia University Press, 1935.

Goodrich, Carter. "National Planning and Internal Improvements," *Political Science Quarterly,* March 1948.

———, editor. *Canals and American Economic Development.* New York: Columbia University Press, 1961.

Gray, Ralph D. *The National Waterway: A History of the Chesapeake and Delaware Canal, 1769–1965.* Urbana, Ill.: The University of Illinois Press, 1967.

Hamlin, Talbot. *Greek Revival Architecture in America.* New York: Oxford University Press, 1944.

Hammond, John Martin. *Quaint and Historic Forts of North America.* Philadelphia: J. B. Lippincott, 1915.

Hawthorne, Nathaniel. "The Custom House," introduction to *The Scarlet Letter.* Boston: Ticknor, Fields and Reed, 1850.

Holland, Francis Ross. *America's Lighthouses: Their Illustrated History since 1716.* Brattleboro, Vermont: The Stephen Green Press, 1972.

Kiley, John N. "Operations of the United States Subtreasuries Establishment, Abolishment, and Transfer of Functions to the Federal Reserve Banks." Rutgers University graduate thesis, June 1956.

Landy, Jacob. "The Washington Monument Project in New York," *Journal of the Society of Architectural Historians,* December 1969.

Lewis, E. R. *Seacoast Fortifications of the United States.* Washington, D.C.: The Smithsonian Institution Press, 1970.

Miller, J. Jefferson. "The Designs for the Washington Monument in Baltimore," *Journal of the Society of Architectural Historians,* March 1964.

National Park Service. "Castle Clinton National Monument" (pamphlet). Washington, D.C.: U.S. Government Printing Office, 1972.

National Society of the Colonial Dames of America. *Three Centuries of Custom Houses.* Washington, D.C.: The National Society of the Colonial Dames of America, 1972.

Riepel, Robert, and Athearn, R. G. *America Moves West.* New York: Holt, Rinehart and Winston, 1970.

Torres, Louis, "John Frazee and the New York Custom House," *Journal of the Society of Architectural Historians,* October 1964.

Trollope, Frances. *Domestic ... ners of the Americans, 1832.* Magnolia, Mass.: Peter Smith Publishers, Inc.

U.S., Congress, House of Representatives, Committee on Public Buildings. *Buildings for Treasury and State Departments.* 24th Congress, 1st session, 1836, House Report no. 247.

U.S., Department of the Interior, National Park Service. "Cape Hatteras Lighthouse, North Carolina" (pamphlet). Washington, D.C.: U.S. Government Printing Office, 1963.

U.S., Department of Transportation, U.S. Coast Guard. "Historically Famous Lighthouses." Washington, D.C.: U.S. Government Printing Office, 1972.

U.S., Department of the Treasury. *Report on Roads and Canals.* Washington, D.C.: U.S. Government Printing Office, 1808.

Wettereau, James O. "New Light on the First Bank of the U.S.," *The Pennsylvania Magazine of Biography,* July 1937.

Chapter 3

Atwater, Caleb. *Remarks Made on a Tour to Prairie du Chien, Thence to Washington City, in 1829.* Columbus, Ohio, 1831. (Facsimile reprint, New York: Arno Press, 1975.)

Ault, Phil. *Wires West: The Story of the Talking Wires.* New York: Dodd, Mead and Company, 1974.

Biddle, Ellen McGowan. *Reminiscences of a Soldier's Wife.* Philadelphia: J. B. Lippincott Company, 1907.

Billington, Ray Allen. *Westward Expansion: The American Frontier.* New York: Macmillan Publishing Company, 1974 (reprint of 1949 edition).

Bloom, John Porter, editor. *The American Territorial System.* Athens, Ohio: Ohio University Press, 1973.

Bremmer, Robert H., editor. *Children and Youth in America: A Documentary History,* vol. 2: *Negro, Indian, and Immigrant Children.* Cambridge, Mass.: Harvard University Press, 1971.

Catton, Bruce. *The American Heritage Pictorial History of the Civil War,* edited by Richard M. Ketchum. Garden City, N.Y.: Doubleday & Company, American Heritage Publishing Company, 1960.

Current, Richard N. *John C. Calhoun.* New York: Washington Square Press, 1966.

Frankenstein, Alfred. "The Great Trans-Mississippi Railroad Survey," *Art in America,* January–February 1976.

Frazer, Robert W. *Forts of the West to 1898.* Norman, Okla.: The University of Oklahoma Press, 1965.

Getlein, Frank. *The Lure of the Great West.* Waukesha, Wis.: Country Beautiful Corporation, 1973.

Goetzmann, William H. *Army Exploration in the American West, 1803–1863.* New Haven: Yale University Press, 1959.

———. "Exploration's Nation: The Role of Discovery in American History," in Daniel J. Boorstin, editor, *American Civilization: A Portrait from the Twentieth Century.* New York: McGraw-Hill Book Company, 1972.

Gurney, Gene. *The Smithsonian Institution.* New York: Crown Publishers, Inc., 1964.

Hagan, William T. *American Indians.* Chicago: The University of Chicago Press, 1961.

Hellman, Geoffrey T. *The Smithsonian: Octopus on the Mall.* Philadelphia and New York: J. B. Lippincott Co., 1966.

Hitchcock, Henry-Russell, and Seale, William. *Temples of Democracy: The State Capitols of the USA.* New York: Harcourt, Brace, Jovanovich, 1976.

Kirker, Harold. *California's Architectural Frontier.* New York: Russell and Russell, 1960.

Kuspit, Donald B. "Nineteenth-Century Landscape: Poetry and Property," *Art in America,* January–February 1976.

Lamar, Howard Roberts. *Dakota Territory, 1861–1889: A Study of Frontier Politics.* New Haven: Yale University Press, 1956.

Leech, Margaret. *Reveille in Washington.* New York: Time, Inc., 1962 (reprint of Harper & Brothers 1941 edition).

Leupp, Francis. "Back to Nature for the Indian." *Charities and Commons,* June 6, 1908.

———. See also U.S., Department of the Interior, Bureau of Indian Affairs.

Lowenfels, Walter, editor. *Walt Whitman's Civil War.* New York: Alfred A. Knopf, 1971.

McKee, Russell. *The Last West: A History of the Great Plains of North America.* New York: Thomas Y. Crowell Company, 1974.

Meredith, Roy. *Mathew B. Brady: Mr. Lincoln's Camera Man.* New York: Dover Publications, 1946.

Novak, Barbara. "The Double-Edged Axe," *Art in America,* January–February 1976.

Owen, Robert Dale. *Hints on Public Architecture.* Report of the Smithsonian Building Committee. Washington, D.C., 1849.

Pomeroy, Earl Spencer. *The Territories and the United States, 1861–1890.* Philadelphia: The University of Pennsylvania Press, 1947.

Price, Hiram. See U.S., Department of the Interior, Bureau of Indian Affairs.

Prucha, Francis Paul. *The Sword of the Republic: The U.S. Army on the Frontier, 1783–1846.* New York: The Macmillan Company, 1969.

———. *Broadaxe and Bayonet: The Role of the United States Army in the Development of the Northwest, 1815–1860.* Lincoln, Neb.: The University of Nebraska Press, 1967.

Ravenal, Beatrice St. Julian. *Architects of Charleston.* Charleston: Carolina Art Association, 1945.

Rohrbough, Malcolm. *The Land Office Business: 1789–1837.* New York: Oxford University Press, 1968.

Roper, Laura Wood. *A Biography of Frederick Law Olmsted.* Baltimore: The Johns Hopkins University Press, 1973.

Slotkin, Richard. *Regeneration through Violence: The Mythology of the American Frontier, 1600–1860.* Middletown, Conn.: Wesleyan University Press, 1973.

Taft, Robert. *Artists and Illustrators of the Old West: 1850–1900.* New York: Charles Scribner's Sons, 1953.

Thompson, Robert Luther. *Wiring a Continent: The History of the Telegraph Industry in the United States.* Princeton, N.J.: Princeton University Press, 1947.

U.S., Congress, Senate. *Reports of Explorations and Surveys to Ascertain the Most Practicable and Economic Route for a Railroad from the Mississippi River to the Pacific Ocean, Made under the Direction of the Secretary of War in 1853–4. According to Acts of Congress of March 3, 1853; May 31, 1854; and August 5, 1854.* 13 volumes, 1855–1861.

U.S., Department of the Interior. *Creation of the Department of the Interior, March 3, 1849.* Historical Vignettes Series, 1776–1976. Washington, D.C.: U.S. Government Printing Office, March 3, 1976.

U.S., Department of the Interior, Bureau of Indian Affairs. *Annual Report of the Commissioner of Indian Affairs.* Washington, D.C.: U.S. Government Printing Office, 1880–1936. See especially reports by Commissioners of Indian Affairs R. H. Pratt (1880), Hiram Price (1881), and Francis Leupp (1907–1908).

U.S., General Services Administration. *Lucky Landmark: A Study of a Design and Its Survival,* by Donald J. Lehman. Historical Building Study no. 4. Washington, D.C.: U.S. Government Printing Office, 1973.

The United States Magazine and Democratic Review, July–December 1839.

Washburn, Wilcomb E. *Red Man's Land/White Man's Law: A Study of the Past and Present Status of the American Indian.* New York: Charles Scribner's Sons, 1971.

Whyte, James H. *The Uncivil War: Washington during the Reconstruction, 1865–1878.* New York: Twayne Publishers, 1958.

Wodehouse, Lawrence. "Ammi Burnham Young, 1798–1874," *Journal of the Society of Architectural Historians,* December 1966.

Chapter 4

American Architect and Building News. Issues March 15, 1879; January 11, 1879; January 1, 1876; January 15, 1876; April 7, 1894; July 8, 1876; March 24, 1900.

Atlantic Monthly, April 1879. "The Washington Monument and Mr. Story's Design."

Baedeker, Karl. *United States: 1893.* New York: Da Capo Press, 1971 (reprint of 1893 edition).

Barton, E. E. *Historical and Commercial Sketches of Washington and Environs.* Washington, D.C., 1884.

Beauchamp, Tanya Edwards. "Adolph Cluss and the Building of the U.S. National Museum: An Architecture of Perfect Adaptability." A thesis presented to the faculty of the School of Architecture, University of Virginia, May, 1972.

Bettmann, Otto L. *The Good Old Days—They Were Terrible!* New York: Random House, 1974.

Bryant, William Cullen. *Picturesque America, Or The Land We Live In,* vols. 1 and 2. New York: Lyle Stuart, Inc., 1975 (reprint of original D. Appleton edition).

Coffin, William. "Decorations in the New Congressional Library," *Century Magazine,* March 1897.

Cole, John Y., "The Main Building of the Library of Congress: A Chronology, 1871–1965," *The Quarterly Journal of the Library of Congress,* October 1972.

Combs, Barry B. *Westward to Promontory.* New York: American West Publishing Company, 1969.

Eidlitz, Leopold. *The Nature and Function of Art.* New York: A. C. Armstrong, 1881.

Evans, George Greenlief. *History of the United States Mint and American Coinage.* Philadelphia: G. E. Evans Company, 1888.

Fuller, Wayne E. *R.F.D.: The Changing Face of Rural America.* Bloomington: Indiana University Press, 1964.

———. *The American Mail: Enlarger of the Common Life.* Chicago: University of Chicago Press, 1972.

Hafen, Le Roy R. *The Overland Mail, 1849–1869.* New York: AMS Press, 1969.

Hickson, Howard. *Mint Mark "CC": The Story of the U.S. Mint at Carson City, Nevada.* Carson City, Nev.: Nevada State Museum, 1972.

Hilker, Helen-Anne. "Monument to Civilization: Diary of a Building," *The Quarterly Journal of the Library of Congress,* October 1972.

Hubbard, Gardiner G. "Our Post Office," *Atlantic Monthly,* vol. 39, no. 1 (1875).

Kelly, Clyde M. *United States Postal Policy.* New York: D. Appleton and Company, 1932.

Koeper, Frederick. *Illinois Architecture from Territorial Times to the Present: A Selective Guide.* Chicago: The University of Chicago Press, 1968.

Leslie, Frank. *Illustrated Historical Register of the Centennial Exposition, 1876.* New York: Paddington Press, 1974 (facsimile reprint).

Mateyka, Marsha Perry. "Adolph Cluss: A Study of His Architecture in Washington, D.C." Unpublished research paper prepared for the American University, fall 1972.

Mumford, Lewis. *The Brown Decades: A Study of the Arts in America, 1865–1895.* New York: Dover Publications, Inc., 1955.

Post, Robert C., editor. *1876, A Centennial Exhibition.* Washington, D.C.: The National Museum of History and Technology, 1976.

Powell, John Wesley. *Report on the Lands of the Arid Region of the United States; With a More Detailed Account of the Lands of Utah.* Edited by Wallace Stegner. Cambridge, Mass.: Harvard University Press, The Belknap Press, 1962 (reprint of 1879 edition).

Prokopoff, Stephen S., and Siegfried, Joan C. *The Nineteenth-Century Architecture of Saratoga Springs.* New York: New York State Council on the Arts, 1970.

Rathbun, Richard. *Report of the U.S. National Museum under the Direction of the Smithsonian Institution, for the Year Ending June 30, 1903.* Washington, D.C.: U.S. Government Printing Office, 1905.

Robinson, Frederick B., "The Eighth Wonder of Erastus Field," *American Heritage,* April 1963.

Roper, Daniel C. *The United States Post Office: Its Past Record, Present Condition and Potential Relation to the New World Era.* New York: Funk & Wagnalls Company, 1917.

Ruskin, John. *The Seven Lamps of Architecture.* New York: Farrar, Straus & Giroux, The Noonday Press, 1971 (reprint of 1849 edition).

Searle, Henry R. *Washington Monument Monograph.* Washington, D.C.: Gibson Brothers, undated.

Silver, Nathan. *Lost New York.* New York: Schocken Books, 1967.

Stern, Madeleine B. *We the Women: Career Firsts of the Nineteenth Century.* New York: Shulte Publishing Company, 1963.

U.S., Department of the Interior, Geological Survey. *A Brief History of the U.S. Geological Survey.* Washington, D.C.: U.S. Government Printing Office, 1975.

U.S., Department of the Interior, Geological Survey. *Ferdinand Vendiveer Hayden and the Founding of Yellowstone National Park.* Washington, D.C.: U.S. Government Printing Office, 1976.

U.S., Department of the Treasury. *History, Organization, and Functions of the Office of Supervising Architect,* by H. H. Thayer. Treasury Document no. 817. Washington, D.C., 1886.

U.S., Department of the Treasury, Office of the Mint. *The Mint Story.* Washington, D.C.: U.S. Government Printing Office, 1968.

U.S., General Services Administration. *Executive Office Building.* Historical Building Study no. 3. Washington, D.C.: U.S. Government Printing Office, 1972.

U.S., General Services Administration. *Pension Building.* Historical Building Study no. 1. Washington, D.C.: U.S. Government Printing Office, 1964.

Weymouth, Lally. *America in 1876: The Way We Were.* New York: Alfred A. Knopf, Vintage Books, 1976.

Wilkinson, Henrietta H. "Mints: Where America's Money Was Made," *Historic Preservation,* April–June 1975.

Wodehouse, Lawrence. "Alfred B. Mullett and his French Style Government Buildings," *Journal of the Society of Architectural Historians,* March 1972.

Chapter 5

Alland, Alexander. *Jacob A. Riis: Photographer and Citizen.* Millerton, N.Y.: Aperture, Inc., 1974.

Benjamin, Park. *The United States Naval Academy.* New York: Knickerbocker Press, 1900.

Cameron, William E., editor. *History of the Columbian Exposition.* Chicago: Columbian Historical Company, 1893.

Carlihan, Jean Paul. "Beaux Arts or 'Bozarts'?," *Architectural Record,* January 1976.

The Century Magazine, October 1905. "The New Naval Academy."

The Chicago Tribune, March 9, 1890. "Plan to Put All the World's Fair Exposition Exhibits under one Roof."

Cram, Ralph Adams. *My Life in Architecture.* Boston: Little, Brown and Company, 1936.

Crane, John, and Kieley, James F. *West Point: The Key to America.* New York: McGraw Hill Book Company, Inc., 1947.

Dahl, Curtis. "Mr. Smith's American Acropolis," *American Heritage,* June 1956.

Farr, Finis. *Frank Lloyd Wright: A Biography.* New York: Charles Scribner's Sons, 1961.

Ferejohn, John A. *Pork Barrel Politics: Rivers and Harbors Legislation, 1947–1968.* Stanford, Calif.: Stanford University Press, 1974.

Flinn, John J. *Official Guide to the World's Columbian Exposition.* Chicago: The Columbian Guide Company, 1893.

Handlin, Oscar. *A Pictorial History of Immigration.* New York: Crown Publishers, Inc., 1972.

Hays, Samuel P. *Conservation and the Gospel of Efficiency: The Progressive Conservation Movement, 1890–1920.* Cambridge, Mass.: Harvard University Press, 1959.

Heise, Arthur. *The Brass Factories.* Washington, D.C.: Public Affairs Press, 1969.

Hines, Thomas S. *Burnham of Chicago.* New York: Oxford University Press, 1974.

James, Henry. *The Art of Travel: Scenes and Journeys in America, England, France, and Italy from the Travel Writings* edited by Dauwen Zabel. New York: Doubleday & Company, Inc., 1958.

———. *The American Scene.* Bloomington: Indiana University Press, 1968 (originally published 1907).

Jordy, William H. *American Buildings and Their Architects: Progressive and Academic Ideals at the Turn of the Twentieth Century.* Garden City, N.Y.: Doubleday & Company, Inc., 1972.

Karlowicz, Titus M. "D. H. Burnham's Role in the Selection of Architects for the World's Columbian Exposition," *Journal of the Society of Architectural Historians,* October 1970.

Kidney, Walter C. *The Architecture of Choice: Eclecticism in America, 1890–1930.* New York: George Braziller, Inc., 1974.

Litchfield, Electus D. "Yorkship Village," *Review of Reviews,* 1919.

Lobell, John. "The Beaux Arts: A Reconsideration of Meaning in Architecture," *AIA Journal,* November 1975.

Lovette, Leland P. *School of the Sea.* Toronto: Fred Stokes Company, 1941.

Low, A. Maurice. "Washington: The City of Leisure," *Atlantic Monthly,* December 1900.

Lubove, Roy. "Homes and 'A Few Well Placed Fruit Trees': An Object Lesson in Federal Housing." *Social Research,* vol. 27, no. 4 (1960).

McCleary, James T. "What Shall the Lincoln Memorial Be?," *American Review of Reviews,* September 1908.

McKelvey, Blake. *The Urbanization of America, 1860–1915.* New Brunswick, N.J.: Rutgers University Press, 1963.

Mandell, Richard D. *Paris 1900: The Great World's Fair.* Toronto: University of Toronto Press, 1967.

Marshall, Chauncey A. M. *History of the U.S. Naval Academy.* New York, 1862.

Moore, Charles. *Daniel H. Burnham, Architect, Planner of Cities,* vols. 1 and 2. Boston: Houghton Mifflin Company, 1921.

———. *The Life and Times of Charles Follen McKim.* Boston: Houghton Mifflin Company, 1929.

———. "Theodore Roosevelt's Service to the National Capital," *Architecture,* October 1919.

Morrison, Hugh. *Louis Sullivan: Prophet of Modern Architecture.* New York: W. W. Norton & Company, Inc., 1962.

National Collection of Fine Arts. *Art for Architecture: Washington, D.C., 1895–1925* (exhibit catalog). Washington, D.C.: National Collection of Fine Arts, 1975.

Norris, Walter B. *Annapolis, Its Colonial and Naval History.* New York: Thomas Y. Crowell, 1925.

Novotny, Ann. *Strangers at the Door.* New York: Bantam Books, 1974 (abridged version of 1972 edition).

Peffer, E. Louise. *The Closing of the Public Domain: Disposal and Reservation Policies, 1900–1950.* Stanford: Stanford University Press, 1951.

Roosevelt, Theodore. *California Addresses.* San Francisco: The California Promotion Society, 1903.

Smith, Darnell Hevenor. *The Office of the Supervising Architect of the Treasury.* Baltimore: The Johns Hopkins University Press, 1923.

Smith, Franklin Webster. See under U.S., Congress, Senate.

Stevens, William Oliver. *Annapolis, Ann Arundel's Town.* New York: Dodd, Mead and Company, 1937.

Sullivan, Louis. *Autobiography of an Idea.* New York: Press of the American Institute of Architects, Inc., 1924.

U.S., Congress, House of Representatives, Public Buildings Commission. *Report of the Public Buildings Commission.* 63rd Congress, 2d session, House Document no. 936. Washington, D.C.: U.S. Government Printing Office, 1914.

U.S., Congress, Senate. Committee on the District of Columbia. *Report of the Senate Committee on the District of Columbia on the Improvement of the Park System of the District of Columbia.* 57th Congress, 1st session, Senate Report no. 166. Washington, D.C.: U.S. Government Printing Office, 1902.

U.S., Congress, Senate. *The Aggrandizement of Washington, D.C.,* by Franklin Webster Smith. 56th Congress, 1st session, Senate Document no. 209. Washington, D.C.: U.S. Government Printing Office, 1900.

U.S., General Services Administration. *Agriculture Administration Building.* Historical Study no. 1. Washington, D.C.: U.S. Government Printing Office, 1964.

U.S., Lincoln Memorial Commission. *The Lincoln Memorial: Washington.* Washington, D.C.: U.S. Government Printing Office, 1927.

U.S., Military Academy. *Annual Report of the Superintendant of the United States Military Academy.* Washington, D.C.: U.S. Government Printing Office, 1898, 1909.

U.S., Shipping Board Emergency Fleet Corps. *Types of Housing for Shipbuilders.* Washington, D.C.: U.S. Government Printing Office, 1949.

Wetmore, James A. "Land Buying for Uncle Sam." *The Federal Architect,* April 1937.

Whitaker, Charles Harris. "Our Stupid and Blundering National Policy of Providing Public Buildings," *AIA Journal,* February 1916 (part 1); March 1916 (part 2).

Wiley, Farida A. *Theodore Roosevelt's America: Selections from the Writings of the Oyster Bay Naturalist.* New York: The Devin-Adair Company, 1955.

Wright, Frank Lloyd. *An Autobiography.* New York: Duell, Sloan and Pearce, 1943 (1st edition, 1932).

———. *In the Cause of Architecture.* New York: Architectural Record Books, 1975.

Chapter 6

Allen, Frederick Lewis. *Only Yesterday: An Informal History of the 1920s.* New York: Harper & Row, 1964 (reprint of 1931 edition).

American Battle Monuments Commission. *American Memorials and Overseas Military Cemeteries.* Washington, D.C.: American Battle Monuments Commission, 1974.

Augur, Tracy B. "City Planning and Civic Progress," *Architectural Forum,* September 1931.

Betts, Benjamin F. "Is the Government Treating Architects Fairly?," *American Architect,* February 1931.

———. "The Government Should Get Out of the Architectural Business," *American Architect,* May 1931.

Brockway, A. L. "Governments and Architects," *Architectural Forum,* September 1931.

Childs, Marquis. "Mr. Pope's Memorial," *Magazine of Art,* April 1937.

The College of Architecture, University of Nebraska, Lincoln. *The Nebraska Capitol and Environs Plan.* Lincoln, Neb.: The University of Nebraska, 1975.

Cret, Paul P. "Ten Years of Modernism," *The Federal Architect,* July 1933.

Dean, Robert J. *Living Granite.* New York: The Viking Press, 1949.

Eberhard, Ernest. "Fifty Years of Agitation . . . for Better Design of Government Buildings and Government Employment of Private Architects," *American Architect,* June 1931.

The Federal Architect, articles 1930–1946

October 1930. "Can Modern Architecture Be Good?"

October 1930. "The Kitty Hawk Memorial."

January 1931. "Independence Square, Washington, D.C."

July 1931. "Specialization in Architecture: Design of Federal Buildings Introduces Exacting Problems."

October 1931. "The City of George Washington, Abraham Lincoln, and the American People."

April 1932. "What Are the Outstanding Buildings? The Federal Architect Conducts Poll to Obtain Opinion of Nationally Prominent Architects."

October 1932. "A Modern Pueblo. The Veterans Administration Hospital at Albuquerque, New Mexico."

April 1933. "Exhibition of Federal Architecture: Jury of Award Chooses Excellent Examples."

October 1933. "The V.A. Home, Biloxi, Mississippi."

April 1934. "The V.A. Facility."

January 1937. "Letter from Judge Wetmore."

April 1937. "Washington Completed" (entire issue).

October 1938. "Directory of Federal Construction" (entire issue).

July 1940. "Association of Federal Architects: Constitution and By-Laws."

January–March 1942. "Louis A. Simon" (entire issue).

April 1942. "Mr. Cret as a Guest."

October 1944. "Veterans Administration" (entire issue).

Final number under Editor Edwin Bateman Morris 1946. "Paul P. Cret" (entire issue).

Fite, Gilbert C. *Mount Rushmore.* Norman, Okla.: The University of Oklahoma Press, 1952.

German Library of Information. *A Nation Builds: Contemporary German Architecture.* New York: German Library of Information, 1940.

Gutheim, Frederick. "The Quality of Public Works," *Magazine of Art,* April 1934.

Hale, William Harlan. "The Grandeur That Is Washington," *Harper's Monthly,* April 1934.

Heath, Ferry K. "The Federal Building Program," *Architectural Forum,* September 1931.

Hudnut, Joseph. *Architecture and the Spirit of Man.* Cambridge: Harvard University Press, 1949.

———. "Twilight of the Gods," *Magazine of Art,* August 1937.

Kopp, Anatole. *Town and Revolution: Soviet Architecture and City Planning, 1917–1935.* New York: George Braziller, Inc., 1970 (originally published in French by Editions Anthropos, Paris, 1967).

Lane, Barbara Miller. *Architecture and Politics in Germany: 1918–1945.* Cambridge: Harvard University Press, 1968.

Leisenring, L. M. "Quarters for the Army," *The Federal Architect,* July 1937.

L'Orange, H. P. *Art Forms and Civic Life in the Late Roman Empire.* Princeton, N.J.: Princeton University Press, 1965.

Magazine of Art, articles 1937–1938

April 1937. "Field Notes: Jefferson Protest."

May 1938. "Letters: Kimball on the Jefferson Memorial."

June 1938. "Facts from the Fine Arts Commission."

Morgan, Arthur C. *Dams and Other Disasters: A Century of the Army Corps of Engineers in Civil Works.* Boston: Porter Sargent Publishers, 1971.

Morris, Edwin Bateman, "The City of Washington Today," *Architecture,* October 1933.

Potts, Vladimir. "The Romanization of Washington," *Vanity Fair,* October 1931.

Price, Willadene. *Gutzon Borglum: The Man Who Carved a Mountain.* Mclean, Va.: EPM Publications, Inc., 1961.

Reed, Henry Hope. *Golden City.* New York: W. W. Norton & Company, Inc., 1970.

Risch, Erna. *Quartermaster Support of the Army: A History of the Corps, 1775–1939.* Washington, D.C.: Quartermaster Historian's Office, U.S. Government Printing Office, 1962.

Speer, Albert. *Inside the Third Reich.* New York: The Macmillan Company, 1970.

Taylor, Robert R. *The Word in Stone: The Role of Architecture in the National Socialist Ideology.* Berkeley, Los Angeles, London: University of California Press, 1974.

Vosburgh, Frederick. "Wonders of the New Washington," *National Geographic Magazine,* April 1935.

Warne, William E. *The Bureau of Reclamation.* Washington, D.C.: Praeger Library of U.S. Government Departments and Agencies, 1973.

Wearin, Otha D. "Wanted: Competitions for Federal Buildings," *Magazine of Art,* May 1938.

White, Theodore B. *Paul Philippe Cret, Architect and Teacher.* Philadelphia: The Art Alliance Press, 1973.

Chapter 7

Abbott, Berenice, and Mc-Causland, Elizabeth. *New York in the Thirties as Photographed by Berenice Abbott.* New York: Dover Publications, 1973 (reprint of *Changing New York,* E. P. Dutton, 1939).

Agee, James, and Evans, Walker. *Let Us Now Praise Famous Men.* Boston: Houghton Mifflin Company, 1960 (1st edition, 1939).

American City, April 1935. "An Outstanding Subsistence Homesteading Project."

Architectural Forum, articles 1939–1943

August 1939. "Dams and Design."

January 1941. "Building for Defense: Headway and Headaches."

January 1941. "Farm Security Administration."

January 1943. "Pentagon Building."

June 1943. "Federal Building, The New York Fair."

January 1943. "U.S. Government Building, The San Francisco Fair."

Aronovici, Carol, editor. *America Can't Have Housing.* New York: The Museum of Modern Art, 1934.

Baldwin, Sidney. *Poverty and Politics: The Rise and Decline of the Farm Security Administration.* Durham, N.C.: The University of North Carolina Press, 1968.

Bauer, Catherine. "Toward Postwar Housing in the U.S.," *Transatlantic,* December 1944.

Bitterman, Eleanor. *Art in Modern Architecture.* New York: Reinhold Publishing Company, 1952.

Bruce, Edward, and Watson, Forbes. *Art in Federal Buildings: An Illustrated Record of the Treasury Department's New Program in Painting and Sculpture,* vol. 1: *Mural Designs, 1934–1936.* Washington, D.C.: Art in Federal Buildings, Incorporated, 1936.

Bush, Donald J. *The Streamlined Decade.* New York: George Braziller, Inc., 1975.

California Historical Society. *Japanese Americans.* San Francisco: California Historical Society, 1972.

Callahan, Sean, editor. *The Photographs of Margaret Bourke-White.* New York: Bonanza Books, 1972.

Conrat, Maisie, and Conrat, Richard. *Executive Order 9066: The Internment of 110,000 Japanese Americans.* Cambridge, Mass.: The MIT Press for the California Historical Society, 1972.

Cornfield, Jerome, and Weber, Marjorie. "Cost of Living: Housing of Federal Employees in the Washington (D.C.) Area in May 1941," *Monthly Labor Review,* November 1941.

Craig, Lois. "Beyond 'Leaf-Raking': WPA's Lasting Legacy," *City,* October–November 1970.

Cutler, Phoebe. "On Recognizing a WPA Rose Garden or a CCC Privy," *Landscape,* Winter 1976.

Dreyfuss, Henry. "The City of Tomorrow," *Popular Mechanics,* March 1939.

Duffus, R. L. *The Valley and Its People: A Portrait of TVA.* New York: Alfred A. Knopf, 1944.

Dunning, N. Max. "Dallying Down in Dallas," *The Federal Architect,* July 1936.

Estill, Calvert L. "Blunders at Arthurdale—Puts Burden on Miner and Taxpayer," *The Washington Post Magazine,* August 12, 1934.

The Federal Architect, articles 1934–1947

July 1934. Editorial.

October 1938. "Federal Emergency Administration of Public Works."

September–December 1941." Defense Housing" (entire issue).

April–June 1942. "Temporaries in the District of Columbia."

January–April 1943. "The Pentagon Building."

July 1943. "Unusual Problems Encountered by Architects in the Navy Department."

July 1943. " Temporary Federal Office Buildings in Washington."

April–July 1945. "The Bureau of Yards and Docks of the Navy Department."

April–July 1945. "National Housing Agency, Federal Public Housing Authority."

October 1946. "Greenbelt Towns."

October 1946. "History of Public Housing Developments."

January 1947. "Architectural Design."

January 1947. "Federal Administration of Public Housing."

Fortitudine, Spring 1975. "Historic Sites."

Fortune, May–June 1937. "Unemployed Artists . . . and How the Government Employs Them . . . An Account of WPA's Four Arts Projects."

Freidel, Frank, editor. *The New Deal and the American People.* Englewood Cliffs, N.J.: Prentice-Hall, Inc., 1965.

Frome, Michael. *The Forest Service.* Washington, D.C.: Praeger Library of U.S. Government Departments and Agencies, 1971.

Gard, Wayne. "The Farmers' Rebellion," *The Nation,* September 7, 1932.

Garver, Thomas H., editor. *Just Before the War: Urban America from 1935 to 1941 as Seen by Photographers of the Farm Security Administration.* Balboa, California: Newport Harbor Art Museum, 1968.

Gelfand, Mark I. *A Nation of Cities: The Federal Government and Urban America, 1933–1965.* New York: Oxford University Press, 1975.

Giedion, Siegfried. "Can Expositions Survive?," *Architectural Forum,* December 1938.

Goodman, Jack. *While You Were Gone: A Report on Wartime Life in the United States.* New York: Simon and Schuster, 1946.

Grattan, C. Hartley. "Reconversion," *Transatlantic,* December 1945.

Groueff, Stephane. *Manhattan Project.* Toronto: Little, Brown and Company, 1967.

Gurney, Gene. *The Pentagon.* New York: Crown Publishers, 1964.

Gutheim, Frederick. "Buildings at the Fair," *Magazine of Art,* August 1939.

———. "Roland Wank: 1898–1970," *Architectural Forum,* September 1970.

Haskell, Douglas. "Architecture of the TVA," *The Nation,* May 17, 1941.

Hegemann, Werner. *City Planning and Housing.* New York: Architectural Book Publishing, 1937.

Hildebrand, Grant. *Designing for Industry: The Architecture of Albert Kahn.* Cambridge, Mass.: The MIT Press, 1974.

Holland, Kenneth, and Hill, Frank Ernest. *Youth in the CCC.* Washington, D.C.: American Council on Education, 1942.

Hoyt, Ray. *We Can Take It: A Short Story of the CCC.* New York: American Book Company, 1935.

Hurley, F. Jack. *Portrait of a Decade: Roy Stryker and the Development of Documentary Photography in the Thirties.* New York: Da Capo Press, 1977 (reprint of 1972 edition published by Louisiana State University Press).

Huxley, Julian. *TVA: Adventure in Planning.* London: The Architectural Press, 1943.

Ickes, Harold L. *The Autobiography of a Curmudgeon.* New York: Reynal and Hitchcock, 1943.

———. *The Secret Diaries of Harold Ickes.* New York: Da Capo Press, 1974 (reprint).

Johnson, A. N. "The Impact of Farm Machinery on the Farm Economy," *Agricultural History,* January 1950.

Johnson, Vance. *Heaven's Tableland: The Dust Bowl Story.* New York: Farrar, Straus and Giroux, 1947.

Keith, Nathaniel S. *Politics and the Housing Crisis Since 1930.* New York: Universe Books, 1974.

Knapp, Sally. *Eleanor Roosevelt.* New York: Crowell and Company, 1949.

Kyle, John H. *The Building of TVA: An Illustrated History.* Baton Rouge: Louisiana State University Press, 1958.

Leighton, Alexander H. *The Governing of Men.* Princeton, N.J.: Princeton University Press, 1945.

Leuchtenberg, William E. *Franklin D. Roosevelt and the New Deal, 1932–1940.* New York: Harper & Row, 1963.

Lilienthal, David E. *TVA: Democracy on the March.* New York: Harper and Brothers, Publishers, 1953.

———. *The Journals of David E. Lilienthal: The TVA Years, 1939–1945.* New York: Harper & Row, 1964.

Lord, Russell. *Behold Our Land.* Boston: Houghton Mifflin Company, 1938.

———. *To Hold This Soil.* Washington, D.C.: U.S. Government Printing Office, 1940.

MacDonald, William F. *Federal Relief Administration and the Arts.* Columbus, Ohio: Ohio State University Press, 1969.

McKinzine, Richard D. *The New Deal for Artists.* Princeton, N.J.: Princeton University Press, 1973.

McWilliams, Carey. "Japanese in America," *Transatlantic,* January 1944.

Maass, Arthur. *Muddy Waters: The Army Engineers and the Nation's Rivers.* Cambridge, Mass.: Harvard University Press, 1951.

Mallory, Keith, and Ottar, Arvid. *The Architecture of War.* New York: Random House, 1973.

Manchester, William. *The Glory and the Dream: A Narrative History of America, 1932–1972.* Boston: Little, Brown and Company, 1974.

Mayer, Albert. *Greenbelt Towns Revisited* (report of the Urban Planning Research and Demonstration Project, HUD). Washington, D.C., October 1968.

Melvin, Bruce L. "Housing Standards for Subsistence Housing," *Architectural Record,* January 1935.

Morgan, Arthur E. *The Making of the TVA.* New York: Prometheus Books, 1974.

Mumford, Lewis, "The Sky Line: Fiftieth Anniversary, Georgian Post Office," *The New Yorker,* February 29, 1936.

The Museum of Modern Art, New York, exhibit catalogs, 1936–1945

Architecture in Government Housing. New York: The Museum of Modern Art, 1936.

Art in Our Time: An Exhibit to Celebrate the Tenth Anniversary of the Museum of Modern Art and the Opening of Its New Building, 1939. New York: Arno Press, 1972 (reprint of 1939 edition).

Built in USA: 1932–1944, edited by Elizabeth Nock, and *Post-War Architecture,* edited by Henry-Russell Hitchcock and Arthur Drexler, in one volume. New York: Arno Press, 1968 (reprint of 1944 and 1952 editions).

Modern Architecture: International Exhibition. New York: Arno Press, 1969 (reprint of 1932 edition).

Wartime Housing. New York: The Museum of Modern Art, 1942.

Myer, Dillon S. *Uprooted Americans.* Tucson, Ariz.: University of Arizona Press, 1971.

Myhra, David. "Rexford Guy Tugwell: Initiator of America's Greenbelt New Towns, 1935–1936," *American Institute of Planners Journal,* May 1974.

National Resources Committee. *Our Cities: Their Role in the National Economy.* Washington, D.C.: National Resources Committee, 1937.

Newsweek, February 15, 1943. "Race Between Claustrophobia and Agoraphobia for Those Pent Up in Washington's Pentagon."

Newsweek, September 18, 1944. "No Place Is Home."

Nichol, William. "Exposition Discovered at Dallas." *The Federal Architect,* October 1936.

Norton, Paul F. "World's Fairs in the 1930s," *Journal of the Society of Architectural Historians,* March 1965.

O'Connor, Francis V. *The New Deal Art Projects.* Washington, D.C.: Smithsonian Institution Press, 1972.

———. *WPA: Art for the Millions.* Greenwich, Conn.: New York Graphic Society, 1968.

Odegard, Peter. "Pressure Politics," *Transatlantic,* August 1944.

Owen, Marguerite. *The Tennessee Valley Authority.* Washington, D.C.: Praeger Library of U.S. Government Departments and Agencies, 1973.

Owings, Nathaniel Alexander. *The Spaces in Between: An Architect's Journey.* Boston: Houghton Mifflin Company, 1973.

Partridge, William T. "Impressions at a Century of Progress," *The Federal Architect,* October 1933.

Perkins, Dexter. *The New Age of Franklin Delano Roosevelt, 1932–45.* Chicago: The University of Chicago Press, 1957.

Pratt, Fletcher. *War for the World.* Vol. 54 of Chronicles of America, edited by Allen Johnson and Allan J. Nevins. New York: United States Publishers Assn., n.d.

Public Works Historical Society. "The Relevancy of Public Works History: The 1930s, a Case Study." Georgetown University Department of History, September 22, 1975.

Redstone, Louis G. *Art in Architecture.* New York: McGraw-Hill Publishing Company, Inc., 1968.

Rice, Millard Milburn. "Footnote on Arthurdale," *Harper's Magazine,* March 1940.

Robinson, George O., Jr. *The Oak Ridge Story.* Knoxville, Tenn.: Southern Publishers, Inc., 1950.

Rollins, Alfred Brooks Jr., editor. *Depression, Recovery and War, 1929–1945.* New York: McGraw-Hill Book Company, 1966.

Schlesinger, Arthur M., Jr. *The Age of Roosevelt: The Crisis of the Old Order, 1919–1933.* Boston: Houghton Mifflin Company, 1957.

———. *The Age of Roosevelt: The Coming of the New Deal.* Boston: Houghton Mifflin Company, 1958.

Scott, Mel. *American City Planning Since 1890.* Berkeley, Calif.: The University of California Press, 1971.

Shannon, David A., editor. *The Great Depression.* Englewood Cliffs, N.J.: Prentice-Hall, Inc., 1960.

Sheppard, Richard. "U.S. Wartime Housing," *Architectural Forum,* August 1944.

Short, C. W. and Stanley-Brown, R. *Public Buildings: A Survey of Architecture.* Washington, D.C.: U.S. Government Printing Office, 1939.

Silcox, F. A. "Our Adventure in Conservation: The C.C.C.," *Atlantic Monthly,* December 1937.

Skidmore, Louis. "Expositions Always Influence Architecture," *American Architect,* May 1932.

Steinbeck, John. *The Grapes of Wrath.* New York: The Viking Press, Inc., 1939.

Stout, Wesley W. "The New Homesteaders," *The Saturday Evening Post,* August 4, 1934.

———. *Secret*.* Detroit, Mich.: Chrysler Corporation, 1947.

Stuart, Reginald. "TVA Swept by a Flood of Criticism," *The New York Times Magazine,* January 12, 1975.

Transatlantic, November 1943. "The Home Front: Manpower."

Transatlantic, June 1945. "War Efforts, U.S. and U.K."

Tugwell, Rexford G. "Parts of a New Civilization," *The Saturday Review of Literature,* March 1940.

U.S., Bureau of the Budget. *The United States at War: Development and Administration of the War Program by the Federal Government.* Washington, D.C.: U.S. Government Printing Office, 1946.

U.S., Department of Agriculture. *1940 Yearbook of Agriculture.* Washington, D.C.: U.S. Government Printing Office, 1940.

U.S., Federal Works Agency. *First Annual Report, 1940.* Washington, D.C.: U.S. Government Printing Office, 1940.

U.S., Federal Works Agency. *Second Annual Report, 1941.* Washington, D.C.: U.S. Government Printing Office, 1941.

U.S., Federal Works Agency. *Third Annual Report, 1942.* Washington, D.C.: U.S. Government Printing Office, 1942.

U.S., Federal Works Agency. *Final Report on the WPA Program, 1935–1943.* Westport, Conn.: The Greenwood Press, 1964 (reprint of 1947 edition).

U.S., Housing and Home Finance Agency, Office of the General Counsel. *Chronology of Major Federal Actions Affecting Housing and Community Development, 1892–1963.* Washington, D.C.: U.S. Government Printing Office, 1964.

U.S., Public Works Administration. *America Builds: The Record of PWA.* Washington: U.S. Government Printing Office, 1939.

U.S., Works Progress Administration, Federal Writers' Project. *The Building of Timberline Lodge.* Portland, Ore.: Works Progress Administration, 1937.

Victoria and Albert Museum, London. "The Compassionate Camera: Dustbowl Pictures" (exhibit brochure for a traveling exhibition) London: Victoria and Albert Museum, 1973.

Waithman, Robert. "Realities of Rationing," *Transatlantic,* May 1945.

Wilhelm, Donald. "America's Biggest Boom Town," *The American Mercury,* September 1941.

Woltersdorf, Arthur F. "Carnival Architecture," *American Architect,* July 1933.

Chapter 8

Ackerman, James. "Listening to Architecture," *Harvard Educational Review,* vol. 39, no. 4 (1969).

———. "Transactions in Architectural Design," *Critical Inquiry,* December 1974.

AIA Journal, March 1962. "The FDR Memorial Competition." Articles by Edmund N. Bacon, Francis Biddle, Thomas H. Creighton, William F. Pedersen, Paul Thiry.

AIA Journal, June 1963. "The New Federal Architecture: Will the New Frontier Bring Forth a New Look?" Articles by Arthur J. Goldberg, Frederick Gutheim, Leonard L. Hunter, and Karel Yasko.

Albright, Horace. "The National Park System," *Transatlantic,* May 1945.

Allardice, Corbin, and Tarpnell, Edward R. *The Atomic Energy Commission.* Washington, D.C.: Praeger Library of U.S. Government Departments and Agencies, 1974.

Allison, David. "Fallout Shelters at Once," *Architectural Forum,* February 1961.

———. "Great Balloon for Peaceful Atoms," *Architectural Forum,* November 1960.

Antarctic Journal, March/April 1975. "A New Research Station at the South Pole."

Architectural Forum, articles 1959–1971
January 1959. "Citizens and Architects."

January 1959. "A New Public Architecture."

March 1959. "The State Department's Modern Design Program. . . ."

June 1959. "U.S. Air Force Academy."

September 1959. "Moscow Looks at U.S. Architecture."

March 1961. "Controversial Building in London."

May 1961. "Air Academy Chapel Shapes Up."

November 1961. "Presidential Palaces."

April 1962. "The Slow Progress of Architecture in Washington."

June 1962. "Seattle Fair."

September 1963. "Building for the Moon Launch: A Study in Size and Speed."

November 1963. "New Tower To Grace Airports."

January 1964. "New York World's Fair."

August–September 1964. "Sinewy Drum for Dublin."

June 1967. "Expo-67."

October 1968. "The U.S. at Osaka."

September 1970. "The Infinitely Expandable Future of Air Structures."

January–February 1971. "Washington, D.C.: Trauma and Tenacity Prevailed in the Design of a Federal Office Building."

July–August 1971. "Overlook in a National Park."

April 1971. "Housing Abandonment."

Architectural Record, December 1962. "Air Force Academy Chapel."

Architectural Record, February 1975. "New Prisons Reflect New Reforms and New Attitudes."

Arendt, Hannah. *The Human Condition.* Chicago: The University of Chicago Press, 1958.

Baker, Russell. "Moods of Washington," *The New York Times Magazine,* March 24, 1974.

Barnes, Wilham, and Morgan, John Heath. *The Foreign Service of the U.S.: Origins, Development and Functions.* Washington, D.C.: Department of State, Bureau of Public Affairs, 1960.

Blair, Ed. "Built-ins for George Air Force Base," *Airman,* November 1971.

Blake, Peter. "Cape Kennedy," *Architectural Forum.* January/February 1967.

———. "Expo-70," *Architectural Forum,* April 1970.

———. "What Is Government Character?," *Architectural Forum,* January 1959.

Breckenfield, Gurney. "The Architects Want a Voice in Redesigning America," *Fortune,* November 1971.

Bridges, The Right Hon. Lord. "The State and the Arts," lecture delivered June 3, 1958, Oxford University, Oxford, England.

Canty, Donald, and Haskell, Douglas. "Pennsylvania Avenue," *Architectural Forum,* July 1964.

Carlson, David B. "Buildings for the Space Age," *Architectural Forum,* September 1960.

Chalk, Warren. "Hardware for a New World," *Architectural Forum,* October 1966.

Clay, Grady. "The Competitors," a monograph prepared for the Joint Center for Urban Studies of MIT and Harvard University, 1960–1961.

———. "The Influences of the Frontier on American Urban Development," Salzburg Seminar in American Studies paper, January 1968.

Commanders Digest, August 28, 1975. "How Military Construction Supports Defense Readiness" (entire issue).

Crawford, William. *Report on the Penitentiaries of the United States.* Montclair, N.J.: Patterson Smith, 1969 (original edition, 1835).

Creighton, Thomas H. *The Architecture of Monuments: The Franklin Delano Roosevelt Memorial Competition.* New York: Reinhold Publishing Company, 1962.

Daughterty, Charles Michael. *City under the Ice: The Story of Camp Century.* New York: The Macmillan Company, 1963.

Design and Environment, Fall 1976. Special issue on the National Park Service.

Dietz, Albert G. H. "U.S. Pavilion in Moscow," *Modern Plastics,* December 1959.

Dix, Dorothea. *Remarks on Prisons and Prison Disciplines in the United States.* Montclair, N.J.: Patterson Smith, 1967 (reprint of 1845 edition).

Bibliography

562–563

Engineering News-Record, articles 1966–1976

August 18, 1966. "Air Force Academy Works Out Its Growing Pains."

August 29, 1974. "New Fabrics, Design Expertise Give Air Structures a Lift!"

June 19, 1975. "Corps of Engineers is 200."

August 28, 1975. "GAO Urges Closer Scrutiny of Government Design Contracts."

August 28, 1975. "U.S. Contractors Balk at a Multi-Billion Dollar Market."

May 18, 1976. "Fault Fixers Ready Keyway of 4,510 ft. Arch."

Fine, Lenore, and Remington, Jesse A. *The Corps of Engineers: Construction in the United States.* Washington, D.C.: Office of the Chief of Military History, U.S. Army, U.S. Government Printing Office, 1972.

Franklin, Herbert M. "Will the New Consciousness of Energy and Environment Create an Imploding Metropolis?," *AIA Journal,* August 1974.

Frome, Michael. "The Most Thoroughly Dammed Nation on Earth," *Architectural Forum,* April 1968.

Gustaitis, Rosa. "The Emperor of Capitol Hill," *Architectural Forum,* September 1968.

Hamilton, Lee David. "'Moon Colony' on Earth," *Architectural Forum,* December 1962.

Herzog, Thomas, et al. *Pneumatic Structures.* New York: Oxford University Press, 1976.

Gutheim, Frederick. "Washington Perspective," *Progressive Architecture,* October 1953, September 1954, February 1955, May 1955.

———. "Washington Report," *Progressive Architecture,* December 1955, May 1956, April 1959.

Heyer, Paul. *Architects on Architecture: New Directions in America.* New York: Walker and Company, 1976.

Hirsch, Richard, and Trento, Joseph J. *The National Aeronautics and Space Administration.* Washington, D.C.: Praeger Library of U.S. Government Departments and Agencies, 1973.

Holland, Laurence B., editor. *Who Designs America?* New York: Doubleday & Company, Inc., Anchor Books, 1966.

Houstoun, Lawrence O., Jr. "Evaluation: Housing the Department of Urban Development," *AIA Journal,* April 1977.

Huxtable, Ada Louise. "J. Edgar Hoover Builds His Dreamhouse," *Architectural Forum,* April 1972.

———. *Will They Ever Finish Bruckner Boulevard?* New York: The Macmillan Company, 1963.

Interior Design, October 1976. "Air and Space Museum."

Johnston, Norman. *The Human Cage: A Brief History of Prison Architecture.* New York: Walker and Company, 1973.

Koehler, Robert E. "Our Park Service Serves Architecture Well," *AIA Journal,* January 1971.

Kuh, Katherine. "Must Monuments be Monumental?," *Saturday Review,* September 2, 1961.

Lethbridge, Francis D. "The Federal City As a Client," *AIA Journal,* May 1965.

Levenson, Sam. "America's Penal System," *Transatlantic,* August 1945.

Lewis, Jo Ann, "A Modern Medici for Public Art," *Art News,* April 1977.

Lewis, O. F. *The Development of American Prisons and Prison Customs, 1776–1845.* Montclair, N.J.: Patterson Smith, 1967 (reprint of 1922 edition).

Moholy-Nagy, Sibyl. "Washington: A Critique of 'The Plan for the Year 2000'," *Architectural Forum,* December 1961.

Montgomery, Roger. "Expo 74: Nature Festival," *Progressive Architecture,* August 1974.

Moore, Charles. "You Have to Pay for the Public Life," *Perspecta 9/10,* The Yale Architectural Journal, 1965.

Moynihan, Daniel P. "Pennsylvania Avenue," *AIA Journal,* January 1963.

———. "What Are the Esthetic Responsibilities of Government, Business and Institutions?," *AIA Journal,* June 1962.

Museum of Modern Art, New York. *Twentieth Century Engineering.* New York: The Museum of Modern Art, 1964.

Pollock, Richard. "The Mysterious Mountain," *The Progressive,* March 1976.

Rose, Barbara, and Kluver. Billy. *Pavilion Experiments in Art and Technology.* New York: E. P. Dutton and Company, 1972.

Sampson, Arthur F. "GSA Sees Building Boom for Private Sector," *Consulting Engineer,* March 1972.

Schlitz, William P. "The New Air and Space Museum's Milestones of Flight," *Air Force Magazine,* August 1976.

Schmertz, Mildred. "Getting Ready for the JFK Library: Not Everyone Wants to Make It Go Away," *Architectural Record,* December 1974.

Sennett, Richard. *The Fall of Public Man.* New York: Alfred A. Knopf, 1977.

Shepherd, Jack. "A New Environment at Interior," *New York Times Magazine,* May 8, 1977.

Stephens, Suzanne. "Big Deals and Bitter Endings: The Hirshhorn Museum and Sculpture Garden," *Artforum,* February 1975.

Tanner, Ogden. "The FDR Competition," *Architectural Forum,* February 1961.

Temko, Allan. "The Air Academy Chapel: A Critical Appraisal," *Architectural Forum,* December 1962.

U.S., Ad Hoc Committee on Federal Office Space. "Guiding Principles for Federal Architecture," Report to the President by the Ad Hoc Committee on Federal Office Space. Washington, D.C.: June 1, 1962.

U.S., Atomic Energy Commission. *Nuclear Power Plants.* Oak Ridge, Tenn.: USAEC Division of Technical Information, 1969.

U.S., Commission on Organization of the Executive Branch of Government. *Real Property Management.* Washington, D.C.: U.S. Government Printing Office, 1955.

U.S., Congress, House of Representatives. *To Provide for the Acceptance and Maintenance of Presidential Libraries, and for Other Purposes.* Hearing before a Special Subcommittee of the Committee on Government Operations, House of Representatives, 84th Congress, 1st session, June 13, 1955.

U.S., Department of Defense. *Industrial Architecture: Fallout Shelters.* Washington, D.C.: Office of Civil Defense, 1964.

U.S., Department of Justice, Bureau of Prisons. *U.S. Federal Detention Headquarters.* Washington, D.C.: U.S. Government Printing Office, 1959.

U.S., General Accounting Office, Comptroller General. *Savings Available by Use of Conventionally Designed Traffic Control Towers at Low-Activity Airports.* Washington, D.C.: U.S. Government Printing Office, 1966.

U.S., General Services Administration. *Inventory Report on Real Property Owned by the United States Government throughout the World.* Washington, D.C.: U.S. Government Printing Office, June 30, 1972; June 30, 1973; June 30, 1974.

Venturi, Robert. *Complexity and Contradiction in Architecture.* New York: The Museum of Modern Art, 1966.

Von Eckardt, Wolf. *A Place to Live: The Crisis of the Cities.* New York: Delacorte Press, 1967.

———. "The Age of Anti-Architecture," *Arizona Architect,* February 1965.

Warnecke, John Carl. "The Federal City: A Practitioner's View," *AIA Journal,* November 1958.

Zube, Ervin, Palmer, James F., and Crystal, Joseph H. "Visitor Center Design Evaluation: A Study Prepared for the Denver Service Center, National Park Service." Washington, D.C.: U.S. Government Printing Office, 1976.

ILLUSTRATION SOURCES AND CREDITS

Credits for pages with more than one illustration read left to right, top to bottom unless specified otherwise.

LC = Library of Congress
NA = National Archives

Prologue

xvi LC
xvii Charles Eames

Chapter 1

2 LC
3 LC
8 Courtesy of the New York Historical Society, New York City
9 Courtesy of the New York Historical Society, New York City; British Museum
10 Both from LC
11 (See caption); LC
12 New York Historical Society; Museum of the City of New York
13 LC; Courtesy of the Henry Francis du Pont Winterthur Museum
14 LC; National Gallery of Art, Washington, D.C., Index of American Design; LC
15 LC
16 (See caption); LC; Maryland Historical Society
17 The Papers of Benjamin Henry Latrobe, Maryland Historical Society; LC; LC
18 American Antiquarian Society, Worcester, Mass.
19 LC
20 Minor Congressional Committee (NA)
21 LC; National Gallery of Art, Washington, D.C.
22 Both from LC
23 LC
24 LC; Musées Nationaux de France, Versailles
25 Both from LC
26 LC; Massachusetts Historical Society
27 Both from Massachusetts Historical Society
28 Top: Jefferson Papers, University of Virginia Library; bottom: University of Virginia Library
29 Maryland Historical Society
30 AIA Foundation/The Octagon, Washington, D.C.; LC; LC
31 LC; Maryland Historical Society
32 LC; The John Carter Brown Library, Brown University; LC
33 LC; LC; Maryland Historical Society
34 Collection of the Architect of the Capitol (LC)
35 All from LC
36 LC; Collection of the Architect of the Capitol (LC); LC
37 LC
38 The Papers of Benjamin Henry Latrobe, Maryland Historical Society
39 The Corcorcan Gallery of Art, Washington, D.C.
40 Both from LC
41 LC
42 All from LC
43 Both from The I. N. Phelps Stokes Collection of American Historical Prints, The New York Public Library

Chapter 2

46 Courtesy of The New York Historical Society, New York City
47 LC
52 LC
53 Both from LC
54 LC; LC; Sir John Soane's Museum, London
55 LC
56 LC; from the original diary in the possession of Moise H. Goldstein, New Orleans, Louisiana, reproduced from H. M. Pierce Gallagher, *Robert Mills, Architect of the Washington Monument, 1781–1855* (New York: Columbia University Press, 1935)
58 Maryland Historical Society; LC
59 Reproduced from G. W. Warren, *History of the Bunker Hill Monument* (Boston: R. Osgood and Co., 1877); Courtauld Institute of Art; LC
60 Both from LC
61 Jack E. Boucher, Historic American Buildings Survey (LC)
62 Ronald Comedy, Historic American Buildings Survey (LC); LC; LC
63 Stephen C. Millett, Jr., Frick Art Reference Library; The Toledo Museum of Art
64 LC; Avery Library, Columbia University; New York Public Library
65 All from the Historic New Orleans Collection (negatives by Betsy Swanson)
66 Oregon Historical Society; NA; National Park Service
67 Courtesy of the Essex Institute, Salem, Mass.; LC
68 Courtesy of the A. H. Robins Company; Jack E. Boucher, Historic American Buildings Survey (LC)
69 Army Photographic Agency, Washington, D. C.; U.S. Army Engineer Museum, Ft. Belvoir, Va.; U.S. Army Engineer Museum, Ft. Belvoir, Va.
70 LC; Courtesy of The New York Historical Society, New York City
71 West Point Museum Collection; LC; Gulf Island National Seashore Library
72 LC
73 LC; Roger W. Toll, National Park Service, U.S. Department of the Interior; Official U.S. Navy Photograph (document, courtesy of Norman Littell)
74 Both from U.S. Coast Guard (NA)
75 Both from U.S. Coast Guard (NA)

76 U.S. Coast Guard Official Photo; by permission of the Houghton Library, Harvard University, gift of Henry Richardson Shepley
77 National Library of Medicine, Bethesda, Md.
78 Both from LC
79 National Library of Medicine, Bethesda, Md.; National Library of Medicine, Bethesda, Md.; LC
80 All from LC
81 LC
82 LC
83 LC
84 LC
85 Both from LC

Sources and Credits

Chapter 3

88 Chicago Historical Society
89 Chicago Historical Society
94 (See caption)
95 Both from LC
96 NA; LC; LC; LC
97 Smithsonian Institution; Jack E. Boucher, Historic American Buildings Survey (LC); Smithsonian Institution
98 LC; NA; Smithsonian Institution
100 LC
101 LC; Bancroft Library, University of California, Berkeley; LC
102 West Point Museum Collections; LC; LC
103 Reproduced from U.S. Secretary of the Treasury, *Annual Report of Secretary of the Treasury on the State of the Finances,* 1859
104 Public Buildings Service (NA); NA; LC
105 Both from LC
107 LC
108 The I. N. Phelps Stokes Collection of American Historical Prints, New York Public Library
109 Both from LC
110 LC; General Services Administration
111 LC
112 LC
113 National Collection of Fine Arts
114 Coe Collection, Yale University; NA
115 Courtesy of the Missouri Historical Society
116 West Point Museum Collections; LC; NA
117 LC
118 All from LC
119 All from LC
120 Walters Art Gallery; The State Historical Society of Colorado
121 Quartermaster General (NA); LC
122 NA; LC; Oregon Historical Society
123 LC
124 Both from LC
125 LC; Oklahoma Historical Society
126 LC; Photo Archives, Buechel Memorial Lakota Museum, St. Francis, S.D.
127 NA
128 The Mariners Museum, Newport News, Va.
129 Courtesy of Olmsted Associates, Inc.; LC

130 All from LC
131 Both from LC
132 Both from LC
133 LC
134 Both from Collection of the Architect of the Capitol (LC)
135 Both from Collection of the Architect of the Capitol (LC)
136 LC; Office of the Secretary of Agriculture (NA)
137 Collection of the Architect of the Capitol (LC); LC; LC; LC
138 Both from LC
139 All from LC
140 Collection of the Architect of the Capitol (LC); LC
141 Both from LC

Chapter 4

144 LC
145 Astor, Lenox and Tilden Foundations, New York Public Library
150 LC
151 Both from Washington National Monument Society Papers (NA)
152 Both LC
153 LC
154 Public Buildings Service (NA); LC; LC
155 Courtesy of the late William Mullett, Bethesda, Md.
156 LC
157 All from LC
158 LC; Photograph by Berenice Abbott, Federal Art Project, "Changing New York," Museum of the City of New York
159 LC; NA
160 U.S. General Services Administration; George Cserna; George Cserna
161 Wanda von Ezdorf; Office of Public Buildings and Grounds (NA); Office of Public Buildings and Grounds (NA); Office of Public Buildings and Grounds (NA)
162 Office of Public Buildings and Grounds (NA); NA; Public Buildings Service, U.S. General Services Administration
164 Chicago Historical Society
165 Public Buildings Service (NA); Museum of Art, Carnegie Library of Pittsburgh
166 Both from LC
167 LC
168 Walter M. Sontheimer; NA
169 Top to bottom, left to right: Author's collection; LC; LC; LC; LC; LC; author's collection
170 National Park Service, U.S. Department of the Interior
171 LC
172 Both from LC
173 Nevada State Museum; Nevada State Museum; LC
174 Public Buildings Service (NA)
175 Both from LC
176 Both from LC
177 The Morgan Wesson Memorial Collection, Museum of Fine Arts, Springfield, Mass.; LC
178 All from LC
179 Both from Smithsonian Institution
180 LC
181 Fine Arts Commission (NA); LC; LC
182 LC
183 Both from LC
184 LC

185 Both from LC
186 LC; Veterans Administration (NA)
187 George Eisenman, Historic American Buildings Survey (LC); Jack Boucher, Historic American Buildings Survey (LC); author's collection; LC
188 Fine Arts Commission (NA)
189 All from LC
190 Both from LC
191 LC; LC; David Blume; LC
192 Both from LC
193 LC
194 Both from LC
196 Three designs all reproduced from *American Architect and Building News,* April 7, 1894; LC
197 LC; Fine Arts Commission (NA); The Cincinnati Historical Society
198 Public Buildings Service (NA); LC; Public Buildings Service (NA)
199 LC; reproduced from *American Architect and Building News,* January 19, 1884; Smithsonian Institution
200 Courtesy of the Quincy Society of Fine Arts, Quincy, Ill.; LC; LC
201 LC; Public Buildings Service (NA)
202 LC
203 LC
204 LC

Chapter 5

208 LC
209 U.S. Signal Corps (NA)
215 Chicago Historical Society
217 U.S. Signal Corps (NA); LC
218 LC
219 M.I.T. Historical Collections; LC
220 LC
221 Courtesy of Burnham Library, The Art Institute of Chicago; reproduced from *Journal of the Society of Architectural Historians,* October 1970
222 LC
223 Both from LC
224 LC
225 NA; LC
226 California Historical Society
227 LC
228 U.S. Naval Academy Museum; LC
229 U.S. Naval Academy
230 Both from LC
231 U.S. Army Photograph; LC; LC
232 LC
233 Public Buildings Service (NA); Public Buildings Service (NA); Glenn E. Dahlby, Chicago Historical Society
234 LC; Nathaniel Lieberman
235 Both from Nathaniel Lieberman
236 William Gellman
237 Public Buildings Service (NA); LC
238 Fine Arts Commission (NA); U.S. Information Agency (NA)
239 LC
240 LC
241 LC
242 Stimson Photo Collection, Wyoming State Archives & Historical Department
244 Author's collection
245 Both from LC
246 LC; LC; White House Historical Association
247 LC
248 Both from LC
249 Both from LC
250 Dennis Reeder; Dennis Reeder; Public Buildings and Parks of National Capital (NA)
251 Both from LC
252 LC
253 Both from LC
254 Both from LC
255 Courtesy of Burnham Library, The Art Institute of Chicago; Fine Arts Commission (NA)
256 LC
257 Fine Arts Commission (NA); Public Works Administration (NA)
258 Fine Arts Commission; LC
259 Permission secured

260 LC
261 Both from NA
262 LC
263 Public Buildings and Parks of National Capital (NA); LC; LC; Robert Lautman
264 LC; Columbia Pictures Corporation, 1939, The Museum of Modern Art/Film Stills Archive
265 LC
266 Smithsonian Institution; The Chicago Historical Society
267 LC; LC; Reproduced from National Park Service records
268 LC; Courtesy of American Museum of Immigration, Statue of Liberty N.M., National Park Service
269 Brown Brothers; LC
270 LC
271 LC
272 LC; *Des Moines Register and Tribune*
273 Both from U.S. Signal Corps (NA)
274 U.S. Housing Corporation (NA); LC; LC
275 Both from LC

Chapter 6

278 LC
279 Public Works Administration (NA)
283 Western History Collections, University of Oklahoma Library
284 Western History Collections, University of Oklahoma Library
285 Both from Western History Collections, University of Oklahoma Library
286 All from LC
287 LC
288 All from LC
289 LC
290 Both from LC
291 Both from Herman Manasse, courtesy of the American Battle Monuments Commission
292 Both from LC
293 LC; Reproduced from *Pencil Points,* July 1932
294 National Academy of Design; courtesy of John S. Harbeson (partner)
295 Both courtesy of John S. Harbeson (partner)
296 LC; Courtesy Harbeson Hough Livingston & Larson; Courtesy Harbeson Hough Livingston & Larson
297 Courtesy Harbeson Hough Livingston & Larson; American Battle Monuments Commission; American Battle Monuments Commission
298 Reproduced from *The Federal Architect,* July 1939
299 Reproduced from *The Federal Architect,* July 1930; October 1946; October 1930; April 1933; January 1931; October 1934
300 LC
301 Reproduced from *The Federal Architect,* January 1939, n.d.
302 Reproduced from *The Federal Architect,* January–March 1942
303 United Press International Photo
304 LC
306 Don Morrow, U.S. Bureau of Indian Affairs
307 Fine Arts Commission (NA); Public Works Administration (NA); Public Works Administration (NA)
308 Reproduced from *The Federal Architect,* July 1936; Veterans Administration; Veterans Administration (NA)
309 Fine Arts Commission (NA)
310 Public Buildings Service (NA)
311 Both from LC
312 LC

314 Dennis Reeder; Dennis Reeder; Michael Bruce; Dennis Reeder; Dennis Reeder; Dennis Reeder
315 Dennis Reeder; LC
316 Both from LC
317 Reproduced from *The Federal Architect,* April 1937
318 LC
319 Public Works Administration (NA); reproduced from *The Federal Architect,* April 1937
320 LC
321 LC
322 Edwin L. Wisherd, © National Geographic Society; LC
323 LC
324 LC
325 Fine Arts Commission; Columbia Pictures Corporation, 1950, The Museum of Modern Art Film Stills Archive
326 Both from LC
328 Reproduced from *The Federal Architect,* January–March 1942
329 All from Public Buildings Service (NA)
330 All from Public Buildings Service (NA)
331 NA
332 Both from LC
333 LC
334 LC; Reproduced from *Pencil Points,* September 1939; Reproduced from Arthur Voyce, *Russian Architecture: Trends in Nationalism and Modernism* (New York: Philosophical Library, 1948)
335 Dr. Richard D. McKinzie, courtesy Maria Ealand
336 Both from Public Buildings Service (NA)
337 Both from Public Buildings Service (NA)

Chapter 7

340 Soil Conservation Service (NA)
341 LC
346 (See caption)
347 (See captions)
348 Both from LC
349 Public Works Administration (NA); Public Buildings Service (NA); Public Works Administration (NA)
350 (See caption); Life Picture Service
351 Life Picture Service; Public Works Administration (NA)
352 Top to bottom, left to right: Franklin D. Roosevelt Library; Franklin D. Roosevelt Library; Public Works Administration (NA); Public Works Administration (NA); Public Works Administration (NA)
353 Work Projects Administration (NA)
354 Both from Work Projects Administration (NA)
355 All from Work Projects Administration (NA)
356 Both from Work Projects Administration (NA)
357 Work Projects Administration (NA)
358 Work Projects Administration (NA)
359 Both from Work Projects Administration (NA)
360 Civilian Conservation Corps (NA)
361 Work Projects Administration (NA); FDR Gift Collection (NA)
362 Both from Civilian Conservation Corps (NA)
363 Finger Lakes State Parks Commission, Trumansburg, New York; Civilian Conservation Corps (NA)
364 Work Projects Administration (NA)
365 Both from Work Projects Administration (NA)
366 WPA Photograph Collection, Archives of American Art, Smithsonian Institution; Photographic Archives, The Museum of Modern Art, New York (Gift of Burgoyne Diller via William Seitz); Work Projects Administration (NA)
367 Holger Cahill Papers, Archives of American Art, Smithsonian Institution

368 Both from Work Projects Administration (NA)
369 Holger Cahill Papers, Archives of American Art, Smithsonian Institution; all posters from WPA Photograph Collection, Archives of American Art, Smithsonian Institution
370 Photograph by Berenice Abbott, Federal Art Project, "Changing New York," Museum Of The City Of New York
371 Both from Work Projects Administration (NA)
372 Public Buildings Service (NA)
373 Dr. Richard D. McKinzie, courtesy Maria Ealand; NA
374 Both from Public Buildings Service (NA)
375 All from Public Buildings Service (NA)
377 LC
378 Both from LC
379 All from LC
380 Both from LC
381 LC
382 Both from LC
383 LC
384 Both from Smithsonian Institution
385 Both from Smithsonian Institution
386 Both from LC
387 All from LC
388 All from LC
389 Both from LC
390 LC
391 LC
392 LC
393 LC
394 Both from LC
395 Tennessee Valley Authority
396 Tennessee Valley Authority
397 All from Tennessee Valley Authority
398 Tennessee Valley Authority
399 All from Tennessee Valley Authority
400 Both from Tennessee Valley Authority
401 Both from Tennessee Valley Authority
402 Tennessee Valley Authority; Tennessee Valley Authority; LC
403 Tennessee Valley Authority
404 Courtesy Haines Lundberg & Waehler, New York
405 The Lawrence G. Zimmerman World's Fair Collection
406 International Conferences, Commissions and Expositions (NA); LC
407 United Press International; The Lawrence G. Zimmerman World's Fair Collection
408 Author's collection; Work Projects Administration (NA)
409 LC

410 WQA Photograph Collection, Archives of American Art, Smithsonian Institution
411 Both from LC
412 Tennessee Valley Authority; courtesy of Lee Krasner Pollock
413 R. Buckminster Fuller Archives; photo courtesy of Albert Kahn Associates, Inc., Detroit; LC
414 Both from LC
415 LC; Eliot Noyes
416 LC
417 LC
418 United Press International; LC
419 LC
420 U.S. Army Photograph; LC
421 *Seattle Post-Intelligencer*
422 War Relocation Authority (NA)
423 All from War Relocation Authority (NA)
424 War Relocation Authority (NA)
426 U.S. Energy Research and Development Administration, Oak Ridge Operations Office
427 U.S. Energy Research and Development Administration, Oak Ridge Operations Office
428 Both from U.S. Energy Research and Development Administration, Oak Ridge Operations Office
429 Both from U.S. Energy Research and Development Administration, Oak Ridge Operations Office
430 U.S. Energy Research and Development Administration, Oak Ridge Operations Office; Hedrich-Blessing, Chicago
431 U.S. Army Photograph; Hedrich-Blessing, Chicago
432 U.S. Army Photograph; Hedrich-Blessing, Chicago
433 Skidmore, Owings & Merrill

Chapter 8

436 California Department of Transportation
437 A. Y. Owen, Life Picture Service
442 Courtesy Niles Bond; Sune Sundahl, Atelié Sundahl
443 Source unknown; U.S. Department of State
444 Rondal Partridge, courtesy of Edward Durell Stone Associates; courtesy of Edward Durell Stone Associates
445 Norman McGrath, courtesy of Johansen and Bhavnani
446 The Press Association Ltd.; U.S. Department of State
447 U.S. Department of State; courtesy of Mitchell/Giurgola Architects
448 Louis Reens, courtesy of The Architects Collaborative, Inc.; U.S. Department of State
449 Asahi Photo
450 Both from Jack Masey
451 Courtesy George Nelson & Company; Charles Eames
452 Stephen F. Rosenthal; Todd Lee, courtesy of Cambridge Seven Associates, Inc.
453 Jack Masey; Architect/ designers: Davis, Brody, Chermayeff, Geismar, De Harak (a joint venture)
454 Jack Masey
455 Courtesy of Victor Lundy
456 Charles R. Pearson, courtesy of Naramore, Bain, Brady & Johanson; courtesy of Naramore, Bain, Brady & Johanson
457 U.S. Army Corps of Engineers
458 Reproduced from Charles Michael Daugherty, *City Under Ice: The Story of Camp Century* (New York: The Macmillan Company, 1963)
459 Both from Office of Polar Programs, National Science Foundation
460 Arthur Whitman, Black Star
461 National Aeronautics and Space Administration
462 Balthazar Korab, U.S. Department of Transportation
463 U.S. Department of Transportation
464 Tennessee Valley Authority; U.S. Corps of Engineers
465 Shin Koyama
466 National Aeronautics and Space Administration
467 Both from National Aeronautics and Space Administration
468 National Aeronautics and Space Administration
469 Both from U.S. General Services Administration

470 Top: Wayne Thom; bottom: architects and engineers: a joint venture of Daniel, Mann, Johnson, & Mendenhall; Max O. Urbahn; and Seelye, Stevenson, Value and Knecht
471 R. Barry Johnson, U.S. Air Force Photo
473 Columbia Pictures Corporation, 1964, Museum of Modern Art/Film Stills Archive
474 U.S. Air Force Photo: courtesy of Robert Osborn
475 David Wallis, New York Times Pictures; U.S. Air Force Photo
476 Harry Naltchayan, *The Washington Post*
477 Courtesy of Skidmore, Owings & Merrill
478 Stewarts Commercial Photographers Inc., courtesy of Skidmore, Owings & Merrill
479 Stewarts Commercial Photographers Inc., courtesy of Skidmore, Owings & Merrill
481 J. Alexander, courtesy of John Carl Warnecke; U.S. Department of Defense
482 U.S. Department of Defense; G. Wade Swicord
483 Lyles, Bisssett, Carlisle & Wolff; Lyles, Bissett, Carlisle & Wolff; U.S. Department of Defense
484 Both from U.S. Department of Defense
485 Connecticut Historical Society
486 LC; Bureau of Prisons, U.S. Department of Justice
487 National Park Service Photo; courtesy of Andrew Delano
488 Both from Bureau of Prisons, U.S. Department of Justice
489 Bureau of Prisons, U.S. Department of Justice; courtesy of Moritz Kundig; Hedrich-Blessing
490 Bureau of Prisons, U.S. Department of Justice
491 Both from Bureau of Prisons, U.S. Department of Justice
492 National Park Service Photo, U.S. Department of the Interior
493 Both from National Park Service, U.S. Department of the Interior
494 Both from National Park Service, U.S. Department of the Interior
495 Both from National Park Service, U.S. Department of the Interior
496 Both Alexandre Georges, courtesy of Mitchell/Giurgola Architects
497 George Cserna; National Park Service, U.S. Department of the Interior; National Park Service, U.S. Department of the Interior

498 © 1976 Mark Cohn (NPS); National Park Service, U.S. Department of the Interior
499 Robert O. Blechman, reproduced from *Architecture Plus*, March/April 1974; Wide World Photos
500 Courtesy of Claes Oldenburg
501 Roxanne Everett; U.S. General Services Administration
502 Both from U.S. General Services Administration
503 U.S. General Services Administration
504 U.S. General Services Administration
505 U.S. General Services Administration
506 Soichi Sunami, courtesy Isamu Noguchi
507 George Cserna
509 Ben Schnall
510 Truman Library Collection; Dwight D. Eisenhower Library; Frank Wolfe
511 John F. Kennedy Library; Charles O'Rear, *The Washington Post*
512 J. Alexander, courtesy John Carl Warnecke Associates
513 M. Woodbridge Williams, National Park Service Photo, U.S. Department of the Interior; Robert Arteaga, National Park Service Photo, U.S. Department of the Interior
514 Collection of Philip Johnson, photo courtesy of Claes Oldenburg
515 Louis Checkman; Offical U.S. Navy Photograph
516 Courtesy of John Corkill, Jr.
517 Photograph courtesy of the D.C. Department of Housing and Community Development
518 Pennsylvania Avenue Development Corporation; reproduced from *Progressive Architecture*, July 1973
519 J. Alexander, courtesy of John Carl Warnecke
520 Hirshhorn Museum, Smithsonian Institution
521 Barbara Martin, courtesy Hellmuth, Obata & Kassabaum; Y. Futagawa, © Retoria
522 Robert C. Lautman; source unknown
523 (See caption)
524 Source unknown; courtesy of Marcel Breuer & Associates
525 Robert C. Lautman
526 Michael Bruce; Paul Myatt, Washington Metropolitan Area Transit Authority
527 Ronald Thomas
528 Both from Michael Bruce
529 All from Michael Bruce
530 Wide World Photos

531 *Washington Evening Star;* Smithsonian Institution; Byron Schumaker, *Washington Evening Star*
532 Associated Press; Wide World Photos
533 Bernie Boston, *Washington Evening Star;* Joseph Silverman, *Washington Evening Star*
534 John Bowden, *Washington Evening Star;* Craig Herndon, *The Washington Post;* Roland L. Freeman
535 From the motion picture, "All the President's Men," courtesy Warner Bros. Inc. © 1976
536 Robert C. Lautman
537 Harry Naltchayan, *The Washington Post; The Washington Post*
538 The Metropolitan Museum of Art, George A. Hearn Fund, 1956
539 Balthazar Korab
540 Both from William Gellman
541 James Readle; Ronald Thomas
542 Nick Chaparos; Nick Chaparos; Ronald Thomas; Nick Chaparos
543 Ronald Thomas

Epilogue

546 National Aeronautics and Space Administration
547 Harry Naltchayan, *The Washington Post*

INDEX

Index

Graphic design copyright © 1978 by
The Massachusetts Institute of Technology

This book was set in VIP Optima by DEKR Corporation
and printed and bound by Halliday Lithograph Corporation
in the United States of America.

Library of Congress Cataloging in Publication Data

Craig, Lois
  The Federal presence.

  Bibliography: p.
  Includes index.
  1. United States—Public buildings. 2. Architecture
and state—United States. I. Federal Architecture
Project. II. Title.
NA4205.C7   725'.1'0973   78–15366
ISBN 0–262–03057–8